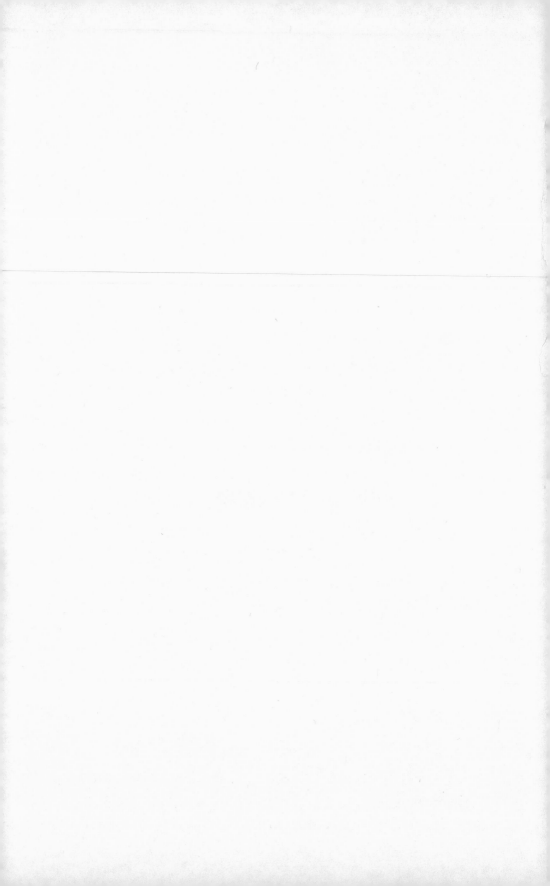

Eyewitness to
Irish History

Peter Berresford Ellis

WILEY

John Wiley & Sons, Inc.

Published by John Wiley & Sons, Inc., Hoboken, New Jersey
Published simultaneously in Canada

Design and production by Navta Associates, Inc.

For general information about our other products and services, please contact our Customer Care Department within the United States at (800) 762-2974, outside the United States at (317) 572-3993 or fax (317) 572-4002.

Wiley also publishes its books in a variety of electronic formats. Some content that appears in print may not be available in electronic books. For more information about Wiley products, visit our web site at www.wiley.com.

Library of Congress Cataloging-in-Publication Data:
Ellis, Peter Berresford.
 Eyewitness to Irish history / Peter Berresford Ellis.
  p. cm.
Includes bibliographical references and index.
 ISBN 0-471-26633-7 (Cloth)
 1. Ireland—History—Sources.   I. Title.
 DA905.E44 2004
 941.5—dc21   2003014214

Printed in the United States of America

10 9 8 7 6 5 4 3 2 1

Sing to me the history of my country,
It is sweet to my soul to hear it.

Aoibhinn, aoibhinn Echtgé árd
Flann mac Lonáin (c. A.D. 850–918)

Contents

Acknowledgments

Each quotation is followed by its source and is thereby acknowledged throughout this book. Every effort has been made to contact the owners of any material that still may be within copyright, but in some cases, the passage of time, often seventy years after the death of the writer, made these efforts difficult. For those who have given their permission, without fee, for the purpose of presenting a unique insight to Ireland's troubled history, I acknowledge a particular debt of gratitude.

To Mo Mowlam and Hodder and Stoughton, for permission to quote the extract from *Momentum* (2002); Cormac O'Malley and Rena Dardis of Anvil Books, for permission to quote from *On Another Man's Wound* (1937, Anvil edition) and *The Singing Flame* (1978); also to Rena Dardis of Anvil Books for permission to quote from *My Fight for Irish Freedom* (1923, Anvil edition) by Dan Breen, and *Guerrilla Days in Ireland* (1949) by Tom Barry; to Clodagh Feehan of Mercier Press (Ireland), copyright holders for *One Day in My Life* (1983) by Bobby Sands; the Francis Hussey Estate; and others, I would like to express my thanks. My acknowledgment to the late Terry de Valéra, copyright holder of Dorothy Macardle's *The Irish Republic* (1937), who expressed his willingness to quote from Miss Macardle's work before his death.

Attempts to contact Fred Holroyd, for permission to quote *War Without Honour* (1989) have proved unsuccessful, as have attempts to contact Marie McGuire to quote from *To Take Arms* (1972).

I would also like to place on record my special appreciation to my researcher, Elizabeth Murray; Liz Curtis; Fr. Desmond Wilson; Silvia Calamati; Fr. Joe McVeigh; Frances Mary Blake; Bernadette McAliskey; Jack Lane; David Sexton; and, of course, my wife, Dorothy, without whom my task would have been made that much harder.

Introduction

Ireland has one of the oldest traditions of historical continuity in Europe. From the evidence of its ancient texts, it claims over three millennia of oral and written history. Irish literature began to blossom in the sixth century A.D. with its poetry, mythology, legal texts, chronicles, and annals. Calvert Watkins, professor of linguistics at Harvard, wrote: "Irish has the oldest vernacular literature of Europe; our earliest monuments go back to the sixth century." Professor David Greene of the Dublin Institute for Advanced Studies clarifies this statement by pointing out that although Greek and Latin have considerably older literatures, the writers of those languages were often not native speakers of them. Latin and Greek were used as lingua franca but were not necessarily mother tongues.

For example, many early Latin writers were, in fact, Celts. Caecilius Statius (fl. c. 225–165 B.C.) became the chief comic dramatist of Rome, with forty-two titles of his plays still known. But he was an Insubrean Celtic warrior from Mediolanum (Milan) who was taken captive at the Battle of Telemon in 225 B.C. when the Romans defeated the Celtic armies of Aneroestes and Concolitanus. As a slave in Rome, he learned Latin, began to write, and finally won his freedom. He was one of many Celts who were to make their literary mark in Latin, just as many Irish writers in the eighteenth, nineteenth, and twentieth centuries have used the English language in which to make their literary reputations.

Ireland, or Éire in the Irish language, is an island that lies immediately west of Great Britain, separated from it by the North Channel, the Irish Sea, and the Celtic Sea. It comprises some 32,598 square miles or 84,429 square kilometers. Today it remains partitioned between the independent Republic of Ireland and Northern Ireland, which is part of the United Kingdom of Great Britain and Northern Ireland. The Republic of Ireland together with Northern Ireland (as a component of the United Kingdom) are part of the European Community. The island's population, given in the 2001 (U.K.) and 2002 (Irish Republic) Census, is just over 5.6 million, with 3.9 million living in the Republic and nearly 1.7 million living in Northern Ireland. The first official language of the Republic is the Irish language. The 2002 Census reported that nearly 1.5 million speak Irish, and English is the second official language. However, English is the predominant one. In Northern Ireland, the Irish language was discouraged by the government until 1991 and now has some recognition under the "peace process." The 2001 Census showed that 167,480 citizens of Northern Ireland speak Irish, but English remains the official and predominant language.

The island of Ireland is composed of a large, fertile central plain roughly enclosed by a highland rim. The highest mountain is Carrantuohill (Corrán Tuathail, signifying an inverted reaping hook), standing 3,414 feet high (approximately 1,040 meters) in the range known as MacGillycuddy's Reeks, which rises to the west of the lakes of Killarney, County Kerry. The island's longest river is the Shannon (An tSionna, "the old one," named after the ancient goddess Sinann), which flows 224 miles southwest from a spring under the Cuilach Mountain, in County Cavan, to the Atlantic Ocean. During its last 70 miles it forms a wide estuary. The capital of the Republic of Ireland is Dublin, or, in Irish, Baile Átha Cliath (town of the hurdle ford). The principal city of Northern Ireland is Belfast, or Beal Feirste (mouth of the river Feirste).

The earliest inhabitants arrived in Ireland around 7000 B.C. and the earliest man-made structure, situated in County Derry, is said to date from this time. In the subsequent millennia, settlements proliferated; cattle herding and forest clearing, crop growing, and even cheese making began. The great structures, built with astronomical alignments, such as Newgrange, Dowth, and Knowth, were constructed around 3200 B.C., which makes them older than the Egyptian pyramids.

Tara, or Teamhair, in County Meath (Midhe, "the middle province"), was being used by 2100 B.C., and it evolved into the chief center of the high kings of Ireland. According to the *Lebor Gabála Erenn*, or *The Book of Invasions*, the earliest complete text of which survives from the twelfth century, Tara took its name from Téa, wife to Éremon, the first Gaelic ruler of Ireland, having displaced the earlier name of Druim Caín (Caín's ridge). It is generally accepted that the Gaels, a branch of the greater Celtic peoples whose civilization spanned Europe from Ireland in the west to the central plain of Turkey in the east, north from Scotland and Belgium, south to southern Spain, and across the Alps into the Po Valley in Italy, arrived in Ireland during the first millennium B.C. The date given in the ancient origin tales contained in the *Lebor Gabála Erenn,* using the Anno Mundi system ("year of the creation of the world"), works out at c. 1015 B.C. This does coincide with some archaeological evidence whereby a change in culture is noticed by the discovery of Hallstatt-devised, or Hallstatt-influenced, artifacts as used by the Continental Celts. Whereas the *Lebor Gabála Erenn* talks of invasion and conquest, new theories by archaeologists and those interested in DNA science argue that the cultural change might be due to small groups who intermarried and whose language became dominant.

We may positively state that when Ireland emerged into recorded history, it was a Celtic country. Moreover, its language and culture were of the Goidelic branch (or Q-Celtic) of the Celtic people. Celtic is a linguistic definition, not a racial one. A Celt is someone who spoke (or still speaks) a Celtic language. That "racial" definitions cannot apply is made clear by the descriptions of a "typical" Celt given by the classical writers. The physical attributes range from tall, gangling, blond Gauls to short, stocky, dark Silurians, with various ethnic types in between.

Linguists argue that the Celts, emerging from the Indo-European common cultural pool sometime before 2000 B.C., once spoke a "common" Celtic language, which then split into two distinct dialects—what we now call Goidelic (Q-Celtic) and Brythonic (P-Celtic). The Goidelic group is represented today by Irish, Manx, and Scottish Gaelic. Brythonic is represented by Welsh, Cornish, and Breton. Goidelic is said to be the oldest form of Celtic, because Brythonic, developed at a later stage and closely related to Gaulish, had simplified its case endings and dropped the neuter gender and dual number. Differences also occurred in the matter of initial mutation and aspiration. Above all, there is the famous substitution of P for Q, resulting in the naming of the two groups by linguists. For example, the word for "son" in Goidelic is *mac,* while in Brythonic it becomes *map.*

In spite of the increasing dialectical divergence between the two groups, the Celts shared a common pre-Christian religion, basic mythological motifs, social system and kingship structures, and a law system. The conservativeness of the Irish language, culture, and social structure, surviving because Ireland was little influenced by Rome until the Christian period—and even then it adapted Christianity to its own cultural needs—has caused great parallels to be drawn with other early Indo-European languages such as Sanskrit and Hittite, and particularly with the Hindu myths and law system. Ireland, in terms of its early written forms and its culture, gives scholars one of the greatest supports for the Indo-European hypothesis.

This concept presupposes the existence at some period in remote antiquity of a unified, primitive Indo-European parent language whose dialects developed into the ancestors of the present major groups as waves of migrants, moving from a point between the Baltic Sea and the Black Sea, carried it westward to Ireland and eastward into Asia. Thus, Germanic, Celtic, Romance, Greek, Albanian, Armenian, Baltic, Slavonic, Iranian, and Indo-Aryan are all Indo-European-language groups. Hittite, although now dead for millennia, is known from tablets found at Boghazkoy in 1905, written in an Akkadian cuneiform syllabery, and was the language of the Hittite Empire that flourished in Asia Minor between 1900 and 1400 B.C. It is the earliest known surviving written Indo-European language. It has been compared to Sanskrit and to Old and Middle Irish forms. Ireland, therefore, represents an old and sophisticated culture.

Ireland's Golden Age of Learning came about when most of Europe had fallen into the Dark Ages. From the sixth to the twelfth centuries, Ireland had become one of the primary educational centers of Europe. At Durrow, an ecclesiastical university established by Colmcille about A.D. 553, students are listed in the mid-seventh century as attending from no less than eighteen different nations. Hugh de Lacey destroyed the great abbey in A.D. 1186 for the purpose of building a castle. The great illustrated Gospel Book, *The Book of Durrow,* now in Trinity College, Dublin, was produced there. It was compiled on the order of the high king Flann Sinna Mac Maelsechnaill (d. A.D. 916) to honor St. Colmcille.

But as well as attracting students from many lands, including the sons of Anglo-Saxon kings such as Aldfrith, who became king of Northumbria (c. A.D. 665–705), three of whose poems in Irish have survived, Irish missionaries and educationalists began to spread through Europe. They set up establishments in the Anglo-Saxon kingdoms, in what is now France, Belgium, Germany, Switzerland, Austria, and Italy. From Kiev in the east to Iceland in the north, and to Taranto in southern Italy, went the Irish *peregrinato pro-Christo.*

Irish literature in both the native language and in Latin; Irish art not only in the form of the illuminated Gospel Books but in metal work and jewelry; and Irish medical men, philosophers, geographers, and cosmologists were at the forefront of European achievement.

However, the Irish system of decentralized government, of its hereditary electoral system of kingship, which precluded the concept of primo-
geniture, caused a weakness in political and military structures. This left
the country prey to stronger outside forces. First came the sea-raiders, the
Norsemen, or Vikings, who were finally defeated by the high king Brían
Bóroimhe at Clontarf in A.D. 1014 and who became absorbed into the
Irish cultural ethos. Then came the Normans, who were also absorbed
into the Irish nation, adopting the language and social system. When
Henry VIII summoned a parliament in Dublin in 1541, the earl of
Ormonde had to translate the words of Henry's new lord deputy, Sir
Anthony St. Leger, into Irish so that the great Anglo-Norman lords of
Ireland would understand him. The English Tudor conquests in the sixteenth century and the Cromwellian Conquest in the seventeenth century
were more genocidal than any previous conquests, removing entire populations, slaughtering them, or selling them as slaves to the colonies,
notably Barbados. Even then, within a few years, the new colonists had
also become Irish in speech, although imposing their own law and governing system, as opposed to the old Irish kingship system.

Finally, the Williamite Conquest (1689–1691) and the enactment of
Penal Laws deprived everyone of civil and religious rights except members
of the Anglican (Episcopalian) Church. Catholics and Dissenting
Protestants were barred from holding lands; serving in any public office
such as law, army, customs, and municipal services; receiving education at
any level; and intermarriage. The Irish language was to be totally eradi-
cated and anyone caught with one of the ancient native Irish law books,
even in the late eighteenth century, would be severely punished. Such law
books were buried or even put in lakes as a means of hiding them.

Over the centuries, the conquests caused a diaspora of immense proportions as countless Irish left Ireland in search of freedom. They went
first to the European mainland, making major contributions to those
countries in which they settled. Irish migrants produced a president of the
French republic (Patrice MacMahon), a prime minister of Spain
(Leopoldo O'Donnell), high chamberlains and other senior officials of the
Austro-Hungarian Empire, and many more. The daughter of Irish immi-
grants in France married the king of Sweden. Irish military service to
many nations became proverbial. In the Heroes Gallery of the Hermitage
in St. Petersburg, Russia, hangs the portrait of the man who turned
Napoleon's army from Russia in 1812, Count Joseph Kornilevitch

O'Rourke of Breifne, who was general in chief of the Russian army in 1812. Escaping from the English, George Thomas of Roscrea, County Tipperary (1756–1802), was made commander of the army of the Begum of Sirdhana in India and appointed rajah of one of his territories.

From the Irish Brigade of the Spanish army, Irishmen moved to Latin America. It was the last Spanish viceroy to Mexico, Juan O'Donoju (O'Donoghue), who devised the plan that gave Mexico its independence in 1821. Bernardo O'Higgins became the Liberator of Chile, and later "Che" Ernest Guevarra Lynch also became a revolutionary icon. As Ireland started to become Anglicized, the Irish also began to settle in every corner of the English-speaking world, from the United States and Canada to Australia, and from South Africa to New Zealand. Ireland suffered one of the biggest diasporas in human history, but its loss was the gain of the many countries in which its refugees settled.

Colonial landlordism was the cause of famines being visited on the rural population of Ireland. Between 1728 and 1845, there were no less than twenty-eight major famines. But these famines were artificially contrived because Ireland held enough foodstuffs, both in livestock and grain, to feed two and a half times its population in every famine where they suffered. Landlords and their agents, backed up by the army and later by armed police, simply refused to distribute food to people who could not pay the commercial prices for it. The period 1845–1848 was known to the Irish as An Ghorta Mhór (The Great Hunger), in which the population loss, in real terms, was 2.5 million through death and immigration.

After the major insurrection of 1798, in which Dissenting Protestants and Catholics joined forces against the English, the English government decided to unite the colonial parliament of Dublin into its own at Westminster. The Union was achieved in 1801, by which time Penal Laws against Dissenting Protestants had been dropped in order to create a bulwark between the ruling class and the majority Catholic population.

As the nineteenth century proceeded, with insurrections in 1803, 1848, 1867, and the Land War of the 1880s, more rights were gradually conceded to the Catholic Irish. Catholic emancipation in 1829 was tempered by an alteration in the minimum sum that people had to have before being accorded the franchise, which resulted in a reduction of those qualified to vote from 230,000 to 14,000. At least Catholics could now be elected to the Westminster Parliament in England. With voting reforms, the limited franchise for the Irish people began to be increased. In 1872, the U.K.

Ballot Act allowed the vote to be conducted in secret so that people could cast a vote without fear of subsequent victimization. In 1874, fifty-nine members of Parliament were returned, this being the majority of Irish seats, demanding Home Rule, a domestic self-government for Ireland within the United Kingdom state.

For the next forty years, the pro-self-government members of Parliament held four-fifths of all Irish seats, only to be thwarted time and again in processing their claims with Home Rule Bills because they were outnumbered by English members of Parliament. This lack of constitutional progress by democratic votes had been planned for as early as 1799 when the concept of the Union was discussed. Edward Cooke, undersecretary at Dublin Castle, had pointed out: "By giving the Irish a hundred members in an Assembly of six hundred and fifty, they will be impotent to operate upon that Assembly, but it will be invested with Irish assent to its authority."

The 1916 uprising became inevitable and the brutal repression that followed it ensured the victory of Sinn Féin, then being a political party standing for a sovereign independent republic at the 1918 general election. Out of the 105 seats representing Ireland in the Westminster Parliament, Sinn Féin won 73, with the Irish Party holding only 6 seats and the Unionists increasing their representation to 26, 8 seats of which were held on split votes between Sinn Féin and the Irish Party.

In accordance with their manifesto declaring they would make a unilateral declaration of independence (UDI), Sinn Féin invited all elected Irish members to Mansion House, Dublin, and on January 21, 1919, instituted Dáil Éireann, the Irish Parliament. Members issued its UDI and elected government ministers. London declared this an illegal assembly. Thirty-four elected Irish members of Parliament were now jailed. English troops were sent in and the War of Independence began, which was to last until 1921. The controversial treaty negotiations that resulted in the acceptance by the Dáil by sixty-four votes to fifty-seven votes, giving Ireland a Free State within the British Commonwealth but with part of its territory partitioned and remaining within the United Kingdom, inevitably led to civil war. On May 24, 1923, the republican forces, facing defeat, were ordered to "dump arms" and cease fire but not surrender.

The Irish Free State came into being on December 6, 1922. On December 7, the Unionist Parliament in Belfast petitioned King George V for permission to withdraw the Six Counties from the Free State, in accordance with the treaty, and establish them as a self-governing part of the

United Kingdom. In 1923, the Irish Free State joined the League of Nations. The Irish Republic was to eventually emerge on April 18, 1949, and deemed to have left the British Commonwealth of Nations. Due to the United Kingdom's hostility, the Republic was not allowed to join the United Nations until 1956. Partition of the country by means of a new Ireland Act of 1949, enacted by the U.K. Parliament, was then guaranteed as being permanent. From 1922, partition remained a focus of deep anger and frustration that led to continued violence in the north of the island. Leaving aside the all-Ireland election results before the enforcement of partition and taking the province of Ulster by itself, only four of Ulster's nine counties had voted to remain in the United Kingdom. Five of the nine counties had voted for the Republic. As four counties would not constitute a viable economic unit, Unionists were allowed to take arbitrary control of two Republican counties—Fermanagh and Tyrone—using force, arresting their elected representatives, and abolishing local government there. A sectarian statelet arose in the six counties of northeast Ulster whose Special Powers laws were admired by both Adolf Hitler and Johannes Vorster (one of the architects of apartheid in South Africa).

Turning from campaigns of violence, the frustrated disenfranchised Catholics chose Civil Rights demonstrations and marches from 1967 to 1969. When those were suppressed with great brutality by the Unionist regime, the U.K. Labour government sent in troops in August 1969. Their initial task was to protect the Catholic ghettos. With a change of government in the United Kingdom, the new Conservative administration fell back on its historical role, harassing the Nationalists (mainly Catholics), which led to the reactivation of the Irish Republican Army. The disastrous introduction of internment without trial in August 1971; torture of internees, which was denounced by the European Court of Human Rights; and shooting of unarmed Civil Rights demonstrators in 1972 saw many young Irish men and women flocking to join the Republican movement.

At the start of the conflict, Paul Johnson, writing in the *New Statesman,* had said: "In Ireland over the centuries, we have tried every possible formula: direct rule, indirect rule, genocide, apartheid, puppet parliaments, real parliaments, martial law, civil law, colonisation, land reform, partition. Nothing has worked. The only solution we have not tried is absolute and unconditional withdrawal."

It was a solution that no one in any U.K. government could ever be persuaded to try. However, after thirty years of bloody conflict, a Peace

Process was finally agreed upon, but whether this will lead to a real peace and the reunification of the island is for a future historian to judge.

Ireland, then, since the arrival of the conquerors, has suffered a brutal history, particularly in the centuries following 1541, when Henry VIII of England made himself king of Ireland. Only in recent years has the Republic of Ireland begun to shake off its poor-neighbor attitude and take a leading role in both the European Community and the United Nations.

Eyewitness to Irish History is no more than an introductory work. It is neither a detailed history of Ireland nor even a compilation of eyewitness accounts of every major or influential event that has occurred in Ireland's long march through history. It is merely a series of snapshots: accounts of events, comments, instructions written by people who were there, eyewitnesses, or contemporaries of people who were there and heard their stories firsthand. The further into the past we go, of course, the less there are firsthand eyewitnesses, but we can accept some of the accounts that survive from later periods that are said to have originated at the time of the event. Indeed, when we rely on Julius Caesar as an eyewitness to his campaigns in Gaul and Britain, we should bear in mind that the earliest copy of his work only survives from the ninth century A.D., almost one thousand years after the events. On this basis, we can also accept many of the early Irish accounts as eyewitness forms.

In examining this work, let us not be misled that this or any other history book is written from the standpoint of academic objectivity. Such a history does not exist, for all history is subjective and dependent on the experiences and motivations of the individual historian and the choice of material on which the historian builds his or her interpretation. There is much to be said in support of the cynicism of Paul Valéry in "De l'histoire," *Regards sur le monde actuel,* 1931: "History justifies whatever we want it to."

History is not simply about the enumeration of facts. It is about the moral interpretation of those facts. Indeed, the very form in which the historian relates the facts conveys judgment and prejudice. For example, let me take what, on the surface, is a simple statement of fact. The bottle is half empty. It is a quantifiable fact that surely cannot be argued. Yet if the same fact is put another way—the bottle is half full—it provides us with an entirely different concept or interpretation of that same fact.

History, more than most disciplines, is one in which the historian is thought to sit in splendid isolation as a judge, viewing the events that are paraded before the historian, who, it is expected, will view the events objectively and dispassionately. But the historian is just as caught up, involved, and biased as any of the historical actors who parade before his or her eyes. Consciously or subconsciously, historians will contribute to those historical characters something of themselves, giving their own values, judgments, and reactions. Very few historians can empathize totally and fully understand what motivates the historical characters.

Often a history book will tell us more about the historian than it does about the historical facts. Historical narratives are full of the personal judgments of the historian. And as historians have their biases, whether they admit it or not, so, too, do all the historical players who tell of their experiences and their views. So in this book, the snapshots that are presented are expressions of individual bias.

Between the snapshots, I have inserted matters of explanation and continuity. Admittedly, this will tell the reader how I, as an individual, look at Irish history, by demonstrating what events have caught my eye through thousands of years. Readers might remark that much of the history dwells on Ireland's struggle to rid itself of the colonial power of its neighbor. It is not to be wondered at when every succeeding generation of the Irish nation, since the Tudors began their policy, best summed up by Sir William Parsons (d. 1650) as "to set up in them obedience to the laws and to the English Empire," has risen up in arms to reassert its independence and nationhood.

The Irish playwright George Bernard Shaw (1856–1950) tried to explain this dynamic in his "Preface for Politicians" when his play *John Bull's Other Ireland* was first published in 1906: "A healthy nation is as unconscious of its nationality as a healthy man is of his bones. But if you break a nation's nationality it will think of nothing else but getting it set again. It will listen to no reformer, to no philosopher and no preacher, until the demand of the Nationalist is granted. It will attend to no business, however vital, except the business of unification and liberation."

One hundred years after Shaw's writing, there are still many who regard Ireland with some feigned astonishment, claiming they cannot understand why there are such problems. The major events of the last four centuries of Irish history have turned on the anticolonial struggle, and there is an awesome feeling of déjà vu as we read of the hardship and suffering of people four hundred years ago and those in recent years. Those who ignore that continuity, which *is* history, are blind. Instead, we must learn from it. Only when we understand it can we deal with it, and we can then awaken from the cyclical nightmare that it has laid on the Irish nation.

1

Ancient Ireland

T he Lebor Gabála Erenn, *commonly called* The Book of the Invasions of Ireland, *is a compilation of Irish origin stories, a mixture of legends and oral history from earliest times. The earliest complete surviving text of the* Lebor Gabála Erenn *dates from the twelfth century, but there is abundant evidence that the text was first put down in writing many centuries before that. The surviving version has a Christian gloss, as it synchronizes the myths, legends, early history, and genealogies within the framework of biblical exegesis. It begins Irish history with the biblical flood in the year of the world 1104 Anno Mundi, a date hotly argued even by the very early commentators.*

Cesair, granddaughter of Noah, and her father, Bíth, and her followers are the first to reach Ireland. Then comes Partholón, descendant of the biblical Magog, and his followers. These are clearly additions to Irish legendary origins made after Christianity took hold in the country. Cesair's settlements are quickly destroyed. Nemed and his followers then arrive from the Caspian Sea. They are destroyed by the Fomorii (fo = under and mor = sea, i.e., "dwellers under the sea"). With the appearance of the Fomorii, who are also called the Tuatha De Domhnan, we find the first indication of native Celtic deities, but these are the gods and goddesses of evil. They appear in the texts but not as invaders or settlers.

The next group to land in Ireland are the Fir Bolg, short, dark people who come to Ireland fleeing oppression. They are said to have eventually been driven to the Aran and Rathlin Islands. Then come the Tuatha Dé Danann, the Children of Danu, the mother goddess, and it is clear that we have now encountered the pantheon of

Celtic Irish gods and goddesses of light and good, as opposed to their bitter enemies, the Fomorii.

The last invasion of which the Lebor Gabála Erenn *speaks is that of the Milesians, named after Míl Easpáin (soldier of Spain), whose real name is Golamh, and he is the progenitor of the Gaels who land in Ireland and establish their dominance. Whether there is any significance in this sequence of mythical invasions is still the subject of scholastic debate.*

Nevertheless, the arrival of the Milesians from the northwest of the Iberian Peninsula does fit with what we know of the movements of historic Celts during the first millennium B.C. *Some of the Celtic people were settled in the Iberian Peninsula from early times. Greek and Phoenician traders attest to this fact, as do the Romans in the third century* B.C. *Stories of the Celtic wanderers in Egypt, serving as mercenaries to the pharaohs, are also historically documented. Míl Easpáin's wife is said to be Scota, the daughter of the pharaoh Nectanebus, and there were two pharaohs of that name. She was killed during the invasion of Ireland and is said to be buried in Scota's Glen, 3 miles from Tralee in County Kerry. Moreover, at the time that this invasion is said to take place, circa 1000* B.C., *archaeology has noted the introduction of some Hallstatt, early continental Celtic, artifacts. Can these legends of the arrival of the Gaels have a foundation in fact?*

The Naming of Ireland

And they, the sons of Míl with the children of the Gael, landed and came thereafter on to Sliabh Mis, where Banba met them with her Druid and her host. Amairgen, son of Míl, asked her: "What is your name?" "Banba," said she, "and from me is this island named." Thereafter they made their way to Sliabh Eibhline where Fotla with her Druid and host met them. Amairgen asked her name. "Fotla," said she, "and from me is this island named." Then they came to Uisnech of Midhe and there found Éire and her Druid and her host. Amairgen asked her name and she told him and said it was from her that the island was named.

But Éire said: "Warriors, welcome to you; long is your coming hither known to my Druid. Yours shall be this island forever, and there shall be no island of like size that shall be better between this and the East of the World. There shall be no people more perfect than your people forever." "That is good," said Amairgen, and thanked her for her courtesy. But Donn, the elder son of Míl, said: "Not to her is it right to give thanks, but to our gods and to our strength of arms." So Éire answered him: "You Donn shall have no profit from this island nor shall your progeny. But a

gift to me, fair minded Amairgen, that my name shall be on this island for-
ever." "Your name shall be the chief name of the island forever," promised
Amairgen. And he likewise promised Éire's two sisters, for such were
Banba and Fotla, that their names would also be immortalised. Thus it
was—Éire is the name of the island but the poets do also recourse to
Banba and Fotla when the island's praises are sung.

> *Lebor na hUidre* (Book of the Dun Cow, also called the Book of Clonmacnoise), written at
> Clonmacnoise c. A.D. 1100, compiled by Mael Muire Mac Ceileachair (d. A.D. 1106)

Notable Early High Kings

*Much has been written on the lives and adventures of the high kings and provincial
kings of Ireland from the time of Eremon and Eber Foinn, the two sons of Golamh or
Míle Easpain, who brought the Gaels to Ireland. Obviously none of the accounts
could be deemed as eyewitness. But the records we have were made by scribes writing down a long, sophisticated tradition of oral historians, and most scholars believe
that the basic information is trustworthy.*

*The earliest written materials concerning the genealogy of Irish kings come from
the seventh century A.D. and are the oldest fragments of Irish poetry, known as forsundud, or praise poems. Four such genealogical poems were collected by Professor
Kuno Meyer, one of them giving a genealogy of the Munster king Cathal Cú cen-
máthair (d. A.D. 641). Professor Myles Dillon has pointed out that the forsundud
are, therefore, the oldest surviving form of Irish poetry, and has compared them to
other ancient Indo-European poetic forms, such as the Sanskrit Vedic narasamsyah,
songs in praise of princes. The forsundud were handed down for a thousand years or
so before being committed to writing in the Christian era. Among the ancient Irish
kings, the following are notable.*

Ollamh Fodhla, *whose dates are put at 754–714 B.C. and who was said to have died
"a natural death within the ramparts of Tara." His name means "high poet of
Fódhla" (Ireland). Lost sources quoted in the seventeenth century claim he was a
man of wisdom who first gathered the ancient laws of the country, the Laws of the
Fénechus, or free land-tillers, and also organized the Festival of Tara to be held every
three years at the feast of Samhain (November 1) to discuss and update the laws and
ensure the annals were kept up to date.*

> Ollamh Fódhla, fierce in valour,
> Marked out the Scholar's Rampart,
> The first mighty king with grace
> Who convened the Festival of Tara.

Fifty years, it was tuneful fame,
was he in the High Kingship over Ireland
so that from him, with fortunate freedom,
Ulaidh (Ulster) received its name.

He died a natural death within his capital [rampart].

Lebor Gabála Erenn

Macha Mong Ruadh, *Macha of the Red Hair, is claimed as the only female high king, and the date in which she began her reign was 377* B.C. *However, her traditions were mixed with the myths about goddesses of war and sovereignty; in fact, there are at least four Machas appearing in Irish myth, so it is difficult to separate reality from mythology.*

Macha Mong Ruadh, daughter of Aodh Ruadh, son of Badharn, son of Airgedmhar, son of Siorlamh, son of Fionn, son of Bratha, son of Labhriadh, son of Cairbe, son of Ollamh Fodhla, held the sovereignty of Ireland seven years. And it was in her time that Ard Mhacha, that is Macha's Height [Armagh] that is named after her, as is Emain Mhacha [Navan].

Dinnseanchas, Rennes Library, ed. Whitley Stokes, *Revue Celtique,* vols. 15 and 16

Bron Bherg [House of Sorrow], haven of the sick, was built by her word.

Banshenchus, ed. M. Dobbs, *Revue Celtique,* 1930, 1931, 1932

Bron Bherg, the first recorded hospital, was destroyed in A.D. *22. Ireland had an ancient and advanced medical system with laws on the running of hospitals, which were available to all who needed treatment irrespective of rank.*

Macha, red-hair daughter of Aedh Rúad mac Badarn, was seven years in the kingship of Ireland after Cimbáeth, till she fell by the hand of Rechtaid Ríderg of Munster.

Lebor Gabála Erenn

Tuathal Techtmhair *(Tuathal the Legitimate), whose reign was given as* A.D. *130–160. He is considered important because he decreed that the high king should not have his home in any of the four kingdoms (Ulster, Leinster, Munster, or Connacht), but being king over them all and not favoring one kingdom, he should rule from an independent territory called the middle kingdom or province. He* created this as Midhe (middle) around the palaces of Tara, Teltown, Tlacghtga, and Uisneach. Midhe is modern Meath and Westmeath.

Then Túathal Techtmar fell thereafter in Dál Araide, in Moin in Chatha, the place where are Ollar and Ollarba, at the hands of Mál son of Rochraide, after completing thirty years in the kingship of Ireland, in the reign of Antonius, King of the World. In his time the festival of Casc [Easter] was adopted by Christians, and in his time the Bóroimha [the fine leveled against the kingdom of Leinster] was extorted.

Lebor Gabála Erenn

Cormac Mac Art. *The start of his reign is usually given as c. A.D. 227–266. He was the son of Art the Solitary and grandson of Conn of the Hundred Battles. He was nicknamed Ulfhada (long beard). His bodyguard was the Fianna commanded by Foinn Mac Cumhail (Finn MacCool). The cycle of stories and adventures that grew up around them became highly popular in the medieval period.*

Cormac had thrice fifty stewards. There were fifty warriors standing in the king's presence as he sat at his meal. There were three hundred cup-bearers in the fortress, and thrice fifty goblets of carbuncle, of gold, and of silver. The total of his household amounted to one thousand and fifty men. . . .

Cormac, son of Art the Solitary, was forty years in the kingship of Ireland until he died in Tech Cleitig, after the bone of a salmon stuck in his throat; or it is phantoms that slew him after he had been cursed by Máel-Cenn.

Lebor Gabála Erenn

Niall Naoi-Ghiallach *(of the Nine Hostages). His dates are usually given as A.D. 379–405, although some evidence has put his death as late as A.D. 454. His name comes from Nél (cloud). His role in the political history of early Ireland is a crucial one, and he is the eponymous progenitor of the Uí Néill, descendants of Néill who dominated the high kingship for centuries and also the Irish struggle against England until the mid-seventeenth century. The traditions of his rule abound in stories of the socially weak triumphing over those who think themselves strong and in Niall's raids against other lands.*

Niall went into Alba with a large host to strengthen and to establish the Dál Riada and the Irish people in Alba who were at this time gaining supremacy over the Cruithin who are called the Picti; and he was the first to give the name Scotia to Alba ... and it was through veneration for Scota, daughter of the Pharaoh Nectanebus, who was wife of Golamh called Míl Easpain, from whom they themselves sprang.

Lebor Gabála Erenn

On one such raid he was slain by Eochaidh, a son of the Leinster king Éana Cinselach, who was said to have taken refuge among the Saxons. Niall's body was brought back by ship to Ireland and taken to Ochann (Faughan Hill, near Navan, in County Meath) for burial. His court poet was Torna Eigeas (the Learned), of whom three poems are said to have survived.

> Saxons with overwhelming cries of war, hosts of
> Jutes from the continent
> From the hour in which the King fell, Gael and
> Picts are in a sore straight

> Darling hero of the shinning host, whose tribes
> Are vast, a beloved band;
> Every man was under his protection when we used to
> Go to foregather with him

Torna Eigeas (the Learned), fl. A.D. 400, in Lebor na hUidre,
translated in Eugene O'Curry,
Manners and Customs of the Ancient Irish vol. 2, Dublin, 1873

Ireland's Early Historians

The first identifiable secular Irish historian was Sinlán mocco Min, abbot of Bangor, who died there in A.D. 607. His annals no longer exist as a separate or distinguishable document. Cenn Faelad (d. A.D. 670), of whose writings only fragments remain, studied at Tuaim Dreacain (Toomregan), which was one of the great universities and medical schools in ancient Ireland. The evidence that we have shows that Irish society already had a literary structure and there was a bardic assembly, which appointed a chief bard. One of the earliest chief bards whom we can identify is Dallán Forgaill of Connacht (b. c. A.D. 540, d. A.D. 596), some of whose poems still survive. He was succeeded in that office by another Connacht poet, Seanchán Torpéist (c. A.D. 570–647), who is said to have saved the epic Táin Bó Cuailgne from oblivion, and this explains the survival of apparently sixth-century verses known as rosc in the otherwise eighth-century verses of the text. Another early historian was

Rumann mac Colmáin (d. A.D. 748 at Tullamore, County Offaly), who was hailed as "the Homer and the Virgil of Ireland."

The earliest known secular book is Cín Dromma Snechta (Book of Drumsnat). This contained several heroic tales written in the first half of the eighth century. It was known to writers of the medieval period but no longer exists. The eighth century saw the rise of the Golden Age of Irish culture and the expansion of its influence in Europe. Much of this great learning and scholastic endeavor has been lost due to the attempted destruction of Irish cultural achievement during the colonial period.

It is not until the tenth and eleventh centuries that we start to have any surviving extensive historical works. Mael Muru of Fathan (c. A.D. 820–886), Cormac mac Cuileannáin (A.D. 836–908), Eochaidh Ua Flainn (fl. A.D. 950–984), Cenaed Ó hArtagáin (c. A.D. 910–975), Muirchertagh Mac Conchertaigh, Mac Liag (b. c. A.D. 960, d. 1015), Cuán Ó Lothcháim (c. A.D. 970–1024), Flann Mainistreach (b. c. A.D. 1000, d. 1056), and Giolla Caoimhin (fl. A.D. 1025–1072) were the leading historians of this period whose works are known. Mac Liag was actually secretary to High King Brían Bóroimhe (Brian Boru) and wrote Cogadh Gaedhel re Gallaibh, about the war against the Danes or Vikings. He was killed with Brían at the battle of Clontarf and his work was finished by Erard Mac Coise (b. c. A.D. 960–1022), who was chief poet to Maelsechnaill Mac Domnaill, who resumed the high kingship after Brían's death and ruled from 1014 to 1027.

2

Early Christian Ireland

The conversion of Ireland to Christianity began in earnest in the early fifth century A.D. It is recorded that Pope Celestine I (A.D. 422–432) appointed Palladius as "first bishop to the Irish believing in Christ," which implies that there were already Christian communities in Ireland. Palladius seems to have died before arriving in Ireland, and Patrick (c. A.D. 385–461) was appointed in his place. But one of the most influential pre-Patrician missionaries was a native of Munster, Ailbe mac Olcnais, who founded his religious center at Emly (Imleach Iubhair, "the borderland of yew trees") in County Tipperary, which became one of the great Irish religious centers. Ailbe became patron saint of Munster. Emly remained an influential cathedral city until 1587, when it was combined with the See of Cashel. The buildings at Emly were destroyed in 1607 after the Irish defeat at Kinsale.

Ailbe was at the christening of King Oenghus Mac Nad Froich (d. c. A.D. 490) of Cashel. His death is given in most of the annals as c. A.D. 527. But if Patrick had died in A.D. 461, the dating would make Ailbe exceptionally old if he had been ministering in Ireland prior to Patrick.

The Birth of Ailbe

Ailbe, bishop of the men of Munster, most blessed father, and second patron of the whole island after Patrick, came from the eastern part of the region of Cliath, which is in Munster. His father, who was named Olcnais, was in the household of King Crónáin in the region of Artrige [Araid Cliach, northeast Limerick]. There he went in by night to the king's female attendant named Sanclit and slept with her. Olcnais then knowing that she had conceived from him, and fearing that the king might kill him, fled. She gave birth to his son, holy Ailbe. Seeing his female's attendant's baby, the King Crónáin said: "This child cannot live under my roof nor be fostered with my sons."

And the king told his servants that the boy should be killed. But the Holy Spirit inspired the servants not to kill the boy; instead they hid him under a certain rock and left him there; and his name is honoured there to the present day. There lived under this same rock, a wild wolf, who loved the holy boy and, like a gentle mother, fondly nourished him among her own cubs.

One day, however, while this wild beast was out hunting prey in the woods, a certain man named Lochán, a man of natural goodness, saw the boy among the wolf cubs under the rocks and took him out and brought him to his own home. As soon as the wild beast returned and saw the boy was missing, she searched frantically, with breathless anxiety, for him. And as Lochán approached his home, the animal seized his cloak and would not let him go until she saw the boy. At which Lochán said to the beast: "Go in peace. This boy will no longer be among wolves, but will stay with me." Then that wild animal, weeping and howling, returned sorrowfully to its cave.

"The Life of St. Ailbe," in *Vitae Sanctorum Hiberniae* vol. 1, ed. C. Plummer, 1910

Patrick's Own Account of His Life

Patrick was born around A.D. 385. From the clues he gives us, it seems that he was a British Celt from the area near what is now Carlisle (then Caer Liwelyd, which the Romans called Luguvallium, "the city of the god Lug"). During his youth, it was part of a northern kingdom ruled by Coel Hen. This was a time long before the arrival of the ancestors of the English, so the popular modern jibe that Patrick was an Englishman is nonsense.

My father was the deacon Calpornius, son of the late Potitus, a priest of the town of Banna Venta Berniae. He had a small estate nearby, where I was taken captive.

I was then barely sixteen. I had neglected the true God, and when I was carried off into captivity in Ireland, along with a great number of people, it was well deserved. For we cut ourselves off from God and did not keep His commandments, and we disobeyed our bishops who were reminding us of our salvation. God revealed His being to us through His wrath: he scattered us among foreign peoples, even to the end of the earth, where, appropriately, I have my own small existence among strangers.

Patrick, *Confessio (Declaration)*, in *Libri Espistolarum Sancti Patrici Esposcopi*, ed. L. Bieler, 1952

Patrick Sets Out to Meet with the Míliucc, Chief at Sliabh Mis (Slemish, County Antrim)

Míliucc, however, heard that his [former] captive was about to arrive in his presence to force on him, as it were, new ways for which he had no desire at the end of his days. Not wishing to be made subject to his own (former) servant, he followed the devil's inspiration and committed himself to the flames; having gathered all his valuables and belongings around him in the house in which he had lived as a chieftain, he set everything on fire. Patrick then stood on that previously mentioned spot on the southern slope of Sliabh Mis from which, when he arrived, he could see the region in which he had gained such grace as a servant.

Bishop Tirechán's account of *St. Patrick's Journey in Ireland* (written in the seventh century), in *The Patrician Texts in the Book of Armagh*, ed. L. Bieler and F. Kelly, 1979

Patrick Converts the Daughters of the High King Laoghaire

The one prominent person in Ireland whom Patrick could not convert to Christianity was the high king, Laoghaire mac Néill (d. c. 463), a son of Niall of the Nine Hostages. The hagiographers are agreed that he died holding his pre-Christian beliefs and was buried in traditional manner, standing upright with his weapons and facing his hereditary enemies, the kingdom of Leinster. However, his daughters did convert.

Afterwards, then, before sunrise, Patrick came to the well that is called Clébach [now Ogulla, near Tulsk in County Roscommon] on the eastern slopes of Cruachu. They sat down beside the well, and suddenly there appeared the two daughters of the High King, Laoghaire—Ethne the Fair and Fidelma the Red. These had come, as is the women's custom, to wash in the morning. They found the holy gathering of bishops with Patrick by the well, and they had no idea where they were from or what was their nature or their people or their homeland; but they thought that they were men of the *sidh* [fairies] or of the gods of the earth or phantoms.

The girls said to them: "Are you really there? Where have you come from?"

Patrick replied to them: "It would be better for you to confess faith in our true God than to ask questions about our origin."

The first girl asked: "Who is God, and where is God, and whose God is he, and where is his house? Has your God sons and daughters, gold and silver? Is he alive forever? Is he beautiful? Have many people foster his sons? Are his daughters dear and beautiful to the men of this world? Is he in heaven or on earth, in the sea, on mountains, in valleys? Give us some idea of him; how he may be seen, how loved; how he may be found—is he found in youth or old age?"

Bishop Tirechán's account of St. Patrick's Journey in Ireland

St. Brigid—Mary of the Gael

Kildare (Cille Dara, "Church of the Oaks") was a conhospitae, where, in Celtic custom, men and women dwelt and worked, raising their children in Christian tradition. Brigid had invited a bishop called Conláeth to establish the abbey with her. A monk of Kildare named Cogitosus wrote her first biography, produced within fifty years of her death.

Nor must one be silent about the miracle of the rebuilding of the church in which the bodies of that glorious pair, the Bishop Conláeth and the Holy Brigid, lie right and left of the ornamented altar placed in shrines decorated with a variegation of gold, silver, gems and precious stones, with gold and silver crowds hanging over them.

In fact, to accommodate the increasing number of the faithful, of both sexes, the church is spacious in its floor area, and it rises to an extreme height. . . . When the ancient door of the left hand entrance, through which Brigid was accustomed to enter the church, was set on its hinges by the craftsmen [rebuilding the church after her death] it did not fill the new entrance of the rebuilt church. In fact, a quarter of the opening was left unclosed and agape. If a fourth part, by height were added, then the door could be restored to fit the opening. The artificers deliberated and discussed whether they should make a completely new and larger, door, which would fill the opening, or whether they should make a timber piece to attach to the old door to bring it to the required size. The gifted master, who was in all these matters the leading craftsman of the Irish, gave wise advice. "We ought," he said, "in this coming night, alongside Brigid, to pray faithfully to the Lord so that she may indicate in the morning what we should do." And so he spent the whole night praying before St Brigid's shrine.

And having sent on his prayer, he rose in the morning and brought the old door and placed it on its hinges. It closed the opening completely. There was no gap, no overlap.

> Cogitosus, a monk of Kildare, writing c. A.D. 620
> "Life of St. Brigid the Virgin," in *Triadis Thaumaturgae*, 1647

The Codification of the Laws of Ireland (A.D. 438)

The tenth year of the reign of Laoghaire. The Senchus and the Fénechus of Ireland were purified and written, the writings and old books of Ireland have been collected and brought to one place at the order of the High King. For three years Laoghaire, the High King, Corc, King of Muman [Munster], Dáire, King of Ulaidh [Ulster], with the ecclesiastics Patrick, Benignus and Cairneach, and the three Brehons, Dubhtach, Chief Brehon of Laoghaire, Rossa and Fearghus, met and considered them.

> *Annals of Tigernach* (earliest surviving complete copy was started in A.D. 1088;
> fragments of earlier copies are in the Bodleian Library, Oxford), ed.
> Whitley Stokes, *Revue Celtique*, 1895, 1896, 1897

What did not clash with the word of God in the written Law and in the New Testament, and with the consciences of the believers, was confirmed in the laws of the Brehons by Patrick and by the ecclesiastics and the princes of Erin; and this is the *Senchus Mór*.

> Introduction to the *Senchus Mór*
> Facsimile ed., Irish Manuscript Commission, Dublin, 1931

Colmcille's "Farewell to Ireland"

In A.D. 561, Colm Mac Fedhlimidh (later known as Colmcille, "Dove of the Church"; b. Donegal, c. 521, d. Iona, 597) went to stay with St. Fintan at the abbey of Maghhile (Moville, near Newtownards). Fintan possessed a copy of The Gospel Book of St. Martin *(of Tours), which he coveted. Each night Colm went to the abbey library and worked on copying the book. Fintan discovered this and was furious. He took the case before the high king, Diarmaid Mac Cearbhaill, and his chief, Brehon (judge). The judgment was "to every cow belongs her calf, so to every book belongs its offspring book." This Brehon law thus delivered the first known copyright law.*

Colm refused to be bound by the judgment. He was a proud descendant of Niall of the Nine Hostages of the Uí Néill dynasty of Cenél Conaill. He took his grievance to his clan, who rose up against King Diarmaid, and a battle was fought at Cul Drebne (modern Culdrevny, under Ben Bulben, County Sligo).

A.D. 561: The battle of Cul Drebne, gained over Diarmaid Mac Cerbhaill, in which 3,000 fell. Fergus and Domnall, two sons of Mac Erca, and Ainmire, son of Setna, and Nainnid, son of Duach . . . were victors, with Aedh, son of Echa Tirmacha, king of Connacht. Through the prayers of Colmcille they conquered.

> *Annála Ulaidh* (Annals of Ulster)
> Compiled by Cathal Mac Maghnusa Mheg Uidhir, 1498,
> published in Dublin, 4 vols., 1887, 1893, 1895, 1901

Although Diarmaid was defeated in this battle, Colmcille went into exile in Scotland, settling on the small island of Iona, where he built up the monastery there as one of the great centers of Christianity whose missionaries spread south into the pagan Anglo-Saxon kingdoms to convert them to the new faith and bring them literacy. Colmcille became bishop of the Dál Riada in what was to become Scotland. Of surviving writings, his twenty-two–verse poem on his exile is regarded as a classic.

> Great is the speed of my coracle
> And its stern turned upon Derry:
> Grievous is my errand over the main,
> Travelling to Alba of the beetling brows.
>
> I stretch my glance across the brine
> From the firm oaken planks:
> Many are the tears of my bright soft grey eye
> As I look back upon Erin.

> *Ancient Irish Poetry,* Kuno Meyer, London, 1913

High King of Ireland Declares Dál Riada (Scotland) Independent (a.d. 575)

And this is the judgement that he gave: that the Dál Riada of Erin [in County Antrim] and its service in war [hostings] belong to the sovranty of Ireland, because military service [hostings] goes always with the land, but the Dál Riada of Erin must pay taxation and tribute to the sovranty of Dál Riada of Alba [Scotland], if not paid their *muir-coblach* [ship service or sea fleet] belongs to the sovantry of Dál Riada [Alba]. All else, however, concerning the Dál Riada of Erin belongs to the sovranty of Ireland.

Amra Coluim Chilli (Preface), Dallán mac Forgall, A.D. c. 540–596

Irish Clerical Humor

The Irish had adopted the Latin alphabet after, it seems, a short experimentation with a peculiar form called Ogam, named after the pagan god of literacy, Ogma. There are 369 known Ogam inscriptions on stones. Some 249 of these inscriptions are in the counties of Kerry, Cork, and Waterford, and record personal names. They seem to belong to the fifth and sixth centuries. The form of Irish is archaic even for the period. An essay on the script was contained in The Book of Ballymote, *compiled in 1390 by Maghnus Ó Duibhgánáin.*

The Latin alphabet gave a freedom to Irish writing at the height of Ireland's Golden Age of learning, producing such scholars and poets as Sedulius (c. A.D. 820–880), whose name was Siadhal mac Eradach of Kildare, settled in Liége, where his poetry and scholarship made him famous; physicians such as Maeldor Ó Tinnrí (d. A.D. 860); and geographers such as Dicuil (d. c. A.D. 775), who wrote of a fellow Irishman, Brother Fedhlimidh (Fidelis), who had been to Egypt and measured the pyramids. Dicuil also wrote astronomical works in prose and verse. Eriugena (Johannes Scotus; b. c. A.D. 810–880) was appointed head of the palace school of Charles the Bald of the Franks and was the foremost western philosopher of his day, writing De Divisione Naturae *and many other works.*

And with Irish scholarship came wit and humor.

> To go to Rome,
> No profit, much pain
> The master you seek in Rome, you find at home
> Or seek in vain

Anonymous, ninth century
Thesaurus Palaeohibernicus, vol. 2, p. 296
Translated by Frank O'Connor, in *A Book of Ireland*, London, 1959

One of the best-known poems translated from eighth-century Irish by Robin Flower (1881–1946) concerned a scholar comparing his activities to those of his cat. The following are two of the several verses:

I and Pangur Ban, my cat,
'Tis a like task we are at;
Hunting mice is his delight,
Hunting words I sit all night.

Practice every day had made
Pangur perfect in his trade;
I get wisdom day and night
Turning darkness into light.

Anonymous, eighth century
Translated by Robin Flower, in *Poems and Translations*, London, 1931

And a final comment on the nature of scholarship and religion:

'Tis sad to see the sons of learning
In everlasting Hellfire burning
While he that never read a line
Doth in eternal glory shine.

Anonymous, ninth century
Translated by Robin Flower, in *Poems and Translations*, London, 1931

3

The Viking Terror

The First Appearance of the Vikings in Ireland

A.D. 795: The Island of St Patrick [near the Skerries, County Dublin] was burnt by the Danes, they made great taxation on the land and stole the holy relics of St Dochonna [bishop of Connor who had died in A.D. 725].

A.D. 830: The Danes, intending full conquest of Ireland, continued their invasions from time to time, using all manner of cruelties. . . . If the owner of the house where a Dane lodged had no more in the world to live upon but one milch cow for the maintenance of himself and family, he was compelled presently to kill her to meet the Dane's demands, if he could not otherwise pay money or some other token approved of. The houses of religion were generally turned into brothels, stables and houses of "easement." Indeed, the sacred altars of God, that saints had in great reverence built, were broke, abused and cast down by them most scornfully.

Untitled manuscript, Trinity College Library Cat. F.3,19
Referred to as the Annals of Clonmacnoise

Bitter and wild is the wind tonight
It tosses the ocean's white hair;

Tonight I fear not the fierce warriors of Norway
Coursing on the Irish Sea.

Anonymous, ninth-century Irish verse in margin of the St. Gall manuscript, p. 112
Translated by Kuno Meyer, in Ancient Irish Poetry, London, 1913

Defeat of the Vikings at Limerick (c. A.D. 937)

Then Suilleabháin with his one hundred and fifty brave, valiant swords-men arrived to his [King Cellachán Caisil of Munster] defence and he made a breach of savage ferocity through the centre of the horde of Lochlannachs [Vikings]. Then arose the unviolated pillar and unsubdued hero and the lion unconquered until that day—namely the long-haired, high spirited Morann of the fierce people [Vikings], the son of the Fleet-King of Leodhas [Lewis] with his warriors around him. And when these chiefs met they smote each other fiercely. Suilleabhán planted his spear through the boss of the buckler and beneath the rim of the helmet and into the Viking prince, so that it passed quickly into his neck, and placed the head in the power of the Irish warrior, And he beheaded the brave Viking and brought the head with him to King Cellachán to boast of his triumph. And many Vikings fell in that fight.

Prince Donnchad met the brave Magnus together in battle. They struck off the points of their broad grooved swords and battered their shields into pieces with their war clubs and wounded their bodies with their javelins. Magnus, however, fell before the great Donnchad.

Then Lochlann and Riordan engaged in battle and Lochlann inflicted a terrible wound on Riordan. When the warrior was wounded and pierced through, and when he perceived that his weapons took no effect on this veteran warrior who was his enemy, Riordan made an heroic rush upon Lochlann, and left his sword, and his long bladed spear, and he put in his mind his sharp iron-blue mail coat and laid dextrously hold of the lower part of the cuirass of the Viking with his left hand and gave the champion a sudden pull, so that he maimed the broad bosom of the war-rior, and that his bowels and entrails fell out of him. And he beheaded the champion and lifted his head in triumph.

Nevertheless, there fell these four valiant champions of the Viking heroes and the other warriors left their places and the soldiers were over-thrown and made for Limerick to shut themselves up there. And it was through the rear of the Vikings that the nobles of Munster went into the town so that the Vikings were not able to close the gates and they were killed in houses and in towers. They brought their wives and children and people in captivity to the nobles of Munster and collected the gold, silver and various riches of the town, and brought the heads, trophies and battle spoils of the Vikings to King Cellachán and the heads of the four who were the most noble of the Vikings were exhibited to him.

Caithreim Cheallachain Chaisil (The battles of King Cellachán of Cashel), written c. A.D. 1127–1138, manuscript at Royal Irish Academy, Dublin, printed version ed. A. Bugge, University of Christiana, Denmark, 1905

Battle of Clontarf (A.D. 1014)

King Brian had come up to the fortified town [Dublin] with his entire army and on Friday the army [Danes] issued from the town. Both armies arranged themselves in battle array. Brodhir commanded one wing and King Sigtrygg [Danish King of Dublin] commanded the other. We must say that King Brian did not wish to give battle on Good Friday; therefore a shield-wall was set about him and his army stationed in front of that. Ulf Hraeda commanded the wing facing Brodhir and Ospak and his sons headed the wing facing Sigtrygg but Centhialfadh stood in the middle and had the flag about him.

Brodhir had tried to learn by means of sorcery how the battle would turn out, and the answer was this; if the battle was fought on Good Friday, King Brian would win the victory but die; and that if it was fought before that time, then all who were against him would fall. Then Brodhir said that they should not fight before Friday.

The Njalssaga, thirteenth century, ed. G. Webbe Dasent, Edinburgh, 1861

The Death of the High King Brian Boru (A.D. 1014)

While the High King was engaged in conversation at his tent, his attendant saw a party of foreigners approaching them . . . the High King unsheathed his sword. For it was Jarl Brodhir and some men escaping from the battle-field. Brodhir would have passed him by unnoticed but one of those with him, who knew the High King by sight, cried out "This is the King!"

Brodhir said: "Surely it is a noble priest?" "Not so," cried the man. "It is the great King Brian himself!" Then Brodhir turned with his battle-axe gleaming in his hand.

The High King gave him a sword blow that cut off the left leg at the knee and turning gave another, which took the right leg at the foot. Jarl Brodhir gave the High King one stroke, which crushed his head utterly, and they fell mutually by each other.

There was not done in Erin, since Christianity—except the beheading of Cormac Mac Cuilinan—any deed greater than this. Brian was, in truth, one of the three best kings that ever were born in Ireland and one of the three men who caused Ireland to prosper . . . for it was he that released the men of Ireland and its women from the bondage and iniquity of the Foreigners and the Vikings. It was he that gained five and twenty battles over the Foreigners and who killed them and banished them. In short, Ireland fell by the death of Brian.

"Cogadh Gaedhel re Gaillaibh," in the *Lebor na Nuachonghbala*
(Book of Leinster), compiled by Fionn MacGormain, 1150

4

Ireland and the Angevin Empire

Preparing the Way

Mael Maedoc ua Morgair (St. Malachy, c. 1094–1148) was a reforming priest from Armagh. He disapproved of the native liturgy and social system and wanted the Irish Church to embrace the rule of Rome. He had already been driven out of the abbey of Bangor, having enraged the people by his actions. However, he was appointed archbishop of Armagh, but he was so opposed that it was some years before he could actually establish himself there. He resigned in 1137 and in 1139 went to Rome to seek the support of Pope Innocent II in his attempt to change the Irish Church.

Innocent II made Malachy his papal legate in Ireland, and Malachy returned to set up the first Cistercian house in Mellifont and introduce canons regular. He became a friend of St. Bernard of Clairvaux and stayed with him during his journeys. In 1148, Malachy set out again to see the pope but died in Clairvaux. St. Bernard wrote his Life *and mentioned Malachy's views of his native land.*

He discovered it was not to men but to beasts that he had been sent; in all the barbarians which he had yet encountered, he had never met such a people so profligate in their morals, so uncouth in their ceremonies, so impious in their faith, so barbarous in laws, so rebellious in discipline, so filthy in life—Christians in name but Pagans in reality . . . [how could] so saintly and loveable man [as Malachy] come out of such a race?

Bernard of Clairvaux, *The Life and Death of St. Malachy the Irishman*
Translated by Robert T. Meyer, Cistercian Publishers, 1978

Malachy had alerted Rome to the fact that the Irish Church paid little heed to the temporal power of Rome. In the latter part of the twelfth century, the Angevin Empire of Henry FitzEmpress included Anjou, its principal seat from which the Angevin Empire took its name; Maine; Touraine; Aquitaine; Gascony; overlordship of Brittany; the original territory of Normandy; and England; with claims over Scotland and Wales. England was merely one of the provinces over which the Angevin emperor, as Henry II, ruled, and he, like the dukes of Normandy before him, hardly spent any time there, being born in Le Mans and dying in Anjou. Richard I, Coeur de Lion (the Lion Heart), spent only six months of his entire life in England. It was only with John, nicknamed "Lackland" for obvious reasons, that the Angevin Empire broke up and the Norman kings were forced to use England as their power base. Thus the idea that England conquered Ireland in the twelfth century is erroneous. The Angevin emperor was Rome's choice to bring Ireland into the Roman fold. Adrian IV—Nicholas Breakspear from what is now Hertfordshire in England—had been born a subject of the Angevin Empire. He had been elected pope on December 4, 1154, and died in 1159.

Henry II's Plan to Conquer Ireland Approved by Pope Adrian IV

Whereas, then, well-beloved son in Christ, you have expressed to us your desire to enter the island of Ireland in order to subject its people to law and to root out from them the weeds of vice, and your willingness to pay an annual tribute to the blessed Peter of one penny from every house, and to maintain the rights of the churches of that land whole and inviolate; We therefore, meeting your pious and laudable desire with due favour and according a gracious assent to our petition, do hereby declare our will and pleasure that, with a view to enlarging the boundaries of the Church, restraining the downward course of vice, correcting evil customs and planting virtue, and for the increase of the Christian religion, you shall enter the island and execute whatsoever may tend to the honour of God and the welfare of the land; and also that the people of that land shall receive you with honour and revere you as their lord; provided always that the rights of the churches remain whole and inviolate, and saving to the blessed Peter and the Holy Roman Church the annual tribute of one penny from every house.

Adrian IV, quoted in Giraldus Cambrensis, *Expugnatio Hibernica*, c. 1185
Giraldus Cambrensis Opera, ed. J. S. Brewer, London, 1861–1891

Deposed King Diarmada Mac Murchadha of Leinster Appeals for Aid to Henry II

Dermot MacMurrough (Diarmada Mac Murchadha Uí Cennselaig) was elected to the kingship of Leinster in 1125. Records show that in his early years he was well regarded, and St. Bernard of Clairvaux, the friend of Mael Maedoc ua Morgair (St. Malachy of Armagh), wrote him a letter of praise. Dermot then made a mistake by falling in love with Dearbhorgaill (Dervogilla, 1108–1193), wife of the king of Breifne, Tigernán Ua Ruairc, and eloping with her. High King Ruairaidh Ó Conchobhair eventually marched on Dermot's kingdom, defeated him, and demanded that Dermot pay compensation to Ua Ruairc. Dearbhorgaill went to the Cistercian Abbey of Mellifont, County Louth, where she spent the rest of her life. In his desire for revenge, Dermot went abroad to Anjou, having heard the power of the Angevin emperor to ask for aid against the high king.

God, who dwells on high, guard and save you King Henry! May He in the same manner give you heart, courage and the inclination to avenge the shame and the misfortune, which my own people have brought upon me!

Noble King Henry, hear of where I was born, of what country. Of Ireland I was born a lord, in Ireland I was acknowledged a king. But wrongfully my own people have cast me out of my kingdom. To you, good Sire, I come to make complaint in the presence of the barons of your empire.

From henceforth onwards, for all the days of my life I will become your liegeman on condition that you be my ally, so that I will not lose everything. I will acknowledge you as sire and lord in the presence of your barons and earls.

Giraldus Cambrensis, *Expugnatio Hibernica*, c. 1185
Giraldus Cambrensis Opera, ed. J. S. Brewer, London, 1861–1891

Henry II Decides to Use Diarmada as a Cat's-Paw to Invasion

Henry, King of England, Duke of Normandy and Aquitaine, Count of Anjou, to all his liegemen, English, Norman, Welsh and Scots, and to all nations subjects to his sway, greeting. Whatsoever the letters shall come unto you, know that we have received Dermot, Prince of Leinster, unto our grace and favour. Wherefore, whosoever within the bounds of our territories shall be willing to give him aid as our vassal and liegeman, in recovering his dominion, let him be assured of our favour and licence in that behalf.

Giraldus Cambrensis, *Expugnatio Hibernica*, c. 1185
Giraldus Cambrensis Opera, ed. J. S. Brewer, London, 1861–1891

High King Ruadri Warns Diarmada (1169)

Contrary to the conditions of our treaty of peace, you have invited a host of foreigners into this island, and yet as long as you kept within the bounds of Leinster we bore it patiently. But, now, forasmuch as, regardless of your solemn oath, and having no concern for the fate of the hostage you gave, you have broken the bounds agreed on, and insolently crossed the frontiers of your own territory—either restrain in future the irruption of your foreign warbands, or we will certainly have your son's head cut off and we will send it to you.

High King Ruadri Ó Conchobhar to Dermot Mac Murrough, king of Leinster, in 1171
Giraldus Cambrensis, *Expugnatio Hibernica*, c. 1185
Giraldus Cambrensis Opera, ed. J. S. Brewer, London, 1861–1891

Diarmada Initially Defeated in 1168 by the High King

Diarmait Mac Murchadha arrived in Ireland with an army of Foreigners and he retook the kingship of Hy Cennselaig [Leinster]. A week was the High King of Ireland in his house before he heard that Mac Murrough had found great strength and returned to power in Leinster. The High King and King of Breifne and the King of Meath and men of Dublin with them, marched to Ferdorcha and encamped a week awaiting envoys from Diarmada. A party of warriors left the camp to seek combat and six of them were killed by the Foreigners. Whereupon the High King's army issued forth and put to flight Diarmada and his Foreigners at which Diarmada submitted to the High King and paid tribute, hostages and gave Ó Ruairc five score ounces of gold for compensation for his wife.

Annals of Tigernach, ed. Whitley Stokes, *Revue Celtique*,
vols. 16, 17, and 18, Paris, 1895–1897

Massacre of Baginbun Point (May 1170)

On May 1, 1170, Raymond le Gros led his Norman army against a combined army of the Irish and Norse-Irish from Waterford. One thousand Irish were killed, wounded or taken prisoner.

Thus nobly retracing his steps [Raymond] while he dealt a terrible blow, and shouted his war-cry, he encouraged his followers to stand on their defence, and struck terror into the enemies' ranks ... the enemy took flight and dispersing themselves over the country, were pursued and slaughtered in such numbers that upwards of five hundreds fell by the sword and when the pursuers ceased striking from sheer weariness, they threw the vast numbers from the edge of the cliffs into the sea underneath.

... having gained the victory, they kept seventy of the principal townsmen [of Waterford] prisoners in the camp, for whose ransom they might have obtained the city itself or an immense sum of money.

Giraldus Cambrensis, *Expugnatio Hibernica*, c. 1185
Giraldus Cambrensis Opera, ed. J. S. Brewer, London, 1861–1891

Of the Irish there were taken quite as many as seventy. But the noble knights had them beheaded. To a wench they gave an axe of tempered steel and she beheaded them all. And then threw their bodies over the cliff because she had that day lost her lover in the combat. Alice of Abervenny was her name, who served the Irish thus.

"Le chansun de Dermot e li Quens Riccard fitz Gilbert" *(The song of Dermot and the earl)*
Translated by Goddard H. Orpen, Clarendon Press, Oxford, 1892

"Strongbow" Richard, Earl of Pembroke, Lands at Passage (August 23, 1170)

The beginning of Erin's evil, to wit, Robert Fitz Stephen came into Ireland with sixty mailcoats [knights] and there was Earl Richard, son of Gilbert, and they had two battalions, both knights and archers, came to help Mac Murchada. And they entered Waterford by force, and left some of their people there, and they invaded Loch Carman [Wexford] by force, and captured Mac Gillie Mhuire, commander of the fortress, and Ua Faelain, the Prince of the Deisi, and his son, and slaughtered the garrison of the fortress, so that seven hundred of them fell.

Annals of Tigernach, ed. Whitley Stokes, *Revue Celtique*,
vols. 16, 17, and 18, Paris, 1895–1897

Defeat of the High King on September 1, 1171 (an English View)

Roderick [Ruadri] took his ease and pleasure, and was bathing himself [with his generals and troops] in the Liffey, but when the alarm was up, and he saw his men, on every side, fall to the ground, he never tarried or called for man or page to array him, but took his mantle and ran away, all naked.

Meredith Hanmer, Chronicles of Ireland, London, 1571, quoting the
Book of Howth (then in Lambeth Palace Library)

The Conflict from an Irish View

Ruadri Ua Conchobhair, Tighernan Ó Ruairc and Muirchertagh Ó Ceabhaill, King of Oriel, marched to Dublin to besiege [Strongbow] Richard, Earl of Pembroke, and Miles de Cogan. For the space of a fortnight there were conflicts and skirmishes between them. Then the High King marched to meet the troops of Diarmada Mac Murchada [Mac Murrough], leaving the troops of Leth Cuinn in camp. The cavalry troops of Ó Ruairc and Ó Cearbhaill went to cut down the enemy's corn and supplies. While this was happening the Earl and Miles de Cogan attacked the camp of Leth Cuin and killed a multitude of camp followers and some warriors, carried out their provinces, their armour and horses.

Ó Ruairc met with Miles de Cogan and fought a battle in which Ó Ruairc was routed and Aedh, son of Tighernán Ó Ruairc, tanaist [heir apparent] was killed along with Ó Donnchadha and Donnchadha Ó Cuinn and many nobles of Oriel.

Annals of Tigernach, ed. Whitley Stokes, Revue Celtique,
vols. 16, 17, and 18, Paris, 1895–1897

After that Diarmada Mac Murchadha mustered with the Foreigners in order to overcome Dublin. Then the High King of Ireland, Ruadri Ua Conchobhair, gathered his troops to the Green of Dublin and remained there, awaiting battle, for three days and three nights, till lightning struck Dublin and demolished it. Thereafter the Foreigners assented to the burning of the town, since they perceived that to be with Mac Murchada [Mac Murrough] was ready to revolt against the King of Ireland. Then the King of Ireland returned with his army unhurt after Mac Murchada and the Foreigners had refused to give him battle. Then Mac Murchada and the Foreigners went and overcame Dublin by force and made captives of all that were therein.

Annals of Tigernach, ed. Whitley Stokes, Revue Celtique,
vols. 16, 17, and 18, Paris, 1895–1897

Henry II Lands in Ireland on October 17, 1172

Henry II, King of England, Duke of Normandy, Earl of Anjou, and lord of many other countries, came to Ireland this year with a fleet of two hundred and forty ships, and landed at Waterford.

Annales Ríoghachta Éireann (Annals of the kingdom of Ireland)
Compiled by Micheál Ó Cléirigh (c. 1632–1636), 7 vols., Dublin, 1849–1851

Henry II arrived in Ireland at Waterford a week before Samhain [November 1] and Diarmait Mac Carthaigh, King of Desmond, submitted to him. Thence Henry went to Dublin and received the submission of the kingship of Leinster and that of Meath, Breifne, Oriel and Ulster.

Annals of Tigernach, ed. Whitley Stokes, *Revue Celtique,*
vols. 16, 17, and 18, Paris, 1895–1897

Henry II's Conquest Approved by Pope Alexander III

Adrian IV's successor as Pope, Alexander III, formerly Rolando Bandinelli of Siena (1159–1181), was delighted that the Angevin emperor was finally making a move to bring Ireland into the Roman fold.

By frequent report and trustworthy evidence and with much joy, we have been assured how that, like a pious king and magnificent prince, you have wonderfully and gloriously triumphed over the people of Ireland, who, ignoring the fear of God, in unbridled fashion at random wander through the steeps of vice, and have renounced all reverence from the Christian faith and virtue, and who destroy themselves in mutual slaughter, and over a kingdom which the Roman emperors, the conquerors of the world, left (so we read) untouched in their time, and, by the ill of God (as we firmly believe) have extended the power of your majesty over that same people, a race uncivilised and undisciplined.

Alexander III, bishop of Rome, writing to Henry II, Tusculum,
on the twelfth Kalends of October 1172
One of three letters of congratulations
quoted in Thomas Rhymer, *Foedera,* London, 1811

The Death of Tigernán Ó Ruairc, King of Breifne (1172)

Tigernán Ó Ruairc, King of Breifne and Conmaine, a man of great power for a long time, was killed by the Normans and by Donal, son of Annadh Ó Ruairc of his own people along with them. He was beheaded by them and his head and body were carried ignominiously to Dublin. The head was raised over the door of the fortress—a sore, miserable sight for the Irish. The body was hung in another place with the feet upwards.

Annála Ulaidh (Annals of Ulster)
Compiled by Cathal Mac Maghnusa Mheg Uidhir, 1498
Published in Dublin, 4 vols., 1887, 1893, 1895, 1901

The Surrender to Henry II (Treaty of Windsor, October 6, 1175)

This is the agreement which was made at Windsor in the octaves of Michaelmas [October 6] in the year of Our Lord 1175 between Henry, King of England, and Roderic [Ruadri], King of Connacht, by Catholicus [Cadhla Ua Dubhthaig], archbishop of Tuam, Cantordis, abbot of Clonfert and by Lawrence [Lorcan Ó Tuathail], Chancellor of the King of Connacht, namely:

The King of England has granted to Roderic [Ruadri], his liegeman, King of Connacht, as long as he shall faithfully serve him, that he shall be king under him, ready to his service, as his man. And he shall hold his land as fully and as peacefully as he held it before the lord king entered Ireland, rendering him tribute. And that he shall have all the rest of the lands and its inhabitants under him and shall bring them to account, so that they shall pay their full tribute to the King of England through him, and so that they shall maintain their rights. And those who are now in possession of their lands and rights shall hold them in peace as long as they remain in the fealty of the King of England. And continue to pay him faithfully and fully his tribute and the other rights which they owe to him by the hands of the King of Connacht, saving in all things the right and honour of the King of England, and of Roderic. And if any of them shall be rebels to the King of England and to Roderic and shall refuse to pay the tribute and other rights of the King of England by his hand, and shall withdraw from the fealty of the king of England, he, Roderic, shall judge them and remove them. If he cannot answer for them by himself, the constable of the King of England in that land [Ireland] shall, when called upon him, aid him to do what is necessary.

And for this agreement the said King of Connacht shall render to the King of England tribute every year, namely, out of every ten animals slaughtered, one hide, acceptable to the merchants both in his land as in the rest: save that he shall not meddle with those lands which the lord king has retained in his lordship and in the lordship of his barons; that is to say, Dublin with all its appurtenances; Meath with all its appurtenances, even as Murchat Ua Mailethlachlin [Murchadh Ó Melaghlin] held it full and freely or as others held it of him; Wexford with all its appurtenances, that is to say, the whole of Leinster; and Waterford with its whole territory from Waterford to Dungarvan, including Dungarvan with all its appurtenances.

And if the Irish who have fled wish to return to the land of the barons of the King of England they may do so in peace, paying the said tribute as others pay it, or doing to the English the services which they were wont to do for their lands, which shall be decided by the judgement and will of their lords. And if any of them are unwilling to return and their lords have called upon the King of Connacht, he shall compel them to return to their land, so that they shall dwell there in peace.

And the King of Connacht shall accept hostages from all whom the Lord King of England has committed to him, and he shall himself give hostages at the will of the King.

The witnesses are: Robert, Bishop of Winchester; Geoffrey, Bishop of Ely; Laurence [Lorcan], Archbishop of Dublin; Geoffrey Nicholas and Roger, the King's chaplains; William, Earl of Essex; Richard de Luci [Lacey]; Geoffrey de Purtico and Reginald de Courtenes.

Latin text in Howden, Chronica Magistri Rogeri de Houedene, ed.
W. Stubbs, 4 vols., London, 1868–1871

The Treaty in Irish Eyes (1175)

Cadhla Ua Dubhthaig [Archbishop of Tuam] came out of England from Henry II, having with him "the peace of Ireland and the kingship thereof," both Foreigner and Irishman, to Ruadri Ua Conchobhair, and to every provincial king, his province, from the King of Ireland, and their tributes to Ruadri.

Annals of Tigernach, ed. Whitley Stokes, Revue Celtique,
vols. 16, 17, and 18, Paris, 1895–1897

Even while Henry II had only a tenuous foothold in Ireland, the pro-Roman Irish clerics held a synod at Cashel, the capital of the Desmond kingdom, whose King Diarmait Mac Carthaigh submitted in October 1172. Giraldus Cambrensis, in Expugnatio Hibernica, *reports the Irish bishops accepted Henry as "conqueror of Ireland," and drew up a new constitution for the Irish Church, bringing it into a new rapprochement with Rome. Celtic customs, as we call them in retrospect, were to be abolished. Lorcan Ó Tuathail (Lawrence O'Toole), archbishop of Dublin, who had negotiated the treaty, was a leading member of the Cashel Synod. In 1179, he went to Rome and was appointed papal legate. He died at Eu, near the mouth of the Bresle, in 1180 on his return journey. He became a saint of the Roman Church.*

5

Irish Princes and Norman Lords

D uring the thirteenth century, the Irish rulers and nobility found they had to live side by side with a number of Norman lords who had carved out territory in the Irish kingdoms and set themselves up with their retainers. Most of them, however, soon adopted the Irish language and sought redress in the local law system rather than implanting their own customs and cultural attitudes. The native church, however, gave way to Rome, and Dominicans established themselves in 1224, followed by Franciscans in 1231, Carmelites in 1270, and Augustines in 1280. In 1297, the lord of Ireland called the first Norman-style Parliament in Dublin.

Irish Law to Be Abolished by Edward I

Edward, King of England, Lord of Ireland etc., to his faithful Robert de Ufford, his justiciar in Ireland, greeting.

. . . we wish you to know that, after diligent discussion and fullest deliberations with our Council in the matter and inasmuch as the laws which the Irish use are detestable to God and contrary to all law so much so they ought not to be deemed law, it seems to us and our Council expedient to grant them the laws of England, provided however that in this the common asset of the people or at least of the prelates and magnates of that land, who are well disposed, should uniformly concur.

Liber Munerum Publicorum Hiberniae I, part IV, p. 3 (dated 1277)

The Battle of Bunratty (1311)

On Ascension Thursday, May 20, 1311, a battle in the struggle for dynastic power was fought in the kingdom of Thomond. It was part of the struggle between Donnchadh Uí Bríain (Ó Bríen) and a claimant, Diarmait Uí Bríain. What made this struggle significant is, instead of appeals to Brehon law, Richard de Clare of Bunratty Castle, situated at the mouth of the river Raite [Ratty], had decided to throw his military support behind Diarmait's claim. King Donnchadh sought aid for William de Burgo (Burke), the Norman lord of Connacht. De Burgo was worried about the territorial ambitions of de Clare and supported King Donnchadh.

Seán Mac Ruadhri Mac Craith (fl. 1300–1350), who was from a family of hereditary bards and historians to the Thomond kings, witnessed the dynastic conflict. He wrote a unique history of the struggle entitled Caithréim Thoirdhealbhaigh *(Wars of Turlough) that presents a fascinating eyewitness to a medieval Irish kingdom at war.*

On the Wednesday after the killing of Mac Conamara, he [William de Burgo, called Mac William Burke in the text] taking the same former clear and open road with all speed came to Ó Brían [king of Thomond]. The pair being thus reunited and on one ground, that night they tarried so; diligently from all airts [quarters of the compass] they summoned to them the people of the country, with first light of the morrow's silent morn they rose [the day precisely being Ascension Thursday], and made a resolute push for Bunratty, where they occupied the adjacent hill.

As for de Clare with his troops of horse and companies of foot, both Irish and Norman; as a great cloud big with fire, edged with scintillation, through the massive fortress-gates they issued and, with intent to engage Ó Brían, already posted there, march to crown the above-named eminence. The parties now being well up each to other and on the scene of action, the Norman nobles' courage was exalted; like embers all faces of the Irish chiefs flushed red; no veteran but his hair bristled on end, while striplings at this their first essay felt their hearts turn and be perturbed in them. The lines charged after a fashion such that we needs must liken their contact with the enemy to some particular horror of the universal Doom. Now was many a golden diadem made to fly, many a comely visage to darken, many a shield was held up for shelter; swords were busy shearing, spears trans-piercing; at last victory declared for Ó Brían and Mac William Burke as against de Clare and his friends and partisans, until Mac William Burke was shrewdly hit and, being taken a disadvantage with but a few attendants, captured. On hearing that their leader and noble lord was actually led into de Clare's castle to be fettered, with single impulse Mac William Burke's men all set their faces to their own land, and far and fast ran a well contested race home into Connacht.

Mac William Burke being thus unluckily made a prisoner, and Donnchadh, the supreme chief, consequently reduced to give up the fight in disorder and fly; de Clare exulted hugely; notwithstanding that, if we leave out Mac William Burke, the losses sustained on de Clare were more than those inflicted on King Donnchadh. At Donal Mac Conmara's earnest exhortation to take the offensive, Brían Bán and Brían Ruadh came in; over the whole region of St Cronán's coarb he sent out flying parties to maraud and back to Bunratty they brought the noble preys [prisoners] thus taken.

> Seán Mac Ruairdh Mac Craith, *Cáithreim Thoirdhealbhach*, ed. and introduction by
> Robin Flower, Standish Hayes O'Grady, London, 1929

The annals mention that King Donnchadh returned to his base at Cocomore, around modern Kilfernora, and here he was assassinated by Murchad, son of Mathgamin, son of Domnall Connachtach Ó Bríain; "and that crime was a great calamity," says the Annals of Innisfallen, *a book initially started by Maelsuthan Ua Cerbaill (d. 1010), the tutor to High King Brían Bóromhe, then kept by other scribes to 1326. The entry continues:*

Although de Clare and Diarmait were in Thomond at that time on a hosting, the murder was not committed by either of them, for according to report, they had no great hand in it, as it was committed because of an old enmity. And Thomond immediately gave pledges and hostages to Diarmait and to de Clare and Diarmait was made full king by the foreigners and the Irish.

> *Annals of Innisfallen*, ed. R. I. Best and Eoin MacNeill, Dublin, 1933

Irish Princes Plead to Pope John XXII (1317)

Lest the sharp-toothed and viperous calumny of the English and their untrue representations should to any degree excite your mind against us and the defenders of our right, which God forbid, and so that there may be no ground for what is not well known and is falsely presented to kindle your displeasure, for our defence we pour into your ears with mighty outcry by means of this letter, an entirely true account of our origin and our form of government, if government it can be called, and also of the cruel wrongs that have been wrought inhumanly on us and our forefathers by some kings of England, their evil ministers and English barons born in Ireland, wrongs that are continued still; and this we do in order that you may be able to approach the subject and see in which party's loud assertion the truth bears company. And this being carefully and sufficiently informed so far as the nature of the case demands, your judgement, like a naked blade may smite or correct the fault of the party that is in the wrong.

. . . when by perfidy and guile some Englishman kills an Irishman, however noble and inoffensive, whether cleric or lay, regular or secular, even if an Irish prelate should be killed, no punishment or correction is inflicted by the said court on such a nefarious murderer; nay more, the better the murdered man was and the greater the place he held among his people, the more his murderer is honoured and rewarded by the English, not merely by the populace but even by English religious and bishops, and most of all by those to whom it falls through their positions to inflict just punishments and due correction on such evil-doers.

Letter to Pope John XXII, 1317, from Domhnall Uí Néill, king of Cenel Eoghain (Ulaidh)
Quoted in the *Scotichronicon* of John Fordun, Harle, manuscript in British Museum
Fordun's Scotichronicon, ed. W. F. Skene, Edinburgh, 1871

King Edward III Concerned at Absorption of Colonists in Ireland (1360)

As many of the English nation in the Marches [borderlands between colonists and native Irish areas] and elsewhere have again became like Irishmen, and refuse to obey our laws and customs, and hold parliaments after the Irish fashion, and learn to speak the Irish language, and send their children among the Irish to be nursed and taught the Irish language, so that the people of English race have for the greater part become Irish; now we order 1) that no Englishman of any state or condition shall—under forfeiture of life, limbs and everything else—follow these Irish customs, laws and parliaments; 2) that any one of English race shall forfeit English liberty if, after the next feast of St John the Baptist he shall speak Irish with other Englishmen and meantime every Englishman must learn English and must not have his children at nurse amongst the Irish.

Translated from French; Edward III to the Sheriff of the Cross and
Seneschal of the Liberty of Kilkenny
Red Book, Archives of the Diocese of Ossory

Revival of Irish Cultural Enterprise

Gofraidh Fionn Ó Dálaigh (1320–1387) of Cork attended the great feast of Uí Maine for the Brehons, the bards and harpers of Ireland, in 1351. He listened cynically to the boasting of the poets and wrote:

In the foreigners' poems we promise that the Irish shall be driven from Ireland: in the Irishmen's poems we promise that the foreigners shall be routed across the sea.

Instead of Irish culture being destroyed, a resurgence of learning began, showing the deep involvement and patronage of the Norman lords in Irish culture. An example is Gearóid Iarla, the third earl of Desmond (c. 1335–1398), justiciar of Ireland from 1367 to 1369, who composed much courtly romantic poetry in Irish, fostered his son, James, with the king of Thomond (Ó Bríen), and ran things according to Brehon law rather than English law. Native learning was reinforced by Irish scholars returning from European universities such as Salerno, Bologna, Padua, and Montpellier bringing in the new Arabic learning: Arabian medicine, philosophy, and astrology. Great medical textbooks were to be produced, so by the eighteenth century, the Irish language contained one of the largest collections of medical texts written in any single language at that time.

Historians produced new powerful narratives such as one by Seán Mac Ruadri Mac Craith, who was eyewitness to the events in Caithréim Thoirdhealbhaigh *(Wars of Turlough) concerning the struggle for the supremacy of the kingship of Thomond. Another historian, Giolla Iosa Mac Firbhisigh (d. 1418), compiled the* Lebor Buidhe Lecain *(Yellow Book of Lecan), and what is now called* Leabhar Mór Mhic Fhir Bhisigh Leccain *(Great Book of Lecan). Poetry continued to flourish and even beautiful prose tales, such as* Trí Truagha na Scéaluidheachta *(Three sorrowful stories), whose author is unknown but is suspected to be someone in the Mac Firbisigh family. It was a period in which the* Fenian Cycle, *the tales of Fionn Mac Cumhaill and the elite band of warriors, the Fianna, was highly popular. The cycle of stories has been considered as Irish creative literary genius at its best. At this time, Arthurian tales as well as tales from other lands were being adapted into Irish forms.*

Two centuries of steady prosperity saw Ireland coming to grips with the Norman set-
tlers and paying scant regard to the lords of Ireland. But this time was about to end.

Richard II Attempts to Conquer Ireland (1395 and 1399)

The Irish provincial kings had been winning back their independence in spite of var-
ious campaigns that had been unleashed since Richard II, at age 10, had succeeded
his grandfather, Edward III, on June 21, 1377. In June 1394, seeking distraction after
the death of his wife, Anne of Bohemia, Richard decided to lead an army to Ireland
and assert himself as lord of Ireland, seeking the submission of the Irish kings and
lords. Landing at Waterford on October 2, 1394, with an army, estimated by Jean
Froissart (c. 1338–1410), a French aristocrat, poet, and chronicler, at thirty thou-
sand archers and four thousand men-at-arms (knights), he was faced by King Art
Mac Murrough of Leinster, known as Art Mór Mac Airt (ruling 1375–1417). He had
restored the kingdom of Leinster almost to its pre-Norman days and exacted an
annual tribute from the Anglo-Norman settlers who remained there, and even mar-
ried a Norman, Elizabeth Veele.

Henry Castide's Tale of the 1395 Conquest

Ireland is one of the evil countries of the world to make war upon, or to
bring under subjugation. For it is closed strongly and widely with high
forests, and great waters and marshes and places uninhabitable. It is hard
to enter to do them of the country any damage, nor you shall find neither
towns nor persons to speak withal. For the men draw to the woods and
dwell in caves and small cottages under trees and among bushes and
hedges, like wild savage beasts. And when they know that any man makes
war against them, and is to enter into their country, then they draw
together to the straits and passages and defend it so that no man can enter
into them. And when they see their time, they will soon take advantage on
their enemies, for they know the country and are light people. For a man
of arms being never so well horsed, and run as fast as he can, the Irishman
will run on foot as fast as he and overtake him, yes, and leap up upon his
horse behind him and draw him from his horse; for they are strong men
in the arms, and have sharp weapons with large blades with two edges,
after the manner of dart heads, where with they will slay their enemy; and
they believe not a man dead till they have cut his throat and opened his
belly and taken out his heart, and carry it away with them. Some say, such

as know their nature that they do eat it, and have great delight therein; they take no man to ransom. . . .

I shall show you somewhat of their rudeness, to the intent that may be a sample against people of other nations; I know it well, for I have proved it by themselves. For when they were at Dublin I had the governance of them about a month, by the King's commandment and his Council, to the intent that I should teach them to use themselves according to the usage of England and because I could speak their language as well as French and English, for in my youth I was brought up among them. I was with the Earl of Ormonde, father to the Earl that now is, who loved me right well, because I could then ride and handle a horse pretty well. And it was my fortune one time that the Earl, who was then my master, was sent with three hundred spearmen and a thousand archers into the marshes of Ireland to make war with the Irishmen, for always the Englishmen have had war with them, to subdue and put them under.

And on the day, as the Earl went against them, I rode a goodly horse of his, light and swift. Thus I rode and followed my master; and the same day the Irishmen were laid in an ambush, and when we came near them, they opened their ambush. Then the English archers began to shoot so eagerly that the Irishmen could not suffer it, for they are but simply armed, therefore they recoiled and went back. Then the Earl, my master, followed in the chase and I that was well horsed, followed him as nearly as I could. And I fortuned so that my horse was afraid and took his bridle in his teeth and ran away with me, and whether I would or not, he bore me so far forward among the Irishmen that one of them with lightness of running, leapt up behind me, and embraced me in his arms and did me no other hurt, but so led me out of the way, and so rode still behind me the space of two hours, and at the last brought me to a secret place, thick of bushes and there he found his company, who were come thither and escaped all dangers, for the Englishmen pursued not so far. Then he showed he had great joy of me, and led me into a town, a strong house among the woods, waters and mires. The town was called Harpely and the gentleman that took me was called Brian Costeret [probably Mac Oistgín, sometimes Mac Costagáin, whose territory was in the Waterford area]. He was a goodly man, howbeit very aged. This Brian Costeret kept me seven years with him [as a hostage] but gave me his daughter in marriage of whom I had two daughters. I shall show you how I was delivered.

It happened at the end of the seven years, one of the Kings named Arthur Mackemur, King of Leinster [Art Mór, or Airt Mac Murrough] raised an army against Duke Lyron [Lionel] of Clarence, son to King Edward of England and against Sir William Windsor. And not far from the city of Leinster, the Englishmen and Irishmen met together, and many were slain and taken on both sides, but the Englishmen obtained the victory, and the Irish fled. And the King Art saved himself, but Brian Costeret, my wife's father, was taken prisoner under the Duke of Clarence's banner. He was taken on the same courser [horse] that he took me on.

The horse was well known among the Earl of Ormonde's folks; and then he showed how I was alive and was at his manor of Harpelyn [sic], and how I had wed his daughter, whereof the Duke of Clarence, Sir William Windsor, and the Englishmen were right glad. Then it was shown him that if he would be delivered out of prison, that he should deliver me into the Englishmen's hands, and my wife and children. With great pain he made that bargain, for he loved me well, and my wife, his daughter, and our children. When he saw he could get his freedom no other way, he accorded thereto, but he retained my eldest daughter still with him. So I and my wife and our second daughter returned into England, and so I went and dwelt beside Bristol on the River Severn.

My two daughters are married, and she in Ireland has three sons and two daughters, and she that I brought with me has four sons and two daughters. And because the language of Irish is as ready to me as the English tongue, for I have always continued with my wife, and taught my children the same speech, therefore the King my sovereign lord, and his Council, commanded me to give attended on these four Kings, and to govern and bring them to reason, and to the usage and customs of England, seeing that had yielded them to be under his obedience, and of the Crown of England, and they were sworn to hold it forever. And yet I ensure you for all that, I did my power to teach them good manners, yet for all that, they be right rude and of gross deportment; much pain I had to make them to speak anything in fair manner; somewhat I altered them but not much, for in many cases they drew to their natural rudeness.

Told to Jean Froissart, in Sir Jean Froissart, *Chronicles*
Translated by Sir John Bourchier, Lord Berners (1523–1525),
ed. W. P. Ker, London, 1903

The Irish kings, princes, and nobles who submitted to Richard II in the early months of 1395 seem to have done so by the influence of Niall Mór Ó Néill, the former Ulster ruler. His son, Niall Óg, was then acting as king of Ulster. Niall Mór had urged a national act of submission to avoid the ravages of war. He had written to the English king saying that he would make submission. On January 20, 1395, Niall Mór met Richard II at the Dominican house at Drogheda and presented letters patent from his son in Latin.

I, Niall Óg Ó Néill, Captain of my Nation, have ordained in my place my beloved father, Niall Mór, giving him power in my name to appear before the illustrious prince Richard, King of England, and Lord of Ireland, and before my lord Roger de Mortimer, Earl of March and Ulster, and to treat of peace with them for me and my nation and subjects, and to surrender whatever lands, liberties, services, and customs, I unjustly possess or allow others to possess, and especially the bonnaght of the Irish of Ulster.

Sir Jean Froissart, Chronicles
Translated by Sir John Bourchier, Lord Berners (1523–1525), ed. W. P. Ker, London, 1903

Bonnaght is the anglicization of buannacht, *signifying an Irish mercenary soldier as opposed to a* gallowglass, *from the Irish* gall óglaigh, *signifying a Scottish mercenary serving in Ireland. Niall Óg himself as "captain of his nation" went to Drogheda on March 16, 1395, and formerly submitted.*

The rest of the Irish kings followed his lead along with all the prominent nobles. Brían Ó Bríain, "Princepts Tothomonie" (king of Thomond), submitted on March 1, at St. Thomas's Abbey, Dublin. Tadgh, The MacCarthy Mór, king of Desmond, submitted to Richard on April 6. Turloch O'Connor Don appeared on April 20 at the Friars Minor house in Waterford. He had been prompted to submit, as he claimed to be the true king of Connacht, and he feared that his rival and cousin, The O'Connor Roe, would be favored as king by Richard.

The King, my sovereign lord's intent was, that in manner, countenance, and apparel of clothing, they should use according to the manner of England, for the King thought to make them all four knights; they had a fair house to lodge in Dublin, and I was charged to abide still with them and not depart. And so two or three days I suffered them to do as they pleased, and said nothing to them, but follow their own appetites. They would sit at the table and make countenance neither good or fair. Then I thought I should cause them to change that manner. They would cause their minstrels, their servants and varlets, to sit with them and to eat in their own dishes, and to drink of their cups, and they showed me that the usage of their country was good, for they said, in all things, except their beds, they worked and lived as common men.

So the fourth day I ordained other tables to be covered in the hall, after the usage of England, and I made these four kings to sit at the high table, and their minstrels at another table, and their servants and varlets at another beneath them, whereof by seeming they were displeased and beheld each other and would not eat, and said how I would take from them their good usage, wherein they had been nourished. Then I answered them smiling to appease them, that it was not honourable for their estates to do as they did before, and that they must leave it, and use the custom of England, and that it was the King's pleasure they should do so, and how he was charged so to order them.

When they heard that they suffered it, because they had put themselves under the obedience of the King of England, and persevered in the same as long as I was with them, Yet they had one custom which I knew well was used in their country, and that was they did with no britches. I had britches of linen made for them. Much ado I had at first to cause them to wear gowns of silk, furred with miniver [white ermine] and grey; for before these Kings thought themselves well apparelled when they had on a mantel. They rode always without saddles and stirrups, and with great pain I made them to ride after our usage. And on a time I demanded them of their belief, wherewith they were not content, and said how they believed in God and on the Trinity, as well as we. Then I demanded on what Pope was their affection. They answered me, on him of Rome. Then I demanded if they would not gladly receive the order of knighthood, and that the King of England should make them knights, according to the usage of France and England and other countries. They answered how they were knights already and that sufficed for them.

I asked where were they made knights, and how and when. They answered that at the age of seven years they were made knights in Ireland, and that a King makes his son a knight. And if the son have no father alive, then the next of his blood may make him a knight. And then this young knight shall begin to joust with spears, such as they may bear with their ease, and run against a shield set on a stake in the field; and the more spears that he breaks the more he shall be honoured.

I knew their manner well enough, though I did demand it. But then I said that the knighthood that they had taken in their youth suffice not to the King of England. But I said he should give them after another manner. They demanded how. I answered that it should be in the holy church, which was the worthiest place. Then they inclined somewhat to my words.

Within two days after the Earl of Ormonde came to them, who could right well speak the language, for some of his lands lay in those parts; he was sent to them by the King and his Council; they all honoured him and he them. Then he fell in sweet communication with them, and he demanded of them how they liked me. They answered and said—well, for he has well shown us the usage of this country, wherefore we ought to thank him and so we do. This answer pleased well the Earl of Ormonde. Then he entered little by little to speak of the order of chivalry, which the King would they should receive. He showed it them from point to point, how they should behave themselves, and what appertained to knighthood. The Earl's words pleased much these four kings, whose names were these: First, the great "Anneal, kyng of Mete" [Ó Neil of Meath, Meath being synonymous with the high kingship], the second "Brine of Thomonde, kyng of Thomonde" [Ó Bríain, king of Thomond], the third "Arthur of Mackequemur, kyng of Lynster" [Art Mór Mac Murrough, king of Leinster], the fourth "Conchue, kyng of Cheveno and Darpe" [O'Conor Don, king of Connacht]. They were made knights by King Richard of England, in the cathedral church of Dublin dedicated to St John the Baptist; it was on Our Lady Day in March as then it fell on a Thursday.

These four kings watched all night before in the church, and the next day at High Mass time, with great solemnity they were made knights; and with them Sir Thomas Orphen, Sir Joatas Pardoe and his cousin Sir John Pardoe. These kings sat that day at the table with King Richard, they were regarded of many folks, because their behaviour was strange to the manner of England, and other countries, and ever naturally men desire novelties.

Sir Jean Froissart, Chronicles
Translated by Sir John Bourchier, Lord Berners (1523–1525), ed. W. P. Ker, London, 1903

In fact, King Art Mór of Leinster had made a submission on January 7, 1395, at Tullow. Part of the deal, as Art and his army were hard men to subdue, was that Richard would pay Art eighty marks a year forever, and confirm the inheritance of Art's wife, Elizabeth. With submissions made by all the Irish kings and most of the leading nobles, only The Ó Donnell and The Maguire stood aloof from these proceedings, Richard II left Ireland from Waterford on May 15, in a ship called Le Trinitie. *Whatever Richard thought that he had gained during his eight months in Ireland,* the fact was that it had all been symbolic. The Irish merely wanted to be rid of him and be allowed to carry on as before. When Roger Mortimer, earl of March and viceroy in Ireland, marched against King Art to remind him of Richard's authority, he was slain in a battle on June 10, 1398. Furious, Richard raised a new army and went back to Ireland, landing at Waterford on June 1, 1399. King Art was not intimidated by Richard II's strength and harassed the English king on his march to Dublin. The poet and chronicler Jean Creton observed a meeting between the earl of Gloucester, Richard II's emissary, and King Art.

He was a fine, large, handsome man, marvellously agile yet stern of countenance and indomitable mien. He wore a high, conical cap covering the nap of the neck and parti-coloured cloak, long coat and undercoat all of gay yellow, crimson and blue. He rode a very swift horse of great value, valued that of four hundred milch cows, having neither saddle nor house, but could rush down a hill faster than a deer or hare. After divers discourse Art told my lord: "I am rightful King in this land, thereby it is unjust to deprive me of what is my land and country by force of conquest." He bid the king withdraw from that which he claimed be his realm.

Jean Creton, *Histoire du roy d'Angleterre Richard*, 1399
Ed. J. Webb, *Archaeologia*, vol. 20, London, 1827

Richard offered a hundred marks for Art, alive or dead, but then news of an uprising in England led by Henry Bolinbroke, duke of Derby, against his rule came to him. Richard II departed Ireland on August 13, 1399, in a vain attempt to secure his own kingdom. Six days after landing, Richard II was forced to surrender and abdicate, and he is said to have met his death by starvation at Pontefract Castle, Yorkshire. For the next one hundred and fifty years, England made no further attempts to conquer Ireland, and the Anglo-Norman lords continued to merge into the Irish nation.

6

The Tudor Conquests

Henry VIII Advised to Conquer Ireland (1521)

After my poor opinion, this land shall never be brought to good order and due subjection, but only by conquest; which is, at your Grace's pleasure, to be brought to pass two manner of ways. One way is, if your Grace will one year set on hand to win one country, and another year, another country, and so continue, till all at length be won. After my opinion, the least number that your Grace must occupy, can be no less than 2,500; for it is not to be doubted, that whensoever the Irishmen shall know that your Grace intendeth a conquest, they will all combine together, and withstand the same to the best of their power. And over and above their own power, undoubtedly they may have three or four thousand Irish Scots, whensoever, and as often as they will call for them; and they be not distant from the north parts of this land, four hours' sailing. Also I think the Earl of Argyll, and divers others of those we call English Scots, will come, if they be desired.

And if your Grace will, in more brief time, have your purpose brought to pass, and to set upon the conquest in divers places, at one time; then, after my poor opinion, 6,000 men is the least number that your Grace must occupy. But to advertise your Grace, in how many years either the one number, or the other, should accomplish and prefect the conquest, the matter is so high and uncertain, that I dare not meddle therewith. Undoubtedly this land is five times as much as Wales; and when King Edward I set on hand to conquer the same, it cost him ten years before he won it all. Wherefore, considering the long time he was in conquering the same, and for the most part being present in his own person, and no sea being between England and Wales, as is between England and this land, I fear, and cannot believe it will be so soon won, as Wales was. For undoubtedly, the countries here be as strong, or stronger, as Wales, and the inhabitants of the same can and do live more hardily, than any other people, after my opinion, in Christendom or Turkey. Whereof a part Master Peche hath seen, and can inform your Grace more largely, as he hath heard by the report of others who hath not only, since his coming hither, taken continual pains in riding about with me, but also continually searched to attain to the knowledge of the state and manner of this land, and disposition of the people of the same, than any man that ever came hither, that continued no longer here, than he hath done.

Also, if it shall like your Grace to set on hand with the said conquest, your Grace must furnish the most part of the number of victuals and carriage for the same, out of England, or some other country; for here is much to do, to furnish this company that is now here. And ever, as the countries shall fortune to be won, strong towns and fortresses must be builded upon the same.

And after my poor opinion, unless your Grace send inhabitants, of your natural subjects, to inhabit such countries as shall be won, all your charges should be but wastefully spent. For if this country's people, of the Irish, should inhabit, undoubtedly they would return to their old ill-rooted customs, whensoever they might see any time to take their advance, according as they have ever yet done, and daily do. And if all the people of this land should be compelled to fall to labour (which they will never do, as long as they may find any country in the land to go unto), yet, after my opinion, there should not be found number sufficient to inhabit well the third part of the land.

And how few English habitants be now within these four shires (of the Pale), Master Peche can inform your Grace, for he hath seen a good part thereof. And if your Grace should inhabit such countries, as should be won, with Spaniards, Flemings, Germans, or any other nation, save only your own natural subjects, I fear, at length, they will rather be obedient to the prince of their native country, than to any other. The premises considered, after my poor opinion, the difficulty to conquer this land resteth in these three articles ensuing:

First, to furnish the army, that your Grace will have here, with money, until the conquest be perfected.

Secondly, how to furnish the said number with victuals, and carriage for the said victuals, ordnance, artillery, and all other stuff that must be occupied in building of strong fortresses.

Thirdly, how to find inhabitants in sufficient number, that will continue true subjects to your Grace, and your noble successors.

> Thomas Howard, earl of Surrey (third duke of Norfolk), to Henry VIII, June 1521
> *State Papers, Henry VIII*, vol. 2, 1543, pp. 73–75

[There are] more than 60 countries, called territories *[regionis]* in Ireland, inhabited with the King's Irish enemies . . . where reigneth more than 60 chief captains whereof some calleth themselves Kings, some Kings' peers in their language, some princes, some dukes, some archdukes . . . and obeyeth to no temporal person.

> Report in *State Papers, Henry VIII*, vol. 2, 1543, pp. 1–31

The King of Thomond to the King of Spain (1534)

The last king of this land [an incorrect reference to Brían Bóroimhe] was of my blood and of my name; and ever since that time we have ceased not to oppose the English intruders; we have never been subject to English rule, or yielded up our ancient rights and liberties; and here is at this present, and for ever will be, perpetual discord between us, and we will harass them with continual war.

> Conchobhar (Conor) Ó Bríain, prince of Ireland, written at our castle at
> Clare, July 21, 1534, to Charles V of Spain
> Manuscript archives, Brussels; printed in J. A. Froude, *Pilgrim*, London, 1861, appendix

Lord Deputy Opens Attack on King of Thomond (August 1536)

Conchobhar had become king of Thomond in 1528, and his brother, Murrough, was nominated as tanist *(heir-elect). Alarmed by the attempt to secure a Spanish alliance, Leonard Grey, the lord deputy, conducted a military campaign in 1536–1538 to quell Conchobhar. The son of the king of Thomond, Donough, had turned against his father and offered his services to the English lord deputy.*

The King's Deputy . . . with all the army, resorted to this city of Limerick; and being here, we consulted together to set forth to the winning and breaking of O'Brien's Bridge. [Ó Bríen's Bridge is now a village on the west bank of the Shannon, County Clare, just below a large lake formed by the Parteen dam. It was a strategic crossing into the heart of the Thomond kingdom.] On Friday we marched with all the army and such other ordnance as we had, towards the bridge, and by the conduct of the said Donough [Ó Bríen] and his friends, we were brought to it in a secret and an unknown way, on this side of the water, where never English host, nor carts, came before; whereby we achieved our purpose with less danger than we could have done on the other side. On Saturday we came to the said bridge, and after the host was encamped, the Deputy with the gunners viewed the same. On this side [of the Shannon] was a strong castle, builded all of hewn marble; and at the other end another castle, but not of such force, both built within the water, somewhat distance from the land. At this end they had broken four arches of the bridge, betwixt the castle and the land. The gunners bent all the ordnance upon the great castle, on this side, shooting at it all that day; but the castle was of such force, that the ordnance did in manner no hurt to it, for the wall was at the least twelve or thirteen feet thick, and both the castles were well warded with gunners, gallowglass and horsemen, having made such fortifications of timber, and hogsheads of earth, as the like have not been seen in this land.

They had one great piece of iron, which shot balls, as great in manner as a man's head. They had also a ship piece, a "Portingall" [Portuguese] piece, certain hagbusshes [harquebuses], and hand guns. And the Deputy, perceiving that the King's ordnance did little hurt to the castles, and also that the shot was spent, against the Sunday in the morning, he caused every man of the army to make a faggot of a athom in length to fill that part of the water twixt the land and the castle, and devised certain ladders to be made; which done, he appointed certain of his own retinue, and a company of Master Saintlowes to give the assault; which we assure you they executed hardily so as with plain manhood and force they scaled the bridge, which the other [the garrison] perceiving, escaped at the other end thereof, by footmanship [into Thomond]; and so they lost both bridge, the castles, their ordnance, and all that was else therein; which castles and bridge the Deputy and we have caused to be broken down to the ground. There was slain of the army two gunners and drivers hurted; and at the loosing of the joints of the timber bridge, a great part of it did fall, and the Mayor of this city of Limerick, with divers others, about the number of thirty persons, standing upon the same. Albeit, thanks be to God, there perished no more, but a servant of Master Saintlowes and one of this city; and all the others, by swimming and one boat, which we had gotten there, were saved.

> Report endorsed by the Council of Ireland to Thomas Cromwell
> (c. 1585–1540), August 9, 1536
> State Papers, Henry VIII, vol. 2, 1543, pp. 351–352

Conchobhar finally surrendered in 1537 to Grey and they signed a treaty at Limerick. He was to die c. 1540 and was succeeded by his brother, Murrough.

Henry VII Declares Himself King of Ireland (1541)

Forasmuch as the King our most gracious dread sovereign lord, and his Grace's most noble progenitors, Kings of England, have been Lords of his land of Ireland, having all manner kingly jurisdiction, power, pre-eminence, and authority royal, belonging or appertaining to the royal estate and majesty of a king, by the name of Lords of Ireland, where the King's Majesty and his most noble progenitors justly and rightfully were, and of right, ought to be Kings of Ireland. . . . His Majesty, his heirs and successors, be from henceforth named, called, accepted, reputed, and taken to be Kings of this land of Ireland, to have, hold and enjoy the said style, title, majesty and honours of King of Ireland, with all manner pre-eminencies, prerogatives, dignities, and all other the premises unto the King's Highness, his heirs and successors for ever, as united and knit to the imperial crown of the Realm of England.

> An Act That the King of England, His Heirs and Successors Be Kings of Ireland
> 33 Hen. VIII c. I, Irish Statutes, 1786, I. 176

On June 26, 1541, Sir Anthony St. Leger, lord deputy, reported to Henry VIII that on June 13, in Dublin, the Anglo-Norman lords had met in a parliament and the act was read to them.

Which proposition was right well and prudently answered by your Highness's Chancellor here [earl of Ormonde]; and, after, both the effect of the proposition and answer was briefly and prudently declared in the Irish tongue, to the said lords, by the mouth of the Earl of Ormonde, greatly to their contention.

There were present two earls, three viscounts, sixteen barons, two archbishops, twelve bishops, as well as Donough O'Brien, heir to the king of Thomond, and other Thomond representatives, including Dr. O'Nolan and a bishop, O'Reilly, and "many other Irish captains" (princes and nobles).

And the said Sunday, all the lords and gentlemen rode to your Church of St Patrick's, where there was sung a solemn Mass by the archbishop of Dublin, and after the Mass, the said Act proclaimed there in presence of 2,000 persons and *Te Deum* sung, with great joy and gladness to all men.

Sir Anthony St. Leger to Henry VIII, June 26, 1541
State Papers, Henry VIII, vol. 3, pp. 304–305, Public Records Office, London

Surrender and Regrant Policy

Henry VIII's initial policy was that now that he had become king of Ireland, the kings, princes, and other nobles of Ireland would surrender their titles to Henry and he would regrant English feudal titles from earl downward to baronets. The rulers, and therefore the people of Ireland, would abandon the native law system, the Brehon law, and also the Irish language, in favor of English law and the English language.

Many of the lesser nobles in the Leinster area began to surrender their titles. Typical of what they had to promise is seen in the agreement made by The Mac Giollaphádraig (MacGilpatrick) of Upper Ossory.

First, the said MacGilpatrick doth utterly forsake and refuse the name [title] of MacGilpatrick; and all claim which he might pretend by the same; and promises to name himself, for ever hereafter, by such name as it shall please the King's Majesty to give him.

Also:

The said MacGilpatrick, his heirs and assignees and every other the inhabiters of such lands as it shall please the King's Majesty to give unto him, shall use the English habits and manner, and, to their knowledge, the

English language, and they, and every of them, shall to their power, bring up their children after the English manner, and the use of the English tongue.

Irish Fiants of the Tudor Sovereigns, ed. Edmund Burke, Dublin, 1994

The King of Ulster Gives Up His Title (1542)

Conn Bacach O'Neill traveled to Henry VIII's royal palace at Greenwich, and on October 1, 1542, formerly submitted and accepted the English title of earl of Tyrone in place of his Gaelic title as The O'Neill, king of Ulster. His son, Ferdorcha (called Matthew by the English), would be styled as baron of Dungannon and primogeniture heir to Conn Bacach.

The Queen's Closet at Greenwich was richly hanged with cloth of Arras, and well strewed with rushes, and after the "sacring" [consecration of elements in the mass] of the High Mass, these Earls [*sic*] in company went to the said closet, and there put on their robes of state. And immediately after the King's Majesty, being under the cloth of state, accompanied with all his noblemen, councillors and others, came in, the Earl, led between the Earl of Oxenford, and the Earl of Hertford, the Viscount Lisle bearing before him his sword, the hilt upwards, Garter before him, bearing his letters patent; and so proceeded to the King's Majesty, who received the Garter, the letters patent, and took them to Mr Wriotselsey, Secretary, to read them openly. And when he came to *cuncturam gladii*, the Viscount Lisle presented unto the King the sword, and the King girt the said sword about the said Earl baudrickwise [belt or girdle] the foresaid Earl kneeling, and the other lords standing that led him. And so the patent read out, the King's Highness took him his letter patent, and he gave him thanks in his language, and a priest made answer of his saying in English; and there the King made two of the men that came with him knights. And so the Earls in order aforesaid took their leave of the King's Highness, and departed unto the place appointed for their dinners, the Earl of Tyrone bearing his letters patent himself, the trumpets blowing before him unto the chamber, which was the Lord Great Master's under the King's lodging. And so they sat at dinner. At the second course Garter proclaimed the King's style, and after the said new Earl's in manner following: *Du très haut et puissant Seigneir Con* [O'Neill], *Comte de Tyrone, en le Royaume d'Irlande.*

October 1, 1542, Calender of Carew Manuscripts, 6. vols., Dublin, 1867–1873

Shame on you, of men of the Gael
Not one of you has life in him:
The foreigner is sharing out your country among themselves
And you are like a phantom host

The O'Neills of Aileach and Navan
The King of Tara and Tailltean
in foolish submission
They have surrendered their kingdom
For the *earldom* of Ulster.

O Nobles of the Island of ancient [King] Art
Evil is your change of dignity.
O ill-guided cowardly host
Henceforth say nothing but "shame"!

Anonymous poet to O'Cearbhaill
"A Sixteenth Century Political Poem," ed. Brían Ó Cuív, *Éigse* 15, 1973–1974

On Sunday, July 1, 1543, Murrough Ó Bríen, fifty-seventh king of Thomond, surrendered. He was given the title earl of Thomond. His son was made Baron Inchiquin, while his nephew, heir apparent under Brehon law, was made Baron Ibrickan and heir to the earldom. "The making of O'Brien an Earl made all that country obedient," wrote Sir Thomas Cusack, the lord justice, in glee, to the duke of Northumberland on May 8, 1533. "Irishmen were never so weak and the English subjects never so strong as now." At the same time that O'Brien surrendered, the powerful Irishized Anglo-Norman Lord Ulick na gCeann, The MacWilliam Uachtar (Upper) of Galway, surrendered his chieftainship to become earl of Clanricade. In Leinster, King Caothaoir Mac Airt Mac Murrough Kavanagh was not persuaded to give up his title until 1554, becoming, as a consequence, only Baron Ballyanne. In Connacht, O'Conor Roe did not surrender until 1567. O'Conor Don, recognized as king of Connacht, died in 1585 without formally giving up the kingship, although that year The Composition of Connacht agreed that the three royal titles, O'Conor Don, O'Conor Rue, and O'Conor Sligo, were "abolished and made extinct forever." The other major Irish kingdom, Desmond, ruled by Donal, The MacCarthy Mór, considered surrender in 1552, but Donal had to be forcibly kidnapped by David Roche, Lord Fermoy, and taken to London, where under duress he accepted the title earl of Clancare.

Thereafter, the lesser nobles of Ireland, with few exceptions, flocked to surrender their titles and get English titles, agreeing to give up native law as well as their language for feudalism.

The Irish Disowned Those Who Had Surrendered

Pride they [the Irish nobles] have bartered for a lowly mind, and bright perception for gloominess; this flaccid disposition of the erstwhile gallant host may in all earnest stand us in lieu of a sermon. They, the flowers of the freeborn clans of Tara's armies, have run out the term of their prosperity; envy has brought down her elbow on them, so that an eclipsing deluge has overwhelmed them. Their wonted good luck they have all forgotten, their Pride they [the Irish nobility] have bartered for a lowly mind, and bright perceptions battle ground and their athletic feats, their ire, their turbulence, their aggressiveness; prowess of clean handed loyal warriors. No stripling now is seen to challenge combat, nor soldier's gear to hang by his pallet, nor sword to suck the hand's palm, while frost congeals the ringlet of the hair. No more the target is seen slung on the broad back, nor hilt grit to the side at coming of the moon, nor smooth soft skin coming into contact with chainmail; still this must once upon a time have been a dream. Their cheerfulness of spirit, their appetite for diversion and their propensity to give away, they have relinquished; likewise their charge in the fight, their industry in depredation so that they being thus are not living men at all.

Anonymous, 16th Irish tract, in Catalogue of Irish Mss in the British Museum,
ed. Standish Hayes O'Grady, London, 1926, p. 473

There was one problem with these surrenders of titles and feudalization of the land. Such agreements were entirely against Brehon law. There was no such concept as primogeniture, and the kingship and all other titles of nobility not only passed through particular families but the holders of titles had to be elected by a minimum of three generations of the family meeting as an electoral college called the derbhfine.

Shortly after returning to Ulster, the new earl of Tyrone and Baron Dungannon found that their derbhfine, *the electoral college of the family, had met and disowned them. Under Irish law, kings and chieftains could hold their titles only as long as they promoted the commonwealth. If they did not, they were removed from office. Three months later, Conn Bacach and Ferdorcha were driven out of the kingdom and took refuge among the English in Dublin. Conn Bacach's youngest son, Seán an Díomais, known to the English as Shane the Proud, was elected king, and his cousin Turlough heir apparent, being installed in Gaelic fashion at Tulach Óg.*

Elizabeth I Gets a Lesson in the Irish Law of Succession

Seán an Díomais, the new king of Ulster, was so powerful that in 1562 he actually made a visit to London to discuss matters with Elizabeth I. According to Ralph Holinshed:

He pretended to be King of Ulster, even as he said his ancestors were, and affecting the manner of the "Great Turk" was continually guarded with 600 armed men, as it were his Janissaries, about him, and had in readiness to bring into the field 1,000 horsemen and 4,000 footmen.

Ralph Holinshed (d. c. 1580)
Chronicles of England, Scotland and Ireland, London, 1577

And now Shane O'Neill came from Ireland . . . with an escort of gallow-glass armed with battle axes, bare-headed, with flowing curls, yellow shirts dyed with saffron . . . large sleeves, short tunics and rough cloaks, whom the English followed with much wonderment as if they had come from China or America. O'Neill was received with all kindness.

When Elizabeth asked how he could consider himself a lawful king when he had overthrown Conn Bacach the King, Seán tried to explain Brehon Law to her.

The surrender made by my father to Henry VIII and the grant which Henry made him by letters patent, was of no value, since Conn had no estate in what he surrendered save for his own life, nor could he yield it without the consent of the chiefs and peoples by whom he had been chosen to the dignity of O'Neill. Such letters patent are of no avail unless the true head of the family is first approved by the oath of twelve men, which in this case was not done.

William Camden (1551–1623)
Annales Rerum Gestorum Angliae et Hiberniae Regnante Elizabethe,
with annotations of Sir Francis Bacon, London, 1615 and 1625

The removal of those kings and nobles who surrendered their titles and lands to Henry VIII happened not only in Ulster but in Thomond and elsewhere. In Desmond, Donal had rejected his English earldom as soon as he was safely back in Ireland. The English, unfamiliar with the principles of the Brehon Law system, could not understand how the Irish nobles were being thrown out of office and new kings and princes simply "elected" in their place. Soon the country was in turmoil as England tried to enforce its edicts. The policy envisaged by Henry VIII of merely absorbing the Irish nation by absorbing its ruling class and changing its language, laws, and customs was now replaced by a genocidal policy by Henry's heirs and successors.

The Bodyguard of The Ó Raghailligh Mór (1579)

Some Irish nobles tried to make terms with the English. Ó Raghailligh (O'Reilly) of Lough Oughter, County Cavan, were powerful and independent princes under the Breifne kings. In the fourteenth century, they had even issued their own coinage. However, in 1541, The Ó Raghailligh Mór had attended the Dublin Parliament of Henry VIII and accepted his surrender and regrant policy and the abolition of his title, native law, and language. His successor was still trying to make this policy work in 1579.

O'Reilly with his brother Philip [Felim], and uncle Edmund [Eamon], and thirty horsemen well furnished, came unlooked for, to present unto me a submission and supplication, in the behalf as well of himself of his whole country . . . to have his people not only frame to English manners, but also his country made shire ground, and subjects to law under Her Majesty's writ. Weighing . . . his gravity in years, and good discretion in government, I thought it good to honour him with the title of knighthood. . . . But how strange the view of these savage personages (most of them wearing glibs [thick mass of matted hair hanging over the eyes], and armed in mail, with pesantes [a gorget or mail plate attached to the helmet] and skulls, and rising upon pillions), seemed to our strangers, I leave to your wisdom to think of. And so myself and the train, together with these strangers, and O'Reilly with his company, being entertained with the said Sir Lucas Dillon, we parted.

Lord Justice Drury to Sir Francis Walsingham, June 26, 1579
State Papers, Elizabeth, vol. 67, No. 12

But O'Reilly was an exception. The new policy had been made clear by Mary Tudor, the Catholic queen.

Queen Mary Tudor Issues Instructions for Colonization (April 28, 1556)

Not being able to overcome the strength of the Irish allegiance to their native law system and social customs, the Tudor monarchy decided that if the Irish would not change themselves by persuasion, then they would have to be changed by force. This was a simple plan. The Irish would be driven from their lands, which would then be planted by colonists from England. The first experiment was to be made in the counties, which are today called Laois and Offaly, and "An Act for the Disposition of Leixe and Offalie" was passed.

Touching the said countries, our special intent and desire is, that the same and the rest of our whole Realm should, by authority of Parliament, be made shire ground and divided into sufficient and reasonable counties as our Realm of England is. . . . We desire also if the Dempsies and those rebels, the Mores and O'Conors, shall call for quarter, and do submit themselves unto order and mercy, that those countries shall then be parted in three parts. . . . And those that have the estate to be found to answer our common laws. . . . The rest of the said two parts we shall distribute among English subjects . . . and none of them to sell or lease his tenement to any Irishman of Irish blood and birth upon pain of forfeiture.

Instructions of Philip and Mary to Thomas Radcliffe, Lord Fitzwalter, their Deputy in
Ireland, touching the countries of Leix (Laois) and Offaly
Cotton Mss Titus B., XI, no. 241, British Museum

Commission to Sir Henry Radcliffe Knt. Lieutenant of the King's and Queen's counties; to parle with, take pledges from and punish with fire and sword the Irish of the said counties otherwise called Leise, Offallery. . . . Also to the said Sir Henry, and Robert Willinson, Henry Cowley, Thomas Smyth and Hugh Lypiat, captains, to execute martial law.

Forasmuch as the O'Mores, O'Dempsies, O'Connors and others of the Irishry, lately inhabiting the countries of Leix, Slewmarge, Irry, Glinmaliry and Offaly, and by their sundry manifest treasons after many pardons granted to them, and sundry benefits showed to them, yet often rebelled . . . their Majesty's Lord Deputy in Ireland, by sword, evicted and reduced the said countries out of and from the wrongful and usurped possession as of right appaertaineth. . . . Be it therefore ordained, enacted and established . . . that the said King's and Queen's Majesty's . . . shall have, hold and possess for ever, as in right of the Crown of England, the said countries.

Acts of 3 and 4 Philip and Mary c. 2. *Irish Statutes,* 1786, I.241-3

Laois (Leix) and Offaly then became Queen's County and King's County until a newly independent Ireland changed them back to the original Irish appellations in 1922.

A horrible and abominable act of treachery was committed by the English of Leinster and Meath upon that part of the [Irish] people of Laois and Offaly that remained in confederacy with them, and under their protection. It was effected thus; they were all summoned to show themselves, with the greatest number they could be able to bring with them, at the great rath of Mullach Maistean [Mullamast, near Athy, County Kildare]; and on their arrival at that place they were surrounded on every side by four lines of soldiers and cavalry, so that not a single individual escaped, by flight or force.

Annales Rioghachta Éireann (Annals of the Four Masters), c. 1632–1636
Compiled by Micheál Ó Cléirigh

In 1579, King Donal, The MacCarthy Mór, and the Anglo-Norman lord Gerald Fitzgerald, earl of Desmond, began a struggle against the forces of Elizabeth I. They were defeated in 1583, and on June 21, 1586, Queen Elizabeth I signed "Articles for Repeopling and Inhabiting the Provinces of Munster in Ireland." A total of 574,628 (English) acres were to be cleared of the Irish and given to English colonists in parcels of 4,000, 6,000, 8,000, and 12,000 acres. The articles decreed: "The heads of every family shall be born of English parents, and the heirs female, inheritable to any the same lands, shall marry with none but with persons born of English parents . . . and no 'mere' Irish to be permitted in any family there." Among the new owners of the largest confiscated Irish estates were Sir Walter Raleigh (1552–1618) and the poet Edmund Spenser (1552–1599).

A Colonist from Nottinghamshire Praises the Munster Colony (1590)

Their soil for the most part is very fertile, and apt for wheat, rye, barley . . . and all other grains and fruits that England anywise doth yield. There is much good timber in many places. . . . There is very rich and great plenty of iron stone . . . also there is great store of lead ore, and wood sufficient to maintain divers iron and lead works (with good husbandry) for ever. A barrel of wheat or a barrel of bay salt containing 3½ bushels of Winchester measure, is sold there for 4s.; malt, peas, beans for 2s. 8d.; barley for 2s. 4d.; oats for 20d. A fresh salmon, worth in London 10s., for 6d.; 24 herrings or 6 mackerel 6d.; sea breams, a fat hen, 30 eggs, a fat pig, 1 lb of butter or 2 gallons of new milk for 1d. A red deer without the skin for 2s. 6d.; a fat beef for 13s. 4s. A fat mutton for 18d.

There be great store of wild swans, cranes, pheasants, partridges ... and all other fowls much more plentiful than in England. You may buy a dozen quails for 3d., a dozen of woodcocks for 4d. and all other fowls rateably. Oysters, mussels, cockles and samphires about the sea coasts are to be had for the gathering, great plenty.... You may buy the best heifers there with calves at their feet, for 20s. a piece, which are nothing inferior to the better sort of Lincolnshire breed. Their chief horses are of as great a price as in England, but cart horses, mares and little hackneys are of a very small price.... You may keep a better house in Ireland for £50 a year than in England for £200 a year.

Robert Payne, A Brief Description of Ireland, London, 1590

Spanish Armada (1588)

With the death of Queen Mary and the accession of the Protestant Elizabeth, King Philip of Spain, Mary's widower, turned his attention to claiming the English kingdom. In May 1588, he sent a fleet to conquer England. It was the greatest battle fleet ever seen, with sixty-five galleons, twenty-five store ships, and thirty smaller vessels. A storm blew up and the fleet was scattered, many trying to return to Spain through the seas around the west coast of Ireland. A great number were driven ashore and wrecked. Many myths about this have arisen: stories that Spanish sailors settled among the Irish; stories that hundreds of Spanish sailors were killed by the "savage" Irish as they sought shelter after being wrecked. In fact, the Spanish sailors were killed by the English garrisons, not by the Irish.

The English Garrison in Ireland Slaughters Survivors of the Spanish Armada (1588)

The men of these ships all perished, save 1,100 or more who were put to the sword, amongst whom were officers and gentlemen of quality to the number of fifty and whose names have been set down in a list. The gentlemen were spared until the Lord Deputy [Sir William Fitzwilliam] sent me specific directions to see them executed—reserving alone de Cordoba and his nephew. . . . I spared them but the Lord Deputy [Sir William] Fitzwilliam came to Connacht and ordered all killed except [Dom Luis] de Cordoba and his nephew who were at Athlone.

Report of Sir Richard Bingham Governor of Connacht
Calendar of State Papers, Ireland, vol. 139, no. 2, p. 25

Irish Save Survivors of Spanish Armada (1588)

Captain Francisco de Cuellar, captain of San Juan de Sicilia, *was wrecked off the coast of Sligo. He managed to get ashore with much hardship, being one of a handful of survivors. English soldiers killed many of the survivors on the shoreline. Captain de Cuellar managed to get to the church of St. Molaise on Inishmurray.*

I went to the church which was forsaken, the images of the saints burned and destroyed, and within were twelve Spaniards hanged by the English Lutherans who were prowling around in quest of us in order to finish with all who had escaped from the disasters of the sea. All the friars had fled to the mountains through fear of these enemies who would have killed them had they caught them, leaving neither church nor friary standing and maiming their watering places for cows and pigs.

De Cuellar found two Spanish survivors who joined him and told him that they had witnessed a hundred Spanish survivors being slain by the English.

We began to see bodies, most miserable and pitiful to look upon, as the sea threw them up from time to time on the strand so that in that place there were more than 400. . . . Some of them we recognised, among them poor Don Diego Enriquez whose body, even in the midst of my distress, I could not bring myself to pass without burying it in a hole which we made in the sand at the water's edge. Along with him we buried another captain much honoured and my great friend. Hardly had we covered them when there came down to us 20 *salvajes* [Irish] to see what we were about. We gave them to understand by signs that we had buried there these men who were our brothers in order that their bodies might not become food for the ravens. We separated from them in search of food along the beach, such as the biscuits which the waves were washing up.

Just then four *salvajes* came upon us and began to take the little clothing I wore, but another of them who seemed to be a leader, pushed them aside and ordered them to leave me alone. This leader put us on a road, which led from the shore to the village where he lived. There was for me the further misery that the road was very rough with big stones so that without pain I could not put one foot beyond the other being in my bare feet and suffering agony as well in one leg in which there was a wound. My poor companions, who were entirely naked and frozen with cold, then very sharp, were more dead than alive and could not render me any assistance. They went ahead, and, little by little, I reached the top of a hill where I discovered some thatched cottages.

De Cuellar fell in with a young man, and their common language was Latin. The man directed de Cuellar to a place where he and his companions would find safety.

God was pleased to bring us to a land of some safety where we found a town belonging to better people, Christian and kindly. In that town were seventy Spanish survivors. The women and children cared for them most charitably. The Chief was not there at this time. Although he is a foreigner, he is a very good Christian and an enemy of the heretics [English] and always fights against them. His name is the Señor de Ruerge [Brían na murtha (of the defenses) Ó Ruairc (Prince of Breifne)]. The Chieftain's wife was exceedingly comely. I told her and the other womenfolk their fortunes as they sat in the sun. I told them a hundred thousand nonsensical things at which they were mightily pleased. But day and night both men and women followed me incessantly asking me to have their fortunes told. . . .

They are always at war with the English who garrison the country, and both defend themselves from them and prevent them from coming into their territory which is all flooded and covered with marshy ponds. . . . Almost all their churches, monasteries and hermitages have been destroyed by the soldiers from the English garrisons and by their own country who have joined them [the English].

Ó Ruairc passed de Cuellar and his men on to a petty chieftain called Mac Fhlannchaidh (MacClancy).

The name of the Chieftain with whom I lived was Manglana [Mac Fhlannchaidh]. This Chieftain was always a great enemy of the Queen [of England] and never loved anything that was hers, nor would he obey her, and therefore the English Governor of this part of the island wanted very much to take him a prisoner.

The English attempted a raid on Mac Fhlannchaidh's territory while de Cuellar was there in November 1588.

When the Chieftain heard of the great force of 1,700 men that was coming against him, knowing he had no means of resistance, he resolved to fly to the mountains, which, in default of an army, were his only means of safety. We Spaniards who were with him already had news of the evil that was coming upon us, and we did not know what to do nor where to turn for safety. One Sunday, after Mass, the Chieftain, blazing with anger, his hair hanging down over his eyes, took us apart and said he could not entertain any hopes of defence and that he had made up his mind to fly with all his people, their flocks and families, and we must look to what we should do to save ourselves. I made answer that if he would wait for a lit-tle while we would give him a reply. I withdrew apart with the eight Spaniards that were with me—they were brave companions—and said to them it was better to die with honour than to wander as fugitives, over the mountains naked and barefoot in the freezing cold. We should, I said, defend the Chieftain's castle to the death. This we could well do against twice as strong a force as that which was coming against us.

De Cuellar and his men held the castle for seventeen days against the force of the English commanded by George Bingham, sheriff of Sligo, brother of the governor of Connacht. Bingham hanged two Spanish prisoners in front of the castle in an attempt to intimidate de Cuellar and his men. Bingham was beaten back. In 1590, Bingham was to attack Mac Fhlannchaidh again and this time caught the chieftain unaware. He was beheaded and his head was taken to Sligo. Bingham reported: "He was a most barbarous creature; his country extended from Grange to Ballyshanning: he was Ó Ruairc's right hand; he had fourteen Spaniards with him, some of whom were taken alive." But de Cuellar and his companions had been passed on to the safe-keeping of the bishop of Derry, Reamoinn Ó Gallchobhair, who was also later cap-tured and executed by the English.

The bishop was a very good Christian. He went about dressed as a savage in order not to be discovered, and I could not hold back my tears when I went up to him and kissed his ring. He had twelve Spaniards with him, meaning to help them cross to Scotland, and he was greatly pleased at my coming, especially when he learned that I was a sea captain. I stayed six days with this bishop who showed me great hospitality and who arranged for a pinnace to take us all to Scotland, a journey which usually took two days. The bishop gave us supplies and said Mass for us in the castle. May God keep him in His protection and deliver him from his enemies! I put to sea in the pinnace in which there were eighteen of us. The same day the wind was contrary and we were obliged to run before it in the direction of the Hebrides where we reached land in the morning—our boat almost full of water and the mainsail torn. From there, after two days of good weather, we began our voyage to Scotland, which we reached in three days—not without danger because the boat took in so much water.

Francisco de Cuellar, writing at Antwerp, October 1589
Manuscript preserved in Biblioteca de la Real Academia de la Historia, Madrid

Native Schools Flourish in Spite of the Conquest

They [the Irish] are sharp-witted, lovers of learning, capable of any study, whereunto they bend themselves, constant in travail.... Without either precepts or congruity they speak Latin like a vulgar tongue, learned in their common schools of leech-craft [medicine] and law, whereat they begin children, and hold on sixteen or twenty years, counting by rote the Aphorisms of Hypocrites and the Civil Institutions, and a few other parings of those two faculties. I have seen them where they kept school, ten in some one chamber, grovelling upon couches of straw, their books at their noses, themselves lying flat prostrate, and so to chant out their lessons by piece-meal, being the most part lusty fellows of twenty-five ears and upwards.

Edmund Campion (1540–1581), in *Historie of Ireland,* 1571, in *Two Histories of Ireland,*
ed. Sir James Ware, Dublin, 1633

Torment is it to me that, in the very clan gathering, foreigners proscribe them that are Ireland's Royal Chiefs, in whose own ancestral territory is given to them no designation but that of a lowly outlaw's name.

Aongus mac Daighre Ó Dálaigh (c. 1540–1600), poet to Ó Broin of County Wicklow
Dia Libh a Laochradh Ghaoidhea (God be with the Irish host),
in *Irish Ministrelsy,* James Hardiman, Dublin, 1831

Baron Münchausen in Ireland (1590)

March 2, 1590

I took an interpreter and a guide in Waterford and a boy to carry my things. We boarded a ship going upstream to Carrick, twelve Irish miles.

March 4, 1590

We walked to the north, thirteen Irish miles. Stayed overnight in the house of an Irish nobleman. Their houses are normally built like towers and surrounded by a wall. They do not live in these, just keep them as a fortress. Next to these, they have another house, badly built, not as good as our farmers; houses in which they light a fire right in the middle. Here, the master of the house takes his place with his wife at the top, the domestic servants following according to their ranks . . . each nobleman is bound to house and feed his servants.

Ludolf von Münchausen (1570–1640), *Diary* for 1590
Translated by Andreas von Breitenbuch, reproduced in *Diaries of Ireland,*
ed. Melosina Lenox-Conyngham, Lilliput Press, Dublin, 1998

English Colonists Absorbed into the Irish Nation

The poet Edmund Spenser, secretary to Lord Grey, the lord deputy, was rewarded with an estate in County Cork and wrote the treatise A View of the Present State of Ireland *in 1596, first published in 1631. It is a conversation between Eudoxus, a learned inquirer, and Irenius, an Englishman with a knowledge of Ireland. Spenser talks of the previous colonists sent to Ireland, who within a few years had adopted the Irish language, laws, and customs.*

Irenius: . . . for the most part of them are degenerated and grown almost mere Irish, yes and more malicious to the English than the very Irish themselves.

Eudoxus: . . . And is it possible that an Englishman brought up naturally in such sweet civility as England affords could find such liking in that barbarous rudeness that he should forget his own nature and forego his own nation? How may this be, or what, I pay you, may be the cause hereof . . . ?

Irenius: . . . the chiefest abuses which are now in the realm are grown from the English, and the English that were are now much more lawless and licentious than the very wild Irish, so that as much care as was then by them had to reform the Irish, so much more must now be used to reform them so much time doth alter the manners of men.

Eudoxus: That seemeth very strange, which you say, that men should so much degenerate from their first natures as to grow wild.

Edmund Spenser, *A View of the Present State of Ireland*, in *Two Histories of Ireland,*
ed. Sir James Ware, Dublin, 1631

The Yellow Ford (August 10, 1598)

In July 1598, the war found Ó Néill and his forces besieging an English garrison in Ulster on the Blackwater River, which was a threat to the heart of his territory. Lord Ormonde sent Sir Henry Bagenal, marshal of the English army in Ireland, with four thousand foot, three hundred horses, and four pieces of artillery to relieve this garrison. The English had muskets, modern flint, and matchlock pieces. The Irish army, while stronger in men, were poorly equipped, with very few guns and no artillery. They relied on bows, spears, and battle-axes.

Bagenal had a personal grievance in closing with Ó Néill. In 1591, Ó Néill had married his sister, Mabel Bagenal, much to Sir Henry's disgust. Sir Henry Bagenal began his march north from Armagh and Ó Néill moved to engage him at the River Callan. While Ó Néill moved on the front of Bagenal's army, Aodh Ruadh Ó Domhnaill moved to cut off any retreat. Accompanying Ó Domhnaill was a young poet and historian, Lugaidh Ó Cléirigh (c. 1570–1620), from Donegal. He was of a chiefly family, under The Ó Domhnaill (O'Donnell), the princes of Tyrconnel, and an uncle to Micheál Ó Cléirigh (1575–1645), who compiled the famous Annála Ríoghachta Éireann *(Annals of the Kingdom of Ireland, better known as the* Annals of the Four Masters*). Lugaidh was one of the outstanding historians and poets of his day, and it is said he accompanied Aodh Ruadh Ó Domhnaill (Red Hugh O'Donnell) on his campaigns. He wrote his outstanding biography,* Beatha Aodha Ruaidh Uí Domhnaill.

When the English army had crossed the first broad, deep trench, which had been dug in front of them, the Irish advanced against them boldly and freely. Their van was obliged to halt, owing to wounds, and stop on account of the shooting. They poured showers of very slender light darts on them, and of sharp pointed arrows, and of heavy leaden balls. The English proceeded to shoot in the same manner from their slender, straight aiming steady guns and from their loud wounding muskets, so that the reports and noise of their discharge was heard in the woods and forests and hollows of the rocks and in the stone fortresses of the neighbouring territory. Many were wounded and hurt in both armies by the shots, but yet the shots of the English reached farther. This was the manner of fighting which the Irish adopted in consequence: they spread themselves about the English all round, and they closed on them and engaged the English at close quarters, so that they drove the winds which were on the outside, and the sharp shooters and soldiers beyond them, into the centre, so that they closed on them and engaged the English at close quarters, so that the English were confused by that and by the shots of the Irish, by the closeness and the compactness of the set order in which their leaders of battle and captains of the fight had placed them. Anger and wrath seized on the soldiers on both sides in consequence of the killing, the slaughtering and the wounding of their friends, their companions, and those dear to them before their faces. They were struggling and slaughtering each other in this way for a good while and a long time, until the closeness and compactness of the English army was thinned out and their leaders and nobles were gapped [separated].

As the glorious God and Almighty Lord ordained victory and triumph for the Irish that day, He allowed a certain English soldier who had spent all the gunpowder he had to go to the nearest barrels of gunpowder carried by them, in the very middle of the army, to refill his pouch once more, and when he stretched out his hand to the powder a tiny spark leapt from the match he had lighting, into the barrel, and from that to each of the barrels in succession, so that whatever was near the place where they were standing, men and horses, arms and armour, and everything which they needed to have by them, was blown up into the regions and clouds of air. The great gun, which they carried with them, was moved from where it was to another place by the force and conflagration of the dry powder, when it blazed up fiercely to the clouds of the heavens. The hill too all round was one mass of dark, black fog for a while after, so that it was not easy for any one to recognise a man of his own people from one of his enemies. However, the General of the English army and their champion of battle, Henry Bagenal, and with him very many of their nobles and leaders were slain. The English were defeated, as is usual with an army whose battle chief, and supplier and counsellor had been taken away. The Irish proceeded to mangle and hack, to kill and destroy in twos and threes, in scores and thirties, in troops and hundreds until they came in over the midmost walls of Armagh. The soldiers and their attendants returned and proceeded to strip the people who had fallen in the battle and to behead those who were severely wounded there. The booty of unusual varied supplies was great. The Irish remained to besiege Armagh at each of the quarters of the town, so that they did not allow anyone in or out for a space of three days and three nights. At that time the English sent messengers to the Irish to ask them to confer with them about surrendering the fortress mentioned [on the Blackwater], where their people had been in garrison for a long time, and that the warders be allowed to go safe to them to Armagh after giving up the place to Aodh Ó Néill, and that he permit both parties to retire from Armagh.

The nobles went to take counsel on that proposal. Some of them said it would be right to allow the English to go on condition they surrendered the fortress, since it was on its account they had engaged them and fought the battle. Many of their [Irish] people were wounded and slain, and their defeat and overthrow was a great triumph to them. Others of them opposed this, and said it was not right to let the English escape from the great straits in which they were, and that they would not be found careless a second time if they escaped from them. However, it was decided by the chiefs at last to let them go away. Terms were agreed on between them on this side and on that to be observed by both, except the Irish did not allow any supplies of food, guns or ordnance, powder or lead to be taken away by anyone out of the fortress except his trunk and his arms which were allowed to the captain who was there. The English thereupon left the fort, and protection and quarter was given them till they came to Armagh. The next day the two bodies of English soldiers went from Armagh to Newry and to their own bases, and they made a census of their army to see what number were missing since they went on their expedition. The number, as their well informed reckoned, was 2,500 besides their General and eighteen captains also of nobles and gentlemen. But all the same, a great number of them escaped luckily without being slain, though they were wounded, and they reckoned the missing as well as those were slain. The battle was fought on the 10th day of August, in the very beginning of harvest. [Other accounts give the date as August 14.]

Meantime, Ó Néill, Ó Domhnaill and the Irish returned to their homes after that victory, and the minds of the nobles were satisfied though their losses were many, and they did not show care or anxiety for those who were slain, for a battle for right is not remembered [with regret] as the proverb says.

Lugaidh Ó Cléirigh, Beatha Aodha Ruaidh Uí Domhnaill (c. 1615),
ed. Paul Walsh, 2 vols., London, 1948 and 1957

The English Account

On Monday, the 14th August, the army marched from Armagh (leaving there all our victuals and some munitions), for the Blackwater, by computation 3,400 foot and some 300 horse. Their form was in six regiments. We marched severally some six or seven score paces distance between each regiment, our way being hard and holly ground, within caliver [a light musket fired without a rest] shot of wood and bog on both sides, which was wholly possessed by the enemy continually playing upon us. After a mile's marching thus we approached the enemy's trench, being a ditch cast in front of our passage, a mile long, some five feet deep, and four feet over, with a thorny hedge on the top. In the middle of a bog, some forty score paces over, our vanguard passed the trench. The battle stood, for the bringing up of the wagons, which stuck fast in a ford, and also for our rear, which being hard set to, retired foully to Armagh. In the meantime, the vanguard passing, one was so distressed as they fell to run, and were all in effect put to the sword without resistance. Up came the Marshal, being Chief Commander, to relieve them, who was killed dead in the head with a bullet; notwithstanding, two other regiments passed over the trench. The battle coming up, two barrels of powder took fire amongst them, by which they dis-ranked and routed; in which while, those two former regiments, being passed the trench were for the most part put to the sword. Then, by the help of our horse, the enemy's main munitions being well spent we brought off the rest into the plain, and so recovered Armagh; where the captains resolved to refresh their men with victuals and munitions, and so to march directly to the Newry. In the meantime the enemy approached, and fell round on all sides of us with their whole force. Then the captains, finding the insufficiency both in mind and means of their men, concluded that the horse should adventure to break forth through the enemy's quarter, and so pass into the Pale, to advertise the State, that present succour might be sent to fetch them off; or else the enemy, seeing the horse gone, might be persuaded that they having a month or two [sic] victuals, which indeed was there, but disposed had not now left meat for above ten days at the uttermost, that the enemy could not keep together, hearing, by a prisoner that was taken, that O'Donnell and Maguire was [sic] then ready to depart. The horsemen, according their desires, performed it with some loss. By the captain's estimation we had killed and run away to the enemy, not less than 1,800 foot, some ten horsemen and thirty horses. The enemy lost, as we heard by some of theirs that we took, seven or eight hundred. There remains of ours about 1,500 in the church of Armagh.

Charles Montague, lieutenant general of the English horse, August 16, 1598, Armagh
Calendar of State Papers, Ireland

Bagenal's army had, indeed, lost two thousand, and a further one thousand were wounded or deserted, and it suffered the total surrender of all artillery, arms, and supplies. *Sir Henry Bagenal was among the slain. Yellow Ford was the worst defeat an English army ever sustained at the hands of an Irish army and the greatest military disaster of Elizabeth's reign. It was not merely a victory for the Irish but a national triumph. Philip III of Spain hailed Ó Néill as the prince of Ireland and Pope Clement VIII wrote that he had commissioned a gold crown to be fashioned in expectation of Ó Néill's coronation as king of the Irish. Indeed, had Ó Néill's subsequent war of liberation been successful, there is little doubt that the old office of high king would have been reconstituted.*

Munster Joins the War (1598)

Many of the Munster men now first about October, 1598 broke into rebellion and joined themselves with Tyrone's forces, spoiled the country, burnt the villages, and pulled down the houses and castles of the English, against whom [especially the female sex] they committed all abominable outrages. . . . The Munster rebellion broke out like a lightning, for in one month's space almost all the Irish were in rebellious arms, and the English were murdered, or stripped and banished.

Fynes Moryson (1566–1630), Itinerary, London, 1617

The cause of this original hate is for that they were conquered of the English, the memory whereof is yet fresh among them and the desire both of revenge and also of recovery of their lands, is daily revived and kindled amongst them by their lords and counsellors; for which they both hate ourselves and our laws and customs.

Edmund Spenser, A Brief Note of Ireland, London, 1598

An Englishman Entertained by Aodh Ruadh Ó Néill (April 1599)

Sir John Harrington, an Englishman best known for his 1591 translation of Orlando Furioso *by Lodovico Ariosto (originally written in 1516), the most influential of the early Orlando poems, visited Ireland in 1599. He was commanding a troop of horse when invited to accompany Sir William Warren, newly appointed lord deputy, to negotiate a treaty with Ó Néill.*

Having expected shipping till the 8th of this month [April] and meeting with none convenient, in respect that all were taken up with sick soldiers, or with my Lord Lieutenant's horses, I was desirous to make some use of the time that I should stay here, and therefore was easily persuaded to go with Sir William Warren . . . to see some part of the Realm northward, and the arch-rebel himself, with whom Sir William was to treat.

But staying at Dundalk till the 15th of this month, and no news certain of the Earl's coming [Ó Néill], I went to see the Newry, and from thence to Carlingford by the narrow water, and was hindered by waters that I could not come back to Sir William Warren before his first meeting with the Earl of Tyrone [Ó Néill], which was on the 17th day; When I came, the Earl used far greater respect to me than I expected, and began debasing his own manner of hard life, comparing himself to wolves, that fill their bellies sometime, and fast as long for it. . . . After this he fell to private communications with Sir William . . . to which I thought it not fit to intrude myself, but took occasion the while to entertain his two sons, by posing them in their learning, and their tutors, which were one Friar Nangle, a Franciscan, and a younger scholar whose name I know not; and finding the two children of good towardly spirit, their age being 13 and 15, in English clothes like a nobleman's sons, with velvet jerkins and gold lace, of good cheerful aspect, freckle-faced, not tall of stature, but strong and well-set, both of them learning the English tongue; I gave them, not without the advice of Sir William Warren, my English translation of *Ariosto,* which I got at Dublin; which their teachers took very thankfully, and soon after shewed it to the Earl, who called to see it openly, and would needs hear some part of it read. I turned . . . to the beginning of the 45th canto, and some other passages of the book, which he seemed to like so well that he solemnly swore his boys should read all the book over to him.

Then we broke our fasts with him, and at his meal he was very merry, and it was my hap to thwart one of his priests in an argument, to which he gave reasonable good ear, and some approbation. . . . Other pleasant and idle tales were needless and impertinent, or to describe his fern table and fern forms spread under the stately canopy of heaven. His guard, for the most part, were beardless boys without shirts; who in the frost, wade as familiar through rivers as water spaniels. With what charm such a master makes them love him, I know not, but if he bid come, they come; if go, they do go; if he say do this, they do it. . . .

This is all I remember any way worthy the writing to you, not doubting but Sir William Warren, that had the sole charge of the business, will give you much better account of the weightier affairs than I, that only went to see their manner of parting.

Sir John Harrington, *Report of a Journey into the North of Ireland Written to Justice Carey (1599)*, in *Nugae Antiqueae*, vol. 1, pp. 247–251

Attack on a Ship in 1601 of Irish Chieftainess Gráinne Uí Máille, Known as Granuaile (1530–1603)

One of the most powerful Irish leaders at this time was Gráinne Uí Máille (Grace O'Malley, c. 1530–1603), only daughter of Dubhdara Ó Máille, whose lands were on the Mayo coast. Her first marriage was to Donal Ó Flaitheartaigh, chief of Iar Connacht (west Connacht), heir to The MacWilliam Iochtar (Burke). She raided English shipping and was captured and imprisoned in Dublin Castle in 1577. Released in 1578, she defeated an English fleet in 1579. Captured again in 1586, she was due to be hanged, but her son-in-law, Risteard de Burgo (Burke), managed to obtain her release. In July 1593, she arrived in London and had a personal audience with Elizabeth I. Returning to Ireland, she was still harried by the English and finally sought refuge with The O'Donnell of Tyrconnell.

The only sail I have seen since I came upon the coast of Ulster and Connaught was a galley I met withal betwixt Teelin and Killybegs, where I made her run on shore amongst the rocks, notwithstanding she rowed with thirty oars, and had on board, ready to, defend her, 100 good shot [marksmen] which entertained skirmish with my [boarding] boat at most an hour and had put her to the worst. But coming up with my ship to her rescue, I quickly, with my great shot, made an end to the affair. This galley comes out of Connaught and belongs to Grany O'Malley [Gráinne Uí Máille], whereof a base son of hers is captain and, as I learned since, this with one other galley, was set out and manned with a people called the Flaherties [Ó Flaithbheataigh] who was purposed to do some spoils upon the countries and islands of McSwyne Fanad [Mac Sweeney Fanad] and McSwyne na Doe [MacSweeny Doe] about Lough Swilly and Sheephaven.

Captain Charles Blessington writing on July 17, 1601, on board Her Majesty's Ship *Tremontaney*, lying at sea off the Blackrock, Ireland, to Sir Robert Cecil, the queen's private secretary *Calendar of State Papers, Ireland*

7

The Flight of the Princes

The Defeat at Kinsale (1601)

The Battle of Kinsale was the last major conflict of the English Tudor Conquest of Ireland. It is regarded as the defining victory of the English, although other engagements occurred. Ó Néill, the Irish leader, finally submitted in 1603 to Charles Blount, eighth Baron Mountjoy, the Lord Deputy Mountjoy. He had conducted one of the most ruthless genocidal campaigns visited on the country, destroying Irish crops in the field, burning houses, and carrying out a slaughter of the population. The English victory marked the defeat of the Irish aristocratic classes and the native law system and social structure.

Toward the end of 1600, the Irish forces in the south were bearing the full brunt of the attack. In September, a token force of four thousand Spanish soldiers, commanded by Don Juan del Aguila, landed near the southern port of Kinsale to help the Munster forces, but Lord Mountjoy managed to besiege the Spanish confined on the Kinsale promontory. The main Irish army of Ó Néill and Ó Domhnaill marched from the north and in turn besieged the English forces.

On the Irish side was Lughaidh Ó Cléirigh (c. 1570–1620), the Donegal historian.

Ó Néill then said he would be slow to attack the English on account of the great strength of the solid, impregnable walls which were all round them, filled in rows with loud-sounding, quick shooting guns, and he said it was better not to relax the siege which they had laid upon the English till they should die of hunger, as many of them had died already, and they would give up their noblest into their mercy and protection at last, and that he did not wish to gratify his enemies, for they were better pleased to fight for their lives and to be killed immediately than to die of plague and hunger. Ó Domhnaill's opinion, however, was that the English should be attacked somehow, for he felt it a shame and disgrace to be taunted with the great straits Don Juan and the Spaniards were in, without making an attempt to relieve them though his death should come of it, and besides, lest the Irish be thought little of and despised by the King of Spain, if they suffered his soldiers to be in hardships and straits from their enemies without being aided as they had requested.

However, this was the outcome. They decided in the end to attack the Lord Deputy and the English as they were asked. They separated thus till the night on which they were ordered to attack the camp. At nightfall they took their tunics of battle and their weapons of war quietly and silently, and they went in order and array as their chiefs and nobles, their leaders and counsellors, directed them.

Ó Cléirigh spent some time analyzing the animosity that had grown up between Ó Néill and Ó Domhnaill, with Ó Néill still thinking that an immediate attack on Mountjoy was unwise due to the fact that the English had more artillery and guns than the more lightly armed Irish forces.

They spent much time in the early hours of the night in dispute and contention, which arose between them. The two noble hosts and armies marched at last side by side and shoulder to shoulder together, until they happened to lose their way and go astray, so that their guides and pathfinders could not hit upon the right road, though the winter night was very long and though the camp which they were to attack was very near them, it was not till the time of sunrise on the net day, so that the sun was shining brightly on the face of the solid earth when Ó Néill's forces found their own flank at the Lord Deputy's camp, and they retired a short distance while their ranks and order would be reformed, for they had left the first order in which they had been drawn up through the straying and the darkness of the night.

As for the Lord Deputy and his army, there had come to him warning and foreknowledge from certain persons from the camp of the Irish that they would be attacked that night, so he and his forces were standing to arms all night long till morning in their chosen passes and their gaps of danger, and on their battlements with their war accoutrements, with all their implements of attack and defence in readiness, when they saw Ó Néill and his forces opposite them in the manner we have said.

In fact, Brían Óg MacMahon, lord of Monaghan, had unwittingly betrayed the Irish plan of battle to Sir George Carew. He knew Carew. The friendship had led to MacMahon sending a veiled warning to his friend to leave the battlefield that night. Carew immediately reported this to Mountjoy.

They were not long considering them till they fired a thick shower of round balls [to welcome the Irish] from clean, beautiful big guns, with well-oiled mechanisms and from finely ridged, costly muskets, and from sharp-aiming, quick firing matchlocks and they threw upon them every other kind of shot and missile besides. Then burst out over the walls against them nimble troops, hard to resist, of active, steady cavalry, who up to that were longing for the order to test the seed of their high galloping horses on the plain. They allowed their foot to follow after, for they were certain that the hail of spherical bullets and the force attack of the troops would make destructive gaps in front of them among their enemies. Both armies were mingled together, maiming and wounding each other, so that many were slain on both sides. But in the end Ó Néill's forces were defeated, an unusual thing with them, and they fled swiftly away from the place, and the way the hurry urged them was to pour in on top of Ó Domhnaill's forces, who happened to be to the east of them and had not yet come to the field of battle. When the routed army of Ó Néill, and the troops of the Lord Deputy's army following them, and swiftly smiting their rear, broke into the midst of Ó Domhnaill's people, wavering and unsteadiness seized on the soldiers, fright and terror on their horses and though it was their desire and their duty to remain on the field of battle, they could not.

Lughaidh Ó Cléirigh, *Beatha Aodha Ruaidh Uí Domhnaill,*
ed. Paul Walsh, 2 vols., London, 1948 and 1957

Those of the battle were almost all slain, and there were (of the Irish rebels only) found dead in the place, about twelve hundred bodies, and about eight hundred were hurt, whereof many died that night; and the chase continuing almost two miles, was left off, our men being tired with killing. The enemy lost two thousand arms brought to reckoning, besides great numbers embezzled, all their powder and drums, and even ensigns, whereof six Spanish. Thus, of the Irish that were taken prisoners, being brought to the camp, though they offered ransom, were all hanged.

And thus were they utterly overthrown, who but the very night before, were so brave and confident of their own good success, as that they reckoned us already theirs, and as we since have understood, were in contention whose prisoner the Lord Deputy should be, whose the Lord President, and so of the rest. The Earl of Clanricade carried himself this day very valiantly, and after the retreat sounded, was knighted by the Lord Deputy, in the field amongst the dead bodies. So did all the rest of the captains, officers and soldiers . . . and especially the Lord Deputy himself, who brake, in his person, upon the flower of the army [of] Spaniards, and omitted no duty of a wise diligent conductor and valiant soldier. Upon the fight ended, he presently called together the army and with prayers gave God thanks for the victory. A victory indeed given by the God of Hosts, and marvellous in our eyes, if all circumstances be duly considered, and of such consequence for the preservation and assurance to Her Majesty, of this deeply endangered Kingdom, as I leave to wiser consideration.

A letter from a soldier of good place in Ireland, to his friend in London,
touching the notable victory of Her Majesty's forces there,
against the Spaniards and Irish rebels, London, 1602

According to the English estimates, there were twelve hundred Irish dead and many more had been wounded. Of nearly nine hundred Irish prisoners taken, all but a few of high rank were executed on the spot. The Spanish prisoners were generally spared and given terms.

Yet though there fell in the defeat at Kinsale so few of the Irish that they would not miss them after a while, and indeed did not miss even then, yet there was not lost in any defeat in recent times in Ireland so much as was lost there. There was lost there, to begin with, one island which was most productive and fruitful, most temperate in heat and cold in the greatest part of Europe, in which there was much honey and wheat, with many fish abounding rivers, waterfalls and estuaries, in which were calm, profitable harbours, as the first man of the race of Gaedheal Glas son of Niul, who came to Ireland gave this testimony, ie Ith, son of Bregon, in the presence of the last kings who were of the Tuatha Dé Danaan over Éire. There were lost there all who escaped of the noble freeborn sons of Míl, valiant impetuous chiefs, lords of territories and tribes, chieftains of districts and cantreds; for it is full certain that there will be in Éireann at any time together people better or more famous that the nobles who were there, and who died afterwards in other countries one after another, after being robbed of their patrimony and of their noble land which they left to their enemies in that defeat. There were lost besides nobility and honour, generosity and great deeds, hospitality and kindliness, courtesy and noble birth, culture and activity, strength and courage, valour and steadfastness, the authority and sovereignty of the Gaels of Ireland to the end of time.

When the forces of the Lord Deputy went away with a shout of victory and triumph, as we have said, the [remnants of] the Irish retreated westward to Inis Eóghain [Inishannon, 12 miles southwest of Cork] and they set to consult hastily, uneasily, blaming and reproaching one another. Some of them said that they ought to close in once more the siege of the Lord Deputy's camp and not raise it at all on account of those of their people who had fallen, and that their war strength was no weaker for their losses, for they were enough for battle without them, if fate and good-luck. Other counsels said that it was best that each prince and each lord of a district should return to defend his own people and protect it against the English as long as he could. Ó Domhnaill, however, said he would not go back to his country, nor would he remain any longer at the siege, and he promised in the presence of the chiefs and of the men of Éireann who were there that he would not stand fast in battle or conflict to maintain warfare along with the Irish alone, especially in the company of a party [Ó Néill] which had been routed at the first blow then; for rage and fury had seized him, and he would have been pleased had he been the first man slain in that defeat rather than witness that calamity which the Irish met. His own people were greatly afraid that he would bring on his death through the suffering which seized him, so that he did not sleep nor eat in comfort for three days and three nights after. It was on the 3rd of January, 1602, that defeat of Kinsale was suffered.

Lughaidh Ó Cléirigh, Beatha Aodha Ruaidh Uí Domhnaill (c. 1615),
ed. Paul Walsh, 2 vols., London, 1948 and 1957

The schism between the two most powerful Ulster princes seemed to be resolved and Ó Domhnaill set out to seek further aid from Spain. He left from Cúan an Chaislein (Castlehaven) on January 6 with some of his retainers and reached the port of La

Coruña, in Galicia, on January 14. He was received with great honor by Philip III, who promised him a new Spanish force. However, while at the royal palace of Simancas, 11 kilometers west of Valladolid, he fell ill suddenly and died on September 10. He had been poisoned.

Sir George Carew, writing to Lord Mountjoy, suggested that the assassin of Ó Domhnaill was an English double agent named James Blake. Blake had served with the Spanish forces in the 1590s but was sending secret reports to Lord Burghley, the English secretary of state. In 1602, Blake had seen Sir George Carew, who wrote to Lord Mountjoy on May 28: "I applauded his enterprise, whereupon he departed from me, and is gone to Spain with determination (bound with many oaths) to kill O Donnell. . . . God give him strength and perseverance." Ó Domhnaill was buried with royal honors at the Franciscan monastery of Valladolid.

In Ireland, Ruaidri Ó Domhnaill (1575–1608), brother to Aodh Ruadh, who had fought alongside his brother, had been appointed heir apparent. On news of his brother's death, he became the new Ó Domhnaill, prince of Tyrconnell, and continued to engage the English in guerrilla war.

Ó Néill, who, after the loss he had sustained, was no weaker, [and] wished to continue the war against the enemy in the old way, but he was wholly unable to get his followers to agree to this. For Ó Ruairc [of Breifne] returned to defend his country against his brother. . . . Ranald [MacDonnell of the Glens of Antrim] followed suit, and others were influenced by their example, and forced Ó Néill also to retire, much against his will.

Philip Ó Súilleabháin Béarra, *Historae Catholicae Iverniae Compendium*, Lisbon, 1621

The Destruction of Dunboy (June 1602)

Donal Cam Ó Súilleabháin Beare (1560–1618), one of the leading Munster nobles, had taken a prominent role in the war against the English. His home territory was the Beara Peninsula in West Cork and Kerry. Following the defeat at Kinsale, he retired to his territory to prepare it for the onslaught that he knew would follow. Sir George Carew (1855–1629), appointed by Lord Mountjoy as president of Munster, left Cork City on March 23, 1602, with the purpose of taking Donal's main castle at Dunboy. Donal, however, was in Ardea and had left the defense of Dunboy in the hands of Risteard MacEochagáin (Richard MacGeoghegan) and 140 men. These included three Spaniards and an Italian. Brother Dominic Ó Coileáin (Collins), a Jesuit, of Youghal was with them. On Sunday, June 6, Carew's two regiments with artillery pieces arrived near the castle. Carew's army eventually numbered 5,000 and was still being reinforced as they prepared their positions. The main attack did not commence until June 17.

The seventeenth [of June], about five of the clock in the morning, our battery, consisting of one demi-cannon, two whole culverins and one demi-culverin, began to play which continued without intermission till towards nine in the forenoon, at which time a turret annexed to the castle, on the south west part thereof, was beaten down . . . with the fall of that tower, many of the rebels were buried therein: that being ruinated, the ordnance played on the west front of the castle, which by one of the clock in the afternoon, was also forced down; upon the fall thereof the enemy sent out a messenger, offering to surrender the place, if they had their lives, and depart with their arms, and a pledge given for the assurance thereof . . . the Lord President [Carew] turned him [the messenger] over to the Marshal by whose direction he was executed.

Thomas Stafford, *Pacata Hibernia*, London, 1633

Carew decided that the time had come for an assault by infantry, which was led by companies of his own regiment commanded by Lieutenant Colonel Henry Skipworth. They managed to storm the walls at one point.

By which passage our men making their descent to the enemy, and gaining ground upon them, they being then in desperate case, some forty of them made a sally out of the castle on the sea side, whither our men pursuing them on the same side, and they being crossed by Captain Blundell with a small party of men (on the outside of the Barbican) on the other side we had the execution of them all there (saving eight which leapt into the sea to save themselves by swimming): But the Lord President supposing before that they would, in their extremity, make such an adventure to escape, had appointed Captain Gawen Harvie, and his Lieutenant Thomas Stafford [the author] with three boats to keep the sea who had the killing of them all, another three leapt from the top of the vault, where our soldiers killed them, amongst which was a brutal rebel Mellaghlen Moore (being the man that laid hands first upon the Earl of Ormonde, and plucked him from his horse, when he was taken prisoner by Owlny Mac Roury) was slain.

The surviving seventy-seven members of the garrison were pushed back into the cellars of the castle "into which," says Stafford, "we having no descent, but a straight winding stone stair, they defended the same against us." They offered to surrender, and Brother Dominic Collins from Youghal actually managed to do so. But they were told to expect no mercy. MacGeoghegan, already mortally wounded, realized that Carew would kill them all and discouraged any further surrenders.

The sun being by this time set, and strong guards being left upon the rebels remaining in the cellar, the regiments withdrew to the camp.

The eighteenth, in the morning, three and twenty more likewise surrendered themselves simply to Captain Blundell, who the night before had the guard, and after their cannoneers being two Spaniards and an Italian (for the rest were slain) likewise yielded themselves. Then Mac Geoghegan, chief commander of the place, being mortally wounded with divers shot in his body, the rest made choice of one Thomas Taylor an English man's son (the dearest and inwardest man with Tyrrell and married to his niece) to be their chief.

Sir Richard Tyrrell was one of the leaders of the Irish forces. The Tyrrell family was of Norman origin, having been settled in Ireland four hundred years, but he is described as "of English race but a bold and unnatural enemy to his country and people." The husband of Tyrrell's niece, Thomas Taylor, was also born and raised in Ireland.

[Taylor] having nine barrels of powder, drew himself and hid into the vault, and there sat down by it, with a lighted match in his hand, vowing and protesting to set it on fire, and blow up the castle, himself, and all the rest, except they might have promise of life, which being by the Lord President refused; (for the safety of our men) his Lordship gave direction for a new battery upon the vault, intending to bury them in the ruins thereof, and after a few times discharged, and the bullets entering amongst them into the cellar, the rest that were with Taylor, partly by intercession, but chiefly by compulsion (threatening to deliver him up if he were obstinate) about ten of the clock in the morning of the same day, constrained him to surrender simply, who with eight and forty more being ready to come forth; and Sir George Thornton, the Sergeant Major, Captain Roger Harvie, Captain Power, and others entering the vault to receive them, Captain Power found the said Richard Mac Geoghegan lying there mortally wounded (as before) and perceiving Taylor and the rest ready to surrender themselves, raised himself from the ground, snatching a lighted candle, and staggering therewith to a barrel of powder (which for that purpose was unheeded) offering to cast it into the same, Captain Power took him and held him in his arms, with intent to make him prisoner, until he was by our men (who perceived his intent) instantly killed, and then Taylor and the rest were brought prisoners to the camp.

Thomas Stafford, Pacata Hibernia, London, 1633

MacGeoghegan had been right to take Sir George Carew at his word. As Stafford said, "The same day fifty eight were executed in the market place." However, Thomas Taylor, Brother Dominick Ó Coileáin (Collins), Toirdelbhach Ruadh Mac Suibhne (Tirlagh Roe Mac Swiney), and twelve other prisoners who had prominent positions were not immediately executed. Brother Dominick, a former soldier who had become a lay brother of the Society of Jesus, was taken to his native Youghal for execution while Taylor was executed in Cork City and the others elsewhere. The English had two officers killed and several wounded and sixty-two soldiers dead or wounded. "So obstinate and resolute a defence had not been seen within this kingdom," said Stafford. "The two and twentieth [of June], the castle of Dunboy was accordingly blown up with powder, the outworks and fortifications utterly destroyed, and the same day Lieutenant Downings, with our men, and boats returned from Dursey to the camp, as also twelve of Tyrell's chief men, formerly spoken of, were executed."

The Long March (December 1602–January 1603)

Donal Cam Ó Súilleabháin, on the north side of the peninsula, in Ardea Castle over-looking the Kenmare River estuary, had been in no position to help the besieged Dunboy. Carew's total troops on the peninsula at the time were in the region of eight thousand men. For six months, Donal Cam managed to hold out, but the English were pursuing a "scorched earth" policy of total destruction of homes, crops in fields, livestock, and people. As Thomas Stafford remarked, "Scarcely a cow could be heard lowing from Dunquin in Kerry to Cashel in Munster." They had now left a force of two thousand men commanded by Charles Wilmot, made governor of the Beara, and Samuel Bagnal. Donal Cam had successes in capturing some of the English gar-risons, but the number of Irish surrenders taking place in Munster was dispiriting him. Pardons for all who deserted him were promised and many Irish leaders accepted.

It was simply a matter of time before Donal Cam was overwhelmed, and he made a decision to take his people to seek protection with Ó Ruairc, prince of Breifne (in modern Leitrim), who was still holding his own against the English. Some of his family and followers had already been dispatched to safety in Spain. Gathering the surviving remnants of his people, some four hundred fighting men, of whom thirteen

were cavalry, and six hundred women and children, he set off on December 31,
1602—a march that takes its place in the annals of human endurance.

All the roads were beset with enemies, and a large sum of money was
promised to whoever would slay him. Hence it came to pass those endured
almost incredible toils and faced tremendous risks. . . .

On the 31st of December, in the year of our Redeemer's birth 1602,
O'Sullivan [Ó Súilleabháin] set out from Glengarriff, and at night pitched
his tents twenty-six miles away in Muskery country, at a place the natives
called Augeris.

On the next day, the 1st of January, 1602, started off in the early morning he reached, before midday, the populous village of Ballyvourney, dedicated to Saint Gobnata.

Philip O'Sullivan Beare, Historiae Catholicae Iverniae Compendium, Lisbon, 1621

The first attack on the refugees came just outside Ballyvourney, and four hours were
spent fighting, according to Philip Ó Súilleabháin. Even so, they covered 24 miles.
The following day, assailed by hunger and lack of sleep, they marched under Slieve
Lougher toward Limerick. Lord Barry and an English garrison disputed the refugees
crossing a river, but Ó Súilleabháin carried the ford with the loss of four men and
some wounded, whom they carried in litters, and accomplished a march of 30 miles
in that day and camped in the woods of Aherlow in County Tipperary. The next day
they were also attacked with such ferocity that the Irish had no time to bury their
dead, and some of their wounded were left behind. The fight lasted eight hours. They
moved on. Near Slievefelim mountains another attack was launched, which they
beat off by a preemptive strike.

Hunger pinching them bitterly, Thomas Burke and Donal M'Malley by
O'Sullivan's order, made a slight detour with six men to look for food.

The enemy suddenly attacked them and Donal and twenty men were
killed. Thomas was captured and the rest routed, but were saved by
O'Sullivan coming to the rescue. Thomas having broken his bonds, his
helmet on but stripped of his sword and dagger, he being pursued and
O'Sullivan rescued him. They halted in the village of Latteragh, and put
his men in a small church and its enclosure. There was in this village a fort
from which they were annoyed the whole night by firing and sallies of the
garrison. They withstood the attack from the fort and O'Sullivan waited
the dawn with drawn sword.

Philip O'Sullivan Beare, Historiae Catholicae Iverniae Compendium, Lisbon, 1621

Crossing the Shannon

It was now the 6th of January, when at dawn, a storm of red-hot balls blazed on O'Sullivan as he advanced. This was, indeed, a daily salutation with which the enemy honoured him; a farewell as they drew off at night; a greeting as they turned up in the morning.

Through the whole of the day his rear column was continually engaged in fight and some fell on both sides, nor was O'Sullivan's only disadvantage that with a few he had to meet many, but, in addition, he had to oppose with wearied and wounded, fresh and stained enemies. The fighting was usually with missiles. Whenever O'Sullivan halted the enemy fled, when he advanced they quickly pursued. Night putting an end to the contest, O'Sullivan reached the village of Brosna.

O'Sullivan seemed to be landed here in a very tight corner, as he could not cross the broad and navigable river Shannon since the enemy had removed all boats and ship, and warned every ferryman under the severest penalties not to carry him over. Moreover, the soldiers were nerveless from want. Every heart was hereupon filled with giant despair. In this critical state of things, my father Dermot O'Sullivan, announced that he would in a short time make a ship and put an end of the soldiers' hunger.

On the following day, which was the 7th of January, they, by Dermot's advice, concealed themselves in the thick and secure wood of Brosna, and having cut down the trees arranged them like a ditch and surrounded themselves with a small trench. In two days they built two ships of osiers and trees, covered with the skins of twelve horses, which they killed, and on whose flesh they all fed except O'Sullivan, Dermot and O' Houlaghan. . . .

These ships were carried by night on the men's shoulders to the bank of the Shannon called Portland, and O'Sullivan began stealthily to ferry his men across in them. Ten of the O'Malleys got into his ship, but it perished in the midst of the river with its men, being too small and imperfectly built to bear the weight. Dermot's ship, which carried thirty men at a time, brought the others across to safety, drawing after them the (remaining) horses swimming and tied to the poop.

At daybreak, after the soldiers had been got over, Donough MacEgan [working for the English], who held the adjoining port of Kiltaroe, surrounded the baggage with an armed band and began to destroy the packs to sprinkle the earth with the blood of the women and children and drive the terror stricken women into the river. Thomas Bure, with about twenty pikes and as many marksmen, had been placed on guard in ambush by O'Sullivan to protect the others until they were brought over the river, and now rousing his men, he unexpectedly attacked Donough with fifteen of his comrades, he slew and routed the rest, nearly all wounded. The locals, attracted by the report of the guns, flocked down to both banks of the river. Hereupon, Thomas with his guards, the women and children, in a great panic, tumultuously pouring into, sank the boat but so near the shore that no one perished and the ship being again floated carried over the guards who, with some of the others, swam across the river; others, not being able to get over on account of the locals coming up, dispersed in different directions and hid themselves. O'Sullivan ordered the ship to be broken up lest it should prove useful to the enemy.

Engagement at Aughrim

Advancing thence, O'Sullivan sent eight armed men in front, the baggage followed immediately after, and he himself with 200 men (for he now had no more), brought up the rear. Here he was obliged by the pursuers' fire to leave behind some worn out beasts of burden, and to abandon some men exhausted by the march, or weakened by wounds. When he reached a place called Aughrim [Eachdhroim, Horse Ridge, County Galway], Henry Malby, an Englishman [governor of Connacht], Thomas Burke, brother of the Earl of Clanricade, and Richard Burke, with five companies of foot and two troops of horse, and a band of native levies, came against him. The neighing of their horses, the sheen of their brilliant armour, the braying of their trumpets, the sound of their pipes, the beat of their drums, all joyously and proudly anticipating victory, unnerved the small band of Irish and struck terror into their souls. The eighty men who were in advance to protect the baggage abandoned it and fled at the first sight of the enemy.

Ó Súilleabháin then addressed his men, urging them to stand fast and fight.

O'Sullivan had scarcely concluded this speech when the enemy cavalry were down full tilt upon him, endeavouring to run the foot through with their spears, to trample them under the horse's hooves and throw their ranks into confusion. O'Sullivan, avoiding the shock of the enemy cavalry, marched his column through the adjacent swampy and boggy ground to a thick low copse wood not far off. The enemy cavalry dismounted and joined their pikemen, and both, running through the bog, tried to get before O'Sullivan and seize the copse, while his column was not fully arranged and his ranks were wide open. The enemy musketeers sharply pressed O'Sullivan's rear. He sent William Burke with forty gunmen against these musketeers but he was driven back by the enemy's numbers with a loss of fourteen musketeers. At this instant O'Sullivan suddenly turned round his division on the enemy's column, which was within a dart's throw, and was followed by his chieftains and the brave, though abandoned by cowards and dastards. This sudden and unexpected *volte face* struck terror into the enemy, and when ordered to fall into line some fled to the rear ranks and, one following another, they wheeled round in a circle. Some fled.

The chief and bravest, however, held their ground against O'Sullivan. Shortly before he came within a spear's length of them, twenty marksmen whom O'Sullivan had posted flanking his front ranks, shot down eleven of the enemy, Forthwith, the advance lines of both parties fell to with drawn swords and couched spears. First of all, Maurice O'Sullivan closed with Richard Burke but before he had got firm ground he was struck on the chest and knocked down by Richard who was standing on firm ground. He was, however, not wounded, being protected by his coat of mail. Donogh O Hinguerdel [sic] with a blow of a sword cut off Richard's right hand as he was making a second thrust and Muiris quickly getting up again ran him through with his lance and Hugh O'Flynn finished him off with his sword as he fell half dead. Dermot O'Houlaghan and Cornelius O'Morrough killed Malby. Then the fight became general, each striking his foe as he met him. The fight going against the enemy, Thomas Burke, who was heavily armoured, was going on his horse by his servants and rode off. And now a heap was formed of bodies and arms and the rest not slowly, but pell mell make for the adjoining fort at Aughrim.

O'Connor, a peer of the bravest in the fight, shouted victory!

This was The O'Connor Kerry, whose seat was at Carrigafoyle Castle, 2 miles from Ballylongford, County Kerry, on the edge of marshes and reed beds on the south shore of the Shannon. Some years before, the English had stormed the castle and executed all the defenders after they had been captured or surrendered. It would also be attacked and more or less destroyed by Cromwell's troops in 1649, but its ruins still stand. O'Connor Kerry had fought at Kinsale.

The conquerors hung on the rear of the enemy. And now those who had not dared to charge with O'Sullivan against the opposing foe, were quick enough to fall on the routed enemy, arrogating to themselves the great blusterings the glory of the victory obtained by others, and anxious by a show of spirit to wipe out the abject disgrace of their ill-timed cowardice.

However, the routed were not pursued far. O'Sullivan ordered a recall to be sounded, having observed John Bostock [an English commander] with some companies coming to the rescue of the fugitives, and who, with the others, betook himself to Aughrim fort. Whilst this was taking place, Malby's musketeers and a crowd of those who, following the Irish divisions, were engaged in plundering O'Sullivan's baggage, and when the English column was routed they also sought safety in flight.

In the battle about 100 enemy fell, the flower of their forces, their general, Malby, Richard Burke, three standard bearers, as many adjutants, more sergeants and the rest were Anglo-Irish and English gentlemen. The Irish lost the fourteen whom I have mentioned. O'Sullivan collecting the enemy's arms and colours, fled that evening, and the following night through a host of surrounding enemies through O'Kelly's country which such haste that he left some soldiers worn out on the road and overcome with sleep.

O'Kelly of Gallagh in Connacht had initially fought against the Elizabethan Conquest, but now in November 1581 had surrendered, had given up his Gaelic title, and had been pardoned and appointed "seneschal of the barony of Kylconnell." The old English title would make Conor na Garroghe O'Kelly of Gallagh the equivalent to the governor of the territory under the English. It was not a place for Ó Súilleabháin to tarry. Philip recounts several more days of struggle before they came to woods, where they lit some fires to warm themselves in the freezing snow.

When the day broke, the locals, coming to investigate the strange fire in such a wilderness, spent a long time talking with O'Sullivan, and then brought him a present of goods, reporting to Oliver Lambert, the English President of Connacht (who had apparently demanded information) that the fire had been lit by labourers. . . .

The darkness of the night, the unknown country, the suspected guide [a man had joined them and offered to guide them to Ó Ruairc's stronghold 15 miles away], multiplied the fears of those groping along. The feet slipping over loose stones, the snow heaped up by the wind, exhaustion, swollen feet, all tried the unhappy fugitives. O'Connor suffered more than anyone did, the causes of his pain increasing. The greater part of his feet and legs was inflamed. Lividness supervened, and in turn gave place to blisters, and these succeeded by ulcers. He was terribly afflicted and only able to bear up because he suffered by Christ Jesus. In the heart of night they reached the little village called Knockvicar [Cnoc an Bhiocáire, County Roscommon] where they refreshed themselves with fire and purchased food. When they decided to move on, O'Connor, whose ulcers had been crustrated by the fire, was not able to stand, much less walk. Four of his comrades carried him on their shoulders until in the twilight they found a stray beast, lank and worn with age, on which they placed him without bridle or saddle, the sharp bone of the lean back pricking the rider. Some led the blind beast, others whacked it along.

Having got over the Curlew hills, they reached a plain, when O'Connor began to walk. After daybreak the guide showed O'Sullivan Ó Ruairc's castle in the distance and bid the rest farewell assuring them all danger was now past. They reached Leitrim fort about eleven o'clock being then reduced to 35, of whom 18 were soldiers, 16 were civilians of which one was woman. The other of the 1,000 who had left Beara had either perished of lingered on the road through weariness and wounds. Some followed in twos and threes. I am astonished that Dermod O'Sullivan, my father, an elderly man near 70 years, and the woman of delicate sex, were to go through these toils which youths in the flower of age and height of their strength were unable to endure. Ó Ruairc received O'Sullivan with most honourable hospitality giving directions to have his sick cured and all necessaries to be supplied.

Philip O'Sullivan Beare, *Historiae Catholicae Iverniae Compendium*, Lisbon, 1621

Ó Súilleabháin Béara had been welcomed by Brían Óg Ó Ruairc, whose father had been betrayed by James VI of Scotland to Elizabeth and had been executed in London. Donal Cam hardly paused to recover, setting out to join Cú Chonnacht Maguire, prince of Fermanagh, who was also still fighting with his brother, Brían. Maguire was also to go into exile, and he died in Genoa, Italy, in 1608. With the news that Ó Néill had surrendered to the English in March 1603, Ó Súilleabháin, having sent his family to safety in Spain, decided to join them. O'Connor Kerry, according to the Annals of the Four Masters, took an entire year before his feet were healed and he was well again.

The Murder of The Ó Súilleabháin Béara
(July 16, 1618)

Among Donal Cam's relatives was his young cousin, frequently thought to be his nephew, Philip, born in Dunboy in 1590. Philip's father had been part of the Long March, and his account was taken from his father as well as from Donal Cam himself and other members of the family. He was to become a scholar and author of Historiae Catholicae Iverniae Compendium, *Lisbon, 1621, the history of the Elizabethan Conquest of his country. Donal Cam felt no option but to join his family in Spain in 1603, and, like the other Irish princes, was welcomed by Philip III, who conferred on him the knighthood of the Order of St. Iago and a pension for life, as well as the title of Conde de Berehaven. This enraged James I, who ordered his minister of state to write to the Spanish court to protest and ask the Spanish king to "forbear to convey any such titulary honour upon any of his subjects without his privity." What the Spanish king replied is not known. Philip wrote:*

But the final strike of evil fortune was that on the 16th of that same month, O'Sullivan, Chieftain of Beare, in whom the Irish had then their greatest hope, perished lamentably in this way.

John Bathe, an Anglo-Irishman, was so favoured by O'Sullivan that he benefited greatly by his influence and patronage. He was treated as such a great friend that he was even received into his home and invited to his table; but, with total disregard for such favours, John acted with effrontery when a trivial argument arose over money given to him by O'Sullivan. This behaviour in no way enhanced the noble lineage of such a great man, or his reputation among the Irish, or among the English from whom he is descended.

Philip, the author of this history, and cousin, was angered by this behaviour and remonstrated with John. Consequently, near the monastery of St. Dominic in Madrid, they attacked each other with drawn swords. From the beginning of the fight, John was struck with such overwhelming fear that, utterly loud cries, he constantly gave ground and Philip wounded him in the face with a sword thrust; he would have killed him had not Edmund O'Moore and Gerald MacMorris, sent by O'Sullivan and two Spanish knights protected him, and had not Philip himself been arrested by an official of the law.

A crowd then gathered from all sides and, among others, came

O'Sullivan, carrying a rosary in his left hand and gloves in his right hand. John, observing him off his guard, unaware of danger and looking in the opposite direction, made his way up to him through the crowd and, stabbing him through the left upper arm, and again striking him in the throat, killed him.

Philip, struggling with the official of the law, escaped and hid himself in the house of the ambassador of France, the Marquis Seneccia. John was thrown into prison together with his relative, Francis Butler, and O'Driscoll, Philip's kinsman who was present at the fight.

O'Sullivan's funeral ceremonies took place in the monastery on the following day in the presence of a large assembly of Spanish nobles, and the expenses were paid through the good offices of the illustrious knight and royal councillor, Don Diego Brochero.

At the time of his death, O'Sullivan was 57 years of age. He was a man of great benevolence, especially towards the poor and needy. . . . In stature he was tall and elegant, with a handsome face and he grew old with dignity.

Philip O'Sullivan Beare, *Historiae Catholicae Iverniae Compendium*, Lisbon, 1621

John Bathe's Account

When he was making his way direct to the palace, as he did every day at the same time, without any thought of trouble and without carrying weapons of any sort, except for his sword, he was attacked by the nephew of the Earl of Birrhaven, by the Earl's major-domo, by the Earl himself, and two Irish soldiers, as well as the Earl's lackey, his page and others, so that he would have been cut to pieces were it not that some Spanish knights took pity on him and came to his aid, although they did know him and had never seen him before.

Don Juan Batheo, September 27, 1620, letter to King Philip III
Biblioteca de la Real Academia de la Historia, Madrid

However, the claim by the Irish political refugees that John Bathe (often written as Rath) was actually an English agent seemed well founded. Once released from the Spanish prison, he took up residence in London, where he received an annual pension from King James I of £500. Ó Súilleabháin, after his march to Leitrim, was regarded as one of the most charismatic of the Irish leaders. It became clear that he was planning to return to Ireland and lead an uprising against the English at the time of his death.

Donal Cam's son inherited, under Spanish law, the title of Conde de Berehaven, and, curiously enough, within a few months of his father's death, he, too, was dead. The title then passed to his second son, Diarmaid (Dernieseo), who had married the daughter of the duke of Sesa. Dermot died in 1659 without male heirs.

The Flight of the Irish Princes (1608)

Usually called the Flight of the Earls, the departure of Ó Néill and Ó Domhnaill from Ulster marked the exit from Ireland of the last independent Gaelic princes, descendants of the ancient kings and high kings. Ó Néill and O'Donnell believed that the English had plans either to assassinate them or arrest them and have them executed. Certainly, assassination of the Irish princes and leaders, even after they had fled to other European countries, was a covert policy of English government.

William Cecil, Lord Burghley, had devised a secret service employing such assassins. Tadhg Mac Carthaigh, son of Mac Carthaigh Mór, king of Desmond, had fled to France for safety and was assassinated there in 1588. He was not the last of the Irish princes to die in such a fashion. Aodh Ruadh (Red Hugh) Ó Domhnaill, the prince of Tyrconnell, had already been murdered by an English agent, James Blake, while in Spain, in 1602.

Cú Chonnacht Maguire, prince of Fermanagh, had gone abroad and returned in August with a Breton ship, which was anchored in Lough Swilly, off Rathmullen in Donegal. On September 4, 1607, Ó Néill and O'Donnell went on board the ship. It would seem that the plan was not to go into permanent exile on the Continent but to await the first favorable opportunity to return and lead the country to liberation. Among their ninety-strong retinue went Tadhg Ó Cianáin (born in Fermanagh, c. 1572; d. possibly in Rome, c. 1625). He was of a family who were hereditary chroniclers to the Maguires, princes of Fermanagh. He kept an eyewitness account of the escape by Ó Néill and O'Donnell written in Irish.

About the middle of the same night they hoisted their sails. . . . They went out a great distance in the sea. The night was bright, quiet and calm, with a breeze from the south-west. . . . An exceeding great storm and very bad weather arose against them, together with fog and rain, so that thy were driven from proximity to land. . . . Afterwards, leaving [coastline of] Tyrconnell on the left, they direct their course past the harbour of Sligo, straight ahead until they were opposite Croagh Patrick in Connacht. Then they feared that the English King's fleet, which was in the harbour of Galway, would meet with them. They proceeded out into the sea to make for Spain straight forward if they could. After that they were on the sea for thirteen days with excessive storms and dangerous bad weather. A cross of gold which O'Neill had, and which contained a portion of the Cross of the Crucifixion any many other relics being put by them in the sea trailing after the ship, gave them great relief.

On Sunday, the thirtieth of September, the wind came right straight against the ship. The sailors, since they could not go to Spain, undertook to reach the harbour of Le Croisic in Brittany at the end of two days and nights. The lords who were in the ship, in consequence of the smallness of their food supply, and also because of all the hardship and sickness of the sea they had received up to that, gave it as their advice that it was right for them to make straight towards France.

They made the Breton French coast, then journeyed on to Rouen.

On the next day, the fifteenth of October, they left Rouen with thirty-one on horseback, two coaches, three wagons and about forty on foot. The Governor of Quillebeuf and many of the gentry of the town came to conduct them a distance from the city. . . .

On Monday, the twenty-second of the same month, they bade farewell to the people of the city [Arras]. They proceeded five more leagues to a famous city called Douai. The people there received them with great respect. They alighted at the Irish College, which was supported by the King of Spain in the town. They themselves stayed in the College and they sent the better part of those with them through the city. They remained there until the following Friday. The reverend father, Flaithrí Ó Malconaire, Irish Provincial of the Friars Minor [Franciscans], and Doctor Robert MacArthur met them here, having come from Flanders. Assemblies of the colleges received them kindly and with respect, delivering in their honour verses and speeches in Latin, Greek, and Irish.

The thirty first of October, O'Neill's son [Henry], the Colonel of the Irish Regiment [this was part of the army of Archduke Albert of Austria, governor of the Spanish Netherlands] came to them with a large well-equipped company of captains and of noble men, Spanish and Irish and of every other nation. On the following Saturday, the Marquis Spinola, the commander in chief, of the King of Spain's army in Flanders came to them from Brussels with a large number of important people and welcomed them. He received them with honour and gave them an invitation to dinner on the next day in Brussels. . . .

Early the next morning they went to Brussels. . . . Colonel Francisco, with many Spanish, Italian, Irish and Flemish captains, came out of the city to meet them. They advanced through the principal streets of the town to the door of the Marquis's palace. The Marquis himself, the Papal Nuncio, the Spanish Ambassador, and he, Duke of Ossuna, came to them from their coaches. . . . Afterwards they entered the apartment where the Marquis was accustomed to take food. He himself arranged each one in his place, seating O'Neill in his own place at the head of the table, the Papal Nuncio on his right, the O'Donnell to his left, O'Neill's children and Maguire next to O'Donnell, and the Spanish Ambassador and the Duke of Aumale on the other side, below the Nuncio. . . . The excellent dinner, which they partook of, was grand and costly enough for a king.

Ó Néill and O'Donnell spent Christmas at Louvain, where they remained until February 28, 1608. Ó Cianáin then describes their journey through Germany and Switzerland, the crossing of the Alps, and the crossing of Lake Lugano by boat.

On Sunday, the twenty-third March, they proceeded to the great remarkable famous city Milan. . . . A great respected earl, Count de Fuentes by name, was chief governor and representative of the King of Spain over that city and over all Lombardy. He sent the King' ambassador at Lucerne, who happened to be in the city, to welcome them and to receive them with honour. On Wednesday, the nobles went in person into the presence of the earl [Fuentes]. He received them with honour and respect. There were many noblemen and a very great guard on either side of him. They remained three full weeks in the city. During that time the earl [Fuentes] had great honour shown them. . . . The lords took their leave of Count de Fuentes on the twelfth of April. . . . He gave them as a token of remembrance a collection of rapiers and fine daggers, with hilts of ornamented precious stones, gilt, and belts and expensive hangers.

Peter Lombard, the Archbishop of Armagh and Primate of Ireland, came [on Tuesday, April 29, at Milvian Bridge, to escort them into Rome] . . . having a large number of coaches sent by cardinals to meet them to that place. . . . Then they proceeded in coaches . . . through the principal streets on Rome in great splendour. They did not rest until they reached the great church of San Pietro in Vaticano. They put up their horses there and entered the church . . . afterwards they proceeded to a splendid palace which his Holiness the Pope [Paul V] had set apart for them in the Borgo Vecchio Santo Spirito.

Paul V (Camillo Borghese of Rome, elected May 16, 1605, died January 28, 1621) received the Irish princes on the Quirinal, the highest of the Seven Hills of Rome, where the Palazzo del Quirinale stands, which was then the summer palace of the popes.

On the Thursday [June 5] of Corpus Christi an order came from the Holy Father to the princes that eight of their noblemen should go in person to carry the canopy over the Blessed sacrament while it was being borne solemnly in the hands of the Pope in procession from the great Church of San Pietro in Vaticano to the Church of St James in Borgo Vecchio and from there back to the Church of Saint Peter. . . . They carried the canopy over the Blessed Sacrament and the People, and never before did Irishmen receive such an honour and privilege. The Italians were greatly surprised that they should be shown such deference and respect for some of them said that seldom before was any one nation in the world appointed to carry the canopy. With the ambassador of all the Catholic kings and princes of Christendom who happened to then be in the city it was an established custom that they, in succession, every year carried the canopy in turn. They were jealous, envious and surprised, that they were not allowed to carry it on this particular day. The procession was reverent, imposing and beautiful, for the great part of the regular Orders and all the clergy and communities of the great churches of Rome were in it, and many princes, dukes and great lords. They had no less than a thousand lighted waxen torches. Following them there were twenty-six archbishops and bishops. Next there were thirty-six cardinals. The Pope carried the Blessed Sacrament, and the Irish lord and noblemen to the number of eight, bore the canopy. About the Pope was his guard of Swiss soldiers, and on either side of him and behind him were two large troops of cavalry. The streets were filled with people behind. It was considered by all that there were no less in number than one hundred thousand.

> Tadhg Ó Cianáin, untitled manuscript, "The Flight of the Earls" (1608), ed. and trans. Father Paul Walsh, in *Archivium Hibernicum*, vol. 5, 1916

The following month, Ruaidri O'Donnell, prince of Tyrconnell, fell sick with a fever and died on July 28, 1608. He was buried in Rome. Rumor had it that he had fallen prey to an assassination attempt. Aodh Ruadh (Red Hugh) Ó Néill continued to live in exile in Rome in a manner befitting a prince. Indeed, in reality he was the last Gaelic king of Ulster. He died on July 20, 1616, and his tomb may still be seen in the church of San Pietro in Montorio, in the Via Garibaldi, in front of the high altar.

The inscription describes him as prince of Ulster. Of his seven sons, Conn died of wounds in 1601; Hugh died unmarried in Rome in 1609; Henry died childless in 1610; John was killed near Barcelona in 1641; Hugo, styled prince of Ulster, had also been killed but at an uncertain date; Conn na Creige died a prisoner in the Tower of London in 1622; and Brian was murdered in Brussels by an English agent in 1617 at age 13. But Aodh Ruadh's nephew, Eoghan Ruadh Ó Néill, was to momentarily raise the fortunes of the family again when, having enlisted in Spanish services in 1618, he was invited to command the Irish armies after the great uprising of 1641 and succeeded in inflicting defeats on the English, most notably the victory at Benburb.

Tonight, Ireland is lonely. The banishment of her true chiefs causes the cheeks of her men and her fair women to be wet. It is strange that this people should be lonely. . . . There is no laughter at children's doings, music is prohibited, the Irish language is in chains. Irish princes, unusually for them, speak not of wine-feasts nor Mass. There is no playing, feasting, nor any pastime. There is no trading or riding horses or turning to face danger. No praise poem is recited, no bedtime story told, no desire to see a book, no giving ear to the family pedigrees. . . . How shall the oppression be lifted from the bright fair-haired race of Conn, since we have no Moses in Ireland? There is none of them [Irish princes] who can lift her up after they have gone. The fact that the royal lines are under heavy oppression is stealing our soul from us.

Aindrias Mac Marcais, in *Talamh Bánaithe* (The deserted land), c. 1610

8

Obedience to the English Empire

We must change their [the Irish] course of government, apparel, manner of holding land, language and habit of life. It will otherwise be impossible to set up in them obedience to the laws and to the English Empire.

Sir William Parsons, lord chief justice of Ireland, *A True Coppie of Divers Letters Sent from the Governors of Ireland*, London, 1641

William Parsons arrived as a penniless adventurer in Ireland at the end of the Tudor Conquest and became surveyor-general by 1601. He became a member of the 1613 Dublin Parliament. An enthusiastic colonist, he was granted a baronetcy in 1620. He then became joint lord chief justice with Sir John Borlase and a privy councillor. He died in London in 1650 and is buried at St. Margaret's Church, Westminster.

The Commissioners for the Plantation of Ulster (1610)

About the end of July last they began their journey into Ulster where they lay in camp nine weeks, and during that time performed two principal things. They took inquisitions. the counties being divided into baronies, they made a description of every barony in a several map. . . . An abstract was made out of many records. . . . The maps were finished, and herein as well the proportions for undertakers [colonists] of all sorts as the Church lands and lands already granted and signed to forts, corporate towns, free schools etc., are distinguished by sundry marks and colours.

"A Brief of the Proceedings of the Commissioners for the Plantation in Ulster Since July Last, March 19, 1610" *Calendar of State Papers, Ireland,* pp. 409–410

Initially 511,465 acres of Irish land had been confiscated in 1607, but then the entire counties of Donegal, Derry, Tyrone, Armagh, Cavan, and Fermanagh were confiscated, totaling 3,785,057 acres.

His Majesty did not utterly exclude the natives out of this plantation, with a purpose to root them out, as the Irish were excluded out of the first English colonies; but made a mixed plantation of English and Irish that they might grow up together in one nation; only, the Irish were in some places transplanted from the woods and mountains into the plains and open countries, that being removed (like wild fruit trees) they might grow milder and bear the better and sweeter fruit.

Sir John Davies, *A Discovery of the True Causes Why Ireland Was Never Entirely Subdued,* London, 1612

In their place [the Irish nobles] we have a conceited and impure swarm: of foreigners' blood—of an excommunicated rabble—Saxons there and Scotsmen. This the land of noble Niall's posterity, they portion out among themselves without leaving a jot of Flann's milk yielding plain but we find it divided into "acres." We have lived to see the clan assembly places emptied; the wealth perished away in the stream; dark thickets of the chase turned into streets. A boorish congregation is in the House of Saints [churches]; God' service [is now performed by the natives] under shelter of simple boughs; poets' and minstrels' bedclothes are thrown to litter cattle; the mountain [allotted to the Irish] all in fenced fields. Fairs are held in places of the chase; hunting there is upon the plain, the open green is crossed by enclosures of twisting fences and the foreigners do not even gather for horse races.

Anonymous Irish writer, *Catalogue of Irish MSS in the British Museum,* ed. Standish Hayes O'Grady, London, 1926

The news here is nothing but [of] continual trouble in these parts. . . . There were never since I came hither so many kerne [Irish guerrillas] out in the woods as now; they are in five or six several companies, so that men can travel no way near any woods without great danger, except they go a good company together, and well provided. The last day of April, Mr Nicholas Elcock, agent for the Clothworkers, was taken by Revelin McCull and his company; he had two men with him, those they left bound and would have killed them had it not been to deliver a letter which they compelled Mr Elcock to write to some of his friends; the effect was that if their pardons were not procured within 14 days, or they had not £100 sterling delivered them by some means at 14 day's end, they would hang him; so they took him into the woods and kept him two days and one night, trailing him from place to place; but the second evening, the country being raised after them and divided many way, some of the country churls by the great goodness of God, happened in a thick obscure place in the woods where Mr Elcock was with a few of the kerne; the rest were gone abroad for more prey, at the sight of whom the kerne fled; so Mr Elcock escaped, almost past hope, blessed be God.

> George Canning, agent of Worshipful Company of Ironmongers, May 13, 1616,
> in J. Nicholl, *Account of the Company of Ironmongers,* pp. 3895–3896

Schools Destroyed

At an end, all at one time, Ulster's schools, Leinster's learned. Of Munster poets, not a tenth alive—that slaughter left no remnant.

> Fearflatha Ó Gnímh (c. 1540–1640), Bard to The Ó Néill Clann Bhuidhe
> "Mo Thruaigh Mar Táid Gaoidhil," in *Irish Magazine & Monthly Asylum
> for Neglected Biography,* vol. 3, Dublin, 1810

Sir Arthur Chichester, Lord Deputy, Plans Colonization in Ulster

I have often said, and written, it is Famine which must consume them [the Irish]; our swords and other endeavours work not that speedy effect which is expected, for their overthrow.

> Written to Lord Burghley, Elizabeth's chief adviser, November 22, 1601, in Moncrieffe,
> *O'Neill Commemorative Journal,* p. 25 c. 1990
> Also in *Calendar of State Papers, Ireland*

Fear of the foreign law does not permit me to tell of Ireland's sore plight; this smooth land of Royal Niall is being wasted with innocent blood.

> Fearflatha Ó Gnímh (c. 1540–1640), Bard to The Ó Néill Clann Bhuidhe
> "Mo Thruaigh Mar Táid Gaoidhil," in *Irish Magazine & Monthly Asylum
> for Neglected Biography,* vol. 3, Dublin, 1810

Peace in Ireland?

And no spectacle was more frequent in the ditches of towns, and especially in wasted countries, than to see multitudes of these poor people dead with their mouths all coloured green by eating nettles, docks, and all things they could rend up above ground. These and very many like lamentable effects followed their rebellion, and no doubt the rebels had been utterly destroyed by famine, had not a general peace followed Tyrone's submission . . . by which the rebels had liberty to seek relief among the subjects of Ireland.

Fynes Moryson, *Itinerary,* London, 1617

Introduction of English Law (1605)

And that they and every of them do henceforth utterly forbear to use . . . those odious and unlawful customs . . . which customs we will and command to be discontinued and abolished forever in this Kingdom, as being barbarous, unreasonable, and intolerable in any civil or Christian commonwealth . . . we do by this present proclamation in his Majesty's name declare and publish, that they and every of them their wives and children, are free, natural, and immediate subjects of His Majesty, and are not to be reputed or called the natives or natural followers of any other lord or chieftain whatsoever, and they and every of them ought to depend wholly and immediately upon His Majesty.

Proclamation of Sir Arthur Chichester, March 11, 1605
Calendar of State Papers, Ireland

The Act of 1587, which deemed all Irish titles would "henceforth ceased, end, determined and be utterly abolished and extinct forever," was supported by a King's Bench judgment in 1606 and 1608 endorsing the abolition of the Brehon law system, and this was followed by "A Royal Proclamation." When a colonial parliament assembled in Dublin in 1613, an act was also passed putting the entire country under English Statute and Common Law and forbidding all forms of Irish cultural expression.

Irish Still Spoken in Central Dublin (1639)

Some curious in the comparisons of tongues, say Irish is a dialect of the ancient British, and the learnedest of that nation in a private discourse I happened to have with him seemed to incline to this opinion, it I can assure your Lordship I found a real multitude of their radical words the same with the Welsh, both for sense and sound. The tone also of both nations is consonant, for when I first walked up and down the Dublin markets me thought I was in Wales when I listened to their speech. I found the Irish tone a little more querulous and whining than the British, which I conjecture proceeded from their often being subjugated by the English.

James Howel, Letter, August 9, 1630
Mercurius Hibernicus, Bristol, 1644

Duelling among the Colonists (1639)

January 20, 1639

This day my son [Lord] Broghhill was at my table at dinner with me. He was secretly called away by a message from Charles Rich, son of the Earl of Warwick, to answer a challenge he brought him from Thomas Howard, son to the Earl of Berkshire. Whereupon Broghill secretly avoided the house bought him a sword and found Jack Barry, whom he made choice of to be his second and went both in Broghill's coach with their seconds into the field, where they fought with their single rapiers and both returned without any wound. Only Broghill took away the fringe of Mr Howard's glove with the passage of his rapier that went through from his hand between his arm and the side of his body, without any other harm and thereupon their seconds parted them, and made them friend and so they came home supped together—and all this for Mrs Harrison.

"Autobiographical Notes, Remembrances and Diaries of Sir Richard Boyle,
First and Great Earl of Cork"
The Lismore Papers, ed. Rev. Alexander B. Grossart, vols. 1–5, 1886

Mrs. Harrison had accepted a proposal of marriage from Roger Boyle, Lord Broghill, youngest son of the great earl of Cork, but had left him for Thomas Howard. Richard Boyle, the first earl of Cork, had been part of the Elizabeth Conquest of Munster in 1588, seized an estate there, and was ennobled.

9

The Insurrection of 1641

A Full Conquest?

There was no way to reduce this kingdom to the English laws and obedience of the Crown, and to free England of the perpetual charge, therefore, but only a full conquest or a political reformation by plantations, as it affirmed in a resolution taken in the reign of Henry the Eighth by the then Lord Deputy and Council.

Sir William Parsons and Sir John Borlase, The Lords Justice and
Council of Ireland, to Secretary of State Vane, April 24, 1641
Calendar of State Papers, Ireland

In spite of the Tudor Conquests and the attempts to clear the Irish off the land, particularly in Ulster, coupled with an attempt to abolish language and law and a destruction of the ruling class, October 23, 1641, saw the Irish rising once more in arms against the English colonial administration. They were led by a descendant of the royal house of Ó Néill, Phelim Ó Néill. The initial step was to be the capture of Dublin Castle, seat of the colonial power. Conor Ruadh Maguire, of Lisnakea, who was now prince of Fermanagh, was charged with its capture, aided by Rory O'Moore and Aodh Mac Mahon. A spy, Owen Connolly, betrayed the plan. They were arrested, held in solitary confinement for eight months, then sent in chains to the Tower of London. They were executed. Maguire was taken to Tyburn, the site of

London's Marble Arch, for the gruesome ritual of being hanged, drawn, and quartered. Father Hugh Burke was in disguise among the crowd witnessing this public execution in 1644.

Execution of Conor Ruadh Maguire, The Maguire, Prince of Fermanagh, Recognized as Baron Maguire of Enniskillen, for His Part in the 1641 Uprising

On February 20, 1644, Lord Maguire, to whom the executioner would have shown some favour by leaving him to hang on the gallows until he should be quite dead, and meanwhile the executioner was busy kindling the fire with which his entrails were to be burned after his death, but so inhuman were the officers that they totally denied Lord Maguire the services of one of our Fathers on the scaffold and they waited not for the executioner but one of them cut the rope with a halberd and let the Lord Maguire drop alive and then called the executioner to open him alive and very ill the executioner did it, the said Lord Maguire making resistance with his hand and defending himself with such little strength he had; and such was the cruelty that for sheer compassion the executioner bore not to look upon him in such torment and, to have done with him, speedily handled his knife well and cut his throat.

Letter from Father Hugh Burke, bishop of Kilmacduagh,
Commissary of the Irish Friars Minor, to his brethren
Archivium Hibernicum, 1949

Conor's brother, Ruaidri, now commanded the Fermanagh contingent. The failure to capture Dublin Castle did not deter Sir Phelim Ruadh Ó Néill (c. 1604–1653), a direct descendant of King Conn Mór of Ulster (1483–1493). He captured Charlemont Castle commanding the Blackwater and took control as commander of the Irish army. The remaining northern chiefs followed a well-coordinated plan and soon their victories spread throughout all Ireland. They were successful at a time when England was preoccupied in the growing tension between the king and Parliament and could not send more than a few thousand men under General Robert Monro to protect their colonial interests. A Confederate Catholic Parliament was established on October 1, 1642, at Kilkenny, with its constitution drawn up by the lawyer Patrick D'Arcy. Exiles were flocking back from the Continent to secure the independence of the country.

General Eoghan Ruadh Ó Néill (1590–1649), who had been serving in the

Spanish forces since going into exile, was invited back to become commander in chief of the Irish forces. He arrived at Lough Swilly in July 1642, the very place from which his uncle Aodh Ruadh had fled into exile in 1608.

Siege of Limerick Castle (1642)

A Confederate Irish army under General Gerald Barry had already marched on Limerick. The city opened its gates and welcomed them. However, the English garrison under Captain George Courtney, with sixty soldiers, civilians, and auxiliaries numbering two hundred, barricaded them in Limerick Castle. An anonymous civilian in the castle wrote an account of the siege.

June 21, 1642

About one of the clock in the morning the upper part of the wall of the bulwark fell down almost as low as the sally port doors, but this was not so great sign of the fire underneath as that which followed the same day, this breach caused a general alarm amongst us, but the enemy (as God would have it) bet not on, or then scarce perceived it, but not long after we perceived that there was fire below under the eastern curtain, by the smell and smoke that broke out in some cabins that were built within the castle against the wall, as also by some smoke that broke up by the side of the trench without, so that then we saw that we were in imminent danger, the increasing whereof we could not prevent, but must go on to an impossibility of our subsisting which I suppose was sufficient cause which moved our Captain to write to the General of the rebels & etc concerning one point of their letter formerly written to him, which was what honourable terms they meant upon which they would have him to yield up the castle unto them, they answered his letter presently desiring him to come forth and parley and they would send in hostages for his safety, to that he replied that he might not go forth of the castle himself, but that he would (if they pleased) send forth two other unto them naming Alderman Lellis an Alderman of the city and A.J. which they refused but wrote to the captain to propose his demands which not long after was done and set down in 9 articles which together with a letter from our Captain was sent unto them, but it was somewhat toward evening and no answer returned that night and we conjectured and probable it was that they stayed to see the event of their fire under our walls which so continued to the increasing of our sorrow that we feared the falling of a great part of our eastern curtain before the next day, and this evening was a brass falcon to be conveyed into one Smith's house for the battering of our gate.

Every hour begat us new cause of fears and we doubted to be assaulted before the next morning, which if they had done, such was our case that without special providence we had been undone from Thursday, June 9, to this Tuesday the 21 were buried 113. So that since we were shut up the number was 223.

June 22, 1642

This day was no shooting from either side as if there had been a formal cessation. In the afternoon the Bishop of Limerick died and in the evening the enemy sent to our Captain that they would accept of the two aforementioned to treat with them and accordingly they went out and after much debate got quarter for life and goods we were to have to accommodation for houses and necessities during our abode in the town and horses and carriages to convey us to Cork we paying for what we took.

June 23, 1642

This day we yielded the castle and carried the Bishop to his grave and buried him in St Munchin's church and every one of us began to carry out our goods out of the castle to houses assigned to us, we had civil usage from the soldiery, and our former acquaintances in the town gave kindly visits.

There died of our company the small time we stayed in the town 57. We did impute the cause of this mortality to our change of diet and so that the number of our dead did in this short time amount to 280.

Anonymous, Diary, ed. M. J. M'Enery
Journal of the Royal Society of Antiquaries, 5th series, vol. 14, 1904

Many of the colonists who had newly arrived in Ireland from England and Scotland, those who had dispossessed the native Irish of their lands, became the victims of harsh treatment. Reports of the massacres of the colonists between November 1641 and May 1642 became the subject of a great propaganda campaign in England. Certainly, massacres took place but were not planned or ordered by the senior Irish commanders. They were manifestations of the hatred felt by dispossessed Irish who had been driven from their homes by the newly arrived colonists.

Some local Irish commanders, such as Tuathail McCann and Art Óg McGinnis, were responsible for massacres in Portadown and Lurgan. However, an examination of the depositions of the survivors taken before commissions in 1641–1642 and again in 1653 shows that the lowest realistic estimate of colonists killed in Ulster was 527 and the highest estimate was 1,259. Robert Maxwell, rector of Tynan, County Armagh, told the credulous propaganda pamphleteers that 154,000 settlers had been massacred. That would have constituted one-tenth of the population of the entire island, and there was not that amount of settlers in all Ireland, let alone the province of Ulster. Neither did Maxwell count the massacres of the native Irish that happened in Ballydavy, near Hollywood, Templepatick, and Islandmagee, County Antrim, which also rose to many hundreds. The colonist propaganda figure is still believed in some quarters today and is often quoted without question by English historians. It was to be the justification for Cromwell's genocidal campaign and settlement.

Even though there were not as many incidents as claimed, the killings unleashed on the colonists were violent and terrible. William Clarke was the only survivor of the Portadown massacre to make a statement both to the 1642 and 1653 commissions.

He was imprisoned for the space of nine days with at the least 100 men, women and children during which time many of them were sore tortured by strangling and half hanging . . . after the time of imprisonment he with an 100 men women or children or thereabouts were . . . driven like hogs about six miles to a river called the Band [Bann] . . . and there [the Irish] forced them to go upon the Bridge naked and with their pikes and swords and other weapons thrust them down headlong into the said river and immediately they perished and those of them that assayed to swim to the shores the rebels stood to shoot at.

William Clarke, January 7, 1641–1642, deposition
Trinity College, manuscript 836

He with such other English as they [the Irish] could find to the number of three score persons which belonged to the said Parish of Loughall and put them all into the Church there and did set a guard over them and from there took them to Porte of Douane [Portadown] . . . and that such English as they met then [they] did take them alongst with the rest which were in all their coming to Porte of Douane about a hundred persons—where were all drowned at that time . . . [Clark] purchased his life then by giving unto them fifteen pounds.

William Clark, February 28, 1652–1653, deposition
Trinity College, manuscript 836

Tuathail (Toole) McRory McCann had been appointed local commander in Portadown by Phelim Ó Néill three days before the massacre. He was captured, and in a deposition of May 5, 1653, said he had not authorized it or seen the killing but had heard of it. He was executed shortly afterward. Phelim Ó Néill was captured in County Tyrone and brought to Dublin to be tried for high treason. He was sentenced to be hanged, drawn, and quartered on March 10, 1653. By this time, more than one hundred prominent Irish leaders had been executed in Dublin, including Theobald Bourke, Viscount Mayo, who was charged with the Shule massacre in which sixty colonists were said to have been massacred on the border of County Galway. Lord Mayo was executed by firing squad on March 29, 1654.

However, in 1643, Lord Ormonde, the king's lord deputy in Ireland, had opened negotiations for peace with the Irish Parliament at Kilkenny. The English parliamentary forces were beginning to have the upper hand over the Royalists in England. Munro, the only effective general opposing the Irish, now expressed allegiance to Parliament. The English Royalists were desperate for allies.

An Italian Welcomed in Kerry (1645)

Monsignor Dionisio Massari (born 1597) was dean of Fermo, Italy, and accompanied the papal nuncio Giovanni Rinuccini. They landed near Kenmare, County Kerry, in October 1645. Massari returned to Italy in November 1646, having written a number of letters reporting his experiences. He became secretary of propaganda to the Holy See.

I an unable to convey an adequate idea of the beauty and wonderful variety of those spots lying amidst the stern mountains of Munster. I particularly enjoyed the sight of several rivulets, one of which sprung out from the summit of a high hill and, falling down a ravine into a deep abyss, at once became a torrent. I noticed woods, springs, beauty spots, and the finest and safest harbours I have ever seen in all my travels. Happening to go ashore one day to enjoy the charm of a valley lying between two noble mountains, I chanced upon a harbour so capacious and secure as to be able to afford shelter and protection to a large fleet against the most violent hurricanes.

As I stood lost in admiration of the marvellous beauty that nature had wrought in this place, I suddenly found myself surrounded by more than four hundred persons, and imagining they were heretics [Protestants] I thought for a moment I was a lost man; but I soon found they were all fine Catholics, men, women and children, who had gathered in from the surrounding districts. They formed a circle round me, and detained me till each one had kissed the crucifix I wore on my breast. They showed me many signs of kindness and affection, lifting their arms to heaven in token of welcome and of thanksgiving to God for our safe arrival. They then led me with gentle persuasion to a cabin in the depths of a wood where I was welcomed by a matron of grave and noble appearance and of most courteous bearing. I was at once put to sit on two feather pillows and I may confess that as I sat down I thought for a moment the ground had given way beneath me. I was then handed a generous noggin of fresh milk, and whether it was owing to the thirst or the excellency of the beverage I took a second drink of it with infinite relish. . . .

Fortunately there was one among them who knew Spanish, and he not only interpreted what they were saying in the Irish tongue, but also conveyed my answers to them to their evident satisfaction.

Even after many hours I had great difficulty in tearing myself away from them, and then all insisted on accompanying me to the waterside. On the way they let me see that they regarded it as a privilege to attend me, give me a hand over difficult places, or even touch the hem of my garments, Some would not part with me till they had waded some distance into the water, while there were others who in a small boat of their own came with me as far as the frigate.

Monsignor Dionisio Massari, "My Irish Campaign," Catholic Bulletin, vol. 7, 1917

The Kilkenny Parliament seemed oblivious to the idea that the Royalists could be defeated by Parliament and opened negotiations with the lord deputy, the earl of Ormonde, in 1643, demanding a full recognition of Catholicism and restoration of all Irish confiscated land. This was supported by Cardinal Rinuccini. Eoghan Ruadh Ó Néill, in June 1646, achieved a major defeat of the Parliamentarian Army of Monro at Benburb on the Blackwater.

There was some degree of optimism for the emergence of a vibrant Ireland. The language had seen new modifications from the Middle Irish period into what is now called early Modern Irish. Writers were beginning to write Irish as it was spoken instead of the literary language taught at the now vanishing bardic schools, with its conventions and archaic prose diction. A literary phenomenon called the Contention of the Bards had run from 1616 to 1624, with professional poets arguing the course of literary endeavor. It was the time when Irish-language books were being produced in Louvain, Brussels, and Antwerp, when the first printed Irish dictionary, Micheál Ó Cleirigh's Foclóir nó sanásan nua (1643), became available, and a new

THE INSURRECTION OF 1641   111

wave of Irish scholars were writing, such as Seathrún Céitinn, from Tipperary (c. 1570–1649), producing his famous Foras Feasa ar Éirinn *(c. 1629–1631) as a counterblast to the distortions of Irish history by English writers. There were now competing catechisms of Catholic and Protestant religions, and the New Testament in Irish was available, while Bishop Bedell had organized the translation of the Old Testament, a task completed about 1642. One foreign observer even noticed the continuation of the Irish medical traditions.*

Irish Doctors in 1648

The Irish nobility have in every family a domestic physician, who has a tract of free land for his remuneration, and who is appointed, not on account of the amount of learning he brings away in his head from colleges, but because he can cure disorders. These doctors obtain their medical knowledge chiefly from books belonging to particular families left them by their ancestors, in which are laid down the symptoms of the several diseases, with the remedies annexed; which remedies are vernacular— the productions of their own country.

J. B. Van Helmont, "Confessio Authoris," in Ortus Medicinae, Amsterdam, 1648

But now the Irish people were to face their greatest challenge. The Civil War in England had been won by the Parliamentary forces commanded by Oliver Cromwell. Charles I had met his death on a scaffold in Whitehall, London, on January 30, 1649. Now the English Parliament could turn its attention to Ireland.

10

The Cromwellian Conquest

O n August 15, 1649, Oliver Cromwell, lord lieutenant and commander
of the Army of the English Commonwealth in Ireland, stepped ashore
from the frigate John in the Liffey estuary. His mission was to reconquer the country.

Drogheda (September 1649)

At 8 A.M. on Monday, September 10, 1649, a note was delivered to Sir Arthur Aston,
the governor of Drogheda.

Sir, having brought the army belonging to the Parliament of England
before this place, to reduce it to obedience, to the end effusion of blood
may be prevented, I thought fit to summon you to deliver the same into
my hands to their use. If this be refused, you will have no cause to blame
me. I expect your answer and rest your servant. O. Cromwell.

Carte Manuscript Collection, Bodleian Library

Although our men that stormed the breaches were forced to recoil, as
before is expressed, yet being encouraged to recover their loss, they made a
second attempt, wherein God was pleased so to animate them that they got
round of the enemy, and by the goodness of God, forced him to quit his

entrenchment's. And after a very hot dispute, the enemy having both horse and foot and we only foot within the wall, they gave ground, and our men became masters both of their retrenchments and the church; which indeed, although they made our entrance the more difficult, yet they proved of excellent use to us so that the enemy could not annoy us with their horse, but thereby we had advantage to make good the ground, that so we might let in our own horse, which accordingly was done, though with much difficulty. The enemy retreated, divers of them, into the Millmount; a place very strong and of difficult access, being exceedingly high, having a good graft and strongly palisade The Governor, Sir Arthur Aston, and divers considerable officers being there, our men, getting up to them were ordered by me to put them all to the sword. And indeed being the heat of the action, I forbade them to spare any that were in arms in the town, and, I think that night they put to the sword about two thousand men.

Cromwell to Sir William Lenthall, Speaker of the House of Commons, London,
September 17, 1949, in Writings and Speeches of Oliver Cromwell,
W. C. Abbott ed., 4 vols., Cambridge, Mass., 1937–1947

The mount [Millmount] was very strong of itself and manned with 250 of their principal men, Sir Arthur Aston being in it, who was governor of the town; which when they saw their men retreat, were so downcast and disheartened, that they thought it vain to make any further resistance, which if they had, they could have killed some hundreds of our men before they could have taken it. Lieutenant Colonel Axtell of Colonel Hewson's regiment with some twelve of hi men went up to the top of the mount and demanded the governor the surrender of it, who was very stubborn, speaking very big words, but at length was persuaded to go into the windmill on top of the mount and as many more as the chiefest of them as it would contained, where they were all disarmed and afterwards all slain.

Anonymous account printed in Perfect Diurnall, October 8, 1949

[Cromwell's] officers and soldiers promising quarter to such as would lay down their arms and performing it as long as any place held out, which encouraged others to yield; but when they had once all in their power and feared that no hurt could be done to them, the word "No Quarter" went round and the [Cromwellian] soldiers were forced many of them against their wills to kill their prisoners.

Lord Ormonde to Lord Byron
Carte Manuscript Collection, vol. 3, p. 412, Bodleian Library

[The Cromwellians] put all they met to the sword, having positive orders from the Lieutenant General [Cromwell] to give no quarter to any soldier. Their works and fort were also stormed and taken and those that defended them put to the sword also, and amongst them Sir Arthur Aston, Governor of the place. A great dispute there was amongst the soldiers for his artificial leg, which was reported to be of gold, but it proved to be of wood, his girdle being found to be the better booty, wherein two hundred pieces of gold were found quilted.

General Edmund Ludlow, in *The Memoirs of Edmund Ludlow, Lt. General of Horse in the Army of the Commonwealth of England,* ed. C. H. Firth, 2 vols., Oxford, 1894 (see vol. 1, pp. 302–303)

[Aston] was believed to have hid away his gold for security in his wooden leg. This they seized upon as a prize, but finding nothing in it, they knocked out his brains with it and hacked his body to pieces.

Anthony Wood, Cromwellian soldier, *Athena Oxonienses,* 2 vols., Oxford, 1791–1796

The rest fled over the bridge where they were closely pursued and most of them slain. Some got in two towers on the wall and some into the steeple but, they refusing to come down, the steeple was fired and then fifty of them got out at the top of the church, but the enraged soldiers put them all to the sword, and thirty of them were burnt in the fire, some of them cursing and crying out "God Damn them" and cursed their souls as they were burning. Those in the towers, being about 200, did yield to the General's mercy, where most of them have their lives and be sent to Barbados. In this slaughter there was by my observation, at least, 3,000 dead bodies lay in the fort and the streets, whereof there could not be 150 of them of our army, for I lost more than any other regiment and there was not sixty killed outright of my men.

Colonel John Hewson, letter, in *Perfect Occurrences,* October 5, 1649

The next day, the other two towers were summon, in one of which was about six or seven score; but they refused to yield themselves and we knowing that hunger must compel them, set only good guards to secure them from running away until their stomachs were come down. From one of the said towers, notwithstanding their condition, they killed and wounded some of our men. When they submitted, their officers were knocked on the head and every tenth man of the soldiers killed, and the rest shipped for the Barbados. The soldiers in the other tower were all spared to their lives only and shipped likewise for the Barbados.

Cromwell to Lenthall, September 17, 1649
Writings and Speeches of Oliver Cromwell, ed. W. C. Abbott, 4 vols.,
Cambridge, Mass., 1937–1947

Five Catholic priests were slaughtered by Cromwell's men at Drogheda: Father Peter Taaffe, Father John Taaffe, Father Dominic Dillon, Father Robert Netterville, and Father Richard Overton ("Five Martyrs of Drogheda," recorded by Rev. Gerard Rice, in Ríocht na Midhe, Records of Meath Archaeological and Historical Society, vol. 9, no. 3, 1997).

I believe all their Friars were knocked on the head promiscuously but two: the one of which was Father Peter Taaffe [brother to Lord Taaffe] whom the soldiers took the next day and made an end of; the other was taken in the round tower under the repute of a lieutenant. And when he understood that the officers in that tower had no quarter, he confessed he was a friar; but that did not save him.

Cromwell to Lenthall, September 17, 1649
Writings and Speeches of Oliver Cromwell, ed. W. C. Abbott, 4 vols.,
Cambridge, Mass., 1937–1947

Cromwellian Period: Sack of Drogheda

When the city was captured by the English, the blood of the Catholics was mercilessly shed in the streets, in the dwelling houses, and in the open fields; to none was mercy shown; not to the women, not to the aged, nor to the young. . . . On the following day, when the soldiers were searching through the ruins of the city, they discovered one of our Fathers named Seán Taaffe, with his brother, a secular priest. Suspecting that they were religious, they [the English] examined them, and finding that they were priests and one of them, moreover, a Jesuit, they led them off in triumph, and accompanied by a tumultuous crowd, conducted them to the marketplace, and there, as if they were at length extinguishing the Catholic religious and our Society, they tied them both to stakes fixed in the ground and pierced their bodies with shots till they expired.

Anonymous Irish Jesuit Father writing to Irish College in Rome (1649),
reporting the fall of Drogheda to Oliver Cromwell
Archivium Hibernicum, 1917–1918

The Fall of Wexford (October 1649)

Cromwell brought his army to Wexford and demanded the surrender of the town on October 3, 1649. Lieutenant Colonel David Sinnot was commander of the garrison. Sinnott played a clever diplomatic game of delaying tactics, so Cromwell wrote on October 4: "Having summoned you to deliver the town of Wexford into my hands, I might well expect delivery thereto, and not a formal treaty." Yet Cromwell was patient until October 11.

As soon as Cromwell came, he sent them a trumpeter to offer conditions, which was denied with great resolution. On which he fell to his Batteries [artillery], and made great breaches in two several places in the wall, and then assaulted and [was] beaten off, and assaulted again with courage and fury, and entered the town, where again the fight was renewed, and continued until those within were hacked down, and some of them, endeavouring to escape, were lost without mercy.

Anonymous Cromwellian officer
The History of the Warr of Ireland from 1641–1653 by a British Officer in the Regiment of Sir John Clotworthy, ed. Edmund Hogan, Dublin, 1873

On the 11th of October we took in Wexford, where the hand of God wonderfully appeared. We were forced to storm Wexford, where the enemy was very strong every way. Our men after battery of the Castle, yielded by Captain Stafford, the Governor, entered upon their flight over the water, and 2,000 were killed and drowned. Colonel Roe's jaw [was] broken with a bullet who is since dead. We lost but five men every way. We have near 80 ships and 100 boats to fish in, of which here is a fine trade. God hath spoiled the spoiler; abundance of plunder and riches. It is a fine spot for some Godly congregation, where house and land wait for inhabitants and occupiers. I wish they would come.

We march to Duncannon, Colonel Tuttle and Colonel Collams Regiments of foot, and my Lords of House are gone thither. We hear Owen Roe O'Neale is upon his March this way. Yours, H. Peters

Hugh Peters, Chaplain
A letter from Ireland, read in the House of Commons, London, 1649

Hugh Peters was later to be executed as a regicide.

Eoghan Ruaidh Ó Néill (Owen Roe O'Neale, as given by Peters) was at Cloughoughter Castle, County Cavan, and indeed marching his army south to join

Ormonde. He died there on November 6, 1649. There is a theory that enemy agents poisoned him.

Lieutenant Col. Wm. Butler escaped out of Wexford by swimming over ye ferry and brought ye news that ye governor was not above two hours in yet town giving orders for ye ferrying over Colonel Mayarts regiment when he was forced by ye enemy who entered ye ports by ye Treachery of one Captain [James] Stafford who commanded ye castle to Endeavour his safety likewise by swimming, but being shot in ye head by some of the enemy he was unfortunately drowned.

David Sinnotts's death recounted in A Narrative After the Defeat of Rathmines,
London, 1649

Fall of Clonmel (May 1650)

Aodh Buidhe Ó Néill (Hugh O'Neill), nephew of Eoghan Ruaidh, had arrived to reinforce Clonmel, County Tipperary, with two thousand infantry. Mayor John White was in charge of civilian resistance. On Saturday, April 27, Cromwell arrived at the north side of the town and positioned his heavy cannon overlooking the town from that side. He now had fourteen thousand men to surround the town. Having called for its surrender, Cromwell's guns opened fire on May 9. Ó Néill proved a capable commander and raided Cromwell's camp, driving the Cromwellians from Clonmel several times.

Letter May 19, 1650

This day we entered Clonmel, which was quit by the enemy last night, after a tedious storm, which continued four hours. Our men kept close to the breach, which they had entered, all the time, save only one accidental retreat in the storm. We lost in this storm Colonel Cullum and some other officers with divers private soldiers, and others wounded.

The enemy had made many great preparations within by a transverse or crosswork; and to beat our men out of the town, and left some few with the inhabitants to make conditions. In the morning our forces pursued and killed all they could light upon.

Bulstrode Whitelocke, Memorials of English Affairs, 4 vols., Oxford, 1853

Yesterday we stormed Clonmel, to which work both officers and soldiers did as much and more than could be expected. We had with our guns made a breach in their works, where after a hot fight we gave back a while;

but presently charged up the same ground again. But the enemy had made themselves exceedingly strong, by double works and transverse, which were worse to enter than the breach; when we came up to it they had cross-works, and were strongly flanked from the houses from within their works, the enemy defended themselves against us that day, until towards evening our men all the whole keeping up close to their breach, and many on both sides were slain. At night the enemy drew out the other side, and marched away undiscovered to us, and the inhabitants of Clonmel sent out for a parley. Upon which articles were agreed on before we knew the enemy was gone. After the signing of the conditions we discovered the enemy to be gone, and very early this morning pursued them, and fell upon their rear of stragglers, and killed above 200 besides those we slew in the storm. And of our party we had slain, Colonel Cullum, Capt. Jordan, Capt. Humphrys and some others are wounded. We entered Clonmel this morning, and have kept our conditions with them; the place is considerable, and very advantageous to the reducing of these parts wholly to the Parliament of England.

Report in *Severall Proceedings*, May 23–June 6, 1649

Colonel Hugh O'Neale governor of the place, with all the garrison, had marched out at the beginning of the night towards Waterford, before the commissioners came out to treat. It somewhat troubled the commanders to be thus over reached [outwitted] but conditions being granted, they thought it their duty to keep them with the town.

General Edmund Ludlow, *The Memoirs of Edmund Ludlow, Lt. General of Horse in the Army of the Commonwealth of England*, ed. C. H. Firth, 2 vols., Oxford, 1894

Cromwellian cavalry killed Father James O'Reilly, a noted poet and theologian, and Father Mylor MacGrath was hanged. On May 26, Cromwell embarked on the frigate President Bradshaw *back to England, leaving Ireton to complete the conquest. Aodh Ó Néill and his men reached Waterford, then moved on to Limerick, but Ó Néill was taken captive in October 1651. He was sent to the Tower of London in January 1652. The Spanish ambassador Alonso de Cardeñas pointed out that Ó Néill had been born in Spanish territory and applied for his release on the grounds of his citizenship. Ó Néill ended his days in Spain sometime after 1660. Cromwell counted Clonmel as one of his worst military disasters and accepted that Ó Néill had outgeneraled him.*

Cromwellian Conquest (February 1652)

I marched with a party of horse and foot into the fastness of Wicklow, as well to make example of such as had not obeyed the proclamation, as to place a garrison there, to prevent the excursion of the enemy. . . . We scoured by different ways the passes and retreats of the Irish, but met not with many of them; our parties being so big that the Irish, who had sentinels placed on every hill, gave notice of our march to their friends, so that upon our approach, they still fled to their bogs and woods.

General Edmund Ludlow, *The Memoirs of Edmund Ludlow, Lt. General of Horse in the Army of the Commonwealth of England*, ed. C. H. Firth, 2 vols., Oxford, 1894

Irish Depopulation (1641–1652)

About 504,000 of the Irish perished and were wasted by the sword, famine, hardships and banishment between the 23rd October, 1641, and the same day in 1652.

William Petty, *The Political Anatomy of Ireland*, London, 1691

Petty had estimated that the population of Ireland in 1641 had been 1,448,000, of which a total of 616,000 had perished by 1652. Of these, 504,000 were natives and 112,000 were colonists and English soldiers. A further 40,000 Irish soldiers were allowed to go abroad into foreign service, and another 100,000 Irish men, women, and children were transported as labor for the colonies. This was a depopulation of nearly 50 percent.

Hell or Connaught

An act of January 23, 1653, stipulated the disarming of all the Irish. Then, on September 26, 1653, a further act set aside the province of Connaught (Connacht) and County Clare for "the habitation of the Irish nation." The border was the river Shannon, and the Irish men and their wives and children were to transplant themselves west of the Shannon by May 1, 1654. Heads of families were to go by January 20, 1654, while families were to follow by the final day.

The transplanting work moves on but slowly; not above six score from all provinces are yet removed into Connaught. The flood gates being shut from transporting [to Spain] and one vent stopped for sending away the soldiery, part of them Irish, they begin to break out into Torying [Irish guerrillas] and the waters begin to rise again upon us.

Mercurius Politicus, July 12, 1654

A further act was passed on June 22, 1654. If the Irish were not transported into Connaught by May 1, 1655, they could be executed or transported to the colonies.

Transport! Transplant! My ears are deafened by English.
Shoot him, kill him, strip him, tear him
A Tory *[toiridh]*, hack him, hang him, rebel,
A rogue, a thief, a priest, a papist.

Eamon Mac Donnchadh an Dúin, 1657, in Cecile O'Rahilly, Five Seventeenth Century Poets, Dublin Institute for Advance Study, Dublin, 1952

Tory (toiridh, the Irish word for a pursuer) was the name given to the Irish guerrillas. On April 19, 1655, as a means to stop the Irish guerrilla attacks, it was decreed that in the vicinity of any English person, or person "under protection," being killed, "four persons of the Irish nation" were to be seized and held for twenty-eight days. If the culprits were not found, the hostages would be transported to the colonies.

We have three beasts to destroy that lay heavy burdens on us. The first is the wolf, on whom we lay five pounds a head if a dog, and ten pounds if a bitch. The second beast is a priest, on whose head we lay ten pounds—if he be eminent, more. The third beast is a Tory [*toridhe* is the native name for Irish guerrilla] on whose head, if he be a public Tory, we lay twenty ponds and forty shillings on a private Tory. Your army cannot catch them. The Irish bring them in; brothers and cousins cut one another's throats.

Major Anthony Morgan, Member of Parliament for Wicklow,
Proceedings of House of Commons, June 10, 1657

Major Anthony Morgan (b. c. 1621) had fought for the Royalists but changed sides in 1645. He studied medicine at Oxford and received his doctorate in 1648. While his main occupation in Ireland was political and administrative, he had permission to receive all executed Irish prisoners for the purposes of dissection. His work was acknowledged in an entry in the Dictionary of National Biography.

Cromwellian Slave Taking

Concerning the young women, although we must use force in taking them up, yet it being so much for their own good and like to be of so great advantage to the public, it is not in the least doubted that you may have such a number of them as you shall think fit to make use upon this account.... As for the young Irish boys, we could well spare them and they might be of use to you; and who knows but it might be a means to make them Englishmen.

> Henry Cromwell, lord deputy, to Secretary Thurloe, September 11, 1655, on progress in
> rounding up Irish women and children to be sent as slave labor to Barbados
> *Calendar of State Papers, Ireland*, ed. J. P. Mahaffy, 1647–1660, HMSO, London, 1903

Young maidens of noble families were despoiled of their possessions and dragged almost naked and piercing heaven with their shrieks to a ship bound for the West Indies.

> Cardinal Giovanni Rinuccini, Papal Nuncio to the Irish Parliament
> of Kilkenny, writing on conditions in 1655
> *Commentarius Rinuccinianus de sedis apostolicae legatione ad foederatos Hiberniae
> Catholicos per annos 1645–1649*, compiled by Fr. Barnabus O'Ferrell
> and Dr. Daniel O'Connell, ed. from the manuscript by Fr. Joannes Kavanagh,
> 6 vols., Irish Manuscript Commission, 1932–1949

It was a usual practise with Colonel Strubber, the governor of Galway, and other commanders in the said county, to take people out of their beds at night and sell them for slaves to the Indies, and by computation sold out of the said country about a thousand souls.

> Anonymous, *A Collection of Some of the Massacres Committed on the Irish*, London, 1660

And soon these heretics [English] caused the poor Catholics to be sent in crowded ships to Barbados and the Islands of America, such that those who did not die in the open remained in perpetual servitude. I believe that some 60,000 were sent there....

Wound follows wound that nothing be wanting to fill the cup of sufferings. The few Catholic families that remain were lately deprived by Cromwell of all their immovable property, and are all compelled to abandon their native estates, and retire into the province of Connaught....

... the design, obviously, is to extirpate gradually the whole nation, since no plan can succeed in shaking the attachment to the Roman Catholic faith.

Some of our Protestant garrisons lately told the Catholics that nothing could stay these persecutions, save the abjuration of the People's authority and Mass, but vain was their labour, their labour now is vain.

Father Thomas Quinn S. J., report to the Vatican in 1656,
Archivium Hibernicum (Maynooth)

Irish Priests in Hiding

An act of May 6, 1653, ordered the expulsion of all Catholic priests, and other religious from Ireland on pain of transportation and death.

We live, for the most part, in the mountains and forests and often, too, in the midst of bogs to escape the cavalry of the heretics [English]. Catholics flock to us, who we refresh by the Word of God and consolation of the Sacraments; here in those wild mountain tracts, we preach to them constancy in faith, and the mysteries of the Cross of Our Lord: here we find true worshippers of God and champions of Christ. In spite of all the precautions used to exercise our evangelical ministry in secret, the Cromwellians often discover it; and then the wild beast was never hunted with more fury, nor tracked with more pertinacity, through mountain, woods and bogs, than the priest! At present it is a common saying among the misbelievers "I am going to hunt priests."

Father Thomas Quinn S. J., report to the Vatican in 1656,
Archivium Hibernicum (Maynooth)

I live a banished man within the bounds of my native soil; a spectator of others enriched by my birthright; an object of condoling to my relations and friend, and a condoler of their miseries.

Ruairi Ó Flaithearta (Roderick O'Flahety), *A Choreographical Description of West or h-Iarr Connaught*, London, 1684

Earl of Ormonde Arrives as Charles II's Lord Deputy in Ireland (1660)

Woe to him who cannot simper English
Since the Earl has come across to Ireland:
So long my life upon Conn's plain continues
I'd barter all my poetry for English

Dáibhídh Ó Bruadair (c. 1625–1698), *Nach ait an Nós*, in *Duanaire Dháibhidh Uí Bhruadair*, ed. and trans. John C. MacErlean, 3 vols., Irish Text Society, 1910, 1913, 1917

Confirmation of Cromwellian Confiscations (1661)

This caps all their tricks, this statute from overseas
That lays the switch on the people of Heber the Fair;
A crooked deal has robbed us of our land
And all our rights in Ireland are swept away

The Gaels are stripped in Ireland now at last
And now let the grave be dug of every man
Or let them get their pass and cross the waves
And promise to stay gone to their dying day

Although the English are stronger now than the Gaels.
And though their fortunes are better for some time here;
Relying on their titles, they will not yield a field,
On their backs God's anger will pour down in streams.

Séafra Ó Donncadha an Ghleanna (Geoffrey O'Donoghue of the Glens, 1620–1678), *Dánta Shéafraidh Uí Dhonnchadha an Ghleanna,* ed. Pádraig Ua Duinnín, Dublin, 1902

11

The Williamite Conquest

The Stuart restoration of Charles II had not helped the Irish nation. Most of the Cromwellian land distribution was simply confirmed, and in 1672 alone some eighty thousand Presbyterian Scottish colonists arrived in Ulster to take over confiscated lands. The accession of James II in 1685 provided momentary hope for those who wished to change the land settlements. In January 1687, Richard Talbot, the leader of the Old English Catholics in Ireland, was named lord deputy. Two years earlier, he had been made earl of Tyrconnell, accepting the title that had once been given to the now exiled O'Donnells. As James II became more estranged from support in England, he tried to build a base among the Old English in Ireland.

In 1688, England stood on the brink of civil war. The rebels against James II invited James's eldest daughter, Mary, to be queen if they rose up. Mary's husband, William Henry Nassau, prince of Orange, pointed out that if his wife were to be queen, then he must be king. He was not content to simply be a consort. On November 5, 1688, William landed at Torbay with an army of forty thousand men. He was supported by the League of Augsburg, an alliance of European rulers who were opposed to the increasing power of Louis XIV of France, who was James II's only ally. The league included Pope Innocent XI as temporal ruler of the papal states. William and Mary soon displaced James II in England. James fled to France, then to Ireland, where Tyrconnell was certain of victory.

James II called a parliament in Dublin in 1689. This enacted legislation abolishing all religious discrimination and passed Acts 13 and 15, which declared that all religions should be equal under the law and that priests and ministers should be sup-

ported by their own congregations; no tithes were to be levied upon any person for support of a church to which he did not belong. Such legislation was deemed essential by James II's secretary of state for Ireland, William Ellis (who died in exile in Rome, 1732). Ellis was Tyrconnell's secretary, a member of the Dublin 1689 Parliament, and in James's Privy Council.

On June 14, 1690, William landed in Belfast Lough with an army comprised of troops from the many countries that formed the League of Augsburg.

The Battle of the Boyne (July 1, 1690)

They [colonial troops] did very bravely at first but espying another great party, whom they took for the enemy, just ready to surround them, they began to fly and did actively put in disorder the Dutch horse and all others that stood in their way. The place was unfortunately full of holes and dung pits and the passages narrow; but, above all, the dust and smoke quite blinded them. His Majesty was here in the crowd of all, drawing his sword and animating them that fled to follow him. His danger was great among the enemy's guns, which killed thirty of the Inniskillingers on the spot. Nay, one of the Inniskillingers came with a pistol cocked to His Majesty, till he called out "what, are you angry with your friends?" The truth is, the clothes of friends and foes are so much alike that His Majesty had had goodness to excuse all that passed.

Sir Robert Southwell to Lord Nottingham, July 1, 1690, from Donore after the battle
Historical Manuscript Commission, *Finch Manuscripts*, vol. 2, pp. 326–329

Although the conflict at the Boyne was not a significant victory in military terms, for the Jacobite army was able to withdraw, regroup, and fight on for another year, James panicked and fled from Ireland back to St. Germain in France, earning him the title among the Irish of Seamus an Chaca (James the Shit).

The Fall of Athlone (1691)

Tuesday, June 30, 1691

Most of the day passed in silence. In the afternoon on a sudden the whole camp was alarmed, and we marched down to the bridge within a mile of Athlone where we understood the town was taken, the enemy [Williamites] having entered both at the bridge and ford without the least opposition made on our side. The Regiments of O'Gara, Cormack O'Neill and others that were in the [defence] works, quitting them at the first onset without firing a shot, so that there was no time for any relief to enter the place. Some of the enemy who ventured without the castle were driven back without any loss, whereupon they retired and secured themselves within, whilst our men who had quitted the town ran in great confusion over the bog. All our army stood at arms near the place but could do nothing, the castle being strong on the land side. In this pasture we continued till towards the night with manifest tokens of fear in most men's faces, as if utter ruin had been hanging over us upon the loss of the place, though the arm was untouched, and except the defence of the Shannon, no loss sustained. At night we returned to the camp, threw down our tents and made all ready to march.

John Stevens, *The Journal of John Stevens*, ed. Robert H. Murray, Oxford, 1912

Aughrim of the Slaughter (July 12, 1691)

The last major battle of the Williamite Conquest was fought at Aughrim, 30 miles east of Galway, on July 12, 1691. Charles Chalmont, Marquis St. Ruth, commanded the Jacobite army. The Williamites were commanded by Godard van Reede, Baron Ginkel. For the Irish nation, the battle was disastrous. Seven thousand men were killed, along with four hundred officers, most of them scions of the Irish and Anglo-Irish nobility. Colonel Charles O'Kelly observed that the Irish had "lost the flower of their army and nation." St. Ruth was also killed.

At the very top of the hill cavalry were mixed with infantry. The firing was so intense that the ridges seemed to be ablaze. As dusk fell the cavalry began to move away and take flight, abandoning the infantry who in turn threw down their arms, left their colours and ran. Terrible scenes followed as the English fell on the rear of the fugitives. Stricken with terror we saw them fleeing in all directions across the countryside into the mountains, woods, bogs and wildernesses. Like mad people, the women, children and wagoners filled every road weeping and wailing. Worse still was the sight after the battle of the many men and horses too badly wounded to get away, who when attempting to rise fell back unable to bear their own weight. Some mutilated and in great pain begged to be put out of their misery, and others coughed out blood and threats, their bloodied weapons frozen in their hands as if in readiness for some future battle. The blood from the dead so covered the ground that one could hardly take a step without slipping. This grisly scene of slaughter remained untouched and unchanged for several days, the horror of which cannot be imagined except by those who saw it.

When the trumpets sounded the recall, the English returned in triumph, stripping the tackle from the horses and clothes and arms from the men. They then stretched out their weary bodies on the battlefield under the open sky, as the tents had not yet arrived, so that for many the bloodied ground was their bed. Others busied themselves in placing corpses as seats in circles around the fires, the light from which lit up the countryside.

Andreas Claudianus, Danish eyewitness
Journal of the Galway Archaeological and Historical Society, vol. 26, 1954

> In Aughrim of the slaughter they rest;
> Their skeletons lying there, without coffins,
> Have caused the women of Ireland to beat their hands,
> The children to be neglected, and the fugitives to wail.

Séamas Dall MacCuarta (1647–1732), "Elegy for Sorley MacDonnell," in Amhráin
Shéamais Mhic Cuarta, ed. Lorcáin Ua Muireadhaigh, Dundalk, 1925

The Treaty of Limerick (October 3, 1691)

On September 23, 1691, the Irish and their French allies, holding out in Limerick, decided that further resistance was useless. Negotiations were opened, and on October 3, the Treaty of Limerick was signed. Prominent in the negotiations on the Irish side was Major General Patrick Sarsfield, first earl of Lucan.

During the treaty a saying of Sarsfield's deserves to be remembered for it is much talked of all Europe over. He asked some of the English officers if they had not come to a better opinion of the Irish by their behaviour during this war; and whereas they said it was much the same that it had always been; Sarsfield answered: "As low as we now are, change but kings with us and we will fight it over again with you."

Bishop Gilbert Burnet, History of His Own Time, London, 1723–1734

On Sunday, October 3, 1691, two treaties were signed at Limerick. A military one allowed twelve thousand Irish soldiers to leave Ireland and seek service abroad in the Irish Brigades of France, Spain, and Austria. Sarsfield, watching the remnants of the Irish army embarking for France, was heard to comment:

These men are leaving all that is most dear in life for a strange land in which they will have to endure much, to serve in an army that hardly knows our people; but they are true to Ireland and have still hopes for her cause; we will make another Ireland in the armies of the great King of France.

Quoted by Gerald O'Connor, Sarsfield's aide-de-camp
Memoir of Gerald O'Connor, ed. William O'Connor Morris, London, 1903

Sarsfield led his troops into the service of Louis XIV and fell during an engagement at Landen in Holland, part of the great battle of Neerwinden, which was a defeat for William of Orange. As he lay dying, he is reported to have said, "If only it was for Ireland." The civil treaty had agreed that the

Catholics of this kingdom, shall enjoy such privileges in the exercise of their religion, as are consistent with the laws of Ireland, or as they did enjoy in the reign of King Charles II, and their majesties, as soon as their affairs will permit them to summon parliament in this kingdom, will endeavour to procure the said Roman Catholics such further security in that particular as any preserves them from any distance upon the account of their said religion.

The civil articles of Limerick exactly printed from the letters patent, Dublin, 1692

12

The Penal Laws

I n 1692, the new lord lieutenant, Henry, Viscount Sidney, convened a parliament in Dublin. But already in 1691 the London Parliament had introduced an Oath of Supremacy incorporating recognition of the English monarch as head of the church. No Catholics could therefore take it in conscience and were thus excluded from sitting in parliament.

That if any persons that now is, or hereafter shall be, a peer of Ireland, or member of the house of peers, or member of the house of commons there, or that shall become a barrister at law, attorney, clerk or officer in chancery, or any other court, and all and every deputy or deputies in any office whatsoever, shall presume to offend, contrary to this act, that then every such peer and member, and such other person and persons so offending, shall be thenceforth disabled to hold or execute any office, or place of profit, trust, ecclesiastical. Civil or military, in any of their majesties realms of Ireland or England, or dominion of Wales, or town of Berwick-upon-Tweed, or in any of their majesty's islands or foreign plantations, to the said realm belonging; and shall be disabled from thenceforth, to sit or vote in either house of parliament of the said realm of Ireland, or make a proxy in the house of peers there, or to sue or use any action, bill plaint, or information in course of law, or to prosecute any suit in any court of equity, or to be guardian of any child, or executor or administrator of any person, or capable of any legacy or deed of gift, and shall forfeit, for every wilful offence against this act, the sum of five hundred pounds.

Statutes of Realm of England (10 vols., 1810–1822), vol. 6, pp. 254–277

No Catholics were allowed to have arms, not even a gun to hunt rabbits, on pain of fines, imprisonment, pillory, and public floggings. Catholics were to be left defenseless at the whim of land grabbers. Catholics were prohibited education. Only Anglican education was allowed. Even after William III confiscated some 1.5 million acres of Irish land for new colonists, Catholics still retained 14 percent of the land. By a series of acts between 1704 and 1709 preventing Catholics from inheriting, purchasing, or leasing land for long periods, debilitating existing landowners, this figure had decreased by 1778, so only 7 percent of the land was left in Catholic hands.

In 1695, an act stated that

No Papist shall be capable to have or keep in his possession, or in the possession of any other, to his use or at his disposition, any horse, gelding or more of the value of £5 or more.

Beginning May 1, 1698, all Catholic priests, including friars, monks, bishops, and archbishops, were ordered out of Ireland.

If any of them remain after that day, or return, the delinquents are to be transported, and if they return again to be guilty of high treason and to suffer accordingly.

That meant execution.

Catholics were not allowed to print and sell newspapers or books. An underground literary tradition continued, with some of Ireland's greatest Irish-language poets writing during this period. Irish cultural endeavor became part of an "Underground Ireland" as described in Daniel Corkery's The Hidden Ireland *(Dublin, 1924).*

Those Irish forced to seek political refuge abroad continued the tradition that began in the seventeenth century by publishing books and smuggling them into Ireland, particularly dictionaries such as Conchobhar Ó Beaglaoich's Irish dictionary published in Paris in 1732, with collaborator Aindrias Mac Cruitín, or John O'Brien's Focalóir Gaoidhilge-Sax Bhéarla, *printed in Paris in 1768. Some Irish exiles, such as Anthony Hamilton (d. 1720), once governor of Limerick, wrote in*

French, and two of his works are considered French classics. The Abbé James MacGeoghegan (1702–1764) wrote Histoire d'Irlande *(1758) in French, while Aindrias Ó Duinnshléibhe published religious works in Irish in 1742 for the use of the soldiers of the Irish Brigade of the French army.*

Anglican Protestants could now pay an Irish Catholic laborer or servant whatever wage they chose. If the laborer or servant refused to work for it, he or she could be fined 2 shillings and flogged in default of payment.

No Catholic could marry a Protestant. Indeed, in 1697, it was also enacted that any Anglican marrying a Catholic was immediately debarred from voting or sitting in Parliament. A Protestant heiress marrying a Catholic lost her inheritance.

Catholics were also prevented from holding government offices, from entering the legal and medical professions, and from holding commissions in the army, navy, custom and excise, and municipal services.

Over the next thirty years, these acts were revised, so any loopholes not covered in previous legislation were eliminated. In 1727, yet another act clarified that "no Catholic shall be entitled or admitted to vote at the election of any member to serve in Parliament or at the election of any magistrate for any city, or other town."

One insidious piece of legislation was that in 1702 it was stipulated that when a Catholic converted to the Established Church, he could take over the ownership of his father's property and throw him out, or, indeed, if any Protestant, convert or otherwise, found he had an interest in any estate or property owned by a Catholic, he could claim it and throw the owners off the property.

Similar Penal Laws were enacted against Dissenting Protestants (particularly Presbyterians). On March 4, 1704, the law expressed intent to deny rights to Presbyterians. Presbyterian ministers were liable to three months in jail for delivering a sermon and a fine of £100 for celebrating the Last Supper. Couples married by a Presbyterian minister could be dragged into an Anglican church and accused of fornication, and their marriage declared illegal. Presbyterians were also excluded from holding offices in law, army, navy, customs and excise, and municipal employment. In 1715, a further act made it an offense for Presbyterian ministers to teach children, and this was punishable by imprisonment. Intermarriage between Presbyterians and Anglicans was illegal. By 1704, nine-tenths of the Irish were effectually reduced to a slave population under complete control of the colonial masters. The broken Treaty of Limerick became a byword for perfidy.

A Colonist Returns (1692)

Elizabeth Freke (1641–1714), cousin of the famous Dr. Nicolas Culpepper, author of London Dispensatory, *married one of her cousins, Percy Freke, in 1672. She went as a settler to Ireland in 1676, where her husband had acquired an estate in Cork called Rathbarry. He was a professional soldier. She left Ireland in 1684 and stayed at her home in Norfolk until after the Williamite Conquest, returning in November 1692. Percy Freke became one of the largest estate owners in Cork from lands acquired from the Commissioners for Sales of Forfeited Estates. He became Member of Parliament for Clonakilty in the Williamite Colonial Parliament in Dublin in 1692.*

November 12, 1692: I came with my servants a horseback to Rathbarry, from whence I had been absent eight years, where, when I came, I found my house quite burnt down, only two little rooms and neither a bed, table or chair or stool fit for a Christian to sit on, dish or plate to eat out of, or meat or drink fit to suffice nature; and on the land . . . only two sheep and two lambs and three or four garron horses, worth about ten shillings a piece. And this was the fifth time I came to bare walls and a naked house since I married.

In this more deplorable condition I stayed till near Christmas when the Irish [colonial] parliament adjourned and Mr Freke came home. . . .

However, in this miserable place I stayed, almost frightened out of my wits for four years and a half, and sick all the time with colic and vapours, so that I hardly went down stairs (but as I were carried to the garden) all the time I were in Ireland . . . and though I have undergone more than mortal tongue can speak. I never knew what vapours were till this prospect gave me in Ireland, the misfortune of which I expected to carry with me to my grave.

"Elizabeth Freke Diary," ed. Mary Carbery
Journal of the Cork Historical and Archaeological Society, vol. 16, 1913

No less than six of Percy Freke's descendants took their seats in the Dublin Parliament and rose to high office, Castle Freke, in Cork, being the family center. They were awarded with a baronetcy in 1713 and later the title of Baron Carbery. Sir John Freke, as Member of Parliament for Baltimore, 1790–1800, voted against the Union in 1799 and 1800.

Irish Language Slowly Absorbs the New Colonists

We cannot so much wonder [at this adoption of native culture] . . . when we consider how many there are of the children of Oliver's [Cromwell] soldiers in Ireland who cannot speak one word of English.

Robert Molesworth, *A True Way to Render Ireland Happy and Secure,* Dublin, 1697

Bardic Schools in Penal Times (1722)

In spite of the privations during the seventeenth century, the bardic colleges were not entirely suppressed. Dr. Douglas Hyde comments: "I doubt if a single college survived into the eighteenth [century], to come under the cruel law which made it penal for a Catholic to teach a school. In the seventeenth century, however, several famous colleges of poetry are still found" (Literary History of Ireland, *1899*). *However, Tomás Ó Súilleabháin of County Tipperary, whose name is anglicized as Thomas O'Sullevan, wrote a preface to put into context the memoir of the fifth marquis of Clanricade (1604–1657) published in 1744. His "Dissertation" was written in 1722. He spoke about bardic colleges from his own experience, so it may be that some colleges did survive until his time.*

Concerning the poetical seminary or school, from which I was carried away to clear other things that fell in my way, it was open only to such as were descended of poets and reputed within their tribes. And so was it with all the schools of that kind in the nation, being equal to the number of families that followed the said calling. But some more or less frequented for the difference of professors, conveniency, with other reasons, and seldom any come but from remote parts to be at a distance from relations and other acquaintances that might interrupt his study. The qualifications first required were reading well, writing the mother-tongue [Irish] and a strong memory. It was likewise necessary the place should be in the solitary recess of a garden or within a sept or enclosure far out of reach of any noise, which an intercourse of people might otherwise occasion. The structure was a snug, low hit, and beds in it at convenience distances, each within a small apartment without much furniture of any kind, save only a table, some seats and a conveniency for clothes to hang upon. No windows to let in the day, nor any light at all used but that of candles and these brought in at a proper season only.

The students upon thorough examination being first divided into classes, wherein a regard was had to everyone's age, genius and the schooling had before, if any at all, or otherwise. The professors (one or more as there was occasion) gave a subject suitable to the capacity of each class, determining the number of rhymes and clearing what was to be chiefly observed therein as to syllables, quatrains, concord, correspondence, termination and union, each of which were restrained by peculiar rules. The said subject (either one or more as aforesaid) having been given over night, they worked it apart each by himself upon his own bed, the whole next day in the dark, till at a certain hour in the night, lights being brought in, they committed it to writing. Being afterwards dressed and come together into a large room, where the masters waited, each scholar gave in his performance, which being corrected or approved (according as it required) either the same or fresh subjects were given against the next day.

This part being over, the students went to their meal. Which was then served up; and so, after some time spent in conversation and other diversions, each retired to his rest, to be ready for the business of the next morning. Every Saturday and on the eve of Festival Days they broke up and dispersed themselves among the gentlemen and rich farmers of the country, by whom they were very well entertained and much made of, till they thought fit to take their leave, in order to re-assume their study. Nor was the people satisfied with affording this hospitality alone; they sent in by turns every week from far and near liquors and all manner of provision towards the subsistence of the Academy, so that the Chief Poet was at little or no charges, but, on the contrary, got very well by it, besides the presents made him by the students upon their first coming which was always at Michaelmas, and from thence till the 25th of March, during the cold season of the year only, did that close study last. At that the scholars broke up and repaired to his own country, with an attestation of his behaviour and capacity from the Chief Professor to those that had sent him.

The reason of laying the study aforesaid in the dark was doubtless to avoid distraction which light and the variety of object represented thereby commonly occasion. This being prevented, the faculties of the soul occupied themselves solely upon the subject in hand and the theme given; so that it was soon brought to some perfection according to the notions or capacities of the students. Yet the course was long and tedious, as we find, and it was six or seven years before a mastery or the last degree was conferred, which you'll the less admire upon considering the great difficulty of the art, the many kinds of their poems, the exactness and nicety to be observed in each, which was necessary to render their numbers soft, and the harmony agreeable and pleasing to the ear.

As every professor, or Chief Poet, depended on some prince or great lord that had endowed his tribe, he was under strict ties to him and family, as to record in good metre his marriages, births, deaths, acquisitions made in war and peace, exploits, and other remarkable things relating to the same. He was likewise bound to offer an elegy on the decease of the said lord, his consort, or any of their children, and a marriage song when there should be occasion. But as to any epic or heroic verse to be made for any other lord or stranger, it was required that at least a *paroemion* or metre therein, should be upon the Patron or the Name in general. . . .

The last part to be done, which was the Action and Pronunciation of the poems in the presence of the Maecenas or the principal person it related to, was performed with a great deal of ceremony in a consort of vocal and instrumental music. The poet himself said nothing, but directed and took care that everybody else did his part right. The bards having first had the composition from him, got it well by heart, and now pronounced it orderly, keeping even pace with a harp, touched upon that occasion; no other musical instrument being allowed for the said purpose than this alone, as being masculine, much sweeter and fuller than any other.

> Thomas O'Sullevan, "Dissertation" as the preface to *Memoirs of the Marquis of Clanricade*, Dublin, 1744

By 1776, a quarter-million Ulster Presbyterians, denied rights under William of Orange's Penal Laws, had fled in search of religious freedom to the New World. They were to play a prominent role in the American struggle for independence. They would be the leading force in bringing the creed of republicanism and the Rights of Man back into Ireland, also playing a prominent part in the United Irish movement. The Ulster Presbyterians would provide four governors for the thirteen breakaway colonies, nineteen American Revolutionary generals, as well as the chairman of the committee drawing up the constitution of the American republic. One person saw the impact of the effect of enacting the Penal Laws against Dissenting Protestants and Catholics. This was Hugh Boulter (1672–1742), who was not merely the Anglican archbishop of Armagh and Primate of All-Ireland but was the lord justice, a privy councillor, and chief adviser to the government in Ireland. He warned as early as 1728 that the continued inclusion of Dissenting Protestants in the same Penal Laws as Catholics was producing a negative political outcome.

The worst of this is that it stands to unite Protestant and Papist and whenever that happens, goodbye to the English interest in Ireland forever.

> Archbishop Hugh Boulter, Lord Justice, *State Papers (Domestic), Ireland,* 1733

The Famine of 1741

In 1741, half a million people died in Ireland from malnutrition and related diseases. As with the other so-called famines, there was enough food in the country to feed twice the population, but the colonial landowners, mostly absentee, exported the grain and livestock to markets in England.

The distresses of the sick and poor are endless. The havoc of mankind in the counties of Cork, Limerick and some adjacent places, hath been incredible. The nation, probably, will not recover this loss in a century. The other day I heard one from the county of Limerick say that whole villages were entirely dispeopled. About two months since I heard Sir Richard Cox say that five hundred were dead in the parish, though in a county, I believe, not very populous. It were to be wished people of condition were at their seats in the country during these calamitous times, which might provide relief and employment for the poor. Certainly, if these perish, the rich must suffer in the end.

Thomas Prior of Dublin, May 19, 1741, in John Mitchell,
The History of Ireland, 2 vols., Dublin, 1868

The Penal Period

Life has conquered; the wind has blown away
Alexander, Caesar and all their power and sway;
Tara and Troy have made no longer stay;
Perhaps the English too will have their day

Anonymous Irish eighteenth-century verse,
Translated by Frank O'Connor, *Book of Ireland,* London, 1959

Art Uí Laoghaire, a Victim of the Penal Laws (1773)

Art Uí Laoghaire of Rathleigh, Macroom, County Cork, born in 1745, who was denied an education and profession under the Penal Laws, went abroad to study and was commissioned to the Austrian service. He quickly rose to be a major in a Hungarian hussar regiment. He returned to Ireland to marry Eibhlín Dubh Ní Chonaill (c. 1748–1800), daughter of one of the O'Connells of Derryvane, County Kerry. Her mother was the daughter of The O'Donoghue of the Glens, one of the few Irish chiefs to remain with his people, living incognito. Art and Eibhlín had three children.

Art made a bad enemy in the former high sheriff of Cork, Abraham Morris. Art brought back from the Continent a horse that was reputed to be a gift from Empress Maria Theresa of Austria. The horse won several races at Macroom. Morris demanded that he sell it for £5, pointing out that under the law no Catholic could own a horse valued over £5 or, indeed, bear arms. Art refused, and on May 4, 1773, his wife found his body near their home at Carraig an Ime. It was obvious that Morris was the murderer, but he was never punished. Eibhlín wrote a poem, Tóramh-Cháindadh Air Uí Laeghaire (Lament of Art O'Leary), which became one of the classics of eighteenth-century Irish poetry. These are selected verses:

> My steadfast love, how well a hat looked on you
> With its band of drawn gold, and a silver hilted sword,
> On a slender, white headed horse, cantering.
>
> The English used to scrape the ground before you
> And not to show you any favour, but from sheer dread of you—
> Though it was to them that you lost your life.
>
> My steadfast love, when they'll came home to me—
> Darling little Conchobhar, and the baby, Fear Ó Laoghaire,
> They ask me straight away, where did I leave their daddy?
> I'll tell them in my anguish that I left him at Cill an Martar,
> They'll call out to their father, and he'll not be there to answer.

Caoine Airt Uí Laoghaire, ed. Seán Ó Cuív, Dublin, 1923

Founder of Methodism in Ireland (1778)

Monday 18 May 1778: There were two roads to Sligo, one of which was several miles shorter, but had some sloughs [hollow filled with mud] in it. However, having a good guide, we chose this. Two sloughs we got over well. On our approaching the third, seven or eight countrymen presently ran to help us. One of them carried me over on his shoulders; others got the horses through; and some carried the chaise. We then thought the difficulty was past; but in half an hour we came to another slough; being helped over it, I walked on leaving Mr Delap, John Carr, Joseph Bradford and Jesse Bugden, with the chaise, which was stuck fast in the slough. As none of them thought of unharnessing the horses, the traces were soon broke: at length they fastened ropes to the chaise, and to the strongest horse; and the horse pulling, and the men thrusting at once, they thrust it through the slough to firm land. In an hour or two after we all met at Ballincurragh.

While I was walking, a poor man overtook me, who appeared to be in distress: he said he owed his landlord twenty shillings rent, for which he had turned him and his family out of doors; and that he had been down with his relations to beg their help, but they would do nothing. Upon my giving him a guinea, he would needs kneel down I the road to pray for me; and then cried out, "Oh, I shall have a house! I shall have a house over my head!" So perhaps God answered that poor man's prayers, by the sticking fast of the chaise in the slough.

John Wesley, Journal, Chicago, 1951

Traces of the Descendants of the Kings of Ireland (1776)

At Clonells, near Castlrea, lives O'Connor [The O'Conor Don], the direct descendant of Roderick O'Connor [Ruaidri Uí Conchobhair], who was King of Connaught six or seven hundred years ago; there is a monument of him in Roscommon Church, with his sceptre, etc. . . . I was told as a certainty that the family were here long before the coming of the Milesians. Their possessions formerly so great, are reduced to three or four hundred pounds a year, the family having fared in the revolutions of so many ages much worse than the O'Niels and O'Briens. The common people pay him the greatest respect, and send him presents of cattle etc., upon various occasions. They consider him as the prince of a people involved in one common ruin. . . .

Another great family in Connaught is MacDermot, who calls himself Prince of Coolavin. He lives at Coolavin in Sligo, and though he has not above one hundred pounds a year, will not admit his children to sit down in his presence. This was certainly the case with his father, and some assured me even with the present Chief. Lord Kingsborough, Mr Ponsonby, Mr O'Hara, Mr Sandford, etc. came to see him and his address was curious: O'Hara, you are welcome! Sandford, I am glad to see your mother's son [his mother was an O'Brien]: as to the rest of ye, come in as ye can.

Arthur Young, A Tour in Ireland, ed. A. W. Hutton, 2 vols., London, 1892

The Anglo-Irish Landlords as Observed by an Englishman (1776)

A landlord in Ireland can scarcely invent an order, which a servant, labourer or cotter dare refuse to execute. Nothing satisfies him but an unlimited submission. Disrespect or anything tending towards sauciness he may punish with his cane or his horse-whip with the most perfect security; a poor man would have his bones broke if he offered to lift his hand in his own defence. Knocking down is spoken of in the country in a manner than makes an Englishman stare. . . . It must strike the most casual traveller to see whole strings of cars whipped into a ditch by a gentleman's footman to make way for his carriage; if they are overturned or broken in pieces, no matter, it is taken in patience.

Landlords of consequence have assured me, that many of their cotters would think themselves honoured by having their wives or daughters sent for to the bed of their master; a mark of slavery that proves the oppression under which such people must live.

Arthur Young, A Tour in Ireland, ed. A. W. Hutton, 2 vols., London, 1892

Hedge Schools (1776)

Many of the common people speak Latin fluently and I accidentally arrived at a little hut, in a very obscure part of this country, where I saw four lads reading Homer, their master having been a mendicant scholar at an English grammar school at Tralee.

Arthur Young, A Tour in Ireland, ed. A. W. Hutton, 2 vols., London, 1892

An Encounter with the "Wild Geese" (c. 1783–1787)

By the end of the eighteenth century, the middle classes of Dublin had been anglicized. Michael Kelly, born in Dublin in 1764, was an actor, tenor virtuoso, and composer. After appearing in Dublin, he trained in Italy, and by 1783 he had become principal tenor in Vienna.

I procured an audience of the Emperor of Germany at Schoenbrunn, and found him with a half dozen of general officers, among who were Generals O'Donnell and Kavanagh, my gallant countrymen. The latter [he was from Borris in the Queen's County] said something to me in Irish which I did not understand, consequently made him no answer. The Emperor turned quickly on me and said, "What! O'Kelly, don't you speak the language of your own country?" I replied, "Please, your Majesty, none but the lower orders of the Irish people speak Irish." The Emperor laughed loudly. The impropriety of the remark made before two Milesian Generals flashed into my mind in an instant and I could have bitten off my tongue. They luckily did not, or pretended not to hear.

Michael Kelly, Reminiscences, London, 1826

Michael Kelly displayed the general attitudes of the Irish middle classes after nearly two centuries of English policies to anglicize the country. He went on to become musical director at the Drury Lane Theatre and died in Margate in 1826. The O'Donnell mentioned by Kelly was Major-General Count Henry O'Donnell, born in Castlebar, County Mayo, in 1726, who had married Leopoldine, Princess Cantacuzne, of the imperial family of the Paleologi of Constantinople, and a close relative of Empress Maria Theresa. Their son, Count Joseph O'Donnell, born in 1756, became finance minister of Emperor Joseph II and president of the Upper House of the Austrian Parliament. The Kavanagh who had asked him the question in Irish, which only "the lower orders" spoke, was General Charles Kavanagh of the Austrian army and governor of Prague. O'Donnell was a descendant of the O'Donnell princes of Tyrconnell, while Kavanagh was of the line of the MacMurrough Kavanaghs who had been kings of Leinster. But such history had been more or less wiped from the minds of the general Irish population by this time. By 1738, Dr. Samuel Madden (1686–1763) was speaking of the Irish language as a dying one when he wrote Reflections and Resolutions Proper for the Gentlemen of Ireland as to the Conduct for Their Service of the Country.

13

The Insurrection
of 1798

*I*n October 1791, the Society of United Irishmen was founded in Belfast.
*Initially it drew its support from the Ulster Presbyterians and progressive
members of the Episcopalian Church who sought parliamentary reform. Many, however, like the young lawyer Theobald Wolf Tone, were inspired by the American War
of Independence, Thomas Paine's* The Rights of Man, *and the French Revolution of
1789. They began to urge for the establishment of an Irish republic.*

*Theobald Wolfe Tone (1763–1798) was born in Dublin and educated at Trinity
College, being called to both the English and the Irish bars. His writing, enthusiastic
activity, and organizational work soon made him into an acknowledged leader. The
United Irish movement was suppressed in May 1794 and moved from an open
organization to a secret, oath-bound movement pledged to revolutionary aims. Tone
was to write*

I soon formed my theory. . . . To subvert the tyranny of our execrable government, to break the connection with England, the never-failing source
of all our political evils, and to assert the independence of my country,
these were my objectives. To unite the whole people of Ireland, to abolish
the memory of past dissensions, and to substitute the common name of
Irishman, in place of the denominations of Protestant, Catholic and
Dissenter, these were my means.

The Best of Tone, ed. Proinsias Mac Aonghusa and Liam Reagain, Cork, 1972

The movement needed support from the new revolutionary government of France. In 1794, Tone opened talks with the French Directory through the intermediary William Jackson. In April 1795, Jackson was arrested and charged with treason. Tone's involvement became known, and in May 1795 he fled from Belfast to America with his family. The U.S. government gave Tone letters of introduction to the French minister to the Committee of Public Safety in Paris. He arrived in France in 1796 and impressed the minister for foreign affairs, Charles Delacroix, with his energy and ability. An invasion force of fifteen thousand troops gathered at the Breton port of Brest under the command of General Lazare Hoche. Admiral Bouvet commanded the fleet of forty-three ships. Tone received the commission as chef de brigade *and was appointed adjutant general of the force.*

Wolfe Tone's Abortive Mission to Bantry Bay (1796)

December 22nd. This morning, at eight, we have neared Bantry Bay considerably, but the fleet is terribly scattered. . . . I am so happy as to arrive there. We are gaining the Bay by slow degrees, with a head wind at east, where it has hung these five weeks. Tonight we hope, if nothing extraordinary happens, to cast anchor in the mouth of the Bay, and work up tomorrow morning; these delays are dreadful to my impatience. I am now so near the shore that I can see, distinctly, two old castles, yet I am utterly uncertain whether I shall ever set foot on it.

December 23rd. Last night it blew a heavy gale from the eastward with snow, so that the mountains are covered this morning. . . . We lie in this disorder, expecting a visit from the English every hour, without taking a single step for our defence, even to the common one of having a frigate in the harbour's mouth, to give us notice of their approach. . . . I am now so near the shore, that I can in a manner touch the sides of Bantry Bay with my right and left and yet God knows whether I shall ever tread again on Irish ground. There is one thing, which I am surprised at, which is the extreme *sang-froid* with which I view the coast. I expected I should have been violently affected, yet I look at it as if it were the coast of Japan; I do not, however, love my country the less, for not having romantic feelings with regard to her. Another thing, we are now three days in Bantry Bay; if we do not land immediately, the enemy will collect a superior force, and perhaps repay us our victory of Quiberon. In an enterprise like ours, everything depends upon the promptitude and audacity of our first movements, and we are here, I am sorry to say it, most pitifully languid. It is mortifying, but that is too poor a word; I could tear my flesh with rage and vexation, but that advances nothing, and so I hold my tongue in general, and devour my melancholy as I can. To come so near, and then to fail, if we are to fail! And everyone aboard seems now to have given up all hopes.

December 25th. These memorandums are a strange mixture. Sometimes I am in preposterously high spirits, and at other times I am as dejected, according to the posture of our affairs. Last night, I had the strongest expectations that today we should debark, but at two this morning I was awakened by the wind. I rose immediately, and, wrapping myself in my greatcoat, walked for an hour in the gallery, devoured by the most gloomy reflections. The wind continues right ahead, so that it is absolutely impossible to work up to the landing-place, and God knows when it will change. The same wind is exactly favourable to bring the English upon us, and these cruel delays give the enemy time to assemble his entire force in this neighbourhood, and perhaps (it is, unfortunately, more than perhaps) by his superiority in numbers, in cavalry, in artillery, in money in provisions—in short, in everything we want—to crush us, supposing we are even able to effectuate a landing at last, at the same time that the fleet will be caught as in a trap. Had we been able to land the first day and march directly to Cork, we should have infallibly carried it by a *coup de main,* and then we should have a footing in the country; but as it is—if we are taken, my fate will not be a mild one; the best I can expect is to be shot as an *émigré rentré* unless I have the good fortune to be killed in the action; for most assuredly if the enemy will have us he must fight for us. Perhaps I may be reserved for a trial, for the sake of striking terror into others, in which case I shall be hanged as a traitor, and embowelled & etc. As to the embowelling, *"je m'en fiche"*; if they hang me, they are welcome to embowel if they please. . . . I see nothing before me, unless a miracle be wrought in our favour, but the ruin of the expedition, the slavery of my country, and my own destruction. Well, if I am to fall, at least I will sell my life as dear as individual resistance can make it. So now I have made up my mind. I have a merry Christmas of it today.

December 26th. Last night, at half after six o'clock, in a heavy gale of wind still from the east, we were surprised by the Admiral's frigate running under our quarter and hailing the *Indomptable* with orders to cut our cable and put to sea instantly; the frigate then pursued her course, leaving us all in the utmost astonishment. Our first idea was that it might be an

English frigate, lurking in the bottom of the bay, which took advantage of the storm and darkness of the night to make her escape, and wished to separate our squadron by this stratagem; for it seems utterly incredible that an Admiral should cut and run in this manner, without any previous signal of any kind to warn the fleet, and that the first notice we should have of his intention should be his failing us in this extraordinary manner with such unexpected and peremptory orders. After a short consultation with his officers (considering the storm, the darkness of the night, that we have two anchors out and only one spare one in the hold), Captain Bedout resolved to wait at all events till tomorrow morning I order to ascertain whether it was really the Admiral who hailed us. The morning is now come, the gale continues, and the fog is so thick that we cannot see a ship's length ahead; so here we lie in the utmost uncertainty and anxiety. In all probability we are now left without Admiral or General; if so, Chérin will command the troops and Bedout the fleet, but at all events there is an end to the expedition. . . . I hope the Directory will not dismiss me from the service for this unhappy failure, in which, certainly, I haven nothing personally to reproach myself with; and, in that case, I shall be rich enough to live as a peasant. If God Almighty sends me my dearest love and darling babies in safety. I will buy or rent a little spot and have done with the world for ever. I shall neither be great nor famous, nor powerful, but I may be happy. God knows whether I shall ever reach France myself, and in that case what will become of my family? It is horrible to me to think of. Oh! My life and soul, my darling babies, shall I ever see you again? This infernal wind continues without intermission, and now that all I lost, I am as eager to get back to France as I was to come to Ireland.

December 27th. Yesterday several vessels, including the *Indomptable* dragged their anchors several times, and it was with difficulty they rode out the gale. At two o'clock the *Revolution,* a seventy-four, made signal that she could hold no longer, and in consequence of the Commodore's permission, who now command our little squadron, cut her only cable and put to sea. In the night the *Patriote* and *Pluton,* of seventy-four each were forced to put to sea, with the *Nicomede* flute, so that this morning we are reduced to several sail of the line and one frigate. An attempt here is now desperate but I still think if we were debarked at the mouth of the Shannon we might yet recover all. At ten o'clock the Commodore made signal to get under way, which was delayed by one of the ships, which required an hour to get ready. . . . The wind, at last, has come round to the southward. And the signal is now flying to get under way. At half after four there being every appearance of a stormy night, three vessels cut their cables and put to sea. The *Indomptable,* having with great difficulty weighed one anchor, we were forced at length to cut the cable of the other and make the best of our way out of the bay, being followed by the whole of our little squadron, now reduced to ten sail, of which seven are of the line, one frigate, and two corvettes, or luggers.

December 28th. Last night it blew a perfect hurricane. At one this morning a dreadful sea took the ship in the quarter, stove in the quarter galley, and one of the deadlights in the great cabin, which was instantly filled with water to the depth of three feet. The cots of the officers were almost all torn down, and themselves and their trunks floated about the cabin. For my part, I had just fallen asleep when wakened by the shock, of which I at first did not comprehend the meaning, but hearing the water distinctly rolling in the cabin beneath me and two or three officers mounting in their shirts as wet as if they had risen from the bottom of the sea, I concluded instantly that the ship had struck and was filling with water, and that she would sink directly. As the movements of the mind are as quick as lightning in such perilous moments, it is impossible to describe the infinity of ideas, which shot across my mind in an instant. As I knew all notions of saving my life was in vain in such a stormy sea, I took my part instantly and lay down in my hammock, expecting every instant to go to the bottom; but I was soon relieved by the appearance of one of the officers, Baudin, who explained to us the accident. I can safely say that I had perfect command of myself during the few terrible minutes which I passed in this situation and I was not, I believe, more afraid than any of those about me. I resigned myself to my fate, which I verily thought was inevitable, and I could have died like a man. Immediately after this blow the wind abated, and at daylight, having run nine knots an hour under one jib only during the hurricane, we found ourselves at the rendezvous, having parted company with three ships of the line and the frigate, which makes our sixth separation. The frigate *Coquille* joined us in the course of the day, which we spent standing off and on the shore, without being joined by any of our missing companions.

December 29th. At four this morning the Commodore made the signal to steer for France; so there is an end of our expedition for the present; perhaps for ever. I spent all yesterday in my hammock, partly through sea-sickness, and much more through vexation. At ten we made a prize for an unfortunate brig bound from Lisbon to Cork, laden with salt, which we sunk.

December 30th/31st. On our way to Best. It will be well supposed I am in no great humour to make memorandums. This is the last day of the year 1796, which has been a very remarkable one in my history.

> Theobald Wolfe Tone, *Diary,* in *Life of Theobold Wolfe Tone Written by Himself and Continued by His Son, with His Political Writings and Fragments of His Diary,* ed. William T. W. Tone, 2 vols., Washington, 1826

The Rising

The country is in a state of rebellion.

> John Jeffreys Pratt, second earl of Camden, viceroy, March 30, 1798, declaring martial law

Because of the near invasion of 1796, Lieutenant General Edward Lake (1744–1808) was appointed military commander in Ulster to root out the United Irish societies. Ulster was considered the main power base of the movement because of the support from the Presbyterians. On paper the movement counted 250,000 members. Lake issued a proclamation in May 1797 and began to move to disarm the United Irish and arrest its leaders. In April, he was appointed commander in chief of the army in Ireland. Because of his increasingly repressive measures, the surviving leadership was driven to a premature uprising. May 23, 1798, was fixed as the date for the insurrection. Ironically, it was the date on which the notorious "hanging judge," the earl of Clonmell, died.

John Scott, first earl of Clonmell (1739–1798), was known as Copperface Jack. He served as solicitor general, attorney general, and lord chief justice. He had an extremely unpleasant reputation as a "hanging judge." Clonmell is thought to have given the information that Lord Edward Fitzgerald (1763–1798) was a leading United Irishman. When Major Sirr and his men cornered Lord Edward in a house on Thomas Street, Dublin, on May 19, he was badly wounded, and he died in Newgate Prison on June 4.

February 13, 1798

The arrival of Lord Moira in this country to throw into confusion, as apprehended, by encouraging the malcontent Papists and Presbyterians. *NB* I think my best game is to play the invalid and be silent; the Government hates me, and are driving things to extremities; the country is disaffected and savage; the Parliament corrupt and despised. Be discreet and silent.

> Earl of Clonmell, *Diary,* in William J. Fitzpatrick, *Ireland before the Famine,* Dublin, 1867

Francis Rawdon, second earl of Moira (later to become the marquis of Hastings, 1754–1826), was Anglo-Irish and a leading advocate of the abolition of the Penal Laws. He was a prominent spokesman for Irish rights in the House of Lords in London and had secretly been supplied with information on the social and political problems by Wolfe Tone. Lord Moira was a distinguished soldier, and rumor had it that he was in league with the United Irish. This was not true. A week after Lord Clonmell had made his observation, Lord Moira returned to London.

Before my God and my country, I speak of what I myself have seen. I have seen in Ireland the most absurd as well as the most disgusting tyranny that any nation groaned under. I have seen troops set full of this prejudice, that every inhabitant of that kingdom is a rebel to the British Government. The most wanton insults, the most cowardly oppression upon men of all ranks and conditions, in a part of the country as free from disturbances as the City of London. Thirty houses are sometimes burned in a single night, but from prudential motives I wish to draw a veil over more aggravated facts.

Lord Moira, *Parliament Record, House of Lords,* London, Monday, February 19, 1798

Protestant Bigotry

Some army officers disliked the bigotry expressed by extreme Protestants and felt it ruined the case of trying to win over the Catholics in the south prior to the rising.

For a man to boast or be proud of his religion was absurd. It was a circumstance in which he had no merit; he was one or the other because his parents were so before him and it was determined for him before he had a choice. Any man might fairly pride himself upon being just and honest, but not on his religion.

Brigadier-General Sir John Moore, *Diary,* March 17, 1798, at Skibbereen
Diaries of Lt. Gen. Sir John Moore, vol. 1, London, 1899–1902, p. 279

A Dublin Lady's View of the Insurrection

Marianne Fortescue (1767–1849) was the daughter of John McClintock of Drumcar, Dunleer, County Louth, Member of Parliament for Enniskillen and Belturbet. She was married to Matthew Fortescue of Stephenstown, but Marianne wrote her diary at the family house on Merrion Street, Dublin, where they were staying when the 1798 uprising broke out. In July 1798, she was able to return to Stephenstown, County Louth.

25 May 1798

Still sad working going on with the United [Irishmen]—Martial Law was yesterday proclaim'd in this town—all yeomen out every night. Jack Fortescue return'd to town & had only got as far as Naas—the Mail [coach] was attacked—the horses very providentially took fright at the firing and ran off—the coach was upset & by that means they all escaped (I mean the passengers) with their lives—there was a shocking battle at Naas. Jack saw thirty-nine laying dead and six hung; we suppose a vast number more must have been kill'd—the army got five pikes from the defenders who dropp'd them in running off—The Mail Jack got safe with him into the Post Office at Naas—where we hope it remain'd safe—Fortescue is pretty well—the children very well—I feel unpleasant from the idea of the dreadful situation we all are in—God send us speedy deliverance.

27 May 1798

We are still going on in the same way—the Rebels are defeated in all the battles hitherto fought—there were three men hung yesterday on Queen's Bridge—God send there may be soon an end to it—the weather is uncommonly fine—I long most amazingly to get down to Stephenstown—The North we hear is quiet—on the door of every house in town there is a list of the inhabitants posed up & we are liable to have our houses searched at any time for fear of conceal'd arms—Fortescue & the children are this day very well.

Marianne Fortescue, *Diary*
Journal of the Louth Archaeological and Historical Society, vol. 24, part 2, 1998

Elizabeth Richards's View of the Insurrection of 1798 in Wexford

Elizabeth Richards (1778–1863) was the daughter of Thomas Richards of Rathaspeck, near Wexford, and Martha Redmond of Killowgowan. She was living with her mother and sister at Rathaspeck when on May 27 the United Irishmen seized control of the area. Her family were Loyalists. She was to survive the insurrection, and on April 15, 1802, she married Count Frederick Willen van Limburg-Stirum (1774–1858), a Dutchman, and made her home at Gravenhage.

Whitsuntide 27 May 1798—Clonard

At church, to my unspeakable astonishment, I heard that Bagnal Harvey, [Lord] Edward Fitzgerald and John Colclough of Bally Feague, had been taken up on suspicion of disaffection to the Government, and lodged in jail, that the rebels in great force had attacked Carlow, nearly destroyed Gullagh-street, but at length had been repulsed. After Divine Service, we walked to Fairfield, the news we had heard was the subject of conversation, it was treated lightly until a service of Mr Sutton's rode up in haste to the hall door and told us that his master and mistress had sent him out to let my mother know that the people at the other side of the water were up, that they judged the country to be very unsafe, and begged we would go to town immediately. Horror struck we ran home. My mother had the lower windows barred, and in breathless anxiety we awaited the return of our servants whom she had sent to town to take the oaths of allegiance.

An hour had elapsed when I saw my nurse running down the avenue. I asked her what was the news. She said: "Good news, the people had dispersed and the danger was over." My mother had the hall door opened and we ventured to come out. At that moment a strange man came from the shrubbery and we were running back to our fortress. My nurse knew him to be one of Mrs Hatton's workmen. I ran to ask him for his mistress. She was at Clonard, he said, and begged we would go to her immediately, she sent to my mother a note she had received from a lady in Wexford; by that we learned that the insurgent were in force and had put to death some men who would not join them. The danger seemed evident to my mother and she determined to wait no longer for the carriage, but to walk across the fields to Clonard with the man who had brought the note. I often turned round to look at Rathaspeck. I fear the sadness with which I gazed at it is prophetic.

In the evening flying reports reached us that a detachment of the North Cork Militia, consisting of 200 men, had been sent against the rebels and was cut to pieces with the exception of Col. Tooke who commanded it, and 5 privates. This was thought to be impossible, too soon we found it to be a dreadful certainty. From the back windows we see several houses in flames. "Good God, what a scene."

Monday 28 May 1798

The morning passes in listening to reports and looking through a spyglass. At about three o'clock George Reade rode out to demand Mr Hatton's fire arms, he confirmed the dreadful intelligence of a second defeat of the King's troops at Enniscorthy, of the burning of part of the town, of the murder of Mrs Burroughs, of d'Arcy Howlin etc.

Tuesday 29 May 1798

The Donegal Militia, commanded by Col. [Richard] Maxwell, is arrived at Wexford, also Col. Colville, captains Young and Soden of the 13th who have volunteered their services for our defence. My mother and sister are gone to Rathaspeck to secure our papers and anything of value that is portable. . . . Towards evening we heard the rebels were collecting on the Mountain of Forth.

Wednesday 30 May 1798

At four o'clock my mother called us—during the night the rebels had collected in great force at the Three Rocks. Through the telescope we plainly saw them in large bodies, marching and counter marching, and tossing their pikes as if in joy; numbers on horseback were also performing a kind of exercise. About six o'clock we saw part of the garrison march towards the rebels, they were met by them [on the high road that leads from Wexford to the mountain of Forth, to Jaghmon], a volley of musketry was fired, we saw an officer fall from his horse, we afterwards learned it was [Lt.] Col. [Jonas] Watson, and in the course of a few minutes the King's troops began a precipitate retreat.

Our distress aggravated by uncertainty of the fate of the army and what our own might be, so near to a conquering mob, at first approached despair. At length a stupid horror pervaded my senses. I feared without being able to think at the extent of our misery—all that was most dreadful.

In the course of this morning a man rode into the courtyard with a white handkerchief tied to his hat, a green bough in the front of him and a drawn sword in his hand: everyone crowded round him, the servants seemed joyful. He demanded, or rather commanded, that provisions should be sent to the camp. "We are starving Ma'am," said he to Mrs Hatton, "send us provisions or"—he struck his sword with violence on the head of a pump, near which he had stopped his horse and without waiting for an answer, rode off. His orders were instantly complied with, though not without objections from Mrs Hatton. "Government may confiscate my property for assisting rebels." "If you do not comply, we shall be murdered," was the reply of all.

An old man was dispatched to the Three Rocks with a car loaded with bacon, potatoes etc etc. For which Mrs Hatton received thanks from the rebel chiefs. Reports now reached us that the Yeomanry had abandoned their posts—gone on board vessels with their families, and the town was nearly deserted. About one o'clock, Mrs Clifford came to Clonard from Wexford, she looked distracted. "Ladies," she said, "I am sorry to be the messenger of bad news, the army has left Wexford, it is in possession of the rebels, every Protestant is to be murdered tonight; you cannot escape, all we have to do is prepare for death." I looked around me with horror. I felt there was no possibility of concealment or flight, the infernal pikes seemed already to glitter at our breasts.—I shrieked and for a moment was all mad. Crowds of the Enniscorthy victors now began to fill the house— some of them wearing the uniforms of the murdered Yeomanry, flushed with victory and glorying in the blood they had shed. They told that they or some of their friends had met the 13th Regt. on its way to Wexford, and that not a man but the Commander had escaped. Some of Mrs Hatton's servants repaired to their victorious confederates. As soon as they knew to a certainty that the army had retreated, the mask was thrown aside. Those men who the Sunday before had solemnly taken the oath of Allegiance [to the Crown] did not hesitate to join the rebels. About six o'clock a vast number of the insurgents on horseback and on foot marched passed by the gate of Clonard, and to our inexpressible satisfaction promised protection to Mrs Hatton. An evening of listless anxiety was followed by a night of apprehension. We could hear shouts—or rather yells of joy, from the town that struck terror to our hearts. I sat up late—death I imagined would have additional horrors, if unthought of, and notwithstanding the assurance of safety that had been given us, to that only did I look forward.

It was one or two companies of the Meath Militia that had been defeated by the rebels. They had two field pieces which were taken by the latter and contributed to the defeat of the Donegal Militia at the Three Rocks.

Thursday 31 May 1798

Mrs Hatton received a threatening letter from a man with whom she had had some money dealings, he required that she should give him up some lands or £700; a rebel guard which had been sent to protect her by Gen. Roche [Edward Roche of Garrylough, local United Irish leader] (a tenant of Mrs Hatton's) confined the bearer of the letter in the garden-house and sent information of the threats contained in it to the rebel camp at the Windmill Mills. The guard was reinforced. One servant, and old cotter, came from Rathaspeck to see us; they wept for thanks; the marks of attachment they showed us made me cry too. Some people who had flown from Wexford to Clonard told us a massacre of the Protestants was intended and would undoubtedly take place. A servant of Mrs Hatton's of the Protestant religious overheard some Papists says that they would first murder the Orangemen, and the Protestants too, although it should be five years afterwards; William Hatton, who is an original United Irishman, assured us there would not be a massacre, but if we were uneasy, he would endeavour to procure a boat to take us to Wales. It is said that Captain Boyd had been taken out and put to death at the Three Rocks. We spent a melancholy evening, although we know him but little, some of our tears were for his sufferings.

Edward Roche was a farmer and maltster, about forty years old, who had served as a sergeant in the Shelmalier Yeoman Cavalry and took a leading part in the engagements in Wexford. "This is not a war for religion but for liberty!" he declared. After the defeat of the United Irish, in August, he was taken prisoner. He and several of his fellow prisoners died suddenly in captivity. No explanation for the deaths was offered by the authorities. The United forces gave blanket immunity and protection to all Quakers in the area but had issued warrants for the arrest of four Wexford magistrates, James Boyd being noted for "cruelty and oppression" of the Irish population. Boyd was a captain in the Wexford Yeoman Cavalry, but rather than being put to death as rumor had it, he had escaped by sea. It was his brother, John, who had been killed on the Wexford quayside while attempting to escape.

Friday 1 June 1798

On foot, unattended, and bearing in our hands green boughs, the emblem of Unity, Mrs Hatton, my mother, my sister and I set out from Clonard, we met several parties of armed men on the road, they suffered us to pass unmolested. The great body of insurgents had been drawn off towards Ross, one or two corps were exercising in the Windmill fields. The town presented a melancholy spectacle, houses quitted. The streets strewn with broken glass, pieces of furniture and articles of ladies dress. Confusion, astonishment, ferocity was alternatively expressed in the faces of those we met, and some viewed us with exaltation, whilst other invoked "the saints and angels to guard and bless us." William Hatton met us and accompanied us into town, he desired us to hide our sorrow—every one succeeded but me.

Saturday 2 June 1798

This morning brought us some consolation, Lord Kingsborough (Colonel of the North Cork Militia) and two officers of his regiment have been taken prisoners by the crew of the armed boat that had been fitted for sea by order of Mr Keagh [Matthew Keogh] the rebel commander of the town; letters found with them which says that 10,000 men had marched from Dublin against the Wexford rebels—Oh, what joy for us.

Mr Keagh came into a lady's house, where we had gone to see some friends, he had Lord Kingsborough's sword; my mother addressed him as "Captain Keagh"—he scarcely noticed what she said, he laid his hand on the hilt of the sword, exclaiming: "I am now Colonel. This is Lord Kingsborough's sword." In a pompous conceited manner he then mentioned his intention of sending an express to Government offering to spare the lives of prisoners the people had taken, if those of their party which were in the hands of Government were protected. Miss Shunt begged he would enclose a few lines from her to her brother, he said he would—adding "make haste and do not write fiddle faddle. I shall be obliged to read what you write." Lord Kingsborough had been conducted to Mr Keagh's house, the mob wanted to see him, and to have him taken. Mr Keagh's authority availed to keep the people quiet, but he could not induce them to disperse. A boy of about 14 of the name of Lett, a relation of Beauchamp Bagnal Harvey, rode up the street, the mob collected round him, asking they should not get a pitch cap for Lord Kingsborough. (A favourite amusement of Lord K. and his Reg't was putting pitch caps on the "Croppies" as the rebels were then called.) "No, no, we will have none of those doings," he replied—and such was his influence, that it was urged no farther.

We returned to Clonard more tranquil now than we had left it, although fully convinced that we were prisoners; no application for our removal from Wexford would be listened to by the Committee. "For some time," said William Hatton, "you must content yourselves here."

George, Viscount Kingsborough, son and heir of Robert, second earl of Kingston, was captured at sea and landed at Wexford on June 2. He commanded the notorious North Cork Militia responsible for several atrocities against the civil population. He was known to use a whip among other methods of torture to extract confessions. Particularly, he was responsible for putting burning pitch on suspects' heads to execute them. This became known in Irish as caip báis *(death cap), and thus* kibosh *entered the English language; "to put the kibosh on" means to dispose of something finally. Kingsborough was protected from the enraged crowd, and when English troops started to land at Wexford, he was released on June 21. Keogh gave him back his sword and he took the surrender, writing a note: "The people here have treated their prisoners with great humanity."*

Wednesday 6 June 1798

Some women who came to Clonard today said that the Barracks and Market House of Ross were still in possession of the King's troops. I was in an ecstasy of joy, I exulted over William Hatton, I reasoned with him, he listened to my loyal arguments with good humour, but without conviction; he provoked me. I left the room and for revenge I pulled the odious green cockade out of my hat, and trampled on it; it was a satisfaction to me to insult the rebel colours.

Monday 11 June 1798

Today we drove to Clonard on a common cart attended by two of our servants armed with swords. Coming out of the avenue gate, we met three women who sneered at us and looked exultingly at our shabby equipage. I was vexed. . . . From Clonard we proceeded to Wexford. Oh, what a dismal scene. The shops all shut, pikemen guarding every avenue to the town. Distrust, fear, anxiety on the countenances of everyone we met. We call to Mrs Sutton, Mr Slay [a rebel chief] had given her a newspaper. Its contents inspired us with hopes, which we did not dare manifest in her presence. . . . Mrs Sutton told me she had heard that the burning of the band of Scullabogue had been ordered by one of the rebel chiefs. That such an action was permitted will be shame, eternal shame to the Irish name.

At Scullabogue, 25 miles west of New Ross, a number of local loyalists had been rounded up and lodged in an empty house and adjoining barn owned by a Captain King. There were one hundred all told, including twenty women and children. They were, contrary to later propaganda, Catholics as well as Protestants. After the first attack on New Ross, a panic-stricken messenger arrived telling the local commander that the king's troops were butchering rebel soldiers, and the loyalist prisoners were to be killed as reprisal. The local commander refused unless he received the order directly from his commander. The messenger left, then returned with a second order, which was also refused. A third order came, supposedly issued by a priest. The guards were no longer restrained by their commander but began the process, shooting four men at a time until thirty-five were shot on the lawn of Scullabogue. The rest of the prisoners in the barn were barricaded in and the barn set afire. A prisoner who had escaped the massacre, Richard Grundy, gave the details in an affidavit of June 23. In spite of later anti-Catholic propaganda, three of the identified assailants, John Ellard, Robert Mills, and John Turner, were Protestants.

Wednesday 13 June 1798

I drew the whole morning, the weather here is too warm to take exercise, it is the finest I have seen in Ireland. How little are our feelings in unison with this bright sunshine. . . . Bagnal Harvey has resigned his chief command to a priest of the name Roach. This is the age of wonders. The rosary is exchanged for the sword and Ministers of the Prince of Peace for the flames of Civil Disorder.

Beauchamp Bagnal Harvey of Bargy Castle (1762–1798) was a lawyer and United Irishman. Like many United Irish leaders, he was a Protestant. He was made commander in chief of the Wexford insurgents and enforced strict discipline on his troops, prescribing punishments for any who plundered, burned houses, or murdered. On June 7, he was appointed president of the Wexford town committee and gave command to Father Philip Roche of Pollpeasty, near Clonroche. Bagnal Harvey was arrested and hanged in Wexford with others. Roche, too, gained a reputation among his enemies for his merciful conduct. He negotiated terms but was hanged on Wexford Bridge.

Thursday 14th June 1798

The insurgence have failed in their attack on Borris. . . . After tea I walked with my mother. The evening was delicious, seated in the elm bower breathing air perfumed with woodbine and syringa. My heat was heavy, all my thoughts gloomy.

Saturday 16 June 1798

A party of ruffians came to search the house for arms. . . . My mother assured them she had not any, but they were welcome to search the house. . . . In a loft they found a blunderbuss covered with dust and without a lock. It served however as a pretext for reproaching my mother with a breach of faith. One Connick, who had found the blunderbuss, insisted on my sister's opening her writing-desk, he thought, he said, it might conceal pocket pistols. The impertinence of this man, and the tone of authority assumed by the whole party, overcame my mother's spirits, she wept bitter. I felt indignation, and a wish to be revenged.

Saturday 17 June 1798

After dinner, my sister and I walked to Fairfield, the Miss Jooles returned with us. There was a strange looking old man at the Lodge. I entered into conversation with him. He spoke of the rising in the North.

Wednesday 20 June 1798

The rebels have been driven from their camp at Lacken. MacDonald with a faltering voice told us so. Such good news, so unexpected, so unhoped for. It has been confirmed by the number of flying trembling wretches who vainly endeavour to conceal their terrors. With exhilarated spirits we walked to Fairfield, from thence through a telescope we plainly distinguished eleven English Ships of War. The entrance of Mr Neyler of Gurtinnanrogue with a sad countenance increased my satisfaction. I guessed he had heard what was good for us, bad news for him. . . . It was late when we left Fairfield, the evening was cold and blustery—at intervals we heard the roar of cannons. Some men we met told us there was an engagement at Fowke's Mill; my mother and I resolved not to go to bed until we knew the event . . . my sister and I sat down in the back parlour, the wind whistled through broken panes of glass, dark clouds flew across the sky. We were silent . . . listening to the sound of musketry, which could be heard now and then in the intervals of the storm. . . . About 11 o'clock we were so anxious to know what the result of the engagement had been that my mother begged the housemaid to go and inquire of the guard that was kept at the cross-road, if they had received any intelligence from Fowke's Mill. She soon returned and brought word that some men she had spoken to said they had left Fowke's Mill, the King's troops were giving way and by this time they supposed they were beaten. It seemed so odd . . . that we gave but little credit to this account.

Thursday 21 June 1798

At two o'clock in the morning, one of our servants and one of the guard . . . returned from Fowke's Mill. The girl who opened the door for them brought us word that the King's troops had been defeated. . . . Despondent and almost heartbroken I threw myself on a chair in my bedroom. I know not how long I remained there. I was stupefied with grief. . . .

After breakfast we walked to Mrs Joole's. There we heard that the rebels had been defeated at Fowke's Mills, this morning at Vinegar Hill and that they were flying in all directions. How happy we were now. About 5 o'clock we walked to the Avenue gate, the green boughs and pikes have nearly disappeared. Many sought refuge at our house; they said the King's troops were encamped at the Windmill Mills, that they plundered every house and shot every man they saw.

We again went to Fairfield, Mr Codd who had commanded the Rathaspeck Corps and a Mr O'Brien, nephew to Mr Corrin the Priest, were there. They wore their swords, cross-belts and green collars. The deep, the manly regret that Mr O'Brien seemed to feel for the overthrow of his party interested me for him. His countenance expressed despair, his arms were folded, his mind seemed abstracted from the surrounding objects; some one observed "we shall now have the blessing of peace restored." "Yes," he replied, with a smile of agony and indignation, "there will be peace, but we shall all be slaves."

O'Brien was sentenced to nine years' transportation to the penal colonies.

Friday 22 June 1798

More troops have marched into Wexford, a body of rebels that had been encamped at Kilinick, and afterwards at Benville, have retreated, they have not been pursued. Two of Lord Mountmorris's Cavalry shot at a man within a short distance of Rathaspeck. . . . All morning we listened to the shrieks and complainings of female rebels. They almost turned my joy to sorrow.

Elizabeth Richards, Elizabeth Richards Diary 1798–1825,
ed. M. de Jong-Ijsselstein, Hiversum, 1993

When Tone heard the news of the uprising in May 1798, he renewed his efforts to persuade the French to send forces to help. The plan was for three French invasion forces to sail for Ireland, the first being commanded by Jean Joseph Amable Humbert with 1,099 officers and men. His troops landed in Killala Bay, County Mayo, on August 23. Seven thousand additional troops were due to be dispatched from Brest and Dunkirk.

General Humbert's landing was effective without opposition and immediately he was joined by five thousand United Irish. He began his advance on Ballina, then to Castlebar, where he defeated an English force, capturing nine pieces of artillery. Colonel Joseph McDonnell was the local Irish commander, under Humbert, and

John Moore was appointed president of the Provisional Government of Connacht. Humbert then tried to link up with the United Irish units to the east. However, on September 8, at Ballinamuck, the new viceroy, Charles, Marquis Cornwallis, having replaced Lake as commander in chief, outmaneuvered Humbert and inflicted a bloody defeat on the French general, forcing him to surrender. The Irish were either cut down or executed immediately. The lives of the French survivors were generally spared. Matthew Tone and Bartholomew Teeling, who had acted as aides to Humbert, were taken to Dublin for execution.

Shortly afterward, James Napper Tandy (1740–1803) arrived at Rutland Island, off the Donegal coast, in the Anacréon, with 270 French troops and Irish émigrés, plus arms and supplies. But friends reported the catastrophe at Ballinamuck and he reluctantly ordered the return to France.

On September 16, Tone had sailed with General Jean Hardy and three thousand men, planning to reach Lough Swilly. Intercepted by a powerful English squadron, after a fierce engagement with the flagship Hoche aground, Hardy surrendered the French fleet on October 12. Tone was taken prisoner and transported to the Royal Barracks in Dublin. Although in French uniform, an officer and citizen of the French Republic, he was court-martialed on November 10. He told the court: "I have regarded the connection between Ireland and Great Britain as the curse of the Irish nation: I felt that while it lasted the country could never be free nor happy!" He was sentenced to be hanged.

Lord Chief Justice Arthur, Viscount Kilwarden (1739–1803), a staunch Unionist, recognized Tone's military trial was illegal. He issued a writ of habeas corpus for the military to hand over Tone to civil jurisdiction. Negotiations seemed under way to exchange Tone for a prominent English prisoner held by the French. Major William Sandys, in charge of the prison, refused to comply. The lord justice then gave orders for the writ to be served again by the sheriff of Dublin with authority to arrest the provost marshal, Major Sandys, and General Craig if the writ was refused. This was delivered on Sunday, November 11. When the sheriff of Dublin arrived at the jail, he was told that Tone had attempted to cut his own throat. Efforts to hand him over to a civilian doctor proved futile. It was reported that he died on Monday, November 19, from the wound. Many considered that it was murder and that the military feared that a civil court would allow Tone to be exchanged for an English prisoner in France. It certainly was the usual custom at the time. His suicide or murder is one of the most debated subjects of Irish history.

With Tone's death in November 1798, the uprising had been successfully quashed. According to the historian Richard Robert Madden, born in Dublin in 1798, the repression that followed cost the lives of seventy thousand Irish men, women, and children and the lives of twenty thousand soldiers and loyalists. Executions and imprisonments continued for some years.

14

Union, 1801; Insurrection, 1803; Catholic Emancipation, 1829

T he colonial Parliament in Dublin had become more and more inde-
pendent of the Parliament in London. That independence was
acknowledged by London in 1782 when the Parliament was under the leadership of
Henry Grattan (1746–1820), a reformer and supporter of abolition of the Penal
Laws. But the Dublin Parliament was still as alien to the ordinary Irish people as
London was. Only two hundred thousand out of the seven million who populated
Ireland could vote prior to the Act of Union. No Catholics were represented there,
and two-thirds of the seats available in the Dublin Parliament were held at the nom-
ination of patrons for whoever could pay them the most money. No Dissenting
Protestants were allowed to sit in the upper chamber of the Dublin Parliament.

The idea of a union of the Dublin and London Parliaments had first been suggested in 1759 as a way of controlling the troubled colony. The idea was considered
seriously again when the 1798 Insurrection was quelled. The first attempt to pass an
Act of Union was put to the Dublin Parliament in 1799 but was firmly rejected. The
colonial "bosses" wanted to maintain their power bases and thus the Orange Order
found itself firmly against the idea of any union with England.

The Method to Achieve the Union (1799–1800)

The viceroy, Lord Charles Cornwwallis (1738–1805), was ordered to secure a reversal of that decision. As 216 seats of the 300-seat Parliament were controlled by the

159

nomination of a handful of the large landowning Anglican Ascendancy, it was clear that only a few of these landowners, such as the duke of Leinster and the earl of Shannon, needed to be persuaded to accept the Union.

My occupation is now of the most unpleasant nature, bargaining and jobbing with the most corrupt people under Heaven. I despise and hate myself every hour for engaging in such dirty work, and am supported only by the reflection that without an Union the British Empire must be dissolved.

Lord Cornwallis, lord lieutenant of Ireland, in W. H. Lecky,
Leaders of Public Opinion in Ireland, London, 1912

Of the 300 members, therefore, 84 "rotten borough" members were paid off from government funds; 72 members held positions controlled by the English administration and were open to "pressure"; 28 others were given immediate peerages. By 1806, U.K. prime minister William Pitt had created a total of 77 new Irish peers as a partial price for the Union. The immediate bill for bribes was £1,250,000. On February 6, 1800, the motion for the Union was passed by 158 votes to 115. The Royal Assent was given on August 1, 1800, and the Union of the United Kingdom of Great Britain and Ireland came into effect on January 1, 1801.

The 1803 Insurrection

The ideals and organizational structure of the United Irish movement had not disappeared. Under a new leadership, another uprising was planned.

The Provisional Government to the People of Ireland:

You are now called upon to show to the world that you are competent to take your place among nations, that you have a right to claim their recognisance of you as an independent country, by the only satisfactory proof you can furnish of your capability of maintaining your independence, your wresting it from England with your own hands. . . . We, therefore solemnly declare, that our object is to establish a free and independent republic in Ireland; that the pursuit of this object we will relinquish only with our lives, that we will never, but at the express call of our country, abandon our post till the acknowledgement of its independence is obtained from England.

Declaration of the Irish Republic of 1803, in Robert Emmet's Papers
quoted in *Trial of Robert Emmet for High Treason,* Dublin, 1803

"Let No Man Write My Epitaph"

Robert Emmet (1778–1803) was the third son of an eminent Dublin physician, Dr. Robert Emmet. His brother, Thomas Addis Emmet (1764–1827), was one of the leaders of the United Irishmen, imprisoned in 1798 and released in 1803. Thomas eventually went to New York and built up a large law practice. Robert had been expelled from Trinity College, Dublin, for political subversion. Although a warrant was issued for his arrest, it was not carried out. In 1802, he met with Napoleon to discuss aid for an uprising. He returned to Dublin in October to prepare for an uprising on July 23, 1803. The orders were confusing and ineffective. Robert fled into the Dublin Mountains but returned to see his fiancée, Sarah Cullen, at Harold's Cross. Hoping to arrange passage to America, he was betrayed and arrested on August 25. On September 19, he was tried at the courthouse on Green Street. Asked why the sentence should not be carried out, he gave a famous speech. In spite of many interruptions by the chief justice, John Toler, first earl of Norbury (1745–1831), Emmet's speech was inspirational. Even in the 1960s, the South African apartheid regime put a recording of it on their banned list.

Let no man dare, when I am dead, to charge me with dishonour; let no man attaint my memory by believing that I could have engaged in any cause but that of my country's liberty and independence; or that I could have become the pliant minion of power in the oppression and misery of my country. The proclamation of the Provisional Government speaks for our views. . . .

My lords, you are impatient for the sacrifice. The blood which you seek is not congealed by the artificial terrors which surround your victim—it circulates warmly and unruffled through the channels which God created for noble purposes, but which you are now bent to destroy, for purposes so grievous that they cry to heaven. Be yet patient! I have but a few more words to say—I am going to my cold and silent grave—my lamp of life is nearly extinguished—my race is run—the grave opens to receive me, and I sink into its bosom. I have but one request to ask at my departure from this world: it is—the charity of its silence. Let no man write my epitaph; for as no man who knows my motives dare now vindicate them, let not prejudice or ignorance asperse them. Let them and me rest in obscurity and peace, and my tomb remain uninscribed, and my memory in oblivion, until other times and other men can do justice to my character. When my country takes her place among the nations of the earth then, and not till then, let my epitaph be written. I have done.

Trial of Robert Emmet for High Treason, Dublin, 1803
Also in Richard R. Madden, *The Life and Times of Robert Emmet,* 1847

At noon on September 20, 1803, Emmet was hanged in public on Thomas Street. His body was then cut down and his head severed.

The Arrest of Anne Devlin and Her Family after the 1803 Insurrection

Anne Devlin (c. 1778–1851) of Croneburg, Rathdrum, County Wicklow, came from a family involved in the 1798 uprising. Her cousin, Michael Dwyer, was an insurgent commander. Her father was held for two and a half years without trial, and, upon his release, settled his family in Rathfarnham, Dublin, where he set up a thriving dairy and horse-hire business. When Robert Emmet was planning his rising, Anne was employed in his house, acting, however, as a messenger between him and his conspirators. With the failure of the rising, all of Anne's family was arrested.

There was no possibility of escape. The house was surrounded by a large party of horse and foot soldiers. . . . We were scarcely allowed time to dress when we were hurried down to the lower part of the house. While we, the females, were dressing, some of the soldiers were pinioning my father and my brothers with the cord reins, which they had cut from our horses. My heart ached when I saw my poor father with his hands firmly tied behind his back.

I stood close behind him, and while the guards were putting the rest in marching order I put my hands under his coat unperceived and cut the cords that bound him, telling him not to draw his hands out of that position in their view. We were then ready for marching. My mother was 50 years of age, my father something more, my elder sister was 25. I was in my 24th year, and my next sister in her 22nd year.

My brother Art was 20, John 18 and James eight or nine. This child was so extremely bad in that terrible disease that his eyes were wholly closed for several days and for a considerable time afterward he could not see. His whole body was one ulcer. Even the soles of his feet were so affected that he could not bear anything to touch them. When my mother saw that he, too, was to be marched off, she said, with indignation, "What? Do you mean to take this child out in this condition? You would act more manly to shoot him."

"No," said my father, "it is not possible to take him, but if you do," he added, as he looked at Mr Walker, "the curse of his innocent blood will be on you."

My mother went and kissed James and said, "My poor child, you are early marked for the slaughter house."

"Come, come, woman," said one of the officers, "we can't be delaying. The whole of you must come."

The Life, Imprisonment, Suffering and Death of Anne Devlin, Dublin, 1851

Anne was released in 1806, having been tortured but refusing to betray her comrades. She was broken by imprisonment and eviction and spent the rest of her life in poverty. She dictated her story to Brother Luke Cullen on behalf of Dr. Richard Madden, who raised funds to erect a memorial on her grave in Glasnevin Cemetery in 1851.

The 1822 Famine

Money, it seems, is wanted in Ireland. Now people do not eat money. No, but the money will buy them something to eat. What? The food is there, then. Pray, observe this: and let the parties get out of the concern if they can. The food is there; but those who have it in their possession will not give it without the money. And we know that the food is there; for since this famine has been declared in Parliament, thousands of quarters of corn have been imported every week from Ireland to England.

William Cobbett, *Political Register*, July 1822

Daniel O'Connell—The Liberator?: Catholic Emancipation (1829)

The Penal Laws, now more removed from restricting the Dissenting Protestants, remained a bane to Irish Catholics. The Catholic Committee was formed in 1805 to press for emancipation, but it was harassed by government and forced to disband. It was reconstituted in 1812 as the Catholic Board, which in turn was dissolved in 1814 by government pressure. In 1823, it was reestablished as the Catholic Association of Ireland, with Daniel O'Connell and Richard Lalor Sheil as leaders. Suppressed again in 1825, it was immediately relaunched as the New Catholic Association.

Daniel O'Connell (1775–1847) was from Cahirciveen, County Kerry, from one of the few wealthy Catholic families. A lawyer (as the law preventing Catholics from becoming lawyers was repealed in 1792), he had studied in France and witnessed the French Revolution but deplored it. While claiming to be a pacifist, he had joined the Lawyers Corps of Artillery and was active in 1798 in helping to suppress the United

Irish uprising. A native Irish speaker, he believed that it was utilitarian that the Irish language be dropped in favor of English.

An entire cessation of Catholic meetings had taken place. There was a total stagnation of public feeling, and I do not exaggerate when I say that the Catholic question was nearly forgotten. No angry resolutions issued from public bodies; the monster abuses of the Church Establishment, the frightful evils of political monopoly, the hideous anomaly in the whole structure of our civil institutions, the unnatural ascendancy of a handful of men over an immense and powerful population—all these, and the other just and legitimate causes of public exasperation, were gradually dropping out of the national memory. The country was then in a state of comparative repose, but it was a degrading and unwholesome tranquility. We sat down like galley-slaves in a calm. A general stagnation diffused itself over the national feelings. The public pulse had stopped, the circulation of all generous sentiment had been arrested, and the country was palsied to the heart.

Richard Lalor Sheil, in *Select Committee on the State of Ireland*, London, 1825

When O'Connell was voted as Member of Parliament in a Clare by-election, in spite of the prohibition on a Catholic being elected as an MP, the government realized emancipation was inevitable, and despite the antagonism of George IV to the idea, the Emancipation Bill became law in April 1829, allowing O'Connell to take his seat in Westminster. The Catholic Association had dissolved itself on February 12 that year in anticipation.

Was this really emancipation? In fact, after the bill was passed, fewer Irish people could vote in elections than before. In 1828, two hundred thirty thousand could vote out of the Irish population of over seven million. But the effect of emancipation meant that the property qualification for a vote rose from forty shillings (£2) to 200 shillings (£10), excluding not only the vast majority of Catholics from voting but, indeed, many Irish people of any religion. Only fourteen thousand people now had the vote after "emancipation."

Dissenting Protestants Allowed to Join the Orange Order (1834)

The Orange Order had been formed in 1795 as an elite Anglican Ascendancy movement to maintain the colonial Ascendancy oligarchy. The Order found natural support in the English royal family, having two royal princes as imperial grand masters and grand masters: HRH Duke of York and HRH Duke of Cumberland. Initially it developed as a Masonic-style movement. It enters history as a High Tory conservative, sectarian, and counterrevolutionary force. The Orange Order was an implacable enemy to the union of 1801, since it stood for the power of the colonial Parliament run by the Ascendancy.

The Order began to lose support after the Union, and His Royal Highness Frederick Augustus, Duke of York, resigned as grand master in 1823. By 1825, the lodges had almost disappeared, and, with the Emancipation Act of 1829 and the Reform Bill of 1832, the Ascendancy decided to open up the dwindling membership to Dissenting Protestants. The Presbyterian leader, Reverend Henry Cooke (1788–1868), was invited to a rally at Hillsborough on Friday, October 30, 1834, which the marquis of Donegall, Lord Downshire, Lord Londonderry, Lord Hillsborough, Lord Roden, Lord Clanwilliam, Lord Castlereagh, Lord Dufferin and Ava, Lord Hill of Down, and countless other Ascendancy grandees attended.

While I appear before you as a Presbyterian, I wish it to be distinctly understood that I do not appear as a representative but merely as a sample of the Presbyterian Church. . . . I trust I see more in this meeting than a mere eliciting of public opinion, or a mere gathering of the clans. I trust I see in it the pledge of Protestant union and cooperation. Between the divided [Protestant] churches, I publish the banns of a sacred marriage of Christian forebearance where they differ, of Christian love where they agree, and of Christian cooperation in all matters where their common safety is concerned.

Henry Cooke, report of Hillsborough speech, *Belfast Newsletter,* November 1, 1834
Quoted in *Orangeism in Ireland and throughout the Empire,* R. M. Sibbett, London, 1937

Cooke forgot to add that his Christian love did not apply to Catholics. The marriage worked. Dissenting Protestants, mainly Presbyterians, now flocked into the Orange Order, swamping the membership. While the Orange lodges were suppressed following an inquiry ordered by U.K. prime minister Lord Melbourne after it was suggested that there was an Orange conspiracy to set up a regency under its grand master, His Royal Highness Ernest Augustus, duke of Cumberland, to prevent Victoria from coming to the throne, the Presbyterians of Ireland followed a new sectarian dimension.

Cobbett Visits Lord Midleton's Estate

There were now some six thousand absentee landlords living in London and Paris, with a few in Dublin, owning 8 million acres of Irish land. Lord Midleton was an absentee landlord, who, nevertheless, was considered one of the better landlords. He drew between £25,000 and £30,000 a year from the estate. Cobbett describes conditions of the accommodation for his workers.

They all consisted of mud-walls, with a covering of rafters and straw. None of them so good as the place where you keep your little horse. I took a particular account of the first that I went into. It was 21 feet long and 9 feet wide. The floor, the bare ground. No fireplace, no chimney, the fore (made of potato-haulm) [haulm are the stalks of the plant used for litter or thatching] made on one side against the wall, and the smoke going out of a hole in the roof. No table, no chair. . . . There was one window, 9 inches by 5, and the glass broken half out. . . . No bed, no mattress, some large flat stones, to keep the bodies from the damp ground; some dirty straw and a bundle of rags were all the bedding. The man's name was Owen Gumbleton. Five small children; the mother, about thirty, naturally handsome, but worn into half-ugliness by hunger and filth; she had no shoes or stockings, no shift, a mere rag over her body and down to her knees. . . . Gumbleton's hog was lying in the room. . . . There is a nasty dunghill (no privy) to each hovel. The dung that the hog makes in the hovel is carefully put into a heap by itself, as being the most precious. This dung and the pig are the main things to raise the rent and to get fuel with.

William Cobbett, *Weekly Political Register*, October 25, 1834

Strange Famine Death of Smith and His Family (1830)

Three persons were interred today who died of corrosive sublimate poisoning (I believe) which was, by mistake, in the soup which they drank. Many are ill for the same reason. It was in charity that Dean Stephenson gave it to them. . . . The poor smith escaped the year's distress, under which the poor of Ireland labour in food-scarce July. . . . It is well it happened that his wife and child departed along with him, that they did not stay behind him, sorrowful, heartbroken . . . gazing vacantly at his forge tools, with no hand to set them to work, to earn for them their daily bread. . . . His hand will no more set a curved shoe on the neighing stallion, on prancing mare, on unkempt gelding, or on kicking fierce colt. . . . The three coffins were side by side on a cart, under white sheets, and men, with bowed heads, drew the cart with ropes to their last resting place, where the smith was buried down on the exposed side, his loving wife by his side and their babe on her breast as was their wont in their marriage bed.

Amhlaoibh Ó Súileabháin (Humphrey O'Sullivan), translated from *Cinn-lae Amhlaoibh Uí Shúilleabháin (1780–1839)*, Irish Texts Society, 4 vols., 1936

15

Repeal, Starvation, and the Insurrection of 1848

Irish Ready to Be "West Briton"

On April 15, 1840, Daniel O'Connell founded the Repeal Association to campaign for the repeal of the union between Ireland and Great Britain and the establishment of a separate legislature in Dublin. Although he was initially supported by Young Ireland, a republican movement, and its newspaper, The Nation, *O'Connell's idea was for a Home Rule domestic parliament, still accepting the Crown of England and continuing its ties with Great Britain.*

The people of Ireland are ready to become a portion of the Empire, provided they be made so in reality and not in name alone; they are ready to become a kind of "West Briton" if made so in benefits and justice; but if not, we are Irishmen again.

> Daniel O'Connell, in William E. H. Lecky, *Leaders of Public Opinion in Ireland*,
> anonymously published, Dublin, 1861

O'Connell declared 1843 to be the Year of Repeal, convinced that in the face of huge support, the London government would accede to it. He began to hold mass meetings throughout the country and was elected lord mayor of Dublin in that year. At Tara, nearly seven hundred fifty thousand came to hear him. The London government became alarmed, and a meeting planned at Clontarf for October 8, 1843, was banned on October 7. O'Connell was arrested and charged with conspiracy.

Sentenced to a year of imprisonment and a fine of £2,000, he served only three months before the House of Lords set aside the verdict.

O'Connell Released from Jail

The unexpected termination of the inquiry into the legality of Mr O'Connell's imprisonment and his liberation have been the most prominent occurrences since our last. The result is different to what had ever been anticipated by the traverses, or their most confident friends, as well as by the Government. It is in direct opposition to the opinion of the Judges.

The law lords who voted for the reversal of the sentence were Lord Denman, Lord Cottenham, and Lord Campbell. Those who were against it were the Lord Chancellor and Lord Brougham. Lord Langdale was absent, but it is understood that if he had attended he would have voted with the majority.

The news of the reversal of the judgement on Mr O'Connell and his companions was received in Dublin about five o'clock on Thursday evening, the 5th inst. Immediately on the arrival of the steamer at Kingstown [Dun Laoghaire] the whole population was thrown into a state of indescribable excitement. "O'Connell is free," was uttered by thousands of voices as the people danced about in almost frantic joy. At Dublin the same scene was exhibited, but upon a more extensive scale. At night, tar barrels were lighted in many parts of the city, and had it not been for the interference of some of the leaders, a general illumination would have taken place.

Mr O'Connell is said to have received the intelligence of his release without betraying the least emotion of surprise. Great numbers of his friends waited upon him to offer him their congratulations.

On Friday evening, the order for the discharge of the prisoners arrived, and at seven o'clock, Mr O'Connell leaning upon two of his sons, left the prison on foot, and proceeded accompanied by an immense assembly, to his house in Merrion Square. The other prisoners subsequently left the Penitentiary, and were loudly cheered.

The liberation of O'Connell and his fellow prisoners has produced an excitement in all parts of Ireland far surpassing the enthusiasm of Tara and Mulagharnasa, or any other of the monster meetings. The long cherished impression that, notwithstanding his late imprisonment, Mr O'Connell was still invulnerable to the law, has derived greater impulse

from the reversal of its sentence than it had received from any other circumstances in his history.

The Repealers held their usual weekly meeting on Monday, in the
Conciliation Hall. The galleries were crowded with ladies by eight o'clock
in the morning; and long before the appointed hour, every available corner of the building was crowded to suffocation. The traverses, on their
respective entrances, were enthusiastically cheered. The Lord Mayor of
Dublin occupied the chair.

Mr O'Connell came forward and was received with the loudest applause.
He entered at great length into a statement of the course which he intends
to pursue with reference to the future, and expressed his readiness to try the
experiment of a Federal Parliament. In the meantime, however, he proposed
the formation of a Preservative Assembly of three hundred gentlemen, to
meet in Dublin and control the proceedings of the Repeal Association,
much in the same way the House of Lords is considered a check upon the
Commons. Each member of the Assembly must prove his title by handing
in 100L [£100], a qualification which Mr O'Connell considered would so far
insure the respectability of the Assembly, that they would be able to treat
with government and stipulate terms.

His next step for the attainment of Repeal is to be the impeachment of
the Irish Judges and Attorney General—the latter for the monstrous indict-
ment, and the former for their conduct during the trials. He also stated his
intention to make a tour of the English provinces for the purpose of stating his case and procuring the assistance of the English people in effecting
the impeachment. He formally entered his notice of motion respecting the
expediency of holding the Clontarf meeting and also with regard to the
impeachment of the legal personages connected with the state trials.

"Liberation of O'Connell," correspondent, *New York Herald*, October 3, 1844

Advice to Westminster on the Catholic Church

You can take the Catholic Church under your care. . . . Are not lectures at
Maynooth cheaper than State prosecutions? Are not professors less costly
than Crown solicitors? Is not a large standing army and a great constabulary force more expensive than the moral police with which by the priest-
hood of Ireland you can be thirstily and efficaciously supplied?

Richard Lalor Shiel, vice president of the Board of Trade, to the House of Commons,
1845, in *Speeches of Richard Lalor Shiel*, ed. Thomas McNevin, London, 1845

His health failing, O'Connell left Ireland in February 1847 to spend time in Rome. He died upon reaching Genoa on May 15, 1847.

Peasant's Conditions in 1848

Michael Doheny (b. County Tipperary, 1805; d. New York, 1863), a lawyer, was involved in the Young Ireland uprising of 1848 and fled to America upon the suppression of the uprising. On the run, he found shelter with peasants in the mountains near Glengarriff in County Cork.

The cabin was ten feet square, with no window and no chimney. The floor, except where the bed was propped in a corner was composed of a sloping mountain rock, somewhat polished by human feet and the constant tread of sheep, which were always shut up with the inmates at night. The fire, which could be said to burn and smoke, but not to light, consisted of a heath sods, dug fresh from the mountain. A splinter of bog-wood, lurid through the smoke, supplied us with light for our nightly meal. The tea was drawn in a broken pot, and drunk from wooden vessels, while the sheep chewed the cud in calm and happy indifference. They were about twelve in number, and occupied the whole space of the cabin between the bed and the fireplace.

Michael Doheny, The Felon's Track, New York, 1849

An Ghorta Mhór: The Great Hunger of 1845–1848

For the twenty-eighth time since 1728, an artificial famine was produced in Ireland in 1845. Famine had become a common feature of life for the poor Irish. In the early nineteenth century alone, in 1800, 1807, 1817, 1821–1822, 1830–1834, and 1836 there had been famines due to colonial mismanagement. The rural population was now deprived, by blight, of its staple food, potatoes. From the introduction of the potato into Ireland at the end of the sixteenth century, it had become the ideal crop for a population dispossessed from the lands and farms and (through the seventeenth century) constantly on the move to avoid the colonial soldiery. Growing underground, the potato was a food crop that could be hidden. It now provided the main diet for the peasantry, which constituted two-thirds of the population. In September 1845 a fungus—Phytophthora infestans—came to Europe from North America and potato crops were destroyed. Appeals for assistance, for the landlords to take into account the situation when demanding their rents from the peasantry, fell on deaf ears.

They may starve! Such in spirit, if not words, was the reply given yesterday by the English viceroy.

Freeman's Journal, November 4, 1845

They are suffering a real though artificial famine. Nature does her duty; the land is fruitful enough, nor can it be fairly said that man is wanting. The Irishman is disposed to work; in fact man and nature together do produce abundantly. The island is full and overflowing with human food. But something ever intervenes between the hungry mouth and the ample banquet.

The Times, London, June 26, 1845

A Doctor's View

[People] starve in the midst of plenty, as literally as if dungeon bars separated them from a granary. When distress has been at its height, and our poor have been dying of starvation in our streets, our corn has been going to a foreign market. It is, to our own poor, a forbidden fruit.

Dominic J. Corrigan, On Famine and Fever as Causes and Effect in Ireland, Dublin, 1846

Immense herds of cattle, sheep and hogs . . . floating off on every tide, out of every one of our thirteen seaports, bound for England; and the landlords were receiving their rents and going to England to spend them; and many hundreds of poor people had laid down and died on the roadside for want of food.

John Mitchell, Jail Journal, or Five Years in British Prisons, New York, 1854

Guarding Food en Route to England

The barges leave Clonmel once a week for this place, with the export supplies under convoy which, last Tuesday, consisted of 2 guns, 50 cavalry and 80 infantry escorting them on the banks of the Suir as far as Carrick.

Government official writing from Waterford, April 24, 1846, in Cecil Woodham Smith,
The Great Hunger, Hamilton, London, 1962

I entered some of the hovels . . . and the scenes, which presented themselves, were such as no tongue or pen can convey the slightest idea of. In the first six famished and ghastly skeletons, to all appearance dead, were huddled in a corner on some filthy straw, their sole covering what seemed a ragged horsecloth, their wretched legs hanging about, naked above the knees. I approached with horror, and found by a low moaning they were alive—they were in fever, four children, a woman, and what had once been a man . . . in a few minutes I was surrounded by at least 200 of such phantoms, such frightful spectres as no words can describe.

Nicholas Cummins J. P., writing on December 15, 1846
The Times, London, December 24, 1846

The actual starving people lived upon the carcasses of diseased cattle, upon dogs, and dead horses, but principally on the herbs of the field, nettle tops, wild mustard and watercress's, and even in some place dead bodies were found with grass in their mouths.

House of Commons Sessional Papers, vol. 29, part 5, 1856, p. 243

It is true, also, that Government did, to a certain small extent, speculate in Indian corn, and did send a good many cargoes of it to Ireland, and form depots of it at several points; but as to this, also, their mysterious intimations had led all the world to believe they would provide very large quantities, whereas, in fact, the quantity imported by them was inadequate to supply the loss of grain exported from any one county; and a Government ship sailing into any harbour with Indian corn, was sure to meet half a dozen sailing out with Irish wheat and cattle. The effect of this, therefore, was to blind people to the fact that England was exacting her tribute as usual, famine or no famine. The effect of both combined was to engender a dependent and pauper spirit, and to free England from all anxiety about "repeal." A landless, hungry pauper cannot afford to think of the honour of his country, and cares nothing about a national flag.

John Mitchell, The History of Ireland, New York, 1868

We have made it [Ireland] the most degraded and most miserable country in the world. . . . All the world is crying shame upon us; but we are equally callous to our ignominy and to the results of our misgovernments.

Lord John Russell, March 23, 1846
Parliamentary Debates (Hansard) House of Lords

Oscar Wilde's Mother Warns of the Consequence

Lady Jane Francesca Wilde, née Elgee (1821–1896), was born in Wexford. Witnessing the famine firsthand converted her to the republican nationalism of the Young

Ireland movement, and she contributed to The Nation *using the pen name Speranza. Her article, "Jacta Alea Est," caused the paper to be prosecuted for sedition. She married an eminent Dublin eye surgeon, William Wilde, who was knighted for his work. She continued to write after her husband died in 1876. Among her successful books was* Ancient Legends of Ireland *(1887). She had three children. The youngest was a daughter who died in childhood. William, the eldest, was a journalist. Her second son was the writer Oscar Fingal O'Flahertie Wills Wilde (1854–1900).*

> Weary men, what reap ye?—Golden corn for the stranger.
> What sow ye?—Human corpses that wait for the avenger.
> Fainting forms, hunger-stricken, what see you in the offing?
> Stately ships to bear our food away, amid the stranger's scoffing.
> There's a proud array of soldiers—what do they round your door?
> They guard our masters' granaries from the thin hands of the poor.
> Pale mothers, wherefore weeping? Would to God that we were dead—
> Our children swoon before us, and we cannot give them bread.

"The Famine Year" [1848] in *The Cabinet of Irish Literature,* ed. T. P. O'Connor, vol. 4, Dublin, n.d.

The Coffin Ships

Over a million Irish men, women, and children fled Ireland, mostly for the Americas, during the famine years. Instead of finding refuge, tens of thousands went to their deaths mainly from typhus or cholera. British North America (Canada) was one major destination. But on Grosse-Ile, in the St. Lawrence River, an island converted into a quarantine station, there is the mass grave of an estimated hundred thousand Irish refugees who did not make it to a new life. At Victoria Bridge, in Pointe Saint-Charles, Montréal, another mass grave of six thousand is marked by a memorial.

The *Syria:* The First Reported Coffin Ship

All the sick now in hospital are from one vessel, the "Syria" being the first and only emigrant vessel that has yet arrived. The vessel left Liverpool on the 24th March, having on board two hundred and forty-one passengers recently arrived from Ireland; many were in a weak state when they embarked, and all were wretched and poor—disease—fever and dysentery—broke out a few days after leaving poor, and has gone on increasing until now—nine died on the passage, and one on landing here, and eighty-four are now inmates of the hospital—and I fully expect that from twenty to twenty-four will have to be admitted.

George M. Douglas, medical superintendent, Quarantine State Grosse-Ile, May 17, 1847,
quoted in Pádraic Ó Laighin, "Grosse-Ile: The Holocaust Revisited," in *The Untold Story:*
The Irish in Canada, ed. Robert O'Driscoll and Lorna Reynolds, Toronto, 1988

Gearóid Mac Aodhagáin, anglicized as Gerald Keegan, was a former student at Maynooth, a hedge school. In the summer of 1847 he decided to emigrate with his uncle and cousins, so he hastily married his fiancee, Aileen, in April 1847 and set sail on April 17. Keegan kept a journal from February to July 1847. Aileen Keegan died first, then Gerald. His Journal *was rescued by his uncle and was published by Robert Sellar in* The Summer of Sorrow *(Huntingdon, Quebec, 1895).*

April 9, We were married Monday morning, and spent three happy days with Aileen's cousin in Limerick. Arrived here in Dublin today. The ship is advertised to sail tomorrow. Took our tickets for second cabin and drive tomorrow morning to where the ship is lying.

April 21, The first death took place last night when a boy of five years succumbed to dysentery. In the afternoon a wail suddenly arose from the hold—a fine young woman had died from the same cause. Both were dropped into the sea at sunset. There are fewer seasick today, but the number ill from dysentery grows.

April 24, We had a dreadful night, and I slept only by snatches. At midnight the tempest seemed to reach its height, when its roar drowned all other sounds. The ship swayed and rolled as if she would capsize, while ever and anon she shipped sea that flooded our little cabin, and threatened to tear the [deck] house, of which it forms part, from its fastenings and carry it overboard,

April 26, A beautiful morning, bright and milder than it has been. Every sail is drawing and the ship is bowling along at a fine rate. I got up early, being anxious about uncle's wife. Found her no better. Worse than that, learned there were five besides her ill the same way. There is not a shadow of doubt that typhus fever is on board. Since we left port, no attempt has been made to clear the steerage, which is filthy beyond description. When I speak to the men to join in and shovel up the worst of the dirt, they despondently ask me, "What's the use?" The despondency engendered of hunger and disease is upon them and they will not exert themselves. The steward is the only one of the ship's company who goes down the hatch-steps, and it would be better if he did not, for his errand is to sell the drink for which so many are parting with the sixpences they should keep for their landing in a strange country. The day being passably warm in the afternoon the children played on deck and I coaxed Paddy Doolan to get out his pipes and set them jigging.

April 29, Uncle's wife died this morning. It would not be correct to say the fever killed her, for it had not reached its crisis. She was weakly when she left home, and the sojourn on the quay, waiting to get on board ship, gave her a bad cold. Her system was so reduced, she could not withstand the onset of the disease.

April 30, The fever spreads and to the other horrors of the steerage is added cries of those in delirium. While coming from the galley this afternoon, with a pan of stirabout for some sick children, a man suddenly sprang upwards from the hatchway, rushed to the bulwark, his white hair streaming in the wind, and without a moment's hesitation, leaped into the seething waters. He disappeared beneath them at once. His daughter soon came hurrying up the ladder to look for him. She said he had escaped from his bunk during her momentary absence, that he was mad with fever. When I told her gently as I could that she would never see him again, she could not believe me, thinking he was hiding. Oh the piercing cry that came from her lips when she learned where he had gone; the rush to the vessel's side, and the eager look as she scanned the billows. Aileen led her away; dumb from the sudden stroke yet without a tear.

May 4, No death today.

May 6, There were three deaths today. If it please God, may this agony soon end.

May 9, Uncle's oldest son died of a fever soon after daylight . . . the body along with two more we dropped overboard when the sailors were at dinner. . . . I told Aileen today she must not even go near the hatchways.

May 10, This was a sad day, five having died.

May 11, A child died today, a sweet girl toddler that Aileen was fond of. Many of the sick are sinking tonight, not one of whom but might have lived with proper sustenance.

May 12, Four deaths and the number of sick greatly increased.

May 13, The evening being calm Aileen got a wrap and we sat watching the darkening waters and the shores that loomed momentarily more faint, until the lights from the house windows alone marked where they were. "What is that?" she suddenly exclaimed, and I saw a shapeless heap move past our ship on the outgoing tide. Presently there was another and another. Craning my head over the bulwark I watched. Another came, it caught in one cable, and before the swish of the current washed it clear, I caught a glimpse of a white face. I understood it all. The ship ahead of us had emigrants and they were throwing overboard their dead. Without telling Aileen, I grasped her arm, and drew her to our cabin.

May 31, Grosse Isle. Fourteen days since I penned a line in this sorrowful record. I wish I had not lived to pen another. [Having been put ashore on Grosse Ile, Keegan recounts how his wife Aileen falls sick.] Why recall the dreadful nights and days that followed? What profit to tell of the pain in the breast, the raging fever, the delirium, the agonising gasping for breath—the end? The fourth day, with bursting heart and throbbing head, I knelt by the corpse of my Aileen. There was not a soul to help; everybody was too full of their own troubles to be able to heed me. The island was now filled with sick emigrants and death was on every side. I dug her grave, the priest came, I laid her there, I filled it in, I staggered to the shed that had sheltered us, and I fell from sheer exhaustion and remembered no more.

Father Moylan from Montréal arrived on the island and persuaded Gerald to help in the work of tending the sick. He also wanted Gerald to go to Montréal as a witness before a committee of inquiry appointed by the legislature on the conditions and treatment.

July 9, This evening I took a walk to the far side of the island and enjoyed the solitude and the peace of nature. Sitting on the beach, I watched the sun sink behind the hills. I have a feeling that my own sun will soon disappear, for I am sad and disheartened beyond all my experience. Dr Fenwick told me the other day I should leave; that I needed a change. I cannot, indeed I will not, for I cherish the secret wish to die where my Aileen left me. A ship has arrived with 31 dead on board; she lost over a fourth of those who embarked on her at Liverpool. Another out of 470 emigrants, dropped 150 into the Atlantic. Sure, tragedies like those ought to direct the eyes of the civilised world to what is happening. My heart is broken at the sight of thousands of my own dear people, men, women and little children, dying for lack of a crust on Canada's shore.

July 14, I think the end has come. Tonight my head throbs and my bones are sore. Bridget, after hovering a long time between life and death, sank to rest this morning, and is buried. Ellen leaves by tomorrow's steamer, and will be in Huntingdon in a few days. I gave her a message to uncle. My life has been a failure. May God have pity on me and on my poor people. Oh, that Aileen were here, that I felt her hand on my racked forehead.

Journal published in *The Summer of Sorrow*, Huntingdon, Quebec, 1895

Gerald's uncle—not the one with whom he had traveled to Canada but Mr. O'Connor of Huntingdon, whose sister was Gerald's mother—arrived at Grosse Ile and was taken to his nephew by Dr. Russell. He was dying and made his uncle take him from the fever shed and lay him in the sunshine under a tree. He gave Mr. O'Connor his bag and pointed out his journal. "It will tell to those unborn what Irishmen and women have suffered in this summer of sorrow." O'Connor buried Gerald on the island.

It occurred to some officials that the fever and dysentery, typhus, and cholera were not being imported from Ireland—that the vast majority of people, although in poor physical condition from malnutrition, were not taking diseases on board the ships with them but succumbing to the diseases from the conditions on the ships themselves. No one realized that the thousands of pauper emigrants shipped from different Irish ports and from Liverpool, worn out with poverty and disease, and laboring under fever of a most infectious and malignant description, had symptoms that did not manifest until after a week on shipboard.

The cooperating influences of poverty and its outcomes on the emigrants existed prior to embarkation as well as afterward: the impurities of atmosphere in the crowded holds of the vessels; neglect of personal cleanliness; impure water; lack of medical attendance and supervision during the passage; and lastly and principally, exposure, impurities, want from insufficient attention, and hospital deficiencies at the quarantine station.

The two types of fever prevalent among the Irish emigrants were both caused by microorganisms entering the human bloodstream, transmitted by lice, or passed on by flies. Many of the ships transporting the emigrants to Canada in their holds had originally taken cargoes of Canadian wood to England, and in the sawdust residue, still in the holds when the emigrants boarded, lived the bacilli and lice that caused the disease to spread among them. The deaths of the emigrants had caused a new meaning to an old Irish proverb: Bíonn súil le mior, ach ní bhíonn súil le huaigh (One looks forward to the sea, but one does not expect to find a grave).

Young Ireland Insurrection (1848)

Disillusioned with Daniel O'Connell and his Repeal Association, a group of young intellectuals launched a newspaper, The Nation, *in October 1842. Out of this they* formed a new movement called Young Ireland, led by Thomas Davies, Charles Gavan Duffy, and John Blake Dillon. For a while they remained allied to the Repeal Association, but William Smith O'Brien and John Mitchel broke with it in 1846. The "Great Hunger" gave impetus to the call for a radical solution to the colonial question. Young Ireland considered the teachings of the United Irish and began to favor physical force by which to establish a sovereign republic. O'Brien (1803–1864) was born at Dromoland, Clare, a direct descendant of the kings of Thomond, and he had been Member of Parliament for Ennis. John Mitchel (1815–1875) was from Dungiven, County Derry, son of a Presbyterian minister and a lawyer. He founded the United Irishman journal. O'Brien and Mitchel began to establish Confederate and Citizen's Clubs to build support.

In April 1848, Thomas Francis Meagher attended a meeting of the Irish Confederation in Dublin. He had returned from Paris, where he had been presented with a gift of a tricolor flag from the citizens of France. The flag was green, white, and orange, symbolic of the union of green for older Ireland and orange for the new tradition, with the white for brotherhood. "I hope to see that flag one day waving as our national banner," Meagher told the meeting attendees. Today it is the national flag of the Irish Republic, expressing the hope of eventual reunification of the two traditions.

Mitchel was arrested early in 1848 and sentenced to fourteen years' transportation to the penal colonies.

O'Brien's Last Address before the Insurrection

Rebel Review. Tuesday evening was appointed by Mr W. Smith O'Brien for his inspection of the Confederate Clubs of this city, and the place appointed as the review field was the piece of ground behind the Corn Market and adjoining the City Park known by the name of the Monerea Marsh. At seven o'clock the clubs began to arrive at the end of the South Terrace, and having been passed by tickets into the salt and lime works yard of J.J. O'Connor, were drawn up according to precedence. They moved up into sections of two deep, each section numbering from 40 to 100, flanked by persons apparently in command, and whose orders were given by signs. Each section, as it arrived at a certain point on the road, passed in review in front of the superior officer. The sections, which continued to march up in quick succession, had all arrived before eight o'clock.

Shortly after that hour a band came up playing a military quickstep, followed by a jingle [a coach], in which were Mr W. Smith O'Brien and Messrs Denny Lane, J. Shea Lawlor and R. Shine Lawlor. Having alighted, they went into the yard for a few minutes, when Mr O'Brien ordered them to march to the Monerea Marsh, and draw up in line. The order being obeyed, they all drew up in military line, and he passed along with his staff, each man as he passed putting the index finger of the right hand to his hat or cap in salute. Mr O'Brien took up a prominent position, and the clubs marched two deep in review before him, headed by their presidents, flanked by the secretaries and vice-presidents. As each club passed the president announced its name, and all gave the salute.

Mr O'Brien watched cautiously to see that each man gave the salute, and whenever a party forgot to do so, he rebuked him occasioning saying "Just touch your hats as you walk along." The St Patrick's Club having halted in front of him for a moment, he cried out "do move along, and when you meet the other club turn to the east, as I want to see what kind of men the patriots of Ireland are." On one of the clubs passing, he remarked on the number of young boys in it, to which Town Councillor Mullan replied, "We are particular to enrol none under sixteen years of age, and all this will be found to come up to that." Mr O'Brien having dis-approved of the order in which one club marched, one of the members said "we want a little discipline yet, sir; but we are willing to learn." To which Mr O'Brien said, in an authoritative tone, "keep your places and be silent!" A woman here rushed forward and explained "three cheers for the King of Munster" to which Mr O'Brien replied "not yet—not yet—no shouting—no shouting." The clubs were composed of tradesmen, with one exception, that of the Mercantile Assistants' Club, the major of whose members were the shop clerks in the drapers' establishments in this city. The review having terminated, Mr S. O'Brien and his staff mounted a heap of rubbish, and, fronting the Lunatic Asylum, he was presented with an address form the southern district. The address was read by Mr Ralph Varian, Secretary of the Southern District. The following are extracts from the documents:

Dear Sir—On behalf of the fifteen Clubs of Cork City, we venture to address you.

The bending slavishness of the aristocracy of this country to the uncurbed power of an English dominancy is unexampled in the history of master and slave classes. The love of country is not only an instinct, but the first of social virtues. The Irish aristocracy have not this institution, which is common to savages. It has either been whipped out of them or bribed out of them. They stand alone in opposing the liberties of their own country. They preferring last in England to being first in Ireland. This is a social sin; it is a political heresy. It damnifies equally the land and the people. It perpetuates the degradation of Ireland. It makes a land of slaves and beggars. Its gods are poor law officials—its sanctified institutions, poor law Bastilles—its revenues, absentee rents and poor rates. This is Ireland of the present under English rule, after half a century of that legislation which we are called upon to uphold, as the perfection of human wisdom, by our blood and bravery—our common sense and common strength.

You have nobly risen against all this. You have pronounced that it is unsanctioned by any law of our being, by any dictate of our reason, by any edict of our morals, by any principle of human truth or human right. When it is condemned by all those forces of reason and religion, you assert, and truly do you say it, that it is lawful and legitimate for the Irish people to oppose it to the death. As all tyrannies must be put down, so must the tyranny of English misrule.

Mr Smith O'Brien then addressed them. He was not sorry that the enemies of this country had an opportunity of seeing such a heart-stirring display, for they desired it to be believed that so much disunion prevailed amongst the Irish people that it would be impossible to collect the united sentiments of such a great city as Cork in such a demonstration as he now beheld; and he was told that seldom, if ever, be the occasion however interesting, was so large a mass of people met together as was upon the present. He had to thank the clubs for the extreme regularity and order and precision which they observed; and for his part he placed very little value upon cheers, but deeply felt the importance of subordination; for shouting was of little avail when the struggle was for liberty, while regularity and order were the great requisites; and therefore they should accustom themselves to control; and this was now the more necessary, for never at any former period were such unjustifiable attempts made by a Whig minister to suppress the liberties of the people as at that present moment.

Having referred to the trial of Mitchel and the arrests of Duffy and the others, he asked them might he tell Duffy and the others now lying in dungeon that the men of Cork were prepared? (Loud cries of "yes and the women too.") Were they prepared to sustain those heroes in every effort to demand, if necessary, and secure the final vindication of the liberties of this country? (Shouts of "yes.") From expedience alone he was anxious to avoid a catastrophe—having the Irish people plunged into unsuccessful strife, for when the effort was made for the independence of the country it must be crowned with success, and he was now bound to tell them that the only fear he entertained of the achievement of that success was precipitation and defeat in the endeavour to vindicate their rights. Therefore he counselled them to accustom themselves to restraint so far as was possible under existing circumstances. He told them not to do nothing [sic] rashly—nothing without the desire of their leaders—nothing without the cooperation of their fellow countrymen, and, trusting in the skill and resolution of their leaders, they would find the struggle conducted to a successful issue.

Mr Denny Lane—Suggest the necessity of all joining the clubs.

Mr S. O'Brien said that they had seen the advantage of club organisation where they had seen 2,000 or 3,000 fellow citizens drawn up in position in an orderly manner and he hoped that after this night they would all get enrolled. He now requested them to move off as quietly as they had come, and above all things to avoid shouting in the streets, and he would now disperse them calling or them to give a hearty cheer for Ireland. (Cheering)

Cork Constitution, Thursday, July 13, 1848

William Smith O'Brien's fear of being precipitated into action by the government was justified. With the suspension of habeas corpus, as the authorities moved to arrest and thus destroy the leadership of the Young Ireland movement, he moved to County Tipperary to meet with other leaders, including Thomas Francis Meagher and Terence MacManus. A force of forty-six armed police arrived to arrest him and the others at Ballingarry, and the 1848 Insurrection ended in what has been called no more than a scuffle.

O'Brien was sentenced to death, but eighty thousand people signed a petition and the sentence was commuted to penal servitude for life. He served five years in Van Dieman's Land in Tasmania but was released in 1854 thanks to continued international pressure. The condition of his release was that he remain outside the United Kingdom. This condition was relaxed to just Ireland in 1856. He died at Bangor in Wales on June 16, 1864.

Thomas Meagher was sentenced to death, but the sentence was commuted to penal servitude for life in Van Dieman's Land. He escaped in 1852 and was given asylum in the United States, where he organized the Irish Brigade that fought for the Union in the Civil War. Meagher gained the rank of brigadier general and was later governor of the Montana Territory. He accidentally drowned in July 1867. Terence Bellew MacManus (1823–1860) was sentenced to death but his sentence was also commuted to penal servitude for life in Van Dieman's Land. He escaped with Meagher and settled in San Francisco.

October 24th—A poor extemporised abortion of a rising in Tipperary, headed by Smith O'Brien. There appears to have been no money or provisions to keep a band of people together two days. And O'Brien, Meagher, O'Donoghue [Pat of Dublin] and Terence M'Manus of Liverpool, all committed for trial to Clonmel gaol for being parties to the wretched business. I cannot well judge of this affair here, but in so far as I can learn anything about it and understand it, O'Brien has been driven into doing the very thing that ought not to have been done—that Lord Clarendon will thank him heartily for doing. An insurrection, indeed, has been too long deferred; yet, in the present condition of the island, no rising must begin in the country. Dublin streets for that. Reilly, Doheny, have fled; and all prominent members of the Confederation in country towns are arrested on suspicion.

What glee in Dublin Castle and the bloodthirsty dens of Downing Street, at this excuse for "vigour"! And, of course, all the world thinks Irish resistance is effectually crushed; and that Ireland's capacity for resistance was tested at this cursed Ballingarry.

John Mitchell, *Jail Journal, or Five Years in British Prisons*, New York, 1854

Mitchell escaped from the penal colony in Van Dieman's Land in 1853 and found asylum in the United States. He became a newspaper editor in New York but took the Confederate side in the Civil War, and his eldest and youngest sons were killed in the Confederate army. He was imprisoned after the end of the war. In 1874, he returned to Ireland to be elected MP for Tipperary, but the government declared him ineligible to sit as an undischarged felon. He was reelected in 1875 but died a few days later in Newry, where he is buried.

16

The Insurrection of 1867 and the Land League

On March 17, 1858, the Irish Republican Brotherhood was founded in Dublin by former members of the Young Ireland movement who had escaped imprisonment. James Stephens (1825–1901) became the leader. He had been wounded at Ballingarry in the 1848 uprising but had escaped to Paris. He returned to Ireland in secret to become known as An Seabhac Súilach (the Wandering Hawk). He went to the United States, where John O'Mahoney had become the IRB's chief representative, on a fund-raising mission. O'Mahoney called members of the movement the Fenians, naming them after Na Fianna Éireann, the semimythical bodyguard of the ancient high kings. The movement, like the United Irish and the Young Irelanders before it, was dedicated to establishing an independent Irish Republic. A newspaper, The Irish People, was launched in November 1863 as its mouthpiece and was suppressed in September 1865. Stephens was arrested on November 11, 1865, but made a spectacular escape from Richmond Prison, Dublin, on November 24, and was smuggled to New York.

With the English authorities closing in and leaders being arrested, two plans were put into action. As the bulk of the trained Fenian army was in the United States, the veterans of both Union and Confederate armies, it was decided to seize part of the territory of the Provinces of British North America to use as a bargaining counter in negotiations with Britain. An army of 25,000 commanded by Major General "Fighting Tom" Sweeney, originally from Cork, and a veteran of the U.S.–Mexican War as well as one of Sherman's divisional commanders, was to launch a three-pronged attack into Upper and Lower Canada. Brigadier Charles Tevis was to cross *from Chicago and Milwaukee with 3,000 men, Brigadier William Lynch was to cross Lake Erie and Niagara with 5,000 men, and the main thrust commanded by Brigadier Samuel P. Spear was to cross with 16,800 from upstate New York and Vermont. The plan was put into operation, but when Britain agreed to pay the United States reparation for supporting the Confederacy, President Johnson agreed to block the Fenian advance, sending General U. S. Grant to cut off supplies and stop the crossings. Even so, the Fenians fought a few successful engagements with the British at Ridgeway and Pidgeon Hill in June 1866. As a result of this attempt, during the following year some of the provinces of British North America confederated into the Dominion of Canada.*

The second plan was the rising in Ireland. Stephens had been replaced as leader in December 1866 by Colonel Thomas Kelly (1833–1908) from Galway, who fought with the 10th Ohio Regiment during the American Civil War, then returned to Ireland to help rescue Stephens from Richmond Jail. Kelly had planned the rising for February 11, but the plan misfired. Several weeks later, the uncoordinated response began in Ireland on March 5, 1867. It was confined to Counties Dublin, Cork, Kerry, Limerick, Tipperary, and Clare and was fairly quickly suppressed.

With profound sorrow have today to record the outbreak of an insane and criminal insurrection in the south of Ireland. The blow has fallen suddenly and unexpectedly.

Cork Examiner, Thursday, March 7, 1867

The Fenian Rising in the South of Ireland—On Tuesday [March 5] night a widespread and formidable insurrection was began by the Fenians in the South of Ireland. The rising was made simultaneously in parts of the counties of Cork, Limerick, Tipperary and Clare. Owing to the general interruption of the telegraphic and railway communication yesterday (the Fenians having cut the telegraphic wires and torn up the track of the Great Southern and Western Railway) we have had much difficulty in collecting authentic details of the events of the last twenty-four hours. . . .

The precise circumstances of the occurrence in Midleton are these: a few minutes before eleven o'clock the Fenians assembled in the Main Street of the town . . . they moved down to the bridge close by the National Bank and here they drew up on the left side of the approach to the bridge. The patrol consisting of Acting Constables Greany, Sub-Constables O'Donnell, Sheedy and O'Brien, passed on towards the bridge at the other side of the road. When they passed slightly beyond the Fenians, they were challenged by, it is believed Daly [Timothy Daly] their leader, and called upon to surrender in the name of the Irish Republic.

The police were then close to Mr Green's gate, and the Fenians were but a few yards away from them, assembled four deep. When the police did not obey the call, Daly seized Sub-Constable O'Donnell's rifle, and presenting a revolver at his head, fired. O'Donnell at the same time pushed Daly slightly from him, and this caused the pistol ball to glance around the back of his head, the power singeing his hair. At the same moment, the party of Fenians fired a volley. A ball entered Sub-Constable Sheedy's breast, low down near the stomach on the right side, and after running a short distance up the chapel road, he fell and bled probably to death. The other policemen fled in the same direction, and O'Donnell, who was wounded in the head, took shelter in a house. As others fled, the Fenians fired after them.

Midleton, County Cork, is called Mainistir na Córann (the monastery of the weir) in Irish, named from a monastery founded there in A.D. 1180, of which nothing remains. The Irish Constabulary was formed in 1836 as an armed force run with military discipline. Housed in barracks, constables were usually not local to the area in which they served and were confined to barracks. Only after seven years of service could they officially marry. Officers, like military officers, had to provide their own horses and equipment. By 1867, the constabulary consisted of twelve thousand men. Royal was added in recognition of their suppression of the 1867 uprising.

The first assembly of the Midleton Fenians was at the Cork road, where they were formed in three divisions, but being there surprised by the police they scattered and subsequently met at the house of a person of some position in the town, at the door of which a sentry was posted, and all persons entering closely scanned. Thence they are believed to have proceeded to the Bank Bridge. The police say they were only armed with pistols, but a gentleman who passed closed to them, says that they had rifles and swords. After the encounter of the bridge they are said to have gone by Ballincurra towards Castlemartyr. The firing in Midleton is described as being as regular as that of disciplined troops.

Castlemartyr, Baile an Mártra, meaning "town of the relics," County Cork, is 10 miles west of Youghal. The ruins of Imokilly Castle, which had been destroyed in the Williamite Conquest, were found there.

At Castlemartyr the arrival of the Fenians, which included the Midleton party, took place about two o'clock in the morning. A haggard [haystack] belonging to Mr Walker, near the village was set on fire. It is believed as a ruse, but the police—five men under Constable O'Connell, having reconnoitred, thought they saw more than a mere fire in the affair, and declining to render any assistance, returned to their barracks, where they made every preparation to resist an attack. They had not long to wait for it when a large body of men—some say as many as 500, but it was impossible to state accurately, the night was so dark—drew up before the station, after having been directed by some person, in stentorian tones, to go and attack the police station at once. Having arrived before the station, some persons called upon the police to surrender.

The party had come in with baggage, all the men seemed to wear haversacks containing provisions, and as well as the police could see them through the windows, they had rifles and fixed bayonets, which they carried "sloped" in true military style. They knocked several times at the door of the barrack, receiving no reply, they commenced firing, the bullets entering pretty thickly through the window shutters & etc. The Fenians called out to the villagers, who looked out of their windows, to keep in their heads. The police returned their fire with interest, and it is thought with effect. The Fenian leader, Timothy Daly (who had come on from Midleton) was found, when the party had departed, lying dead. . . .

The party retreated immediately after Daly was shot and were pursued towards the bridge by the police; but they made a stand forming a breastwork at the bridge, and the police thought it more prudent to retire to their quarters.

Timothy Daly was a Midleton carpenter with a wife and eight children. He was described as "a person of considerable intelligence" and was an officer in the Irish Republican Brotherhood.

A strong force of infantry was despatched by special train to the Limerick Junction of the great Southern and Western Railway, where they are to remain until further orders. The 48th Regiment, which returned to the Curragh Camp for a few days since, from Killarney, have received orders to be in readiness to proceed to the south at a moment's notice, and the executive have taken measures to concentrate troops at any given point with as little delay as possible should the occasion arise.

A man whose capture was eagerly sought for by the police was brought to town [Dublin] last night by the constabulary and lodged in Chancery Lane station house. He was arrested at the Limerick junction on his way to Dublin, and turned out to be no less a person than the functionary known as General Godfrey Massey, who it is stated was invested with great authority, and had been easily engaged for some weeks past at the work of organisation in the western districts of Cork and Kerry. He had been in the Federal army, and returned to this country from America about two months since. He was forwarded this day under the Lord Lieutenant's warrant to Mountjoy prison.

Cork Examiner, Thursday, March 7, 1867

Godfrey Massey was the illegitimate son of William Massey of Castelconnell, County Limerick. His mother, Mary Condon, took him to the United States, where she brought him up under the name Patrick Condon. He fought in the American Civil War and served in the Confederate (not the Federal) Army, reaching the rank of colonel. He joined the IRB and in January was sent with money to procure arms and help plan the uprising, He turned informer after his arrest and his information helped the authorities in suppressing the rising.

It is perfectly clear and admitted upon all hands, even by the most timid, that the Fenian rising which lately frightened our isle from its propriety is now at an end. Never massed on Galtimore, nor scattered through the rural districts, nor threatening the towns, are there Fenian bands of any kind. A tempest of two or three day's duration, in which almost every ill the heavens could combine, in which wind, snow, hail, rain, and one might say frost, have been at work together, had completed the task begun by an overpowering military force.

Cork Examiner, Friday, March 15, 1867

In fact, four thousand men had been active in the Cork area under the command of James O'Brien and William Mackey Lomasney. But by the end of March 1867, the badly coordinated rising had been quashed. Colonel Thomas Kelly, the IRB leader, had been arrested with his aide, Captain Timothy Deasy, in England. Both were rescued as they were being transported to Belle Vue Jail, Manchester, on September 18. During this rescue attempt, a Dubliner, Peter Rice, tried to break the lock of the prison van by firing into it just as Sergeant Charles Brett, a popular Manchester police officer, inside the van, was trying to peer through the lock to see what was happening. He was killed. Rice escaped, as did Deasy and Kelly.

Subsequently, among the sixty Irishmen rounded up as suspects, Edward O'Meagher Condon, Thomas Maguire, William Allen, Michael Larkin, and Michael O'Brien were charged with complicity in the murder. The five were sentenced to death on evidence now seen to be fabricated. Thomas Maguire was a marine serving on a Royal Navy ship and had only just arrived in Manchester on leave. He had no connections with the Fenians and consequently there was some disquiet at his sentence, leading to Maguire's "free pardon" two days before the execution. Condon, who had served as a captain in the U.S. Federal army in the Civil War, had American citizenship. His case was taken up by the United States and a reprieve was secured. He was released on the condition that he could not set foot in any British dominion for twenty years. In 1909, he was granted the freedom of the city of Dublin and he died in New York in 1918. The others were publicly executed on November 23, becoming known as the Manchester Martyrs and the last prisoners to be publicly executed in England.

During April and into the summer of 1867, trials for high treason and sedition were held, but death sentences were usually commuted to penal servitude ranging from life to twelve years. Many of those tried had served in both the Federal and Confederate armies in the American Civil War. Some had achieved high rank, such as Thomas F. Burke of Fethard, County Tipperary (1840–1889), who had been a brevet general in the Confederate forces.

The IRB continued a campaign of bombing in England but in 1873 decided to support all endeavors to bring about independence for Ireland. It was not until 1924 that the IRB dissolved itself.

Disestablishment of the Anglican Church (1869)

U.K. prime minister W. E. Gladstone put forward the Bill for Disestablishing the Anglican Church of Ireland and disendowing its considerable landholdings to be used for the relief of poverty and for education. Embodied in this act passed in both Houses of Parliament in London at the end of July was a general disestablishment of all government connection with religion in Ireland. The Maynooth Grant for Catholics and the Regium Donum for Presbyterians were also abolished.

2 August 1869: The reception of the Bill by the Protestants in this quarter is comical. On Sunday last the Reverend Mr Myles announced from his pulpit at Dunmurray, that England had separated herself from God. "We Irish Protestants," said he, "have always been faithful to her, and now she requites our fidelity with desertion. Caesar has cast us off. I will not preach disloyalty, but I will say this—let Caesar take care of himself for the future without our assistance."

William Joseph O'Neill Daunt (1807–1894), *Diary*, in *A Life Spent for Ireland*,
New York, 1896

Ireland's Most Famous Fenian Prisoner (1871)

Jeremiah O'Donovan Rossa (1831–1915) from Rosscarbery, County Cork, was busi-
ness manager of the republican newspaper The Irish People *and a contributor to its*
columns, writing articles and poetry. He was arrested in 1865, charged with sedition,
and sentenced to penal servitude for twenty years, being transferred to prisons in
England rather than Ireland.

When my twenty-eight days' bread and water had expired, a spell of six
month's penal-class diet commenced, and they gave me oakum to pick in
my cell and an hour in the open air every day. I took the hour, but I did
not pick the oakum, on the grounds that it was against my principle while
undergoing punishment; and for not working they took away my hour's
exercise from me, and put me back every alternative day, and sometimes
two days a time, on bread and water. They capped the climax of their punishment now when, besides putting me on bread and water in the black-
hole for forty-eight hours, they decreed that I was to get no bed at night,
and that I was to be stripped of my body clothes.

Alison came to my cell at locking-up hour and asked me to put out my
clothes. "I will not," said I, "unless I get a bed."

"You can get no bed. That is the order, and we must get your clothes."

"That is assassination work and I will be no party to it. I will not give
my clothes."

"But you must give your clothes, and we will soon see that you must."
Saying which he walked off, and returned accompanied by warders
Hibbert and Giddings.

The foregoing conversation was repeated, and when I definitely said:
"No, I will not give them," the three of them rushed at me. I tried to keep
them away by holding them at arm's length, but made no attempt whatever at striking them, and they struck my hands with their clubs to make
me let go whenever I caught one of them. I was soon overpowered and
lying on the ground, with Hibbert's knee upon my neck. You might have
seen a butcher trying a pig for measles. It was in exactly the same manner
that Hibbert took charge of my head and neck while Alison and Giddings
were pulling the breeches off me. It was necessary to turn me from one
side to the other, the necessary for Hibbert to take his knee off my neck
while this was doing; but, as I was flat of my back, he gave a leap, and with
his knee foremost, came down on my chest.

It was a treacherous, murderous act. The air shot up my throat as it would through the neck of a full-blown bladder if you leaped on it. The sudden compression on the chest caused this, and the blade bones must have been very strong and elastic to bear such a strain.

When they had stripped me, they were leaving the cell, and I proceeded to raise myself from the floor, but Hibbert, who was the last going out, turned back and gave me a kick which threw me in against the wall and cut me in several places. I was so excited that I think I should have shown myself a fighting man that night if I could lay hold of any weapon to strike with.

In the morning I sent for the doctor, and when he brought me from the black hole into the light of the hallway I saw my chest black and blue and swollen. I got some liniment to rub to it, and by degrees the soreness and swelling went away.

As soon as Alison, Giddings and Hibbert saw I was under medical treatment on account of their assault, they entered on the books a charge against me to the effect I had assaulted them in the discharge of their duty.

O'Donovan Rossa, *My Years in English Jails,* New York, 1874

International protests finally led to Rossa's release on the condition that he could not return to Ireland. He went into exile in the United States, where he edited The United Irishmen *and published his journals. When he died in New York in 1915, his body was returned to Ireland for interment in Glasnevin cemetery on August 1. An immense crowd followed the cortege, and at the graveside, Pádraig Pearse, to be the figurehead of the uprising in the following year, ended his funeral oration with the words that have become famous: "The fools, the fools, the fools! They have left us our Fenian deed, and while Ireland holds these graves, Ireland unfree shall never be at peace."*

Assassination of Lord Leitrim (April 2, 1878)

In 1876, there came the start of a series of disastrous harvests. Not having learned from the terrible years of the Great Hunger, the colonial landlords of Ireland began to evict impoverished tenant farmers and their workers. Economic depression in England, reducing the demand for Irish migrant labor, cut off a vital source of income. On April 2, 1878, one of Ireland's biggest landowners, William Sydney Claments, third earl of Leitrim (1806–1878), who had won notoriety for his treatment of the peasantry in Donegal, set out from his estate along Mulroy Bay for the quarter sessions to process eviction orders against a number of his tenants. His driver and clerk were killed by gunfire. He was wounded, then his attackers battered him to death. His funeral in Dublin was a focal point of the anger of the impoverished Irish who correctly saw another great hunger forthcoming.

The crowd closed around the hearse as it approached the graveyard, groaning, cheering and hissing. The occupants of the mourning coaches on descending from their carriages were jostled about and scattered. The police in vain sought to clear a passage for the coffin. . . . Over a quarter of an hour elapsed before the coffin could be finally removed. In the meantime the mob hooted and groaned, and voices came from the worst of them saying, "Out with the old b—"; "Lug him out"; "Dance on him." . . . The last prayers being over, the coffin was borne through the southern door, towards the vaults. . . . Immediately that the bareheaded mourners were sighted by the mob outside the railings, a new howl of execration went up and amid hisses, cheers and indecent jests, the coffin of the unfortunate nobleman was hurried to its last resting place.

The Freeman's Journal, April 11, 1878

The Rise of the Land League

The first organized demonstration was held at Irishtown, County Mayo, on April 20, 1879, as a reaction to a threat to evict the tenants on the estate of Canon Geoffrey Burke, the parish priest, who had recently inherited the estate from his brother. The demonstration was so successful that Burke withdrew the threat of eviction and abated the arrears of rent by 20 percent. On October 21, 1879, the Irish National Land League was formed as a reaction to the worsening conditions experienced by tenant farmers and the agricultural depression that was modeled on the Land League of Mayo. Charles Stewart Parnell, M.P. (1846–1891), leader of the Irish Party at Westminster, was elected president.

On Sunday a very large and enthusiastic demonstration was held at the now well-known village of Irishtown. It was here some twelve months ago that the first Land League meeting was held, and this demonstration was organised to celebrate the anniversary. In point of numbers and enthusiasm this meeting was as important as any previously held. Large contingents arrived from Westport, Balla, Knock, Ballindine, Logboy, Cross, Ballyhaunis, Claremorris and Tuam. From all the surrounding districts the people poured in. The Claremorris and Ballyhaunis brass bands were in attendance, and discoursed national music during the proceedings, such as "Ireland for the Irish," "The Land for the People," "*Is lim an Talam,*" "Stick to your Homesteads," etc. Messrs Parnell, O'Kelly, Davitt, Daly and Louden were most enthusiastically received. A large force of police was present and two Government reporters took short hand notes on the platform.

. . . Mr Michael Davitt then came forward amidst much enthusiasm and said—"Rev. Chairman and men of Mayo, I take the liberty of moving the following resolution for your consideration:

"That in commemorating the initiation of the national land agitation by an anniversary meeting in Irishtown we are manifesting the vitality of that movement which during the past twelve months has shaken the feudalistic system of land laws to its foundation, called forth the inherent and hitherto inert resoluteness of the farmers of Ireland in the assertion of their rights, and demonstrated the power of the democracy of our country by the triumphs achieved over class supremacy, and the intelligence and order exhibited by the people in over one hundred great demonstrations during the past year."

Davitt ended with these words:

"The Land League called upon the farmers to pay no rent until they got a substantial reduction. It called upon the people, as he now called upon them, to look to their interests and the comfort of their homes first, and then give the landlord a rent that they could spare. Now they had triumphed over the Government of England and the landlords of Ireland, and by their action they had made the landlords the weaker party—then in the name of reason, justice and common sense, let the landlords go to the wall (loud cheering)."

The Connaught Telegraph, Saturday, May 8, 1880

A comparison report by a police officer makes interesting reading:

Constable J. O'Rorke reporter, speaker M. Davitt, date 2.5.'80, place Irishtown Co Mayo. Substance of speech:

Anniversary of the initiation of the national Land agitation.

Reviewed the work done by the agitation which he said had shown the tenant farmers their great strength had brought them together in vast numbers, the force of landlordism was nothing against the vast masses of the people, it had convinced them that they had rights to the soil of Ireland—rights far more strong and more superior than the landlords; and it had infused into the people such a spirit that they are resolved to fight for those rights until victory crowned their cause. The Land League had called upon the people to pay no rent until they got a reduction, to look to their own comforts and then offer the landlord what they could spare. You have triumphed over both the landlords and the Govt. and by your action have made the landlords the weaker party. Then in the name of reason, in the name of justice and common sense, let the landlords go to the wall (loud cheering).

Irish Land League and Irish National League
Report of Speeches 1871–1888, County Mayo, no. 18
Police report in State Papers Office, Dublin

Lord Mountmorres, a Small Landowner But a Harsh Magistrate, Was Shot to Death as He Left His Estate at Clonbur, County Galway (September 25, 1880)

The spot where the deceased fell is still marked by a large quantity of clotted blood. The outrage seems to have been well planned. The place chosen for the attack is near the top of a hill—an English mile from Clonbur. The horse should of course walk slowly up the ascent and this afforded the assassins an opportunity of taking deliberate aim. A number of stones were placed under one of the side walls so as to afford facilities for escape. Beside the six bullets which were found in his body, three were found on the road which did not appear to pass thro' his person. They varied in weight and this would go to show that more than one took part in the murder.

The Connaught Telegraph, October 2, 1880

Letter from a Landowner of 900 Acres at Claremorris, County Mayo, to the Rt. Hon. J. Lowerth, Chief Secretary of Ireland, Irish Office, London (July 25, 1879)

As an Englishman and one who served through the whole Crimean War and was here during the Fenian Rising I cannot be well considered an alarmist. Having purchased this property fifteen years since and spent several thousand pounds in improving it and the condition of the Tenants I was considered a Good Landlord and the Tenants paid their rents most punctually. But in the last fortnight I have been calumniated by a Priest at the Claremorris meeting and will be also by the Press of the Secret Society, and my tenants last Wednesday refused to pay their rents except at a reduction of 25 per cent and Rent Receipts altered to make it a permanent reduction.

They do not assert poverty but one of them said they were combined to it and the rest agreed. I know all landlords are ready to give large reductions where necessary but don't like to be compelled in by this Society. Mr Gladstone after disendowing the Irish Church and reducing the Landlords to only receivers of Head Rents, left a coercion act which was a benefit to all except the lawless and this act everybody except the lawless trust the present government will again establish before the close of the session or all the Gentry must leave the country or give an adhesion to this Secret Society as the priests have been forced to do. It is intolerable to live under this illegal government (of a few determined men with revolvers) and whose organisation is spreading daily. There is no fear of any outrages until the winter but the apparent lull in the organisation is more dangerous and will if not checked shortly spread from this comparatively small district to other parts of Ireland. The extra police sent here alarmed the people for the moment but when they found there was no change it passed off. The people in this locality are extremely well dressed and not in any great poverty. There is also a prospect of a good harvest. Trusting you will excuse me addressing you to such a length I remain, Your most obedient servant, J.C. Sheffield JP,

Written from Carradoyne, Claremorris, County Mayo
Chief Secretary's Office, Registered Papers 1879: 129/33
State Papers Office, Dublin

Ennis (Sunday, September 19, 1880)

In his Ennis speech, Land League president Charles Parnell, M.P., had asked his audience what they would do if they encountered a land grabber who benefited from tenants' evictions from their farmsteads and cottages. Several people shouted, "Shoot him," but Parnell went on outlining what was to become the main weapon of the Land League and one, when practiced against the English land agent at Lough Mask, County Mayo, Captain Charles Cunningham Boycott, brought a new word into the English language: boycotting.

When a man takes a farm from which another has been evicted you must shun him on the road side when you meet him, you must shun him in the streets of the town, you must shun him in the shop, you must shun him in the fair green and in the market place, and even in the place of worship. By leaving him severely alone, by putting him into a moral convent, by isolating him from the rest of his countrymen as if he were a leper of old, you must show him your detestation of the crime he has committed.

The Times, London, September 20, 1880

On Monday last Ballinarobe was made the scene of what at one time appeared would end in a regular collision between the military and police on one side, the civilians on the other. The cause of this riotous fray was, it transpired, that Captain Boycott—who has recently rendered himself notoriously obnoxious to the public—appeared at Petty Sessions in three cases in which he got defeated. The gallant Captain's appearance on the street although sheltered behind buckshot warriors, created such wild fury and excitement that he and his bodyguard had to beat a precipitated retreat in the direction of the military barracks. Stones were used freely, Sub Inspector M'Ardle, the RM, and some of the RIC coming in for what may be termed two year old paving stones. The "sojers" and police available had to turn out and guard this universally held captain until they, by some difficulty, allowed him to fly from his pursuers by the Castlebar road. On the announcement being made public, knowing that the "bird had flown," all things went as smooth as a marriage bell until it had been circulated that a volunteer brigade of Ulster Orangemen are expected to come to Loughmask to save the harvest from the aspect of events. Doubtful if they do but they will find it enough to save themselves and not mind the harvest.—Correspondent

The Connaught Telegraph, November 6, 1880

Captain Charles Cunningham Boycott (1832–1897), from Norfolk, England, was land agent for Lord Erne's estate at Lough Mask, County Mayo. He was a bitter enemy of the Land League and opposed any idea of rent reduction. He was an early victim of social ostracizing. No one would work on his estate. Boycott imported fifty Orangemen from the North to work the land, but they had to be guarded by a thousand troops, costing the London government £10,000, or, as Parnell put it, "one shilling for every turnip dug from Boycott's land." Soon his name became synonymous with the weapon of ostracism. He returned to England in 1886.

From the Chief Secretary, William Edward Forster, to Prime Minister Gladstone (January 26, 1881)

Unless we can strike at the boycotting weapon, Parnell will beat us. If we strike a blow at all it must be a sufficiently hard blow to paralyse the action of the League, and for this purpose I think we must make a simultaneous arrest of the central leaders and the local leaders who conduct the boycotting. . . . I see no alternative unless we allow the Land League to govern Ireland.

Quoted in T. Wemyss Reid, The Life of W. E. Forster, London, 1888

By the end of 1881, under the new Protection of Person and Property Act (1881) some one thousand people were being held in jail without trial on suspicion of "agrarian outrage." They included Charles Parnell, M.P., and several other Irish M.P.s.

Proclamation by the Lord Lieutenant of Ireland (October 20, 1881)

Whereas an Association styling itself The Irish National Land League has existed for some time past, assuming to interfere with the Queen's subjects in the free exercise of their lawful rights, and especially to control the relations of Landlords and Tenants in Ireland. . . .

Now we hereby warn all persons that the said Association styling itself "The Irish National Land League" or by whatsoever other name it may be called or known, is an unlawful and criminal Association; and that all meeting and Assemblies to carry out or promote its designs or purposes are alike, unlawful and criminal, and will be prevented and, if necessary dispersed by force.

National Library Proclamations, Dublin, 1881

The Irish National Invincibles (1882)

The draconian methods of the administration caused a breakaway group from the Irish Republican Brotherhood to be formed, called the Irish National Invincibles, who decided on a program of political assassination. The initial targets were Chief Secretary William E. Forster and John Mallon of G Division of the Dublin Metropolitan Police. But on May 2, 1882, Forster had resigned, returning to England, and

Parnell had been released from Kilmainham Jail, following a "treaty" with the London government. On May 6, 1882, a new chief secretary, Lord Frederick Cavendish, had arrived and was strolling outside the Vice Regal Lodge in Phoenix Park with Undersecretary Thomas H. Burke. The Invincibles struck, assassinating them both. J. B. Hall, working on the Evening Telegraph, *which had formerly been the* Evening Freeman, *a main Dublin newspaper published on Princes Street, described events from his perspective.*

Perhaps the most vivid of my random recollections is centred around the Phoenix Park murders of Lord Frederick Cavendish and Mr Thomas Henry Burke, which took place on the 6th May, 1882.

That night, it was a Saturday, I attended a performance of "Maritana" by the Carl Rosa Opera Company. During the first act, Mr Barton McGuckin and Mr Michael Gunn came to my box in a state of great excitement and informed me of the appalling news that had reached them, the only definite fact being that the two men had been murdered— whether shot or stabbed was not at the moment mentioned.

A question arose whether it were judicious or otherwise to have an announcement made publicly from the stage, and to stop the performance; but after a conference it was deemed more prudent, and I think wisely, to avoid even a possibility of panic—the house was packed—not to make such an announcement, but to let the news percolate, as it were; to inform the artistes and the conductor and to shorten the opera as much as possible.

I need scarcely say that my hands were full from that moment. I have never known anything to exceed the wave of excitement which spread throughout the city, an excitement made all the more intense by the fact that the rumours that night were so indefinite, and in many respects so conflicting.

How all hands were turned out for the bringing out of a midnight edition of the old *Evening Telegraph;* how the available staff scurried hither and thither to collect what facts were to be gleaned, and how later on from nearly every house one passed came people straining eagerly to gain tidings of what had really happened.

I remember one strange scene. As I drove home I pulled up after midnight at the old Portobello hotel, now a private hospital, then patronised greatly by theatrical artistes. Within, a weird spectacle presented itself. In the coffee room under a flickering light were gathered a crowd of the principals of the Carl Rosa Company, and in their midst stood [George H.]

Snazelle, the great baritone, reading out from the hastily produced edition, such information as was then available of the details of the tragedy which proved, indeed, to be historical in the annals of Dublin.

On the trials of the Invincibles which long afterwards followed, I am not inclined to dwell; it were an oft-told tale, and I refrain. The one incident, however, which was to me the most dramatic of all was the appearance in the [witness] chair as informer of James Carey, the arch-criminal of all.

It was in Kilmainham Courthouse on February 3rd, 1883, when "James Carey, Town Councillor, builder," and Joseph Brady and a group of six others were put forward and charged with the murders. Evidence was given and an adjournment followed and one informer gave evidence; but on the 17th February, there was consternation in the dock when it was seen that one figure was absent and when James Carey was led forward to the witness chair. Had Joe Brady, who glared at him and stretched forward towards him, been able to reach him, I believe he would have been torn to pieces, for Brady was a powerful young fellow, and for the moment he was for all the world like a tiger on the spring.

Amidst painful excitement and a silence only broken by the voices of counsel and witness, Carey, in graphic language and dramatic manner, described the approach of the victims, the hurrying away of the scouts to warn the gang, the signalling and the group of the assassins. He named the men who were waiting to do the murderous work and described the fatal scene with a calm and callous precision dreadful to listen to.

The arrest of James Carey, Joseph Brady, Timothy Kelly, Michael Fagan and others, had taken place in February, 1883, nine months after the tragedy and the trial of Brady was opened in Green Street before Judge William O'Brien on the 14th of April following. No trial in my experience attracted to it anything approaching the almost feverish excitement, which centred upon this case.

I remember that the prisoner was conveyed from Kilmainham Prison under a mounted escort of military and police, with armed police and Marines following on cars. In a second vehicle were the four informers, James Carey, Richard Farrell, William Lamie and Michael Kavanagh (who had driven the outside car to the Park).

The Judge, who was known as "hatchet face," was of singularly cadaverous appearance. The case for the prosecution was opened by the Attorney-

General, Mr A.M. Porter, afterwards Master of the Rolls, in an extremely calm but powerful speech to which Brady listened with apparent uncon- cern, occupying himself at intervals picking his teeth with the stump of a pencil.

The calling of Carey as a witness created a sensation far exceeding even the earlier scene at Kilmainham. Knowing him, as nearly everyone in Court had done as a Town Councillor and a citizen of repute, and with a reputation for ostentatious piety, there was something indescribable in the effect his presence produced, and with every head stretched forward, and breath almost held, the scene was striking, indeed.

He spoke slowly and calmly as he had done at the preliminary hearing. During his evidence he had occasion to look straight at Brady, and their eyes met, and I can never forget the look of scorn, contempt and hatred with which the prisoner fixed his piercing eyes on the informer. Carey quickly shifted his position and looked at him no more until leaving the table he was brought face to face with him and received the same appalling and loathing look.

The cool description by the informer of the preparations for the mur- der of Mr Burke, the arrival in the Park of the conspirators some on a car driven by Kavanagh and others in a cab driven by FitzHarris ("Skin the Goat"), the arrangements for the signal to be given by Carey and the hideous incident of the flashing knives, the brief struggle of the victims, and the final fatal blows was dreadful to listen to. It is but a mild statement to record that Carey left the witness chair admidst the undisguised disgust of those who had listened to him.

When sentence of death was pronounced on him, Brady, bowing to his counsel (Dr Webb and Mr Adams) thanked them. Brady's father was in court and was deeply afflicted, and a pathetic figure in the front of the gallery was a gentle-faced young girl, said to be his sweetheart, and whose tearful eyes were riveted upon him to the end.

The trial of Tom Kelly, who, according to the informer, had assisted actively in the actual murders, created an interest second only to that of Brady. Kelly was extremely youthful and simple looking, and had an air of bewildered anxiety. He was known to have borne a very good character, and it was with profound dismay astonishment that those who were acquainted with him learned that he was associated in any way with the "Invincibles."

He was tried three times, the jury disagreeing on two occasions. The unhappy boy had been a chorister in one of the Dublin Catholic churches and I was told by the Governor of Kilmainham that the night before his execution he sang in his cell Wallace's pathetic song "The Memory of the Past."

I recall the trial of Michael Fagan especially by reason of the fact that two compositors, engaged on Dublin newspapers, were called by the prosecution to give evidence, but refused at first point-blank to do so—until the Judge threatened to send them to prison for twelve month, when they consented to be sworn, and their evidence went the length of identifying the prisoner as having been in the Park on the evening of the 6th of May.

Both Carey and another informer named Smith mentioned that they had impressed upon the perpetrators to "mind it is the man with the grey suit" (meaning Mr Burke). The defence was an alibi, but it was of no avail and Fagan, who was the least concerned in his demeanour of all the accused, was sentenced to death.

James FitzHarris, alias "Skin the Goat," was twice tried, first for murder and secondly for aiding and abetting the perpetrators by conveying them in his cab to and from the Park. He presented a most remarkable appearance. Although plain to the point of ugliness, there was something almost comical in the expression of his rugged face, and he had a habit of winking to friends whom he recognised in the Gallery, or even to strangers who happened to catch his eye.

One of the English newspaper correspondents, describing his countenance, said it presented the appearance of having at some remote period been "badly battered by contact with a traction engine." He had the reputation of being an honest, decent type of cabman, quite incapable of being a bloodthirsty conspirator.

I enquired how he came by his extraordinary nickname and I was informed that FitzHarris had been the possessor of a very fine goat which he kept in his backyard, and that when he was extremely hard-up and at his wit's end to procure the means of satisfying an "unquenchable thirst," a friend and neighbour told him that the skin of the goat would fetch a tidy sum when the animal died.

FitzHarris ruminated on this remark, and in a rash moment sacrificed the poor goat, sold his sleek and silvery skin, and this gratified the inner man at the expense of those finer feelings which it may be supposed he possibly possessed. Since that occasion he was known as "Skin the Goat."

At his first trial, the jury acquitted him of the capital charge, but on the second he was convicted of aiding and abetting, it was pointed out that notwithstanding the enormous reward of £10,000 offered by the Government, FitzHarris had remained silent. He was sentenced to penal servitude for life, but was released after some years, and led a most exemplary life.

The executions of Joseph Brady, Tim Kelly, Michael Fagan, Daniel Curley and Thomas Caffrey took place at Kilmainham Prison, which was quite surrounded by Grenadier Guards and infantry and police. Marwood was the executioner.

There was a certain feeling of commiseration in the case of the boy, Tom Kelly, on account of his extreme youth and the influences under which he was led into crime, as well as the substantial doubt in the case, and up to the last there were hopes entertained of a reprieve.

I was informed that the unhappy youth received religious ministrations from a Sister of Mercy—a cousin of Mr Burke for whose murder he was hanged.

J. B. Hall, Random Records of a Reporter, Dublin, 1910

The assassination, performed with surgical knives, shocked public opinion in Ireland. Parnell, the leader of the Irish Party as well as the Land League, condemned the killings and felt that his work had been undone. He offered his resignation as leader of the Irish Parliamentary Party to Prime Minister Gladstone, whose wife was a relative of Lord Frederick Cavendish, but Gladstone urged him to remain. Brady, Kelly, Caffrey, Fagan, and Curley were executed at Kilmainham between May 14 and June 9, 1883. Eight others were sentenced to varying terms of imprisonment.

There is yet a sequel to this sad story. After the Invincibles had been disposed of, the Government had James Carey on their hands, and the question was what to do with him. They decided to ship him off secretly to their Colony at Natal in South Africa.

On July 4th, 1883, at Dartmouth [England], he embarked on the *Kilfauns Castle* under the name of James Power. A fellow-passenger was one Patrick O'Donnell. They had no previous knowledge of each other, but on the voyage became acquainted and occasionally had refreshments at the bar.

At Cape Town, O'Donnell was shown a portrait of James Carey the informer. He recognised it at once as that of his acquaintance "Mr Power." Carey sailed in the *Melrose* for Port Elizabeth. So did O'Donnell, and while the two men were in the refreshment saloon together, O'Donnell drew a revolver and fired three shots into Carey's body, killing him almost instantly.

O'Donnell was taken into custody and brought back to London where he was put on trial for murder. I was present at the trial. For counsel he had Sir Charles Russell QC and A.M. Sullivan. On the next day he was convicted and sentenced to death, and was executed in Newgate in December, 1883.

A couple of years after the execution a handsome marble monument was sent from New York to Dublin and set up in Glasnevin Cemetery to his memory.

J. B. Hall, *Random Records of a Reporter,* Dublin, 1910

The Irish National Invincible organizations disappeared in the face of animosity from Irish public opinion.

The Eviction at the Vandeleur Estate at Kilrush, County Clare (July 1888)

In spite of the endeavors of the now proscribed Land League, the landlords of Ireland continued their evictions.

On Friday morning the eviction force started from Kilrush House to turn out Michael Connell of Carhudota. The area of the holding is 40 acres [Irish], valuation £33, non-judicial rent, £33 15s; 2½ years rent due to March, 1887, for which he was decreed. The house was barricaded and the tenant remained outside calmly smoking his pipe, and inside the house, subsequently to be smashed by the battering ram, he left his little children, girls and boys, some scarcely able to walk. I feel bound to offer the most emphatic protest against the policy pursued by Connell, whatever its motive. As much more will doubtless be heard about it, I wish to note here that not only did the parish priest, Father O'Meara, not know of what the tenant had done in connection with the children in the house, but he most strenuously and emphatically condemned it, with tears in his eyes, when it reached his knowledge, and that this was only after the eviction. This episode formed, of course, the chief topic of conversation over that part of the country, and not one of the people said a word of sympathy for this man.

A long delay took place in bringing up the battering ram, for it had to pass many obstacles and be dragged by a strong horse up a difficult slope. Captain Croker, the sheriff, demanded possession formally. A constable stood close to the window, which was suddenly smashed by a blow from inside. More hot water and stirabout were then thrown from the window at the gable end. Col. Turner here said: "I warn these people that the house will be fired into if there is any more of that." A canful of hot meal followed this. Col. Turner ordered up two soldiers and directed them to present arms and added, "if anything more is thrown from that window fire into it." Nothing more for some time was thrown out of the window. The Emergency men placed their ladders to the wall and stuffed straw down into the chimney from which smoke was coming, and the battering ram was now put into position. The tenant meanwhile sat on the hedge smoking and his wife and youngest baby were with some difficulty kept from encroaching too near, while a couple of pigs lapped up the meal from the stones underneath the window. The ram is at least adjusted, and the "boss" emergency man, for so they call him, cries out "Take the word from me—back, away with them!" and thud, thud goes the thundering ram. A breach was quickly made in the walls, when the cries of little children were heard inside. "Back away with them," shouts the emergency man, and again bang goes the beam. Col. Turner stood at the field close by and at once ordered the ram to be stopped. District Inspector Dunning stood close by the breach and Colonel Turner told him to say to the people inside that if they came out quietly they would be dealt with leniently.

The Clare Journal, July 1888

The 1903 Land Act

In Mansion House, Dublin, on January 3, 1903, following a land conference including government and Irish members of Parliament, it was agreed that a system of tenant proprietorship should come into being. The great feudal estates of Ireland would generally be broken up into small holdings. The great landlords, such as the earl of Dunraven with 14,000 acres in Limerick, would receive compensation by annual repayments on purchase loans. As these loans for purchasing properties were generally greater than annual rents, only a small percentage of tenant farmers took the opportunity to buy. Nevertheless, by May 1903, it can be said that a seed change had started. Although the price of land was artificially inflated from the 1903 Land Act with the amending Act of 1909, tenants were able to purchase 9 million acres between 1903 and 1920.

History will ask—Why did not you do it thirty years before? We shall have our answer. We shall point to the divisions and the sharp animosities which have rent and poisoned social life in Ireland, and the misgivings which these divisions and these animosities have, not unnaturally, aroused in English minds here. But after this year, after 1903, after the memorable months through which we have passed, after the occasion offered by the Land Conference, apologists for British statesmen in this respect will seek in vain for defence, explanation or excuse. They will see that the divisions are closing up, that for the social venom an antidote has been found in the general good feeling and in the unity of purpose actuating all by the hope of their common native land. In view of all these conditions, unhoped for but decisive, the load of responsibility will be heavy upon the head of any man who through timidity or callousness or an undue insistence upon some one feature of this many faceted problem tries to impair an opportunity, pregnant, as in my conscience I believe it to be with the best possibilities for that portion of the United Kingdom from which hope and enterprise, the child of hope, have been banished for so long.

George Wyndham, chief secretary of Ireland, Parliamentary Debates (Hansard),
May 7, 1903

Upon independence in 1922, a treaty clause was adopted that the Irish Free State pay twice yearly amounts in compensation to the U.K. government for these loans, a sum of about £5 million per annum. In 1932, the Irish government of de Valéra refused to continue to pay, and the United Kingdom retaliated with an economic war lasting six years. The land annuities dispute, which had harmful effects in Ireland, which was struggling in the worldwide economic depression of the 1930s, was resolved when the Irish Free State agreed to pay a capital sum of £10 million to London.

17

The Insurrection of 1916

By the start of the 1914–1918 Great War, in spite of the Irish Party hold-ing four-fifths of all Irish seats for over forty years, the idea of securing self-government from England by the constitutional means of appealing to the London Parliament seemed remote to most Irish people. Several attempts had been made since 1874 to introduce the Home Rule Bill in Parliament. In 1886, the Irish Party finally succeeded, but the bill was defeated in the House of Commons by 343 votes to 311. In 1893, a second bill passed through the Commons but was then rejected by the House of Lords. In 1912, a third bill was carried, but it was rejected by the House of Lords in 1913. The new Parliament Act of 1911 stipulated that the Lords could delay any parliamentary legislation for only two years.

In 1913, Edward Carson (1854–1935), a Dublin lawyer and Unionist politician, placed his appeal for the Union clearly on a sectarian approach. "Home Rule is Rome Rule" was the slogan. As the Protestants were strongest in the province of Ulster, he helped to form the Ulster Volunteer Force, which pledged to fight the U.K. govern-ment forces if Ireland was allowed self-government. In September 1913, a Provisional Government of Ulster was set up.

"Loyalist" Dealings with the German Kaiser

Sir Edward Carson had the honour of receiving an invitation to launch with the Kaiser last week at Hamburg.

Belfast Telegraph, August 27, 1913

It may not be known to the rank and file of Unionists that we have the offer of aid from a powerful continental monarch who, if Home Rule is forced upon the Protestants of Ireland, is prepared to send an army sufficient to release England of any further trouble in Ireland by attaching it to his dominion, believing, as he does that, if the King breaks his coronation oath by signing the Home Rule Bill he will, by so doing, have forfeited his claim to rule Ireland. And should our King sign the Home Rule Bill, the Protestants of Ireland will welcome this continental deliver as their forefathers, under similar circumstances, did once before.

Irish Churchman (Loyalist Journal), November 14, 1913

In reaction to the formation of the Ulster Volunteer Force (UVF), in November, the Irish Citizen's Army was formed, pledging to fight for a socialist republic. Soon afterward, the Irish Volunteers were formed, initially to fight for Home Rule. The buildup of the UVF alarmed the U.K. government, and orders were given to the army in Ireland to protect military arms depots in Ulster against possible raids. In 1914, fifty-six British army officers led by General Sir Hubert de la Poer Gough (1870–1963) actually mutinied in the military camp at The Curragh. Gough, interpreting the order, declared that under no circumstances would he or his officers enforce Home Rule in Ulster. He even declared that he would rather fight for Ulster than against it. The U.K. government backed down, marking this as the only successful mutiny in the history of the British army.

In April, guns from Germany arrived for the Unionists—thirty-five thousand rifles and five million rounds of ammunition. Lt. Colonel Frederick Crawford (1861–1952), a founder of the Ulster Volunteers and member of the Provisional Government of Ulster, had gone to Hamburg, Germany, to purchase the guns and bring them back to Larne.

I walked up and down the deck, tormented by the thought of all those men waiting for me to bring them the weapons with which to fight for their religion, their liberty and all that was dear to them. . . . I went into my cabin and threw myself on my knees, and in simple language told God all about it; what this meant to Ulster.

Lt. Col. Frederick Crawford, quoted in A. T. Q. Stewart,
The Ulster Crisis, Faber, London, 1967

The Irish Volunteers did not have the finances and contacts of the Unionists, but they, too, negotiated with the Germans for arms. Scraping together donations, they purchased nine hundred rifles and twenty-nine thousand rounds of ammunition, part of which was smuggled into Howth by the novelist Erskine Childers (1870–1922) on

his yacht Asgard. *The* Chotah, *another yacht, brought in the last part of the consign-*
ment that had been transferred from Conor O'Brien's yacht, Kelpie, *which had*
become known to the authorities.

But in August 1914, the start of the Great War presented an ideal opportunity for
the U.K. government and Unionists to persuade the leader of the Irish Parliamentary
Party, John Redmond (1856–1918), to have the Home Rule Act suspended for the
duration of the war. Carson was appointed U.K. attorney general, and, shortly afterward, first lord of the Admiralty. His fellow erstwhile pro-German rebels, named as
the Provisional Government of Ulster, also received U.K. government positions. One
became solicitor general for Ireland, another became lord chancellor of Ireland, others were made high court judges, and several received knighthoods and peerages. It
was a lesson not lost on the nationalists.

The suspension of Home Rule caused an inevitable train of events.

The Sinking of the *Libau* off Queenstown (1916)

Karl Spindler, a lieutenant in the Imperial German Navy, was given command of
Libau in March 1916. He was ordered to sail from Lubeck on April 9, with a cargo
of ten modern machine guns, obsolete Russian rifles, ammunition, and explosives, to
help the Irish Volunteers, secretly controlled by the Irish Republican Brotherhood
with its continuing aim of securing an independent Irish Republic. The ship was dis-
guised as a Norwegian vessel, Aud. *On Good Friday, April 21, Spindler was caught*
by British warships and had to accompany them to Queenstown (Cork) harbor.

The moment, which was to decide our fate, was now at hand. In view of
the dangerous cargo, which we carried above the explosive bombs, I had
to reckon with the fact that when I blew up the ship we might all be blown
to bits. I therefore passed the word that I required our volunteers to blow
up the ship and hoist the German naval flag, but that the others were free
to lower a boat just before the explosion was timed to take place. A unanimous, almost angry, "No!" was the answer. "We will stay with the captain
till the end." It is a great satisfaction to me to express here to my brave crew
my thanks for their fidelity. . . .

The ship's pennant was already waving from the mainmast and next
moment the German naval ensign was run up, bidding defiance to the
British and all their works. . . . Then there was a muffled explosion. The
Aud [Libau] shivered from stem to stern, beams and splinters flew up in
the air, followed by a cloud of dirty grey smoke, and flames burst forth
from the saloon, the charthouse, the ventilators and the forecastle. . . .

It required our utmost efforts to get clear of the sinking ship. While we were busy doing this there was a second violent explosion amidships. Several more followed, accompanied by clouds of thick sulphurous smoke. The munitions were probably catching fire. If we did not get clear soon the whole ship might blow up round our heads. The crew gave way with a will. Suddenly a gun roared. The *Bluebell* [*HMS Bluebell*] had spoken. We could not see where the shell struck, for the forward part of the *Aud* which projected out of the water, interrupted our view. All we could see was that the ships at the quay were steaming towards us.

Any resistance would only lead to foolish and useless bloodshed (for we were defenceless and at the mercy of an infinitely superior foe). I had expressly ordered that a white flag was to be shown immediately if we succeeded in launching the boats—this in accordance with the instructions of my superior officers. The order was carried out. . . .

About five minutes after the first explosion a dull, rumbling noise came from the *Aud*. The cargo and bunkers were shifting. The masts tottered. The blazing bow rose perpendicularly out of the water and next moment the Aud, as if drawn down by an invisible hand, sank with a loud hissing noise. Our good old *Libau* was no more.

Captain Karl Spindler, *The Mystery of the Casement Ship*, Berlin, 1931

Spindler and his crew spent the next two years in a prisoner-of-war camp in England. However, with another German naval officer and an Austrian army officer, Spindler escaped from the POW camp near Derby. They were recaptured near Nottingham.

Proclamation of the Irish Republic (1916)

By noon on Easter Monday, April 24, 1916, the Irish Republican Brotherhood's Military Council had dispatched units of the Irish Volunteers and Irish Citizen Army, now united as the Army of the Irish Republic, to prepared positions in Dublin City. Because of conflicting orders, only a few units outside of Dublin responded to the mobilization. The leaders, including Pádraic Pearse and James Connolly, took positions in the General Post Office building in O'Connell Street as the insurgent headquarters. At 12:45 P.M., Tom Clarke handed the Proclamation of the Irish Republic to Pearse, and, accompanied by an armed guard, he stood on the steps of the GPO and read the Proclamation to the people gathered outside. A young Dublin medical student, Ernan (Ernie) O'Malley (1898–1957), originally from Mayo, went to investigate.

In O'Connell Street large groups of people were gathered together. From the flagstaff pole on top of the General Post Office, the GPO, floated a new flag, a tricolour one of green, white and orange, the colours running out from the mast.

"What's it all about?" I asked a man who stood near me, a scowl on his face.

"Those boyhoes, [sic] the Volunteers, have seized the Post Office. They want nothing less than a Republic," he laughed scornfully. "They've killed some Lancers; but they'll soon run away when the soldiers come."

Thin strands of barbed wire ran out in front of the Post Office. Two sentries in green uniforms and slouched hats stood on guard with fixed bayonets. They seemed cool enough. Behind them the windows had been smashed. Heavy mail bags half-filled the spaces, rifle barrels projected, officers in uniform with yellow tabs could be seen hurrying through the rooms. Outside men were carrying in heavy bundles—"explosives, I bet, or ammunition," said a man beside me. Others unloaded provisions and vegetables and carried food inside. On the flat roof sentries patrolled to and fro. Men on motor bicycles, uniformed and in civilian clothes, arrived frequently and the sentries made a lane for them through the crowd.

I walked up the street. Behind Nelson's pillar lay dead horses, some with their feet in the air, others lying flat. "The Lancers' horses," an old man said, although I had not spoken. "Those fellows," pointing with his right hand toward the GPO, "are not going to be frightened by a troop of Lancers. They mean business." Seated on a dead horse was a woman, a shawl around her head, untidy wisps of hair straggled across her dirty face. She swayed slowly, drunk, singing.

> Boys in Khaki, Boys in Blue,
> Here's the best of Jolly Good Luck to You.

On the base of the Pillar was a white poster. Gathered around were groups of men and women. Some looked at it with serious faces, others laughed and sniggered. I began to read it with a smile, but my smile ceased as I read.

Ernie O'Malley, *On Another Man's Wound*, London, 1936

Poblacht na hÉireann
The Provisional Government

Of the
IRISH REPUBLIC
To the People of Ireland

Irishmen and Irishwomen: In the name of God and of the dead generations from which she receives her old tradition of nationhood, Ireland, through us, summons her children to her flag and strikes for her freedom.

Having organised and trained her manhood through her secret revolutionary organisation, the Irish Republican Brotherhood, and through her open military organisations, the Irish Volunteers and the Irish Citizen Army, having patiently perfected her discipline, having resolutely waited for the right moment to reveal itself, she now seizes that moment, and, supported by her exiled children in America and by gallant allies in Europe, but relying in the first on her own strength, she strikes in full confidence of victory.

We declare the right of the people of Ireland to the ownership of Ireland, and to the unfettered control of Irish destinies, to be sovereign and indefeasible. The long usurpation of that right by a foreign people and government has not extinguished the right, nor can it ever be extinguished except by the destruction of the Irish people. In every generation the Irish people have asserted their right to national freedom and sovereignty; six times during the past three hundred years they have asserted it in arms. Standing on that fundamental right and again asserting it in arms in the face of the world, we hereby proclaim the Irish republic as a sovereign independent state, and we pledge our lives and the lives of our comrades-in-arms to the cause of its freedom, of its welfare, and of its exultation among the nations.

The Irish Republic is entitled to, and hereby claims, the allegiance of every Irishman and Irishwoman. The republic guarantees religious and civil liberty, equal rights and equal opportunities to all its citizens, and declares its resolve to pursue the happiness and prosperity of the whole nation and of all its parts, cherishing all the children of the nation equally, and oblivious of the differences carefully fostered by an alien government, which have divided a minority from the majority in the past.

Until our arms have brought the opportune moment for the establishment of a permanent national government representative of the whole people of Ireland, and elected by the suffrage of all her men and women, the Provisional Government, hereby constituted, will administer the civil and military affairs of the republic in trust for the people. We place the cause of the Irish Republic under the protection of the Most high God, whose blessings we invoke upon our arms, and we pray that no one who serves that cause will dishonour it by cowardice, inhumanity or rapine. In this supreme hour the Irish nation must by its valour and discipline, and by the readiness of its children to sacrifice themselves for the common good, prove itself worthy of the august destiny to which it is called.

Signed on behalf of the provisional government,

Thomas J. Clarke, Seán MacDiarmada, Thomas MacDonough, P. H. Pearse, Eamon Ceannt, James Connolly, Joseph Plunket
National Library Proclamations, Dublin

Monday, April 24, at St. Stephen's Green

The insurgent garrison at St. Stephen's Green was commanded by Michael Mallin of the Citizen Army and by Countess Markiwicz (neé Gore-Booth, 1868–1927), the only woman who fought as an armed combatant in the uprising.

As I drew near the Green (St Stephen's Green) rifle fire began like sharply cracking whips. It was from the further side. I saw the gates were closed and men standing inside with guns on their shoulders. I passed a house, the windows of which were smashed. As I went by a man in civilian clothes slipped through the Park gates, which instantly closed behind him. He ran towards me, and I halted. He was carrying two small packets in his hand. He passed me hurriedly, and, placing his leg inside the broken window of the house behind me, he disappeared. Almost immediately another man in civilian clothes appeared from the broken window of another house. He also had something (I don't know what) in his hand. He ran urgently towards the gates, which opened, admitted him, and closed again.

In the centre of this side of the Park a rough barricade of carts and motor cars had been stretched. It was full of gaps. Behind it was a halted tram, and along the vistas of the Green one saw other trams derelict, untenanted.

I came to the barricade. As I reached it and stood by the Shelbourne Hotel, which it faced, a loud cry came from the Park. The gates opened and three men ran out. Two of them held rifles with fixed bayonets. The third gripped a heavy revolver in his fist. They ran towards the motor car, which had just turned the corner, and halted it. The men with bayonets took position instantly on either side of the car. The man with the revolver saluted, and I heard him begging the occupants to pardon him, and directing them to dismount. A man and woman got down. They were again saluted and requested to go on the sidewalk. They did so.

The man crossed and stood by me. He was very tall and thin, middle-aged, with a shaven, wasted face. "I wanted to get down to Armagh today," he said to no one in particular. The loose bluish skin under his eyes was twitching. The Volunteers directed the chauffeur to drive to the barricade and lodge his car in a particular position there. He did it awkwardly, and after three attempts he succeeded in pleasing them. He was a big, brown-faced man, whose knees were rather high for the seat he was in, and they jerked with the speed and persistence of something moved with a power-ful spring. His face was composed and fully under command, although his legs were not. He locked the car into the barricade, and then, being a man accustomed to be commanded, he awaited an order to descend. When the order came he walked directly to his master, still preserving all the solem-nity of his features. These two men did not address a word to each other, but their drilled and expressionless eyes were loud with surprise and fear and rage. They went into the hotel.

I spoke to the man with the revolver. He was no more than a boy, not more certainly than twenty years of age, short in stature, with close curling red hair and blue eyes—kindly looking lad. The strap on his sombrero had torn loose on one side, and except while he held it in his teeth it flapped about his chin. His face was sunburnt and grimy with dust and sweat.

This young man did not appear to me to be acting from his reason. He was doing his work from a determination implanted previously, days, weeks perhaps, on his imagination. His mind was—where? It was not with his body. And continually his eyes went searching widely, looking for spaces, scanning hastily the clouds, the vistas of the streets, looking for something that did not hinder him, looking away for a moment from the immediacies and rigours which were impressed where his mind had been.

When I spoke he looked at me, and I know that for some seconds he did not see me. I said:

"What is the meaning of all this? What has happened?"

He replied collectedly enough in speech, but with that ramble and errancy clouding his eyes.

"We have taken the city. We are expecting an attack from the military at any moment, and those people," he indicated knots of men, women and children clustered towards the end of the Green, "won't go home for me.

We have the Post Office, and the Railways and the Castle. We have all the city. We have everything."

James Stephens (1882–1950), *Insurrection in Dublin*, New York, 1916

At night the din increased; artillery was being used. I slipped out of bed, got quietly over the back wall and went down town. There were few people out. "It's dangerous to go near O'Connell Street," a man said, "three people have been badly wounded near the Parnell Monument." I reached the monument and turned in to Moore Street. From the GPO came the sound of cheering, then a voice singing:

> Then here's to their memory—may it be
> For us a guiding light,
> To cheer our strife for liberty,
> And teach us to unite!
> Through good and ill, be Ireland's still,
> Though sad as those your fate;
> And true men, like you, men,
> Like those of Ninety-Eight.

Men took up the chorus; their voices echoed through the bullet noise. The unlit streets gave a strange quality to the words, the chorus zoomed in a loud shadow between rifle crashes. I felt I should like to join in that song.

I stood near the Pillar. I heard a voice say, "Run for it, quick," and I ran. The houses on either side of Mary Street swayed.

"We were trying to blow up the Pillar," said a uniformed officer of the Citizen Army in Moore Street. "It's too good a guide to warships in the bay or the artillery over there," pointing across towards the Liffey. But the Pillar remained.

"How's the fight going?" I asked.

"We hold Boland's Mill, the College of Surgeons and posts on the South Side. The English have landed and are trying to fight their way through, but they have been held up."

"And when they get through?"

"Oh, well, when they do it will be hot here." He said goodbye in Irish and walked towards the GPO.

I went back home in the early morning and got into bed, unnoticed, save by my brothers. I felt stirrings of sympathy as I wrote in my diary. I did not feel indifferent now to the men holding Dublin.

The shelling and noise increased. The people seemed a little cowed as if they did not understand what it was all about. Civilians fell wounded here and there; the presence of death was close. Military posts pushed on slowly down the city. Spent bullets fell around and the whirring noise of live ones could be heard. I tried to get down to the centre of the city, but I could not get through the cordons. In the evening I was in a whirl; my mind jumped from a snatch of song to a remembered page of economic history. I walked up and down the garden at the back of our house. Distant sounds of firing had new sounds that echoed in my head. They meant something personal; they made me angry. The men down there were right, that I felt sure of. They had a purpose, which I did not share. But no one had a right to Ireland except the Irish. In the city Irishmen were fighting British troops against long odds. I was going to help them in some way.

Ernie O'Malley, On Another Man's Wound, London, 1936

British Soldiers' Behavior

The South Staffordshire Regiment was accused of perpetrating systematic killings of local residents as they advanced, particularly in the North King Street area. Sarah Hughes and her family lived at 172 North King Street. On April 29, British soldiers advancing into Dublin demanded entrance to her house, where she lived with her husband, Michael, and three children.

I had 18 refugees, namely, Walsh, his wife and four children, one old man, a blind man and his son aged 16 years, Mrs O'Neill and her son, all these people had to leave their homes as they were sent from their houses by the Sinn Féiners [a euphemism for republican insurgents] and I took them in and gave them shelter.

When the military entered my premises, they first thoroughly searched the shop, they then came into my kitchen, they looked around there, and then proceeded upstairs. We were all in the back drawing room to escape the heavy firing as the Sinn Féiners were firing from the distillery.

One of the soldiers that entered my place, a Corporal and a Sergeant, they searched my husband also the man Walsh, one of the soldiers said give those Irish pigs an ounce of lead. . . . The military put all women and children down to the cellars, including myself.

I heard the man Walsh saying what are you doing that for. I understood they were taking the men prisoners and handcuffing them, let any human being think over it, one man taken into the drawing room and shot dead. My poor husband was brought to the top of the house and instantly shot dead for no crime at all, it was murder and cool blooded murder there is no other word for it.

Sarah Hughes's statement, written July 19, 1916, printed in Brian Barton, From Behind a Closed Door: Secret Court Martial Records of the 1916 Easter Rising, The Blackstaff Press, Belfast, 2002

Miss Anne Fennel, also of North King Street, reported that two officers and some thirty soldiers burst into her house.

I nearly fell on the ground and clasped the officer's hand in terror but he flung me off. As poor Mrs Ennis saw her husband [George Ennis] being led upstairs she clung to him and refused to be parted from him, and said, "I must go up with my husband." One of the soldiers pulled her off and put a bayonet to her ear and uttered the foulest language. She said, "You would not kill a woman, would you?" He shouted, "Keep quiet, you bloody bitch." After a long time, it must have been a couple of hours, we heard a noise at the parlour door, and to our horror, poor Mr Ennis crawled in. I will never forget. He was dying, bleeding to death, and when the military left the house he had crept down the stairs to see his wife for the last time. He was covered with blood and his eyes were rolling in his head.

Statement in Sir Matthew Nathan Papers, manuscript, Bodleian Library, Oxford

Sean O'Casey (1880–1964), soon to become a playwright, was an Irish-language enthusiast and Socialist. He had been secretary of the Irish Citizen Army. In 1916, however, he failed to support the insurrection and thereafter claimed that Connolly and the Irish Citizen Army had betrayed their socialism to join the "bourgeoisie nationalists." His Shadow of a Gunman *in 1923 caused riots at the Abbey Theatre. He left for London in 1926 to become a full-time writer. His subsequent plays did not have the success of his first three Dublin plays.*

In the sky the flames were soaring higher, till the heavens looked like a great ruby hanging from God's ear. It was tingeing the buildings like a scarlet glow, while the saints stretched their ears to catch the tenor of the Irish prayers going up, for each paternoster and Ave Maria mingled with the biting snarl from the Howth guns and the answering roar from Saxon rifle, machine-gun and cannon, that were weaving a closer cordon of fire round the Sinn Féiners, the fire creeping towards the group of innocent blessed with arms in their hands for the first time. . . .

The grey-green Volunteer uniforms now no longer looked neat; they were ragged and powdered thick with pulverised mortar clouding from the walls. The fighters now looked like automatons moving unsteadily about, encased tightly in a fog of dust and acrid ashes. They were silent, unshaven, maybe muttering an act of contrition for things done before they went to war, wan eyed, they persuaded their drooping lids to lift again, for drowsiness might mean a sudden and silent death to them.

Sean O'Casey (autobiography), Drums Under the Window, London, 1945

The Murder of Francis Sheehy Skeffington

Francis Sheehy Skeffington (1878–1916) was a Socialist, pacifist, and feminist; a journalist; and an author of fiction and nonfiction. He was editor of The Nationalist *and* The Irish Citizen. *He was a regular contributor to the* Manchester Guardian *(England),* L'Humanité *(France), and* Call *(United States) and was well known internationally. He was sympathetic to the republican movement but had campaigned on a nonviolent platform. When the rising broke up, he tried to organize citizens to stop looting in the city.*

Thursday, April 27, 1916

I met D.H. [Douglas Hyde]. His chief emotion is one of astonishment at the organising powers displayed by the Volunteers. We have exchanged rumours, and found that our equipment in this direction is almost identical. He says Sheehy Skeffington has been killed. That he was arrested in a house wherein arms were found and was shot out of hand.

I hope this is another rumour, for, so far as my knowledge of him goes, he was not with the Volunteers, and it is said that he was antagonistic to the forcible methods for which the Volunteers stood. But the tale of his death is so persistent that one is inclined to believe it.

He was the most absurdly courageous man I have ever met with or heard of. . . .

Later on this day I met Mrs Sheehy Skeffington in the street. She confirmed the rumour that her husband had been arrested on the previous day, but further than that she had no news.

James Stephens, The Insurrection in Dublin, New York, 1916

The facts emerged at an inquiry. Sheehy Skeffington had actually saved the life of
Second Lt. Guy Pinfield of the 8th Hussars, stanching a wound under heavy fire. His
nonviolent beliefs made him help friend and foe alike. Between 6 and 7 P.M. on
Tuesday, April 25, he walked home and was stopped by a British army checkpoint
and taken to Portobello Barracks. A battalion of the Royal Irish Rifles was holding it,
some three hundred men commanded by Major Rossborough. But the senior officer
commanding the barracks was Major Sir Francis Fletcher Vane Bart. He had arrived
to take charge on April 24.

During the first day of the Rebellion it was day and night work, my clothes
were never taken off. . . . The work could not have been done but for the
loyal assistance of the two young officers who came with me, Lieutenants
Maunsell and Kelly. . . .

It was on one of the raids namely to place an observation post on the
Tower of the Rathmines Town Hall, that I first received information about
the shooting of Messrs Sheehy Skeffington, McIntyre and Doyle, on
Wednesday, 26th April. While marching through a semi-hostile crowd on
returning to Barracks, several men with that directness which charac-
terises the Irish, shouted: "Murderer, Murderer!" I have been called many
names in my life, but had up to then never been accused of this offence.
Perhaps this was the reason that it stuck in my memory, and consequently
on arrival in Barracks, made careful inquiries among my young officers.
Then the truth came out that this same morning, Captain Bowen-
Colthurst had gone to the Guardhouse, ordered the three men out, and
had them shot against the wall.

Major Sir Francis Fletcher Vane Bart, in *Agin the Governments:*
Memories and Adventures, London, 1927

Sheehy Skeffington had fallen under the scrutiny of Captain J. C. Bowen-Colthurst
of the Royal Irish Rifles, who upon seeing Skeff's "Votes for Women" badge declaimed
him as a dangerous radical. Sheehy Skeffington was held with two other journalists
named Thomas Dickson and Patrick MacIntyre, both unconnected with the nation-
alist movement in Ireland; in fact, they were editors of pro-Unionist newspapers. On
Tuesday, Bowen-Colthurst took the prisoners on a raid as hostages. At Rathmines
Church, Bowen-Colthurst shot a seventeen-year-old youth named Coade after the
boy's jaw had been broken by a soldier who smashed the side of Coade's face with his
rifle butt; he then wrecked the premises of Alderman James Kelly, wrongly believing
him to be a Sinn Féin Alderman. Another Dublin town councillor, Richard
O'Carroll, was also shot by Bowen-Colthurst and left for dead in the gutter.
O'Carroll later died.

The party returned to Portobello Barracks. At 10:05 A.M., Captain Bowen-Colthurst came to the guardroom and ordered Sergeant William Aldridge to bring the prisoners to the barracks yard. With an escort party, he ordered the prisoners to walk to the wall, then ordered the escort to present arms and fire. Lieutenant Dobbyn, hearing the shots, came into the yard. Bowen-Colthurst was observed to be calm. Dobbyn noticed there was movement in Sheehy Skeffington's leg and reported this. Bowen-Colthurst ordered him to be shot again. Major Vane, now learning these facts, ordered Bowen-Colthurst to be confined to barracks pending an official inquiry.

The next day as will be related, was occupied by the fight for the [South Dublin] Union.

In my absence from Barracks on duty, without informing me, or Major Rossborough, an officer, Colonel A—was sent from Dublin Castle, who took a party of men from my command, with Captain Colthurst, to raid the house of Mrs Skeffington. No doubt this was done to attempt to find proof that the shooting was justified. The responsibility for this irregular action rests entirely with the superior authorities, and is a further proof that they were behind the actions of Colthurst, who was their instrument. The raid was carried out "in the most brutal manner" according to the finding of the Royal Commission, but of that, of course, the writer cannot speak except in so far as what some of the officers and Mrs Skeffington told him. They naturally found nothing, except an old photograph of the Kaiser, for poor Skeffington was a pacifist of the most extreme type—and entirely opposed to the rebellion. His two fellow victims were editors of Unionist papers, I believe!

On Sunday [April 30] a party of Royal Engineers, again without my knowledge, was sent from Dublin castle at night to repair the wall against which the men were shot. They did their work very artistically, for I examined it afterwards, no doubt with the object that the facts might be denied. The next day [May 1] I was summoned to the Orderly Room and then was informed by a Colonel Maccamond, who had taken over command of the troops from Major Rossborough, that I would be relieved of my duties with the Defences, and would hand them over to Captain Bowen-Colthurst! I was neither surprised nor sorry to be freed from this work, especially as my duty was an emergency one, and the Rebellion was over in Dublin, but it was astonishing to be asked to hand over to an officer who, in an ordinary way, should have been under arrest pending Court Martial for four murders. This was placed before the Colonel, stating that

I wished to hand my duty over to a responsible officer—but was informed that he was a capable person and it would be all right. Thence I proceeded to the Royal Hospital to report the murders to General Sir John Maxwell who a few days earlier had been sent to Dublin to take over the Irish command. He either could not or would not see me so I proceeded to the Park Gate Headquarters to report to someone. There I was relegated for my report to a Major [Ivor] Price, Chief Intelligence Officer. Having stated the facts to him (which of course he knew all about) he had the impudence to say that he would note them but he thought that men like Skeffington were just as well out of the way. "Thank you," I said, "then my line of action is clear."

. . . I went to the office of the Adjutant General, a man known to me since boyhood, and asked for eight days' leave to go to London, which was granted. But in a conversation with him I became convinced that they were going to do an even more stupid thing. He said that we are going to have a bloody revenge on these rebels—the leaders had surrendered two days before—which made me sad, remembering in history '98 and other Irish rebellions. Anyway, I left by the night mail on Monday, arriving in London Tuesday morning, 2nd May. There were two reasons, which perhaps should be stated for going at once to London Headquarters. The first and most important was that the Army as a whole should not be blamed for acts of an individual or group of individuals at Dublin Castle.

> Major Sir Francis Fletcher Vane Bart, in *Agin the Governments: Memories and Adventures*, London, 1927

Report of Major-General A. E. Sandbach, commanding British troops in the Dublin area, May 3:

Captain Bowen-Colthurst seems to have carried out his duties with discretion.

> Public Records Office, Kew, W0 30/67

In London, Sir Francis Fletcher Vane Bart managed to use personal connections to secure an interview with Field Marshal Lord Kitchener and Mr. Bonham Carter, private secretary to the prime minister:

Kitchener was very pleasant, but when he was told the facts it was clear he could not at first believe them. "Why have I not been informed?" he said, "and why is the officer not under arrest?" It had happened a week before. To the latter query I could only reply: "That is the very reason why I am in England, to ask you, sir, why he is not under arrest." Lord Kitchener then dictated to Bonham Carter a telegram to be sent to HQ, Ireland, ordering Colthurst to be placed under arrest pending trial by Court Martial. This fact, which I saw with my own eyes, was denied four times by Mr. (now Lord) Forster in the House of Commons.

Major Sir Francis Fletcher Vane Bart, in *Agin the Governments: Memories and Adventures*, London, 1927

Politician Henry William Forster (1866–1936) became Baron Forster in 1920 and was appointed governor general of Australia. On May 18, the lord chief justice of England, Lord Reading, agreed that a military court should deal with the matter in camera so that the government would be spared a public hearing. It was held immediately at Victoria Barracks, Belfast.

Statement of Captain Bowen-Colthurst

I knew of the sedition which had been preached in Ireland for years past and I was credibly informed that unarmed soldiers had been shot down in the streets of Dublin by rebels; on Wednesday morning (26th) all this was in my mind; I was very much exhausted and unstrung after a practically sleepless night. I took the gravest view of the situation and I did not think it possible that troops would arrive from England in time to prevent a general massacre. I was convinced that prompt action was necessary to ensure that these men should not escape and further spread disaffection. It was impossible for me to move the prisoners to a more secure place of confinement owing to the armed rebels having possession of the streets all around the barracks; believing that I had the power under martial law, I felt under the circumstances that it was clearly my duty to order these men to be shot.

Statement Public Records Office, Kew WO 30/67

I never imagined for one moment that the men could actually have been killed by design. But having since read the evidence of Sergt. J. Aldridge the act appears to me in quite a different light and if this latter statement is true, then the officer in question used no discretion.

Major General A. E. Sandbach commanding troops in Dublin
Statement of May 16, Public Records Office, Kew WO 30/67

Found guilty but insane, Captain Bowen-Colthurst was confined to Broadmoor Criminal Hospital for a year, then allowed to emigrate to Canada, where he died in 1965. Mrs. Hanna Sheehy Skeffington was offered £10,000 compensation for the death of her husband, which she refused. As the news began to seep out, Theodore Roosevelt (1858–1919), twenty-sixth president of the United States (1901–1909), could not believe it, and on January 18, 1917, wrote to Major Vane via the U.S. ambassador in London, Walter H. Page, asking for confirmation of the facts: "I have unhesitatingly condemned the Germans for the atrocities they have committed; I have always announced that I would just as strongly condemn atrocities of like character committed by the Allies."

Sunday, April 30, 1916: The insurrection has not ceased.

There is much rifle fire, but no sound from the machine guns or the eighteen pounds and trench mortars.

From the window of my kitchen the flag of the Republic can be seen flying afar. This is the flag that flies over Jacob's Biscuit Factory, and will know that the insurrection has ended as soon as I see this flag pulled down. . . .

It is half past three o'clock, and from my window the Republican flag can still be seen flying over Jacob's factory. There is occasional shooting, but the city as a whole is quiet.

At a quarter to five o'clock a heavy gun boomed once. Ten minutes later there was heavy machine gun firing and much rifle shooting. In another ten minutes the flag at Jacob's factory was hauled down.

James Stephens (1882–1950), *Insurrection in Dublin*, New York, 1916

The estimated cost in life was 254 civilians, 116 British soldiers, 17 Royal Irish Constabulary (RIC), and 60 known insurgents. More than 2,600 people had been wounded. There were 3,430 men and 79 women arrested; 1,836 men and 5 women were interned. Of the insurgents tried by court-martial, 99 were sentenced to death, of which 16 sentences were carried out, 15 of them by firing squad, before public outcry halted the process. Roger Casement was hanged in Pentonville Prison, London, on August 3. His remains were returned to Ireland in 1965, as an act of reconciliation, and given a state funeral. Additionally, 122 insurgents were sentenced to varying terms of imprisonment. The authorities were also beginning to intern suspects.

The Death Sentence of Pádraic Pearse

Pearse (1879–1916), son of an English sculptor who had settled in Ireland and favored Home Rule, was an educationalist and writer (poet, playwright, and essayist) both in Irish and English. Called to the Irish bar, Pearse rejected law and threw his energies into education, founding a bilingual school at Ranelagh, Scoil Eanna, which prospered. A member of the Irish Republican Brotherhood (IRB), he gave the stirring oration at the graveside of O'Donovan Rossa in 1915. He was appointed commander in chief of the forces of the Irish Republic and president of the provisional government. After the surrender, he was executed in Kilmainham Jail on May 3, 1916. His court-martial was presided over by Brigadier Charles G. Blackader, commanding the 177th Infantry Division.

General Blackader Admires Pearse

He came to dinner one night greatly depressed. I asked him: "What is the matter?" He answered: "I have just done one of the hardest tasks I have ever had to do. I have had to condemn to death one of the finest characters I have ever come across. There must be something very wrong in the state of things that makes a man like that [Pádraic Pearse] rebel. I don't wonder that his pupils adore him!"

Elizabeth, countess of Fingall, in *Seventy Years Young*, London, 1937

Joseph Plunkett's Marriage on the Eve of Execution

Joseph Mary Plunkett (1887–1916), an admired poet, was the son of George, Count Plunkett. After graduation from University College Dublin, he traveled in Italy, Egypt, and Algeria. In spite of ill health, he joined the IRB and Irish Volunteers upon his return to Ireland. In 1915, he undertook a mission to Berlin to try and secure arms and aid for the rising. Seriously ill, he nevertheless took his place in the GPO. He had become engaged to the artist and feminist Grace Gifford (1888–1955). Her sister, Muriel, was married to the poet and playwright Thomas McDonagh, who had just been executed on May 3. Grace and Joseph had intended to marry during Easter Week. Joseph made his marriage a last request.

I entered Kilmainham Jail on Wednesday, May 3, at 6 p.m., and was detained there till about 11.30 p.m. when I saw him for the first time in the prison chapel, where the marriage was gone through and no speech allowed. He was taken back to his cell and I left the prison. . . . I went to bed at 1.30 and was wakened at 2 o'clock by a policeman, with a letter from the prison Commandant—Major [W. S.] Lennon—asking me to visit Joseph Plunkett. I was brought there in a motor, and saw my husband in his cell, the interview occupying ten minutes. During the interview the cell was packed with officers, and a sergeant, who kept a watch in his hand and closed the interview by saying "Your time is now up."

Grace Gifford Plunkett interview, in R. M. Fox, *Rebel Irishwomen*, London, 1967

Father Eugene McCarthy had conducted the marriage. Plunkett was executed between 4 and 4:30 A.M. on Thursday, May 4, 1916. Those executed by firing squad were: on May 3, Pádraic Pearse (b. 1879), a poet, playwright, and schoolteacher; Thomas J. Clarke (b. 1857), a former IRB prisoner and a tobacconist/newsagent; and Thomas MacDonagh (b. 1878), a poet and playwright. On May 4, Joseph Mary Plunkett (b. 1887), a poet; Edward Daly (b. 1891), a clerk; William Pearse (b. 1881), an art teacher and Pádraic's brother; and Michael Hanrahan (b. 1877), a journalist and novelist. On May 5, John MacBride (b. 1865), a former major in the army of the Transvaal Republic and official in the Dublin waterworks company. On May 8, Eamon Ceannt (b. 1881), a language teacher; Michael Mallin (b. 1880), a secretary of the Silk Weavers' Union; Con Colbert (b. 1888), a baker; and Seán Heuston (b. 1891), a railway clerk. On May 9, Thomas Kent (b. 1867), a landowner. On May 17, James Connolly (b. 1868), a trade union leader and leading Marxist theoretician and writer; and Sean MacDiarmada (b. 1884), a business manager of the newspaper Irish Freedom.

Casement: The Final Execution

Roger Casement, born in Dublin in 1864, came in for a great deal of vitriol and "black propaganda" still argued over today. He had achieved distinction by reporting on the inhuman treatment of native workers in the Belgian Congo, then on the cruelties practiced on the natives by white traders in the Peruvian rubber plantations. He was knighted in 1911 for his services and retired from the colonial service in 1912. He had never disguised his nationalism, he joined the Irish Volunteers in 1913, and he was instrumental in trying to secure German aid for the uprising. He had landed from the U19 on Banna Strand, County Kerry, on Good Friday, April 20, but was almost immediately picked up, taken to London, and tried for high treason. The prosecuting attorney was, ironically, Frederick Edwin Smith (later Lord Birkenhead, 1872–1920), who had served in the Ulster Volunteer Force as aide-de-camp to Edward Carson.

In Ireland alone, in this twentieth century, is loyalty held to be a crime. If loyalty be something less than love and more than law, then we have had enough of such loyalty for Ireland or Irishmen. Self-government is our right, a thing born in us at birth, a thing no more to be doled out to us or withheld from us by another people than the right to life itself—the right to feel the sun or smell the flowers, or love our kind. It is only from the convict these things are withheld, for crime committed and proven—and Ireland, that has wronged no man, that has injured no land, that has sought no dominion over others—Ireland is being treated to-day among the nations of the world as if she were a convicted criminal. If it be treason to fight against such an unnatural fate as this, then I am proud to be a rebel, and shall cling to my "rebellion," with the last drop of my blood.

Roger Casement, *Speeches from the Dock*, ed. T. D., A. M., and D. B. Sullivan, revised ed., Dublin, 1968

Public outrage at the protracted executions swung opinion in Ireland, especially when James Connolly—badly wounded in the fighting—was carried to the execution yard on a stretcher and strapped to a chair to keep him upright while he was shot. But the change in public opinion and the campaign led by the writer George Bernard Shaw—a friend of Casement's and others—failed to stop his execution. He was hanged in London on August 3, 1916. His body was finally returned to Ireland in 1965 as an act of reconciliation.

George Bernard Shaw Comments on the Rising

An Irishman resorting to arms to achieve the independence of his country is only doing what Englishmen will do, if it be their misfortune to be invaded and conquered by the Germans in the course of the present war. Further, such an Irishman is as much in order, morally, in accepting assistance from the Germans as England is in accepting the assistance of Russia in her struggle with Germany.

George Bernard Shaw, *Daily News*, May 10, 1916

As I was passing a street near the Castle cheer after cheer could be heard. I looked ahead. A regiment was approaching. People were leaning from their windows waving triangular flags and handkerchiefs. "They are cheering the soldiers," I said to my companion. . . . As the main body approached I could see that the soldiers were escorting a large number of prisoners, men and women, several hundreds in all. The people were cheering not the soldiers but the rebels. . . .

I spoke to a little group of men and women at the street corner. "Shure, we cheer them," said one woman. "Why shouldn't we? Aren't they our own flesh and blood?"

I have read many accounts of public feeling in Dublin in these days. They are all agreed that the open and strong sympathy of the mass of the population was with the British troops. That this was so in the better parts of the city, I have no doubt, but certainly what I myself saw in the poorer districts did not confirm this. It rather indicated that there was a vast amount of sympathy with the rebels, particularly after the rebels were defeated.

F. A. McKenzie (a Canadian journalist), *The Irish Rebellion: What Happened and Why?* London, 1916

Frongoch Internment Camp (1916)

Within a few weeks, 3,500 prisoners had been rounded up, including 79 women, but a third of these were immediately released. Although 122 Irish insurgents had been sentenced and were distributed throughout the English prison system, 1,706 were to be interned in England. It was decided to use a camp for German prisoners of war at Frongoch, in Gwynedd, Wales, to take some of the Irish internees. There were two camps, the North Camp and the South Camp, and these were put in the charge of Colonel F. A. Heygate, an Eton-educated soldier who was a poet, novelist, and historian. He was known as "Buckshot" to the Irish internees. By August 1916, there were 600 internees in the camp, including Michael Collins (1890–1922), J. J. "Ginger" O'Connell (1887–1944), and W. J. Brennan Whitmore (1886–1977)—the names read like a roll call of famous leaders in the subsequent War of Independence.

We were roused at 5:30 A.M. by a steam horn in the inner yard. The British Provost Guard unlocked the dormitories almost immediately. It then became the duty of the Staff Officers and Company Commanders in each dormitory to see that all men quitted bed and got ready for morning inspection. By 6:10 A.M. we had the men drawn up in columns of fours in the inner yard, with our Camp Commandant at the head, and the Adjutant and aide-de-camp on the flank.

The British Orderly Officer of the Day, accompanied by a sergeant and three files of the Guard and the Sergeant of the British Provost Guard on duty, then arrived; and having disposed of the three files in advantageous position, the officer and Provost Sergeant proceeded to count us. The Sergeant of the Guard followed the officer pretty closely.

This counting always afforded us amusement. They never got the number right on the first count and frequently had to count us the third time. We always maintained that their inability to count the prisoners correctly accounted for the large number of German prisoners whom they were reported to have captured. One of the Officers of the Guard, a second lieutenant, was a never failing source of amusement to us, He had a vitriolic temper; and was nearly always abusing the Guard. For this reason the prisoners nicknamed him "Brimstone." One morning this officer was counting us, a prisoner gave way to a fit of coughing. Instantly Brimstone yelled out in a voice of thunder: "Stop that damned coughing." He had hardly finished when every prisoner in the guard was seized with a violent fit of coughing. For the best part of ten minutes pandemonium reigned supreme. When at last the hubbub ceased Brimstone yelled out: "I hate idiots; I loathe fools" and shaking his fist at us, took his departure.

Commandant W. J. Brennan Whitmore, With the Irish in Frongoch, Dublin, 1917

18

The War of Independence, 1919–1921

D ue to public misconceptions, the 1916 uprising was wrongly credited to Sinn Féin (We Ourselves, indicating self-reliance). It was a political party that had been formed by Arthur Griffith in 1905 as a dual monarchist party. Griffith (1871–1922) envisaged the Austro-Hungarian concept, in which the separate self-governing states of Austria and Hungary, coming together in 1867, shared power over the old Austrian Empire as a dual monarchy. Griffith, not really a republican, was imprisoned with those who had fought in the Rising. By 1917, public perception of 1916 being a Sinn Féin rebellion caused Griffith to stand down from its leadership and allow the party to adopt the role of a republican party with Eamon de Valéra (1882–1975), the former mathematics teacher and senior surviving Dublin commandant of the Irish Volunteers, as its new president. The U.K. government tried to defuse the situation by establishing an Irish Convention in 1917–1918 to discuss a new Home Rule constitution for Ireland, but Sinn Féin boycotted it.

On November 25, 1918, the London Parliament of the United Kingdom of Great Britain and Ireland was dissolved to prepare for a general election. At that time, the Irish Party, pledged to Home Rule, held the majority of Irish seats, as they had done since 1874. But the Home Rule Act of 1913 was already dead in the water. The Irish Party held 68 seats; the Independent Nationalists held 10 seats, Sinn Féin held 7 seats, and the Unionists held 18 seats. Sinn Féin declared that the subsequent general election in Ireland would constitute a national plebiscite. If they proved successful, they would withdraw from the U.K. Parliament in Westminster and establish an Irish Parliament, Dáil Éireann, in Dublin, and reiterate the Proclamation of the 1916 Republic.

In spite of intimidation of republicans by the British military and police at the hustings and polling booths—no less than 47 Sinn Féin prospective parliamentary candidates were arrested—the general election in Ireland took place. The results were declared on December 28, 1918. Of the 105 Irish seats, Sinn Féin had won 73, the Irish Party had secured only 6 seats (but T. P. O'Connor won a seat for a Liverpool, England, constituency, bringing their total to 7 seats), and the Unionists had won 26 seats, 8 of those on split votes between the Irish Party and Sinn Féin. Indeed, three Ulster counties had returned no Unionists at all, while Unionists were in a minority in Tyrone and Fermanagh.

The meaning of the Irish vote is as clear as it is emphatic. More than two-thirds of the electors throughout national Ireland have endorsed the Sinn Féin programme. . . . They invited the people to join the demand for a Republic as something immediately obtainable and practicable as well as desirable, the declaration that they would accept nothing else and nothing less.

The Freeman's Journal, December 30, 1918

The historian Dorothy Macardle (1899–1958) was in the public gallery when the first Dáil Éireann met in the Round Room of Dublin's Mansion House.

On January 21st, 1919, at 3.30 in the afternoon the First Dail Éireann met.

The non-republican Deputies did not attend.

The President of Sinn Féin [Eamon de Valéra] was in Lincoln Prison; Arthur Griffith was also in jail; Count Plunkett proposed that Cathal Brugha should preside.

Father [Michael] O'Flanagan read in Irish the opening prayer. . . .

The clerks of the Dáil were appointed and the roll was called: *"Fé ghlas ag Gallaimh"* (imprisoned by the foreign enemy) was the answer to name after name. Of the seventy-three Republicans elected thirty-six were in jail.

The Provisional Constitution of the Dáil was read and passed unanimously.

Then, everyone present standing, Ireland's Declaration of Independence was read in Irish and in English as follows.

Dorothy Macardle, *The Irish Republic*, Victor Gollancz, Ltd., London, 1937

Irish Declaration of Independence

Whereas the Irish people is by right a free people:

And whereas for seven hundred years the Irish people has never ceased to repudiate and has repeatedly protested in arms against foreign usurpation:

And whereas English rule in this country is, and always has been, based upon force and fraud and maintained by military occupation against the declared will of the people:

And whereas the Irish Republic was proclaimed in Dublin on Easter Monday, 1916, by the Irish Republican Army, acting on behalf of the Irish people:

And whereas the Irish people is resolved to secure and maintain its complete independence in order to promote the common weal, to re-establish justice, to provide for future defence, to ensure peace at home and good will with all nations, and to constitute a national policy based upon the people's will, with equal right and equal opportunity for every citizen:

And whereas at the threshold of a new era in history the Irish electorate has in the General Election of December, 1918, seized the first occasion to declare by an overwhelming majority its firm allegiance to the Irish Republic:

Now, therefore, we, the elected Representatives of the ancient Irish people in National Parliament assembled, do, in the name of the Irish nation, ratify the establishment of the Irish Republic and pledge ourselves and our people to make this declaration effective by every means at our command:

We ordain that the elected Representatives of the Irish people alone have power to make laws binding on the people of Ireland, and that the Irish parliament is the only Parliament to which that people will give its allegiance:

We solemnly declare foreign government in Ireland to be an invasion of our national right which we will never tolerate, and we demand the evacuation of our country by the English garrison.

We claim for our national independence the recognition and support of every free nation in the world, and we proclaim that independence to be a condition precedent to international peace hereafter.

In the name of the Irish people we humbly commit our destiny to Almighty God Who gave our fathers the courage and determination to persevere through long centuries of ruthless tyranny, and strong in the justice of the cause which they have handed down to us, we ask His Divine blessing on this the last stage of the struggle we have pledged ourselves to carry through to freedom.

National Library Proclamations, Dublin

"Deputies," Cathal Brugha said when the reading was finished, "you understand from what is asserted in this Declaration that we are now done with England. Let the world know it and those who are concerned bear it in mind."

The Deputies, standing, affirmed:

"We adopt this Declaration of Independence and we pledge ourselves to put it into effect by every means in our power."

The Dáil then appointed three Delegates to the Peace Conference—Eamon de Valéra, Arthur Griffith and Count Plunkett. An Address to the Free Nations of the World was read in Irish, French and English, and adopted. It called upon "every free nation to support the Irish Republic by recognising Ireland's national status and her right to its vindication at the Peace Congress" and declared that Ireland was "resolutely and irrevocably determined, at the dawn of the promised era of self-determination and liberty, that she will suffer foreign dominion no longer."

Then was read and adopted unanimously the Democratic Programme of Dáil Éireann, founded on the Easter Week Proclamation:

"We declare in the words of the Irish Republican proclamation the right of the people of Ireland to the ownership of Ireland and to the unfettered control of Irish destinies to be indefeasible. . . ."

The session then concluded. It had lasted two hours—two of the most momentous hours in Ireland's history.

Visitors and journalists from many countries filed the gallery of Mansion House; the Assembly made a deep impression on these. "The proceedings throughout were orderly and dignified, not a word being uttered that could provoke ill-feeling," the correspondent of *The Times* write. But it was a French historian, Monsieur [Y. M.] Goblet, who most clearly realised the significance of the event. He realised that Dáil Éireann was inspired by the spirit of Easter Week. "And those who knew it," he wrote, "partisans or adversaries, divined that a new epoch was beginning, and one that would be terrible."

Dorothy Macardle, *The Irish Republic,* Victor Gollancz, Ltd., London, 1937

Marie Comerford (1893–1982) was another eyewitness to the momentous meeting.

People waiting asked one another "Did you ever think you and I would live to see this day?"

I was with a Wexford contingent.

Never was the past so near, or the present so brave, or the future so full of hope.

We filed into the Round Room and pressed around till every inch of standing room was full.

I don't believe I even saw the seating arrangements that first day, the crowd was so great. . . .

The Dáil met at 3.30. It rose at 5.20, the day's work nobly done.

Some 69 press men from home and overseas reported the proceedings.

Outside, Dawson Street was thronged. Volunteers controlled the crowds, but reinforced D.M.P [Dublin Metropolitan Police] kept the trams moving. Young people were perched at every point of vantage.

Colonel Wedgeworth Johnston CB, Chief Commissioner DMP, and Sir Joseph Byrne, Inspector General of the RIC, were in windows overlooking the street. Detectives were also busy.

A secret instruction went out from the Castle:

"Press Censor to all Irish newspapers: The Press are informed with reference to the Dáil Éireann Assembly, which was held in Mansion House, Dublin, on January 21, that the following are not for publication:

"1: The Democratic Programme

"2: The Declaration of Independence.

"3: Speeches of the proposer and seconder of the Declaration of Independence."

Secret printing presses all over the city pounded out the banned literature.

Marie Comerford, The First Dáil, Joe Clarke, Dublin, 1969

The War of Independence—The First Shots

At Soloheadbeg, County Tipperary, January 19, 1919, a section of volunteers from the Third Tipperary Brigade, commanded by Seán Treacy and Dan Breen, organized an ambush to capture a cart of explosives that was under escort by the Royal Irish Constabulary. The first shots of the War of Independence were fired.

At last dawned the fateful morning of 21 January, 1919. Our scout had his eyes fixed on the Tipperary road. Suddenly the alarm was given. Dashing towards us, he gave the word of warring: "They're coming, they're coming!" and returned to his look out.

"Hands up!" The cry came from our men who spoke as if with one voice. "Hands up!" In answer to our challenge they raised their rifles with military precision and held them at the ready. They were Irishmen, too, and would die rather than surrender. We renewed the demand for surrender. We would have preferred to avoid bloodshed; but they were inflexible. Further appeal was useless. It was a matter of our lives or theirs. We took aim. The two policemen fell, mortally wounded: James Godfrey, the driver of the cart, and Patrick Flynn, the County Council employee, looked on in stupefaction. If we had disarmed the police without firing a shot the matter would not have been so serious. The shots had alarmed the countryside. In a moment men and women would appear at every doorway. Within an hour, hundreds of police and military would be scouring the countryside for us. From the moment we were outlaws with a price on our heads.

Dan Breen, *My Fight for Irish Freedom,* Talbot Press, Dublin, 1924

Murder of Tomás MacCurtain, Lord Mayor of Cork

At 1:10 A.M. on Saturday, March 20, 1920, Tomás MacCurtain, elected Sinn Féin lord mayor of Cork, and his wife, Eilis, were awoken by knocking on the street door of their shop at 40 Thomas Davis Street. They lived above it. Mrs. MacCurtain insisted on going down to answer the door.

When I opened the door a man rushed in with a black face and eyes shining like a demon. One man outside the door then asked where was Curtain, and I said he was upstairs. Six men rushed in the hall, four tall men and two small men; the two small men were about my own height and carried rifles, which they held against their sides. I don't know what the tall men had, they may have had rifles but I didn't see them. . . . One gave orders to hold "that one," meaning me, and the second tall man turned and shoved me towards the door but didn't say a word. He wore a big overcoat and cap. His face was blackened and he turned it from me immediately. He had fair foxy hair. He was a well-built man. . . . They seemed to know the house better than I did myself.

Mrs. Eilis MacCurtain, quoted in Florence O'Donoghue, *Tomás MacCurtain: Soldier and Patriot,* Anvil Press, Tralee, 1955

The men rushed upstairs to the bedroom. Mrs. MacCurtain heard the shots that killed her husband. Her brother, James Walsh, shouted for help out of a window, and

*outside she heard someone order: "Fire again." There was a volley of fire from out-
side at the upper windows. Marks made by the bullets were subsequently found.
Susie and Annie Walsh, Mrs. MacCurtain's sisters, had been awakened, and Susie
called to James, who was in an adjoining bedroom. James takes up the story.*

I went out on the landing and as I got there I heard a voice saying: "Come
out, Curtain." This demand was repeated as I was going round the bend of
the stairs about three steps from the top. I saw two tall men. One had a light
overcoat. Their backs were turned to me and they were facing the Lord
Mayor's room. As I got there the Lord Mayor was at the door. I saw the man
on the right, who was in a light coat and wearing a brownish cap, let go and
two shots were fired. He fired a revolver. I don't know what the man on the
left had in his hand. I only got a glimpse of it. I quenched the candle and
dropped on the stairs. When I was lying down I heart a third shot.

James Walsh, quoted in Florence O'Donoghue, *Tomás MacCurtain: Soldier and Patriot*,
Anvil Press, Tralee, 1955

*Twelve witnesses saw the party of men moving outside and leaving the house of the
lord mayor. John Desmond, a City Corporation lamp lighter, saw the party of men
walking to King Street RIC Barracks and being admitted. The name of District
Inspector Swanzy was linked with evidence that pointed to a police raid on the home
of the lord mayor. On Saturday, April 17, the inquest jury rendered a verdict. It was
unanimous and read by James J. McCabe, the coroner.*

We find that the late Alderman MacCurtain, Lord Mayor of Cork, died
from shock and haemorrhage caused by bullet wounds, and that he was
wilfully murdered under circumstances of the most callous brutality, and
that the murder was organised and carried out by the Royal Irish
Constabulary, officially directed by the British Government and we return
a verdict of wilful murder against David Lloyd George, Prime Minister of
England; Lord French, Lord Lieutenant of Ireland: General Smith of the
Royal Irish Constabulary; Divisional Inspector Clayton of the Royal Irish
Constabulary; District Inspector Swanzy and some unknown members of
the Royal Irish Constabulary. We strongly condemn the system at present
in vogue of carrying out raids at unreasonable hours. We tender to Mrs
MacCurtain and family our sincerest sympathy. We extend to the citizens
of Cork our sympathy in the loss they have sustained by the death of one
so eminently capable of directing their civic administration.

The San Francisco Journal of Commerce, September 13, 1920

The use of the preceding quotation from a publication in San Francisco indicates this momentous jury verdict was reported worldwide. District Inspector Swanzy was hurriedly moved to Lisburn, County Antrim, but was assassinated by republicans on August 22, 1920. MacCurtain was not the only Sinn Féin mayor to be shot dead in his home in front of his wife and family by RIC assassination squads. George Clancy, elected mayor of Limerick in January 1921, and his predecessor, the former mayor Michael O'Callaghan, were both assassinated in March 1921.

Cork (North) No. 2 Brigade Captures Brigadier C. H. T. Lucas (June 1920)

On Saturday, June 26, reports reached Liam Lynch, the officer commanding Cork's No. 2 Brigade, that some senior British officers were observed in the fishing pools along the Blackwater River at Kilbarry, 5 miles east of Fermoy. The senior of them was identified as Brigadier Cuthbert Henry Tyndall Lucas, commanding the Sixteenth Infantry Brigade, whose headquarters was in Fermoy. He was one of the four brigade commanders whose commands made up the Sixth Southern Division, commanded by Major General E. P. Strickland.

On a June evening in 1920, Liam Lynch and three of his staff officers, Paddy Clancy, Seán Moylan and myself [George Power], went by Ford car to a place called Kilbarry on the banks of the Blackwater, about three miles east of Fermoy. It had been confirmed that the British officers had arrived there earlier in the day. A fishing lodge by the river was quietly occupied and the General's personal servant arrested there and handed over to a few local Volunteers who had been detailed to keep the place under observation. The IRA officers then proceeded in search of General Lucas and the two officers who were known to be with him. One of the British officers was encountered a short distance from the fishing lodge. Taken completely by surprise, he offered no resistance and was led prisoner to the lodge. Shortly afterwards the second officer was located, just as he had tied up after the day's sport, and he too, was made prisoner. There was still no trace of General Lucas and, as it was getting late in the afternoon, it was decided that two of the IRA officers should proceed, one up and the other down the river, in search of him.

Coming through the small wood I unexpectedly ran into General Lucas as he was making his way back to the lodge. There was a moment of mutual scrutiny and then I sharply commanded him to drop his fishing rod and put up his hands. He hesitated at first but then complied with my order and allowed himself to be disarmed and marched back to the fishing lodge. On his arrival there he was ordered to join his two friends who seemed much relieved to find their O/C unharmed. At that stage, the IRA officers were not certain of the identity of their first two prisoners, so it was decided to ask General Lucas if he had any objection to naming them. To which he replied: "None," provided he was made aware of the identity of his captors. One of the IRA officers then introduced Liam Lynch as O/C No 2 Brigade and the three officers of his Staff. Lucas responded by pointing out Colonel Danfield of the Royal Artillery, and Colonel Tyrrell of the Royal Engineers, and enquired: "What do you propose to do with us?" He was told that all three would be held prisoner pending instructions from IRA Headquarters. In the meantime they would be given facilities to communicate with their relatives.

The first part of the plan having been brought to a successful conclusion it was decided to move the captives well away from the Fermoy area without delay, as it was fully realised that the military reaction would be swift and far reaching. Accordingly, in addition to the Ford in which the IRA officers had travelled, it was decided to use the British officers' large touring car also. A Volunteer [Owen Curtin of Fermoy] was quickly found to drive the captured car. The arrangement now made was that Seán Moylan and myself would travel with Colonel Tyrell in the Ford, and that Liam Lynch and Paddy Clancy would accompany Lucas and Danford in the other car. The Ford was to travel fifty to one hundred yards in advance of the touring car, but was to keep in touch as closely as possible. Making a detour south of Fermoy the convoy set out on the hazardous journey west, which carried us virtually through British lines. For a time all went well. The Ford maintained its appointed distance ahead, and we kept a watchful eye on the following car. As the main Fermoy-Cork road was approached, however, we lost sight of the second car at a wide sweeping bend in the road. By that time the British officers had realised the seriousness of their situation. Instinct and training urged them to make a bid for freedom, and obviously the attempt had to be made before they were transported further from their familiar surroundings, into the mountainous country which they were now approaching. Lucas and Danford exchanged a few words in a strange language—Arabic, we subsequently learned. Suddenly both prisoners sprang at their captors. The attack was so sudden and the element of surprise so complete that the IRA officers were taken at a disadvantage and almost disarmed before they realised what was happening. In the mêlée the driver lost control of the car which crashed into a ditch and he was knocked unconscious by the impact. It was therefore an even fight between the four men. The struggle between Lynch and Lucas was particularly tough, as both were strongly built, well trained six footers. In the first onslaught Lucas got on top of lynch, and made frantic efforts to wrench the gun from him. He had all but succeeded in doing so when the door of the touring car gave way and both men rolled on to the roadway. There they continued to struggle wildly until Lynch had worn down his opponent and the General surrendered.

Meanwhile Paddy Clancy and Danford were fighting desperately, with Danford on top. He had almost succeeded in throttling the IRA officer when Lynch, having disposed of Lucas, took in Clancy's plight at a glance. "Surrender or I shoot" he shouted to the British officer, but Danford ignored the command and held his savage grip on Clancy's throat. There was no alternative to shooting then and without further hesitation, Lynch fired. Colonel Danford felt the sharp sting of a bullet wound in his jaw and collapsed over his opponent. The fight was over.

In the meantime the Ford had proceeded some distance, Moylan and myself oblivious of the fact that a life and death struggle was taking place in the other car. Several valuable minutes had passed before we realised that something must be wrong, and took the decision to go back on our tracks. Immediately we had rounded the wide bend in the road, an extraordinary scene met our eyes. The big touring car lay almost wrecked in the ditch, the driver still unconscious over the wheel. On the grass verge nearby, lay Colonel Danford with General Lucas bending over him, giving him first aid. Some further distance away Liam Lynch was attending to Paddy Clancy.

We were thus faced by an entirely new and dangerous situation. The large touring car was completely out of action, the Ford was too small and was unreliable, and there was no time to arrange alternative transport. After a hurried conference, it was decided to allow Colonel Tyrell to remain with his badly wounded comrade, and the Volunteer driver who had then fully recovered, was sent to get medical aid for him. I was instructed to return east in the Waterford direction and from there to proceed to Dublin to personally report the whole affair to GHQ. The remainder of the party, including General Lucas, now the only prisoner, crowded into the Ford and resumed the interrupted journal towards the Lombardstown area, close to which Brigade headquarters was located at that time.

Having failed in his bid to escape, General Lucas became quite resigned to his lot and showed no resentment towards his captors. Indeed, whilst he was held in North Cork, Lynch and himself had many interesting discussions on a variety of subjects, but mainly on military matters.

George Power, Adjutant Cork No. 2 Brigade, IRA, in *Rebel Cork's Fighting Story,*
Anvil Press, Tralee, n.d.

On the night of June 28, 1920, the British soldiers ran amok, smashing windows and destroying property, shouting, "We want our f—— general back! Give us back our f—— general!" General Lucas was handed to the East Clare Brigade. On July 29 or 30, near Oola, he made a successful break for freedom and reached his own side. Interviewed by newspapers, he commented of his captors, "I was treated as a gentleman by gentlemen."

Death of the Second Sinn Féin Lord Mayor of Cork

On August 12, 1920, Alderman Terence MacSwiney, the elected successor to Lord Mayor Tomás MacCurtain, was arrested. He claimed that his arrest in the Council Chamber was illegal and refused to take food after being arrested. On August 17, he was taken before a military tribunal in Victoria Barracks, Cork, presided over by Lt. Col. James of the South Staffordshire Regiment. Found guilty of possession of documents found "likely to cause disaffection to His Majesty," he was sentenced to two years' imprisonment and told he would be placed on a British naval sloop and taken to Brixton Prison in London.

The Lord Mayor: I wish to state that I will put a limit to any term of imprisonment you may impose as a result of the action I will take. I have taken no food since Thursday, therefore I will be free in a month.

President of the Court: On sentence to imprisonment, you will take no food?

Lord Mayor: I simply say that I have decided the term of my detention whatever your Government may do. I shall be free, alive or dead, within a month.

Quoted in *Rebel Cork's Fighting Story,* Anvil Press, Tralee, n.d.

Terence MacSwiney remained on his hunger strike in Brixton Prison until October 24, a total of seventy-four days, before he succumbed to death. His most famous aphorism in his inaugural address as lord mayor was:

It is not those who can inflict the most, but those that can suffer the most who will conquer, though we do not abrogate our function to demand that murderers and evil doers be punished for their crimes.

"Black and Tans" Visit Milltown Malbay, County Clare (October 1920)

The burnt houses were still smoking, the people still sleeping out in the fields and woods in terror of a renewal of the attack, the blood of one victim still red on the white wall of a burnt house, the funerals both of police and those slain in revenge for them passed before our eyes, and the uncoffined and unrecognisable remains of an unknown person burnt in one of the cottages were still lying hidden in a calf shed in the rear.

English Quaker sent to observe conditions in Ireland
British Society of Friends, *The Friend*, October 8, 1920

"Bloody Sunday" at Croke Park, Dublin (November 21, 1920)

On the afternoon of Sunday, November 21, units of the Royal Irish Constabulary's "Black and Tans" and members of the Auxiliary Division went to Croke Park Stadium, Dublin, where an all-Ireland challenge Gaelic Athletic Association football match between Dublin and Tipperary was taking place. The football reporter for the Dublin Evening Telegraph *was there.*

The match opened at 2.45 and the stands and grounds were crowded with spectators numbering between 10,000 and 15,000. At about 3.10 P.M., about 12 lorries containing armed forces of the Crown arrived. It is alleged that the grounds were dominated from four points. Machine guns placed on the railway which traversed the end of the field and both gates leading from Jones's Road were forced by the raiders. It is stated the gate money was seized.

As the raiders entered the grounds they immediately opened fire, first into the air and then at the crowd.

The armed forces, according to many present, gave no warning to the spectators to disperse beyond the preliminary volley in the air.

A general stampede followed, men, women and children rushed wildly for shelter.

Michael Hogan, a well-known Tipperary player, was shot dead through the mouth, and many people were wounded or injured in the stampede.

Dublin Evening Telegraph, November 22, 1920

Michael Hogan, the goalkeeper of the Tipperary team, was shot dead. Thomas Ryan of Wexford, who had gone to assist him, was shot dead as he knelt beside him. Another Tipperary player, Jim Egan of Millinahone, was badly wounded. The grim total of players and spectators killed immediately was twelve, including a woman. Nearly one hundred were wounded, eleven of them seriously.

When the armed forces and armoured cars entered the field the scene became indescribable, said another spectator. When the park was encircled, the women and children were told they might go. The men were then all searched, and when any motion took place in the crowd a volley of shots were fired over their heads.

One of the collectors at the gate alleged that a bundle of notes, part of the receipts, were taken when he was being searched.

A gentleman who was convenient to the grounds related how about 17 lorries filled with Crown forces came dashing along, stopping about 20 yards from the canal bridge. Dismounting they opened fire.

The Irish Independent, Monday, November 22, 1920

The London Morning Post, *on November 22, accepted the British army version of events, mistakenly calling the match a "hurling" match and saying that it was at "Crow Park" [sic], that the military and RIC were fired upon, and that those killed had been "gunmen." There is a strange feeling of déjà vu looking back on this event after that of January 30, 1972, when in Derry City the 1st Battalion of the Parachute Regiment opened fire on Civil Rights marchers, killing thirteen immediately; one was to die later, and many others were wounded. The regiment, too, claimed to have been fired upon and that those killed had been "gunmen."*

Mass Resignations from the Royal Irish Constabulary

Through 1920 it had become abundantly clear to members of the Royal Irish Constabulary that they were fighting a guerrilla war against their own friends and families and against the express will of the Irish nation. Many began to resign. When the concerns of RIC men at Listowel were raised, Lt. Colonel Gerald B. Smyth, DSO (1885–1920), an Englishman sent to Ireland to be divisional commissioner in

Munster, went to talk to them. He made it plain that he expected the RIC to shoot first and ask questions later.

If a police barracks is burned or if the barracks already occupied is not suitable, then the best house in the locality is to be commandeered, the occupants thrown out into the gutter. Let them die there—the more the merrier. Police and military will patrol the country at least five nights a week. They are not to confine themselves to the main roads, but make across the country, lie in ambush and, when civilians are seen approaching, shout "Hands up!" Should the order be not immediately obeyed, shoot and shoot with effect. If the persons approaching carry their hands in their pockets, or are in any way suspicious looking, shoot them down.

You may make mistakes, occasionally an innocent person may be shot, but that cannot be helped, and you are bound to get the right parties some time. The more you shoot, the better I will like you, and I assure you no policeman will get into trouble for shooting any man.

Quoted in J. Mee, "Memories," *Reynolds News,* London, 1951–1952
Also reported in *Irish Bulletin,* July 9, 1920

Constable Jeremiah Mee (1889–1953) of Glenmaddy, County Galway, was one of many RIC men who resigned at Listowel following Colonel Smyth's address. Within a few weeks, some six hundred men had resigned. On July 17, 1920, Colonel Smith was assassinated in the Cork Country Club, South Mall, Cork City. British army intelligence tried to retaliate.

Tuesday, 12 October (1920)

Early this morning nine of Wilson's men including Col. Smyth's brother who came over to avenge him, went to arrest two murderers in Dublin— a sad muddled affair, two of our men killed, Smyth was one of 'em, and both gunmen escaped.

The Diaries of Mark Sturgis, in *The Last Days of Dublin Castle,*
ed. Michael Hopkinson, Irish Academic Press, Dublin, 1999

Wilson was Lt. Colonel Walter Wilson, chief of the Special Branch in Dublin, and Major G. O. S. Smyth, D.S.O., M.C., who had been serving in Egypt, applied for a posting to Ireland to seek revenge for his brother's assassination. Wilson led a raid on the "Fernside," Drumcondra, home of Professor John Carolan, who was on the teaching staff of St. Patrick's Training College. It was a republican "safe house," and British intelligence discovered that Dan Breen and Seán Tracey of the 3rd Tipperary Brigade were staying there.

Seán could not find his glasses. This was a severe handicap to him as he was very short-sighted. Worse still, his gun had jammed. I shouted to him to get back to the window. He stepped back, just as another bullet buried itself in the wardrobe. I felt a sharp pain in the region of my spine. Feeling certain that my days were numbered, I told him to make his escape, and that I would join him when I had fought my way through. I raked the landing with my Mauser and heard the sound of footsteps retreating down the stairs. Towards the back of the house I could hear the sharp ping of rifle shots.

I dashed out of the room on to the landing, and saw a group of soldiers coming up the stairs, their electric torches pin-pointing me as a target. One bullet grazed my forehead, another passed through the fleshy portion of my thigh; two hit me in the calves of my legs and one lodged in my right lung. But I still kept my stand and fired at the raiders until the gun was empty. . . . I was going to be killed; but I would sell my life dearly.

Dan Breen, My Fight for Irish Freedom, Talbot Press, Dublin, 1924

As well as Major Smyth, Captain A. L. White, D.S.O., was killed in the attack and a corporal wounded. In spite of his wounds, Dan Breen escaped from the house, was picked up by friends, and was taken to the Mater Hospital. Tracey also escaped. Professor Carolan was shot by the soldiers as a reprisal after the men had escaped. He survived a few days—long enough to tell staff in the Mater Hospital what had happened. Two days later, Seán Tracey was killed in a shootout on Talbot Street with Lt. Price, a British intelligence officer.

Chief secretary for Ireland, Sir Hamar Greenwood, had to admit in the House of Commons that during this period 556 constables—Irishmen—had resigned from the RIC, and, more important, 313 Irish magistrates were not prepared to serve any longer. Special recruits from Britain were then enlisted in the RIC as a means of keeping up the disintegrating force. The new units were known as the Auxiliary Division, and they were supposed to be integrated into the RIC. They were known as "Black and Tans" because they had insufficient uniforms and wore a combination of military khaki and police green.

Kilmichael (November 28, 1920)

The Auxiliary Division of the RIC was recruited solely from former British officers with war experience. They were paid £1 a day plus expenses, with a guaranteed leave of three months per year, making them the highest-paid military force of their time. In spite of ranks ranging from lieutenants to colonels and brigadiers, they were officially called cadets; thus when they were killed in action, British propaganda could present a picture in the public mind of youths being slaughtered rather than the reality of the situation. By November 1920, the Auxiliaries had become known for the ferocity of their reprisal attacks on civilians, and Irish morale was suffering. The Auxiliaries were beginning to have the reputation of invincibility. Kilmichael changed that. Lieutenant Colonel Crake, then holding the rank of district inspector, and sixteen members of the Auxiliary Division of the RIC were ambushed at Kilmichael, County Cork, by Tom Barry and a unit of the No. 3 (West Cork) Brigade. All the Auxiliaries were killed.

We had gone about fifty yards when we heard the Auxiliaries shout "We surrender." We kept running along the grass edge of the road as they repeated the surrender cry, and actually saw some Auxiliaries throw away their rifles. Firing stopped, but we continued, still unobserved to jog towards them. Then we saw three of our comrades on No 2 section stand up, one crouched and two upright. Suddenly the Auxiliaries were firing again with revolvers. One of our three men spun around before he fell and Pat Deasy staggered before he, too, went down.

When this occurred, we have reached a point about twenty five yards behind the enemy party and we dropped down as I gave the order, "Rapid fire and do not stop until I tell you." The four rifles opened a rapid fire and several of the enemy were hit before they realised they were being attacked from the rear. Two got to their feet and commenced to run back past No 2 Section, but both were knocked down. Some of the survivors of our No 2 Section had again joined in and the enemy, sandwiched between the two fires, was again shouting "We surrender."

Having seen more than enough of their surrender tactics, I shouted the order, "Keep firing on them until the Cease Fire." The small IRA group on the road was now standing up, firing as they advanced to within ten yards of the Auxiliaries. The Cease Fire; was given and there was an uncanny silence as the sound of the last shot died away.

Tom Barry, Guerrilla Days in Ireland, Irish Press Ltd., Dublin, 1949

The Burning of Cork City (December 1920)

For me it started just before 9.30 P.M. on the evening of Saturday, December 11, 1920. I'd been visiting my cousin Mickey Hussey in his rooms in the Corn Market. . . . Mickey was worried about me leaving at this hour for the new military curfew was at 10 P.M. It had been introduced on the previous day when General Macready, the British commander-in-chief in Ireland, had proclaimed martial law in Munster. The British had maintained the fiction they were engaged in a "police action" but now the gloves were off . . . !

I wasn't worried. I was working for Crosbie's *Cork Examiner*, a daily newspaper, whose owner was not a Unionist but certainly not a supporter of Sinn Féin. However, as many of the reporters were pro–Sinn Féin we tried to stir a neutral path in reporting, keeping to facts and trying to leave the tub-thumping to the editor. I had been given a special pass that afternoon showing that, as a journalist, I could travel during curfew hours. Major General E.P. Strickland himself signed it. He was commanding the British 6th Division covering the city. So I felt comparatively safe from any unwelcome attention. . . .

As I reached the bottom of Abbey Street, I was stopped by a patrol of the Buckinghamshire Light Infantry. In spite of protests, I was bundled into a car, a Lancia, I think. At first I was taken to King Street RIC barracks, next to the Grosvenor Hotel. There was something said about "muddle" for I was pushed back into the vehicle and we drove to the Union Quay RIC barracks. The place was filled with Auxies who seemed to look at me with some unpleasant smiles of what, I thought, was anticipation. I waved my pass and identification at the sergeant in charge but he "had his orders" and I was held for two hours until a young lieutenant of the regulars, no older than myself but wearing a Military Cross ribbon, interrogated me. He looked embarrassed, especially when I asked why the military were setting fire to the city. He simply muttered something about the Auxiliaries being "out of control." . . .

I was released sometime after three o'clock in the morning. There was still gunfire about the city. I heard it not far away at Bandon railway station [now Albert Quay station] and my idiocy drew me along the quay to see what was going on. I found a unit of the City Fire Brigade actually pinned down by gunfire. When I asked who was firing on them, they said it was a unit of Black and Tans who had broken into the nearby City Hall next to the station. One fireman told me that he had also seen "men in uniform" carrying cans of petrol into the Hall from the very barracks on Union Quay that I had been released from.

Around four o'clock there was a tremendous explosion. The Tans had not only placed petrol in the building but also detonated high explosives.

The City Hall and adjoining Carnegie Library, with its hundreds and thousands of priceless volumes, was a sea of flames.

The firemen with me managed to get a hose on the Carnegie Library as the Tans had evidently given up their game of firing at the firemen. Instead they turned off the fire hydrant and refused to let the fire crews have access to water. Protests were met with laughter and abuse. Soon after six o'clock the tower of the City Hall crashed into the blazing ruins below. I heard that elsewhere in the city the soldiers ran their bayonets through the fire brigade's hose pipes.

Exhausted by that time, I found a wandering fellow reporter who gave me a lift back to Sunday's Well on his motorcycle.

Alan J. Ellis, aide memoir manuscript used as the basis for the article
The Irish Democrat, December 1989, manuscript in author's collection

The center of the city was a smoldering ruin. Over forty business premises and three hundred residential properties were destroyed, many were homeless, and thousands were thrown out of work. The value of property looted by the British military was not assessable, although over £3 million worth of damage (1920 value) had been done. One woman had died of a heart attack when Auxiliaries burst into her house, two young men had been shot dead, and several people had been wounded, including several members of the Cork Fire Brigade. Chief Secretary Sir Hamar Greenwood told the House of Commons that the citizens of Cork had started the fires themselves. Even the Unionist Cork Incorporated Chamber of Commerce and Shipping sent Greenwood a telegram expressing their scorn at this lie. A Labour Party Commission already in Ireland investigating atrocity stories, consisting of two English Members of Parliament, William Lunn and John Lawson, arrived in Cork the next day, and the Auxiliaries showed their colors by threatening to shoot them if they started to investigate. They did take evidence and declared themselves satisifed that the British military was responsible.

The moment the diabolical lie that the Irish had burnt their city was uttered, protests from the city of Cork were received by the more fair-minded and, therefore, more honourably equipped Englishmen—including Mr Asquith and Lord Robert Cecil—asking for an impartial and judicial inquiry.

Brigadier General F. P. Crozier, commandant, Auxiliary Division,
Royal Irish Constabulary, 1920–1921
Ireland for Ever, J. Cape, London, 1932

On December 18, 1920, General Edward Strickland ordered a military inquiry but excluded lawyers, press, and nonmilitary observers.

Mr Lloyd George had promised the House of Commons that he would publish this report, but, when he read it, felt bound "in the public interest, to go back on his word." Wise man! Had he published it he would have been out of office within ten minutes. . . . The burnings were deliberate and unlawful "reprisals" for an ambush carried out by the rebels earlier in the day about which the Government deliberately and consistently lied to save its face.

While holding my conference of commanders I received a telegram in code sent off from Downing Street ordering me to "suspend" a company commander on account of the burning of Cork [which had happened two months previously] which enabled Mr Lloyd George to get up in the House during the Cork debate to say a company commander had been suspended and several individuals had been punished for their share in the destruction.

Nothing much happened to the company commander after the fuss had blown over while nobody had ever been punished for Cork—as nobody was allowed to see the evidence "officially"—the individuals referred to as being punished being some half dozen policemen [Auxiliaries] I had dealt with for various offences such as theft, burglar etc in County Cork and for whose discomfiture I had been so hastily returned to light duty instead of going on sick leave. As I only tumbled to the "frame up" after reading the debate in the newspaper, I could do nothing, but more was to follow. . . .

Five minutes before leaving in a car for Kingstown [Dun Laoghaire] to catch the morning mail boat for Holyhead I was rung up again on the phone from Dublin Castle and asked if I would take the Trim looters back and take over a reorganised Auxiliary corps of two divisions, one to be commanded by General [Alan] Wood, the other by a Colonel Guard. "You then" continued the tempter, "need not come into contact with the returned men and you will thus 'save your face'." "My face!" I replied. "It is not my face which needs saving! It can't be done . . . if you take these men back you will be faced with mutiny the next time someone (it won't be me) deals out 'justice' for some act of indiscipline." "Don't be a fool," replied the tempter, "if you continue to stick your toes in you'll miss the "honours" list at the end of this show. . . . You can have a KBE [Knight Commander of the British Empire] in June. These men if they are not reinstated will play hell in London and upset the Cabinet altogether." "No,"

I replied, putting the receiver down as an officer touched me on the shoulder. "All the greatcoats which were hanging in the hall of the mess have been stolen in the night!" he said, "what are you going to travel in?" "Ha! ... ha!" I laughingly remarked. "General Wood will lend me his if it hasn't been pinched too." "But you can't wear his coat," he replied, "he's huge." "I must," I said, and I did, returning the coat to my treacherous subordinate on my return to Dublin as a Crown witness. The thefts were traced to an Auxiliary policeman who was tried and punished, but I never got my coat back.

I left for Wales to unveil a War memorial, and before going told General Wood on no account to let the men back (an order which he promised to obey) but within twenty-four hours received a telegram from Dublin from a friend saying the men were back and being "petted."

On hearing of the return [to service] of the looters I immediately resigned, after which General Wood was appointed to my vacancy and later signed a lie which was read out by Mr Boar Law in the House of Commons during a "frame up" debate on my resignation to the effect that there had been no condemnation of crime.

Brigadier General F. P. Crozier, Commandant, Auxiliary Division,
Royal Irish Constabulary, 1920–1921
Ireland for Ever, J. Cape, London, 1932

Brigadier General Frank Percy Crozier (1879–1937) had commanded the 119th Infantry Brigadier in 1916 and later was general officer commanding the 40th Division in France. Appointed commandant of the Auxiliary Division of the Royal Irish Constabulary in July 1920, he resigned in February 1921. He became increasingly unhappy with the indiscipline of his men. After a raid by Auxiliaries in Trim, County Meath, on February 9 and events in Drumcondra, Dublin, where two young men were killed, Crozier dismissed the twenty-one Auxiliaries responsible from service. Crozier's superior, Major General Sir Hugh H. Tudor (1871–1965), appointed chief of police in Ireland, ordered their reinstatement. Crozier resigned, thus drawing attention to the violent excesses of the Auxiliaries and the Black and Tans.

Friday, 25 February [1921]

L'affaire Crozier almost monopolises attention. This beauty who is, I am sure, more truly responsible for indiscipline in the Auxiliaries, who he commanded, than anybody else, has seized a golden opportunity to resign posing as the upholder of order who was not supported from above; a glorious party. Poor simple Tudor has been carted again. He often half made up his mind to sack him—pity he didn't quite. There is no doubt he is a perfectly worthless fellow.

The Diaries of Mark Sturgis, in *The Last Days of Dublin Castle,*
ed. Michael Hopkinson, Irish Academic Press, Dublin, 1999

Crossbarry, Cork (March 19, 1921)

In one of the biggest military engagements of the War of Independence, a thousand troops of the Essex and Hampshire Regiments, together with 150 RIC Auxiliaries, began a sweep of the area 9 miles southwest of Cork City in search of the Flying Column of Cork No. 3 (West Cork) Brigade consisting of a hundred men. The plan was to surround the IRA men and kill or capture them.

When the Column mobilised at 2.30 A.M. it had full knowledge of the fact that the enemy was moving to attack it from several sides. Although the numbers of the enemy were not then known, the IRA had no doubt that they were outnumbered by ten to one at least. I had to decide without delay whether to fight or return and attempt to evade action. . . .

After hearing the shots that had killed Charlie Hurley at 6.30 A.M. we waited immovable and silent. The quietness of the breaking dawn was disturbed only by the sounds of the enemy transport, which crept nearer and nearer. About 8 A.M. a long line of lorries carrying troops came slowly on past O'Connell's flanking section and into our main ambush positions. Twelve lorries were between Crowley's section in the centre and O'Connell's flankers but many more stretched back along the road. Liam Deasy and I flattened against the ditch as the leading lorry came on, but suddenly it halted and the soldiers started shouting for unfortunately, despite the strictest orders, a volunteer had shown himself at a raised barn door and was seen by many of the British. The British started to scramble from their lorries but the order to fire was given and Crowley's section opened up at them.

Within ten minutes of the opening of our attack we had smashed the British encircling lines wide open. We could have marched away to the south without fear of interference had I wished to do so. But now confidence in ourselves to meet the attacks we knew were coming from the other British units was mixed with contempt for our enemy's fighting ability.

Commandant Tom Barry, *Guerrilla Days in Ireland,* Irish Press Ltd., Dublin, 1949

Six sections of the Flying Column were in action. The cracking of the rifle fire and the bursting of bombs rent the quiet morning air. . . . The first convoy of the British was getting the worst of it. Nine of their lorries were out of action. The remainder of the convoy "about turned" and fled. Dr Con Lucy used his rifle that day with as much enthusiasm as he had wielded the *caman* on the hurling field. A bomb rebounded off a tree and fell at the feet of Dr Eugene ("Nudge") Callanan. Luckily for him it failed to explode. The sections were now ordered out on the road and fire was opened upon the fleeing soldiers who were escaping down the fields towards the railway. Florrie Begley marched up and down Harold's yard playing the bagpipes.

Back at the rear of the fight was No 5 section, disappointed because the men had heard the din of the fierce battle and the tune of the pipes playing the old war songs, while they themselves had not yet fired a shot. The crack of the rifle fire was incessant at first. After a time it died down and single shots then rang out. The fight on the main road was nearly over and still it seemed that No 5 Section would not be needed that day. Tom Barry had issued an order to collect all guns and ammunition. A Lewis gun was amongst the captures. Then the abandoned enemy lorries were set on fire and were actually blazing when rifle fire broke out at the rear of No 5 Section. At last this section had its wish and was in the fight.

After the shooting at Ballymurphy the British forces from Cork and Ballincollig, 600 strong, had divided into two columns with the definite object of surrounding the entire Column. One division under Major Percival (as General Percival he surrendered Singapore to the Japanese in World War II) of the Essex Regiment, took up positions on the east and south of the IRA. One line of the British extended east to the road to Crossbarry Bridge from Brien's bridge, a point directly one mile north of the ambush position. The other line, reinforced by a contingent from Kinsale, extended from Crossbarry Bridge along the main Cork-Bandon railway line. This line was almost parallel with the position of the right flank of the IRA. Westward of this again three convoys of the enemy who had fled earlier in the day had taken up position, so that in all the southern front of the enemy was about two miles in extent. By attacking the enemy, the Column had succeeded in breaking up the British encircling movement. One of their groups had been nearly wiped out on the Crossbarry-Bandon road.

Now came the other British attacking columns on the right and left flanks. They were met by Christy O'Connell's Section No 7, in the main body of the Column's right flank; by number 4 section under Denis Lorden on the left front flank and by my section No 5 on their left flank. No 7 Section was grandly placed to let them have it, lying on a position that overlooked the crossroads. They blazed at them and drove them back eventually. No 4 Section under Denis Lorden was also heavily engaged by a column of about 150 British. On several occasions the British were driven back before they finally gave up the attempt of breaking through this Section. Here a fine Volunteer, Peter Monohan, was killed, holding he position whilst Dan Corcoran of Newceston was badly wounded in the hip. When Corcoran was wounded, the British were only about twenty yards away, but Dick Spencer of Castletownbere jumped out and brought him to safety on his back—one of the many outstanding feats of bravery by the Volunteers.

> Tom Kelliher, No. 5 section leader, Cork No. 3 (West Brigade),
> in *Rebel Cork's Fighting Story*, Anvil Press, Tralee, n.d.

Again the enemy was met with such heavy fire that they hurriedly retreated once more. The fighting had gone on here for about ten minutes and as there were no British inside anywhere but those being attacked by Kelliher and Murphy, I moved the whole Flying Column back, except O'Connell's Section, to strike at this enemy unit without full strength. But when I reached Kelliher's position all the British had gone and we saw no more of those either.

> Commandant Tom Barry, *Guerrilla Days in Ireland*, Irish Press Ltd., Dublin, 1949

The casualties in this action were 3 IRA men killed and 4 wounded, while 39 British soldiers were killed and 47 wounded. At the time, the British officially announced only 10 soldiers had been killed and 1 wounded.

On June 24, 1921, U.K. prime minster David Lloyd George wrote to President Eamon de Valéra to open negotiations to achieve a peaceful settlement in Ireland. A truce negotiated by General Sir Nevil Macready on behalf of the British military came into effect at noon on Monday, July 11. By this time, according to British figures, 162 British soldiers had been killed and 566 wounded; 366 RIC had been killed and 600 wounded. The Irish casualties were 276 Volunteers and 288 civilians killed.

On the same day as the truce, however, the RIC drove into nationalist districts on Falls Road and York Street, North Belfast, in several trucks and armored cars and opened fire indiscriminately.

In certain districts the streets were literally swept by the fire of the rival snipers and the Crown forces, and it was absolutely unsafe for anyone to be out of doors. . . . From five until seven o'clock the condition of affairs on the Falls and Grosvenor Roads and in the great network of intervening streets was simply appalling, and the ambulances were kept busily engaged in conveying the dead and wounded to the hospitals, while many were also brought in private cars and taxis.

Irish News, July 11, 1921

By the end of the week, twenty-three people had been killed in Belfast, two hundred Catholic houses had been destroyed, and over a thousand homeless Catholics were huddled in empty schools and stables. On July 12, de Valéra and four other members of the Dáil crossed to London for a preliminary meeting. It was not a promising start.

19

The Civil War, 1922–1923, and the Aftermath

I t was not until four months after the truce and many exchanges of letters that the Dáil sanctioned the appointment of plenipotentiaries, with instructions limiting their powers, to negotiate a treaty. They arrived in London on October 9, 1921, and on October 11 met with the U.K. prime minister at Downing Street. They were led by Arthur Griffith, minister for foreign affairs, Michael Collins, minister for finance, Robert C. Barton, minister for economic affairs, together with Edmund J. Duggan, T.D., and George Gavan Duffy, T.D. The British team consisted of Prime Minister David Lloyd George, Lord Birkenhead, Winston S. Churchill, Sir Hamar Greenwood, Austen Chamberlain, L. Worthington Evans, and Gordon Hewart.

Negotiations went on until December. The British side was intransigent. There would be no recognition of the republic. A Free State was offered within the Commonwealth, but the Unionists in the north would have the option of withdrawing their six-county area, outlined in the provision of the Government of Ireland Act, 1920, which arbitrarily partitioned the country if both houses of the newly established Parliament of Northern Ireland submitted an address to the king of England at the end of four weeks after the Free State came into being.

Downing Street, London (December 5, 1921)

I have to communicate with Sir James Craig [leader of the Irish Unionists in Belfast] tonight; here are the alternative letters I have prepared, one enclosing the Articles of Agreement reached by His Majesty's Government and yourselves, the other saying that the Sinn Féin representatives refuse the oath of allegiance [to the Crown] and refuse to come within the Empire. If I send this letter it is war—and war in three days! Which letter am I to send?'

Words ascribed to U.K. prime minister Lloyd George by Sir Austen Chamberlain,
U.K. negotiator in Down the Years, London, 1935

Speaking for himself and his colleagues, the English Prime Minister, with all the solemnity and the power of conviction that he alone, of all men I met, can impart by word and gesture—the vehicles by which the mind of one man oppresses and impresses the mind of another—declared that the signature and recommendation of every member of our delegation was necessary or war would follow immediately.

Irish plenipotentiary, Robert Barton, in Official Report of Dáil Éireann, December 19, 1921

Mr Griffith said, speaking in his soft voice, and with his modest manner, "I will give the answer of the Irish Delegates at nine tonight; but, Mr Prime Minister, I personally will sign this agreement and will recommend it to my countrymen." "Do I understand, Mr Griffith," said Mr Lloyd George, "that though everyone else refuses you will nevertheless agree to sign?" "Yes, that is so, Mr Prime Minister," replied this quiet little man of great heart and of great purpose.

Michael Collins rose, looking as though he were going to shoot someone, preferably himself. In all my life I never saw so much passion and suffering in restraint.

Winston S. Churchill, The World Crisis: The Aftermath, London, 1929

Both Michael Collins and Arthur Griffith at this moment saw the shadow of doom clouding over that fateful paper—their own doom. . . . Michael Collins was not appalled by the spectre of death, but he had the Irishman's fear of encountering that charge which comes so readily to the lips of the oppressed—that of having succumbed to alien will and betrayed their country. . . .

. . . He asked for a few hours to consider, promising a reply by nine o'clock. Nine passed, but the Irish leaders did not return. Ten, eleven, and they were not yet back. We had doubt as to whether we should see them again.

David Lloyd George, Is It Peace? London, 1923

The treaty was signed at 2:15 A.M. on Tuesday, December 6, 1921.

As before, they [the Irish delegates] were superficially calm and very quiet. There was a long pause, or there seemed to be, and then Mr Griffith said, "Mr Prime Minister, the Delegation is willing to sign the agreements, but there are a few points of drafting which perhaps it would be convenient if I mention at once." Thus, by the easiest of gestures, he carried the whole matter into the region of detail and everyone concentrated upon those points with overstrained interest so as to drive the main issue into the background for ever.

Winston S. Churchill, The World Crisis: The Aftermath, London, 1929

The treaty agreed on setting up the Irish Free State within the British Commonwealth of Nations, with all offices taking an oath of allegiance to the English Crown, its heirs, and its successors. Furthermore, it provided a time period when the Unionists, who had set up a parliament in Belfast, annexing two republican counties within their sphere of power, would petition the king, asking to be allowed to withdraw from the Free State and continue with their statelet. However, it also allowed a Boundary Commission that would thrash out the thorny problem of those areas that did not want to be ruled by the Unionists.

December 6, 1921

When you have sweated, toiled, had mad dreams, hopeless nightmares, you find yourself in London's streets, cold and dank in the night air.

Think—what have I got for Ireland? Something which she has wanted these past seven hundred years. Will anyone be satisfied at the bargain? Will anyone? I tell you this—early this morning I signed my death warrant. I thought at the time how odd, how ridiculous—a bullet may just as well have done the job five years ago.

I believe Birkenhead may have said an end to his political life. With him it has been my honour to work.

These signatures are the first real step for Ireland. If people will only remember that—the first real step.

Letter from Michael Collins to John O'Kane, December 6, 1921,
quoted in Rex Taylor, Michael Collins, London, 1958

The Dáil Splits (January 7, 1922)

On December 8, 1921, when the plenipotentiaries revealed the details of the treaty to a meeting of the Irish Cabinet, the treaty was accepted for presentation to the Dáil by only four votes to three: Griffith, Collins, Barton, and W. T. Cosgrave voted in favor, while de Valéra, Cathal Brugha, and Austin Stack voted against.

Following the acrimonious treaty debate in the Dáil on January 7, 1922, where Sinn Féin split, with sixty-four votes for the treaty and acceptance of the Free State remaining in the British Commonwealth, versus 57 votes, attention was focused on the views of the army that had fought the War of Independence against the British. Six divisions as well as the North Wexford Brigade and the Carlow Brigade were in favor of the Free State, while eight divisions, the two Dublin Brigades, and the South Wexford Brigade were against the treaty. Eamon de Valéra and Michael Collins now made strenuous efforts to prevent the slide into civil war as Britain's Lloyd George and Winston Churchill applied threats and pressure to the provisional government now led by Griffith and Collins to attack the republican dissidents.

Saturday, 7 January. It is another milestone but if Ireland—or England—expects that the Golden Age is dawning I hope they won't be too roughly disillusioned. It is a huge gamble and we are groping in the dark.

Tuesday, 10 January. The Castle makes a good propaganda appearance with its gate standing open for the first time for at least two years and soldiers busy removing barbed wire.

Sunday 15 January. I went and had a walk with Warren [Sir Norman Fenwick Warren Fisher, 1879–1948] yesterday morning. History alone will show whether we have done good work for Ireland and England or damn bad. It is clearly now up to Ireland to make a success of it or not. We have done the job we were sent to do and Warren told me that L.G. [Lloyd George] will make a splash of it, so I suppose we will all be Dukes! I am glad of it; it would be a pity to let the whole thing finish up as if the Government were half ashamed of it. I spoke to him especially about Andy [Alfred W. "Andy" Cope, assistant undersecretary]. . . .

This is I suppose that phase as far as I am concerned. If Collins stands up to the extremists all will be well but there was an uneasy tone in the Dáil debate which sounded like a feeling after placation of these gentry which I'm sure is the wrong policy and may wreck the new Government if they go on with it.

Thursday 19 January. Little news. The Provisional government are making some show of governing. I wish they would lose no time in getting the IRA into uniform so that all may know who's who and what's what.

Mark Beresford Russell Sturgis, senior civil servant at Dublin Castle (1884–1949),
Diaries of Mark Sturgis
The Last Days of Dublin Castle, ed. Tim Pat Coogan Dublin, 1999

Griffith and Collins formed a provisional government to implement the treaty, while de Valéra and supporters of the republic refused to recognize it. On June 16, 1922, a general election was called (only in the 26 Counties). Fifty-eight pro-treaty candidates were returned (later to form Cumann na nGaedheal), thirty-five anti-treaty (keeping to their Sinn Féin umbrella), seventeen Labour Party, seven Farmers' Party, four Unionists, and seven Independents. De Valéra and Collins worked unsuccessfully to prevent the slide into civil war.

Opening Shots of the Civil War (June 1922)

The Republicans had made the Four Courts, Dublin, their headquarters on April 13, 1922. Among them was the former commander of the 1st Southern Division, who had now been appointed the Republican director of organization, Earnan O'Malley (1898–1957). At 3:40 A.M. on June 28, Thomas Ennis, commander of the 2nd Eastern Division, demanded that the Republicans march out without weapons and surrender to the Free State by 4 A.M. At 4 A.M., with artillery borrowed from the British, Free State troops commanded by Eoin O'Duffy began to pound the garrison in the Four Courts.

The minutes were slow in coming. Artillery and trench mortars, incendiary shells, armoured cars and tanks, of these I was thinking in a confused jumble, and of my relationship to the section. Would artillery fire shake my knees and confidence, and would I disgrace my section?

"Time's up," said Rory [O'Connor], and as he spoke a machine-gun from outside echoed across the night, to be answered by a shout from each of our sections. A heavy boom came next, and we knew artillery was being used; the crash of an eighteen pound shell announced that those who stood in arms for an independent Ireland were to be attacked by some of their former comrades.

"That's Mulcahy's answer to our last note," I said.

Now that fighting had begun, problems that could have been easily solved a few days ago came up. Communications between the blocks was in the open. The dome area was cut off from Headquarters block, the latter from the Records Office. The space was covered with rifle and machine-gun fire. One man was hit as he crossed behind me. Paddy O'Brien and I found men to work on a sandbag barricade but there were not enough bags to make a covered bullet proof passage between the blocks.

I climbed up the iron ladder of the dome, pausing as I heard a wind sound of bullets crossing its space; they made a shrill whistle as they passed. Up above, dawn was coming up the river, risen to the roofs and spreading slowly towards Kingsbridge. This was the second dawn I had watched from the Courts. I could see the old city rising from the river, gradually in Parliament Street, steeply in narrow Winetavern and streets towards Christ Church and the Castle. Light climbed up the house tops and along the ridge of church spires towards the west; slight flashes, soon indistinguishable with full light, showed sniper's nests. I could follow the quays up to the corner of O'Connell Bridge and down by the older houses to beyond Mendicity Institute. The river bordered the most colourful part of the city, haphazardly pleasant the disparity in roof heights and the colour contrasts of shop fronts. Beyond the corner of Winetavern Street was a gun. I saw its recoil as it fired. This gun was firing with open sights at an east target, the corner of the Courts facing Morgan's Place. Slowly the top storey was crumbled, the stone stairs shot away, and men were lowered to the floor below by using knotted blankets. Behind, on Mary's Abbey side, was a second gun at the end of Chancery Street. It looked as if the enemy could advance and occupy any position they thought necessary; the third and fourth battalions of the Dublin Brigade which might have interfered with enemy positions and guns across the river did not seem to make much of an impression on them.

. . . We had not sufficient men. There were between a hundred and eighty and a hundred and ninety men in the garrison, but to hold the Court under present conditions we would have needed at least two hundred and fifty. Practically all were on duty at a time. The reserves of each section for counter-attack were very small, and we had no central reserve to fall back on. As I walked between sections, the buildings seemed to consist chiefly of windows, about five or six windows to each man. They could not all be barricaded; only a few had been made bullet-proof, but rifle-grenades could always be lobbed in, and movement under fire was a little difficult. The roofs were dominated by buildings close to them, and by snipers from St Michan's tower and from the top of Jameson's distillery, but one tunnel was completed by the end of the following day. We could not make another, as we could not spare the men, the munitions block containing the Record Office was isolated. Paddy O'Brien and his adjutant went the rounds frequently during the day, inspecting the Bridewall prison less than thirty yards away. The passage was narrow. Thompson guns and machine guns spattered as they ran across. I went with him at times. The telephones in the section puzzled at intervals. We answered the operator at the main switch and reported the situation in the sections to our commander. Then the telephone did not work; the service had been cut off.

In spite of the heavy artillery bombardment, the Four Courts garrison refused to surrender. Oscar Traynor, commanding the republican troops outside of the Four Courts, sent in a message: "To help me carry on the fight outside, you must surrender forthwith. I would be unable to fight my way through to you even at terrific sacrifice. . . . If the Republic is to be saved your surrender is a necessity." O'Malley pointed out that the Four Courts command was the general headquarters and outranked Traynor. The senior officers decided to fight on. But with the increased fury of the Free State assault, they reconsidered their position.

The morale of the men had been broken by their crowding together in cellars where they could do nothing but listen to the fire directed against the walls and hear the explosions. I thought for a little. If we allowed some of the garrison to march out and we remained to fight our way out, they would be disgraced. They had all done the best they could; it was we of their Headquarters Staff who had left them here to be trapped. I suddenly thought of the dead. Had we maintained the tradition? What would our dead comrades of the Tan war, the men of 1916, the Fenians and the others think? The majority were not afraid to die. A surrender would be harder but I wanted to fight with men who were volunteers.

"Very well, sir," I said to the Chief of Staff, "we'll go out together and surrender, but let's use up our ammunition first."

Some of the men broke down and cried, leaning on their rifles. Others scattered through the front rooms and fired enraged volleys in the direction of the big guns along the quays and at the houses opposite. A white towel hanging from a sweeping-brush was thrust through a bullet shattered hole in the glass. After a time the firing in front slackened. Father Albert was driven up with green-uniformed soldiers in a motor-car.

"The garrison want to surrender," I said to him as I stood at the gate, "and I wish to discuss terms."

"We will go to Brigadier General Daly," said a green coat. "He's in charge of the attack." I handed Father Albert an envelope. "That is for Daly and I would like a written reply." In the enclosed note I asked Daly if at this late moment we could unite to attack the British before any further blood was split between us.

The response from Brigadier Paddy Daly, himself a 1916 veteran, was that he was not authorized to accept conditions and that the garrison should line up on the quay outside the Four Courts. Neither Liam Mellowes, Rory O'Connor, Joseph McKelvey, nor other members of the headquarters staff wanted to formerly surrender the garrison.

"All right," I said to the Chief of Staff. "I'm OC. I'm responsible, and I'll take the surrender. Company, fall in by sections. We're not going to march out with our arms. The men outside have broken their oath to the Republic. Pile arms and ammunition in the room beyond. Gunners will smash machine-gun parts. Strip automatics and throw the parts in the burning block. Then parade on the quays."

The machine-gunners stripped their guns, jumped on the parts, twisted and battered them; their hands were torn and bleeding but they did not heed, they smashed in a frenzy. The men walked out of the gate in groups. The rifles and revolvers were heaped in a large room. The Courts quartermaster with Peadar Breslin and I remained there to pile them up. Paraffin was slopped around the floor, and then with blinding flashes incendiary grenades were thrown; flames flared on the rifle pyre, licking the butts and the woodwork. We watched for a time, tears of rage in our eyes.

"Let's go," I said; "the men are all outside by this."

We could feel the heat of the burning buildings as we crossed the ground. I stripped my long-barrelled gleaming Parabellum and threw the top mechanism into the flames of Headquarters block. I had scarcely fired a shot.

"Wipe your faces," said Peadar Breslin, "I can see the lines of the tears." We wiped our faces with our handkerchiefs. The handkerchiefs were black and grimy when we had finished.

The men were standing outside watching the flaming buildings. "Fall in," I ordered, "by sections." The sections fell in two deep, dressed, and were numbered off by the section commanders on the quays to the left of Church Street bridge, facing the river. Only when we were on the quays did surrender seem worse than it was inside.

Paddy Daly and Tony Lawlor came up to us, smiling. They wore green uniforms. Daly carried the shoulder tabs of a brigadier-general.

"I am surrendering on behalf of the Republican garrison of the Four Courts," I said. "I want to discuss terms with you."

"There are no terms," said Daly. "This is an unconditional surrender."

"I want terms for the men," I said. "I am surrendering my command as prisoners of war. Are you going to see that they receive prisoner-of-war treatment? And I demand terms for my men."

"I have received my instructions. No terms."

Soldiers in green uniform with fixed bayonets marched up. They stood on guard around us. How hateful the green uniforms seemed now. An officer gave an order to the prisoners to form fours. They looked at him and laughed. He ordered again and was told to "Go to hell. Who do you think you're talking to?"

Amongst the officers was a Clare man. I walked over to him. He was in uniform and carried a captain's tabs. "Hello. I did not expect to see you here." He looked confused and ashamed. "We were rushed into it. We did not realise what we were doing and we were into it before we knew. I'm sorry."

Ernie O'Malley, The Singing Flame, Anvil Books, Dublin, 1978

The Four Courts garrison prisoners were marched to a temporary holding base. O'Malley was approached by one of the prisoners, Seán Lemass (1899–1971), who was to become Taoiseach—prime minister of the Irish Republic from 1959 to 1966. He had spotted an unguarded exit. Lemass, O'Malley, Joe Griffin, and Paddy Rigney escaped and linked up with another garrison member, Paddy O'Brien, who had been wounded but taken to his own house by sympathetic ambulance men, and they made their way to Blessington to rejoin the Republican forces.

The civil war continued until May 24, 1923, when Republican forces were ordered by their chief of staff, Frank Aiken, to cease fire and "dump arms"—not to surrender. Aiken (1898–1983) was to eventually become a government minister and deputy prime minister from 1965 to 1969.

Soldiers of the Republic, Legion of the Rearguard:

The Republic can no longer be defended successfully by your arms. Further sacrifice of life would now be vain and continuance of the struggle in arms unwise in the national interest and prejudicial to the future of our cause. Military victory must be allowed to rest for the moment with those who have destroyed the Republic. Other means must be sought to safeguard the nation's right.

Eamon de Valéra, May 24, 1923, quoted in Dorothy Macardle, The Irish Republic,
Victor Gollancz, London, 1937

The cost in lives was between 600 and 700. In all, 11,316 male and 250 female Republican prisoners were now in jail. Some 77 Republicans had been executed by the Free State as "reprisals," including four of O'Malley's friends and comrades from the surrendered Four Courts garrison: Rory O'Connor, Liam Mellowes, Richard Barrett, and Joseph Mckelvey. Had O'Malley not escaped, he, too, would doubtless have been one of the victims of government reprisal shootings. Of the major figures of the struggle against Britain who were now dead, Arthur Griffith, president of the Dáil, had died at age 51 from stress; Michael Collins, chairman of the provisional government, had been shot in an ambush while visiting his native Cork; Erskine Childers had been executed by the provisional government; Liam Lynch, the Republican chief of staff, had been shot in County Tipperary.

The civil war left behind it a legacy of bitterness that was to shape Irish politics during the rest of the century, giving rise to two modern political parties: Fianna Fáil arose from the Republican side, and Fine Gael emerged from the Free State side.

Saorstát Éireann (the Irish Free State) came into being on December 6, 1922. On December 7, the Unionists issued their address to the English king requesting withdrawal from the Free State. A 26-county state was now in existence, with a two-tier legislature (Oireachtas) made up of Dáil Éireann and the upper house, called An Seanead (the Senate). The Crown was represented by a governor general. The U.K. government did not bother to alter the name of its own state until 1927, when, by Acts 17 and 18, George V c 4, known as the Royal and Parliamentary Titles Act, 1927, the United Kingdom of Great Britain and Northern Ireland came into being at midnight on April 12, 1927 (Constitutional Law, vol. 10, part 2, p. 70).

The Border (1925)

Article 12 of the treaty to which the signatories had agreed allowed a commission to be established to determine "in accordance with the wishes of the inhabitants, so far as may be compatible with economic and geographic conditions, the boundaries between Northern Ireland and the rest of Ireland." Lloyd George had pointed out that in reality only four out of the nine Ulster counties had Unionist majorities. If the Unionists insisted on incorporating Tyrone and Fermanagh, it would be coercion.

There is no doubt, certainly since the Act of 1920, that the majority of people of the two counties prefer being with their "southern" neighbours to being in the Northern parliament. Take it either by constituency or by poor law union, or, if you like, by counting heads, and you will find that the majority in these two counties prefer to be with their "southern" neighbours . . . if Ulster is to remain a separate community, you can only by means of coercion keep them there and, although I am against the coercion of Ulster, I do not believe in Ulster coercing other units.

> D. Lloyd George, British prime minister on the Boundary Commission, quoted in
> Michael Farrell, *Northern Ireland: The Orange State,* Pluto Press, London, 1976

Our Northern area will be so cut up and mutilated that we shall no longer be masters in our own house. The decision of that Commission may be a matter of life and death to us.

> Charles Curtis Craig, Member of Parliament for South Antrim, quoted in
> Dorothy Macardle, *The Irish Republic,* Victor Gollancz, London, 1937

Sir James Craig, the Northern Ireland prime minister, having agreed to the treaty's Article 12, now refused to meet his commitments and appoint a member of the commission.

While the Boundary Commission was in suspense Sir James Craig and his government felt it necessary to maintain between 30,000 and 40,000 armed Special Constables in various degrees of mobilisation. . . . On the basis of their being no settlement they were proposing to me that we should provide for the maintenance of all the Special Constables in their present state of efficiency up to at least September, 1926 . . . but as soon as this settlement was reached Sir James Craig informed me that he would be able to proceed immediately with the winding up of the Special Constabulary.

> Winston Churchill, *United Kingdom Parliament Debates (Hansard) House of Commons,*
> vol. 189, col. 361

The U.K. government made the Unionist appointment to the Boundary Commission. Their nominee was J. R. Fisher, a Unionist newspaper owner. The Free State appointed its minister of education, Eoin MacNeill. The chairman was South African justice Richard Feetham. The commission's findings were supposed to be secret, but after a year of meetings it was clear that if the democratic wishes of the inhabitants were to be taken notice of, then large areas of the republican counties of Fermanagh, Tyrone, also of Armagh together with Derry and Newry, would be encompassed by the Irish Free State. The U.K. government decided to use a heavy hand to warn against this.

It was not intended that there should be large transfers of territory. . . . If by any chance the Commissioners felt themselves at liberty to order the transfer of one of these counties nothing would induce the Ulster people [the Unionists] to accept such a decision and no British Government would be guilty of the supreme folly of trying to enforce such a decision.

> Sir Laming Worthing-Evans, U.K. secretary of state for war in 1921, speaking in
> Colchester, September 29
> *Morning Post,* September 30, 1925

It was clear that the Unionists regarded Article 12 as not worth the paper it was writ-ten on. Fisher, against the protocols agreed by the commission, then told the Morning Post *(November 7, 1925) of the plans. He announced that parts of eastern Donegal would be given to Northern Ireland. Eoin MacNeill resigned from the commission, and the Irish Free State prime minister, W. T. Cosgrave, was summoned to London on December 3, 1925, where he met Sir James Craig, prime minister of Northern Ireland, and Stanley Baldwin, U.K. prime minister. They agreed to suppress the report of the Boundary Commission and accept that the arbitrarily enforced borders would remain the same.*

De Valéra's Republicans Enter the Dáil

On May 16, 1926, Eamon de Valéra and many others split from Sinn Féin and founded Fianna Fáil (Soldiers of Destiny). The differences arose mainly on the ques-tion of abstention from the Dáil. De Valéra led the new republican party into the Dáil on August 11, 1927. The problem so far as Fianna Fáil was now concerned was the Oath of Allegiance to the English Crown.

Mr de Valéra picked up the Bible, which was lying on the book containing the oath, carried it to the other end of the room, and placed it on the couch there. He then went back, signed his name on the line pointed out by the Clerk, at the same time, covering the writing above the line with some papers he held in his hand.

Frank Aiken and J. Ryan, eyewitness statement, September 23, 1927, quoted in Earl of
Longford and Thomas P. O'Neill, Eamon de Valéra, Hutchinson, London, 1970

De Valéra told the clerk, first in Irish, then in English:

I want you to understand that I am not taking any oath nor giving any promise of faithfulness to the King of England or to any power outside the people of Ireland. I am putting my name here merely as a formality to get the permission necessary to enter amongst the other *Teachtaí* [Members of the Dáil] who were elected by the people of Ireland, and I want you to know that no other meaning is to be attached to what I am doing.

Eamon de Valéra to O. W. Bohan, August 10, 1927, quoted in Earl of Longford and
Thomas P. O'Neill, Eamon de Valéra, Hutchinson, London, 1970

On March 9, 1932, Fianna Fáil came to power for the first time with a small major-ity. Less than a year later, de Valéra went back to the country and secured a larger majority before forming a new government on February 8, 1933. The party remained the government party until February 1948. De Valéra then began to work on a new constitution. The Dáil approved the new constitution of Ireland on May 1, 1937. On July 21, de Valéra went to the country seeking approval and secured 686,042 votes for, 528,296 votes against. On December 29, 1937, it became law. The new constitution removed the Oath of Allegiance to the British Crown, abolished the governor general of the Irish Free State, replacing the office with a president of Ireland, and abolished appeals to the British Crown and Privy Council. The constitution was that of a republic without naming it as such. In fact, it was referred to as "the Dictionary Republic." The scholar and writer Douglas Hyde (1860–1949) became the first president, an office he held until 1945.

20

Irish Neutrality and the Irish Republic of 1949

*I*n 1939, the Irish Free State declared that it would pursue a policy of neutrality in the European conflict. During June 1940, U.K. government minister Malcolm MacDonald visited Dublin three times in an effort to persuade Taoiseach Eamon de Valéra to enter the war on behalf of the United Kingdom and its allies. The U.K. government offered no less than the reunification of Ireland as payment.

I got the impression that de Valéra had not passed on to his colleagues the assurance I gave him yesterday that declaration of a United Ireland should settle the issue once and for all, and that there would be no going back on that, for he said that one of the principal reasons why his Cabinet regard the plan as unacceptable is that they believe that United Ireland will not materialise from it.

> Malcolm MacDonald, British secretary for the Dominions, June 27, 1940, to U.K.
> prime minister Neville Chamberlain, quoted in Joseph T. Carroll,
> *Ireland in the War Years 1939–1945*, New York, 1975

FOLLOWING FROM MR CHURCHILL FOR MR DE VALERA. PERSONAL. PRIVATE AND SECRET. BEGINS, NOW IS YOUR CHANCE. NOW OR NEVER. "A NATION ONCE AGAIN." AM VERY READY TO MEET YOU AT ANY TIME. ENDS.

> Telegram from Winston Churchill, British prime minister, to Eamon de Valéra,
> Monday, December 8, 1940, quoted in Joseph T. Carroll,
> *Ireland in the War Years 1939–1945*, New York, 1975

De Valéra refused the "carrot" of a United Ireland, foreseeing that any official alliance with Britain less than twenty years after the bloody war of independence might lead to a renewal of the civil war. The Free State's neutrality caused a lot of English public outrage through misinformation.

Irish neutrality, on which she placed a generous interpretation, permitted the Germans to maintain in Dublin, an espionage-centre, a window into Britain, which operated throughout the war and did incalculable harm to the Allied cause.   Nicholas Monsarrat, *The Cruel Sea*, Knopf, New York, 1951

When Geheimauftrag Irland *(Spies in Ireland, Hamburg, 1961) was published, this was shown to be arrant nonsense. If Ireland placed a "generous interpretation" on its neutrality, it was certainly much in Britain's favor. More recent research showed that Ireland's officially neutral position was more help to the Allied war effort than if she had been a belligerent.*

Some 183,000, and possibly far more, volunteers from the Irish Free State served in the U.K. armed forces. Many Irish citizens simply gave addresses of next of kin in the United Kingdom, thus disguising their origins. One estimate was put as high as 400,000 serving in the U.K. armed forces. An Irish division was actually formed by the British army in 1941, but its Irish appellation was never referred to in public. There was also a high rate of recruitment into the Royal Air Force from the Free State, and Churchill actually ordered a Shamrock Wing to be formed along the lines of the American Eagle Squadron, or the units of Poles, Czechs, and so on. It was thought this might be contrary to international law, compromising Irish neutrality.

However, Free State volunteers won 780 British decorations for valor as well as eight Victoria Crosses, Britain's highest military award. In fact, citizens of the Irish Free State won more decorations for valor than those of some of the officially belligerent countries like the Dominion of Canada. This figure is exclusive of the figures of serving military personnel and decorations won from volunteers from Northern Ireland.

On May 13, 1945, at the end of the European conflict, Winston Churchill, on BBC, marred his victory speech by giving vent to his bitterness about Irish neutrality. Speaking of 1940, he said:

This was indeed a deadly moment in our life and if it had not been for loyalty and friendship of Northern Ireland we should have been forced to come to close quarters with Mr de Valéra or perish for ever from the earth. However, with a restraint and poise to which, I say, history will find few parallels, His Majesty's Government never laid a violent hand upon them though at times it would have been quite easy and quite natural, and we left the Dublin Government to frolic with the Germans, and later with the Japanese representatives, to their hearts' content.

Winston S. Churchill, BBC World Broadcast, in *Great War Speeches*, London, 1957

It was not worthy of a statesman and could not be left unanswered by the Irish government.

May 17, 1945: . . . Saw "R.M." briefly. Back to the flat to listen to Dev's speech. Sometimes he is so damned punctilious that I wonder how he will respond. He could blow it. London newspapers are already having a field day about the stupid protocol visit on the German ambassador. His voice is slow, studied. Says he knows what the Irish people expect him to answer to the old bulldog across the water. Help! Is it war? Then says that Churchill has made it clear that he would violate Irish neutrality and justify it by Britain's necessity. Strange that Churchill does not understand that this would make Britain's necessity into a moral code in which other people's rights were not to count. Excellent stuff!

"Mr Churchill is proud of Britain's stand alone, after France had fallen and before America entered the war.

"Could he not find in his heart the generosity to acknowledge that there is a small nation that stood alone, not for one year or two, but for several hundred years against aggression; that endured spoliation, famines, massacres in endless succession; that was clubbed many times into insensibility, but that each time on returning consciousness, took up the fight anew; a small nation that could never be got to accept defeat and has never surrendered her soul?"

Soon as he finished, I hurried out round the corner into O'Connell Street and at once heard the noise of cheering outside the GPO. Dev was coming out from the radio studio and a large crowd had gathered. I was astounded by the wildness of exultation, the demonstration of enthusiasm of those who had heard his broadcast—the old bulldog and all his arrogance had been put in his place. Dev's finest hour. Well done! Well done!

Frank Hussey, journalist, *Diary 1945*
Private collection, P. Shone, Australia

The Irish Republic Proclaimed (April 18, 1949)

From February 18, 1948, to June 14, 1951, the first Inter Party government took power, led by Taoiseach J. A. Costello of Fine Gael. Although de Valéra's Fianna Fáil Party was still the biggest single party, the combination of a number of minority parties joining with Fine Gael saw the first Coalition Cabinet, which then introduced the Republic of Ireland Act. The Constitution of 1937 was amended, and on Easter Monday, April 18, 1949, at midnight, the 26-County state officially became a repub-

lic. It was celebrated in Dublin with a twenty-one–gun salute, a solemn high mass, and a Te Deum at the Pro-Cathedral in Dublin.

I was a child of twelve at the time as I stood with my mother on the reviewing platform (my father, the general secretary of Fine Gael, had died shortly before), the flags, the *feu de joie,* the marching soldiers, all raised within me emotions which, had I been older, could well have drawn me towards the IRA and its stand against the border.

Tim Pat Coogan, former editor of *The Irish Press* and historian, in *The Irish: A Personal View,* Phaidon, London, 1975

The Dissident Voice

It is said that a brisk trade is being done in the sale of bunting to be used on Easter Monday when the 26 Counties government with the approval of the 26 Counties Dáil and presumably the benediction of the 26 Counties President will declare the 26 Counties a Republic.

The whole business is bunkum pure and simple. The Republic of Ireland was proclaimed in arms on Easter Monday 1916. After an All-Ireland election contest, representatives of the whole country met in Dáil Éireann on January 21, 1919, when the Republic was established in the most solemn manner and its Declaration of Independence sent out to the nations.

It has never since been disestablished; the Declaration of Independence has never been revoked.

Hundreds of men and women have given their lives in defence of the Republic of Ireland; thousands have suffered imprisonment, hunger, torture, poverty and exile because of their fidelity to it; Irish people the world over have been stirred and inspired and edified by the unselfish devotion of its loyal adherents.

It has been suppressed by force for the past 27 years (i.e. since 1922—Ed.) and at times under coercion enactments, the very name of it has been declared illegal.

Why is that suppression not being removed now, the Republic of Ireland, restored, and peace and unity and national self-respect re-established in our midst?

Why set up the scarecrow of a 26 Counties Republic decorated with bunting to make as many people as possible believe that it is what it seems to be?

A little humanity, a little honesty, a little respect for the truth, a little real statesmanship, a little courage could wipe out all the bitterness of 27 years and encourage the best of our young people to go forward bravely and joyously to the final crowning of their country's nationhood.

Bunting and bunkum will never do it.

Brían Ó hUiginn, *Irish Press*, April 7, 1949

Brían Ó hUiginn (Brian O'Higgins, 1882–1963) was from Cill Scire, County Meath. He was a popular ballad writer, using the pen name Brían na Banban. He had fought as part of the GPO garrison in Dublin during the 1916 uprising and in the 1918 general election was elected to the West Clare seat for Sinn Féin. O'Higgins took his seat in Dáil Éireann. Taking the republican side in 1921, he again won the seat in the Second Dáil. He was elected president of Sinn Féin in 1932 but resigned from the party in October 1934. His unremitting republican statement was supported in the following issue of the Irish Press *by Dan Breen, who was then a Fianna Fáil T.D. (Teachta Dála). His words struck a resonance with many nationalist newspapers.*

The reaction from London was predictable. It was deemed that the new Republic of Ireland had left the British Commonwealth, and the British government introduced an Ireland Act of 1949 that declared

That part of Ireland heretofore known as Éire [*sic*] ceased, as from the eighteenth day of April, nineteen hundred and forty-nine, ceased to be part of His Majesty's Dominions . . . that Northern Ireland remains part of His Majesty's Dominions and of the United Kingdom and it is hereby affirmed that in no event will Northern Ireland or any part thereof cease to be part of His Majesty's Dominions and or the United Kingdom without the consent of the Parliament of Northern Ireland.

Ireland Act, 1949, HMSO, London, 1949

The mainly Catholic one-third nationalist population of Northern Ireland felt abandoned and desperate.

21

A Protestant State and Civil Rights

I have always said that I am an Orangeman first and a politician and a member of this parliament afterwards. . . . All I boast is that we have a Protestant parliament and a Protestant state.

Sir James Craig (Lord Craigavon, 1871–1940), prime minister of Northern Ireland, speaking in April 1934
Northern Ireland Parliamentary Debates (Hansard), House of Commons, vol. 16, cols. 1091/1095.

In Ulster, Sir James Craig stood solid as a rock. Imperturbable, sagacious, above hate or anger, yet not without a lively sentient, steady, true, unerring, he brought his people at length out from the midst of indescribable miseries and difficulties back to daylight and civilisation.

Winston S. Churchill, *The World Crisis: The Aftermath*, London, 1929

Ignoring the democratically expressed will of the Irish electorate in the 1918 general election, during the War of Independence, the U.K. government rushed through a Government of Ireland Act in 1920 that repealed the 1913 Home Rule Act. This act arbitrarily partitioned six counties of Ulster from the rest of Ulster and from Ireland, ignoring that two of those counties (Fermanagh and Tyrone) had large republican majorities. Democratic institutions in republican areas, the county councils, rural councils, and other bodies were suppressed by troops and police, and elected members and functionaries were arrested. Against this background, elections were held for

*the new Belfast Parliament while Loyalists supported by police and the army
attacked Nationalist homes.*

After a disinterested investigation, the conclusion one has been forced to
is, that the blame for beginning the trouble lies at the door of the
Orangemen. . . .

On these unfortunate beings the fury of Orange Specials and Orange
mobs falls daily and nightly. These people have committed no offence
unless it be an offence to be born a Catholic. . . . On the simple charge of
being Catholic hundreds of families are being continually driven from
their houses. . . . In these operations the Specials provide the petrol,
firearms and immunity from prosecution.

Manchester Guardian, May 21, 1921

*On June 22, 1921, King George V had opened the Unionist's Parliament in Belfast's
City Hall. There seemed to be a touch of irony in his words when he declared: "The
future lies in the hands of my Irish people themselves."*

*The opening of the Belfast Parliament had seen Loyalists launch fierce attacks on
Nationalist (Catholic) enclaves, leaving many dead and injured. During the next
eighteen months, 428 people were killed, 1,766 wounded, 8,750 driven from their
jobs, and 23,000 made homeless. Partition was being enforced on the population by
guns and bombs with almost as many casualties as in the War of Independence.*

Day after day and night after night—especially night after night—raiders
and violence and terrorism are knocking at their doors. . . . Every night
thousands of people sleep in the fields, under hedges, or haystacks,
because they dare not sleep at home. Every night, if they stay in their
houses, many thousands go to bed in fear and trembling, in a Christian
land, in the 20th Century, in a time of peace.

The Times, London, November 30, 1921

*Once the treaty was approved in Dublin, the nationwide Royal Irish Constabulary
was disbanded and in the Six Counties the new Royal Ulster Constabulary took over,
but as well as regular members, a series of A, B, and C Specials were recruited, com-
prising an additional paramilitary force of over twenty thousand men. Of these, the
B Specials were to become notorious. The first police commander was Lt. Colonel
Frederick Crawford of Larne gun-running notoriety. Sir James Craig, the Northern
Ireland leader, had promised Churchill and the London government that the Specials
would be disbanded as soon as the border had been decided. In 1969, Civil Rights
campaigners were still protesting about the activities of the Specials.*

The Unionists have an important ally, they have a coercive police force of their own. . . . They have become what everybody who knows Ulster perceived they would become—the instruments of a religious tyranny . . . some of them, the A Class, became regular RUC, the rest, the B and C classes parade their districts at night with arms, harassing, threatening, beating and occasionally killing their Catholic neighbours and burning their homes.

Manchester Guardian, May 19, 1921

The Unionists quickly set out to consolidate absolute power in the territory by abolishing proportional representation in elections and introducing voting qualifications, allowing a company vote (a multiple vote for business owners) and gerrymandering of electoral boundaries. This ensured Nationalists were a permanent minority. Discrimination against Catholics was now openly encouraged both for public and private employers.

On April 9, 1922, the Civil Authorities (Special Powers) Act of Northern Ireland was introduced by Sir Richard Dawson Bates, the Unionist minister for home affairs. Bates (1876–1949) was a lawyer, a founding member of the Ulster Volunteer Force, and a member of the provisional government of Ulster. He argued that the draconian legislation was to be a temporary measure, but it was reenacted annually until 1933, when it was made permanent law. It was directed against the Nationalist community and restricted and suspended civil liberties.

The legislation conferred powers of search and arrest without warrant, and powers to detail, intern without trial, hang, flog, prohibit coroners' inquests, and make regulations without consulting Parliament. For example, in 1933 it became an offense to refuse to answer incriminating questions. Everyone over the age of fourteen had to carry identity cards. Interment without trial was introduced from 1922 to 1924, 1938 to 1946, 1956 to 1962, and again in 1971. In case there was anything the authorities overlooked, the Special Powers Act provided:

If any person does any act of such a nature as to be calculated to be prejudicial to the preservation of the peace or maintenance of order in northern Ireland and not specifically provided for in the regulations, he shall be deemed to be guilty of an offence against the regulations.

Civil Authorities (Special Powers) Act, April 1922, Belfast

When introducing a new Coercion Bill in the Apartheid South African Parliament in April 1963, Minister of Justice Johannes B. Vorster commented that he "would be willing to exchange all the legislation of that sort for one clause of the Northern Ireland Special Powers Act."

In 1925, an amending act to the Education Act ensured that there would be segregation in education, with only Protestants being allowed to teach Protestant children.

From 1924, an uneasy peace had descended, but then a pogrom against Catholics took place in 1931, resulting in many deaths and injuries. In 1934, the Council of Civil Liberties sent a Commission of Inquiry to Northern Ireland, which finally reported in 1936:

Through the use of Special Powers individual liberty is no longer protected by law, but is at the disposition of the Executive. This abrogation of the rule of law has been so practised as to bring the freedom of the subject into contempt.

Even with such legislation and brute force, the Unionists found it hard to control the natural growth of population.

The Nationalist majority in the county Fermanagh, notwithstanding a reduction of 366 in the year, stands at 3,604. . . . The Boards and properties are nearly all controlled by Unionists. But there is still this millstone around our necks. I would ask the meeting to authorise their executive to adopt whatever plans and take whatever steps, however drastic, to wipe out this nationalist majority.

E. C. Ferguson, M.P., at the annual Unionist Convention in Enniskillen
Irish News, April 15, 1948

We criticise South Africa [apartheid regime], but are we sufficiently without sin ourselves to cast stones?

Two Nationalist members of Enniskillen Council walked out of a committee meeting because every one of the eighteen houses in a ward was allocated to a Unionist on party vote.

Mr Cahir Healy MP, telling me of the happening, adds: "We have public housing estates in which the tenants are segregated into Catholic and Protestant communities. Doesn't criticism of South Africa sound a little hypocritical in the face of that?"

John Gordon, Sunday Express, London, October 20, 1963

In most parts of Britain people are awarded the keys of a council house for very good reasons.

They have been living in a slum, in over crowded conditions, they have large families, they have been waiting a long time, or they have medical recommendations.

All sound reasons, based on need.

But I found a town last week where another factor is put away ahead of those reasons—religion.

I regret to report that, if you want a house in the town of Dungannon, Co Tyrone, your chances will depend to a great extent on what church you belong to.

Ken Graham, The People, London, October 20, 1963

Our ignorance about Northern Ireland is astonishing. Some of us have been there and experienced this atmosphere of distrust, discrimination, plotting and hate. The silence in England about conditions in "Ulster" almost amounts to criminal negligence.

Martin Ennals, Tribune, London, February 7, 1964

No country deserves the Government you have here. This is the only place in the world you cannot report honestly without silly people kicking up about what is only the truth.

Alan Whicker, BBC presenter, in Belfast Telegraph, January 25, 1964

On January 17, 1964, the Campaign for Social Justice was formed in Northern Ireland for the purpose of bringing the light of publicity to bear on the discrimination against the Catholic population. Its pleas to U.K. prime minster Sir Alec Douglas Home, pointing out that discrimination was a policy by the Stormont regime in Belfast and that the U.K. Parliament had ultimate responsibility for it, were ignored. Stormont was the home of the Northern Ireland Parliament, built in the grounds of Stormont Castle, outside Belfast city. It was an imposing edifice and designed to be so. The Prince of Wales (later Edward VIII and subsequently duke of Windsor) opened it on November 17, 1932. Until that time, the Parliament had been in the City Hall and the Assembly College.

On June 27, 1966, four young Catholic barmen from the International Hotel, Belfast, leaving the Malvern Arms, a public house, were fired on by members of a resurrected Ulster Volunteer Force. Peter Ward, age eighteen, was killed, and two of his companions, Andrew Kelly and Liam Doyle, were seriously wounded. The fourth, Richard Leppington, escaped unhurt. The murders, by Protestant extremists, marked the beginning of a new phase in Ireland's bloody colonial history.

The Northern Ireland Civil Rights Association came into existence in the spring of 1968, inspired by the civil rights marches in the United States. The aims of the Northern Ireland Civil Rights Association were to achieve:

(1) A universal franchise in local government elections in line with the franchise in the rest of the United Kingdom, abandoning Ulster's proprietorial voting qualification.

(2) The redrawing of electoral boundaries by an impartial Commission to ensure fair representation, e.g. to eliminate situations where Protestants could command disproportionate influence on councils.

(3) Legislation against discrimination in employment at the local government level and the creation of machinery to remedy local government grievances.

(4) A compulsory points system for housing to ensure fair allocation.

(5) The repeal of the Special Powers Act.

(6) The disbandment of the B Special Police Force.

(7) The withdrawal of the Public Order Bill.

Max Hastings, *Ulster 1969, The Fight for Civil Rights in Northern Ireland*,
Victor Gollancz, London, 1970

Burntollet (1969)

The Northern Ireland Civil Rights Association began a series of marches along the lines of the American civil rights movement on August 24, 1968. Demonstrations for these basic civil rights by Catholics were supported by progressive sections of Protestants and other religious and nonreligious groups. The Civil Rights demonstrators were immediately attacked by Protestant extremists led by Ian Paisley (1926–), founder of his own Free Presbyterian Church of Ulster in 1951. Paisley was ordained by his father and purchased his degree by sending money to a correspondence school in the United States. With his companion, Major Ronald Bunting, aided by B Specials and even Royal Ulster Constabulary regulars, he was able to attack and even halt some of the marches with impunity while the Unionist regime condemned the Civil Rights movement for violence.

On January 1, 1969, sixty marchers set off from City Hall, Belfast, to march to Derry. This march was instigated by the People's Democracy, established in October 1968 by students at Queen's University, Belfast, who supported civil rights. Among the marchers was a twenty-two-year-old student, Bernadette Devlin, from Cookstown. The march grew in strength as it crossed the country, but on January 4, as it reached Burntollet Bridge, across the River Faughan, it was halted.

And then we came to Burntollet Bridge, and from lanes at each side of the road a curtain of bricks and boulders and bottles brought the march to a halt. From the lanes burst hordes of screaming people wielding planks of wood, bottles, laths, iron bars, crowbars, cudgels studded with nails, and they waded into the march beating the hell out of everybody.

I was a very clever girl; cowardice makes you clever. Before this onslaught, our heads-down, arms-linked tactics were no use whatever, and people began to panic and run. Immediately my mind went back to Derry on October 5th and I remembered the uselessness of running. As I stood there I could see a great big lump of flatwood, like a plank out of an orange-box, getting nearer and nearer my face, and there were two great nails sticking out of it. By a quick reflex action, my hand reached my face before the wood did, and immediate two nails went into the back of my hand. Just after that I was struck on the back of the knees with this bit of wood which had failed to get me in the face, and fell to the ground. And then my brain began to tick. "Now, Bernadette," I said, "what is the best thing to do? If you leave your arms and legs out, they'll be broken. You can have your skull cracked or your face destroyed." So I rolled up in a ball on the road, tucked my knees in, tucked my elbows in, and covered my face with one hand and the crown of my head with the other. Through my fingers, I could see legs standing round me: about six people were busily involved in trying to beat me into the ground, and I could feel dull thuds landing on my back and head. Finally, these men muttered something incoherent about leaving that one, and tore off across the fields after somebody else.

When everything was quiet, and five seconds had gone by without my feeling anything, I decided it was time to take my head up. I had a wee peer round, ducked again as a passing Paisleyite threw a swipe at me, and then got up. What had been a march was a shambles. The first few rows had managed to put a spurt on when the attack came, had got through the ambush and were safely up the road. The rest of us were all over the place. The attackers were beating marchers into the ditches, and across the ditches into the river. People were being dragged half-conscious out of the river. Others were being pursued across the fields into the woods. Others had been trapped on the road and were being given a good hiding where they stood. As I got shakily to my feet and looked round, I saw a young fellow getting a thrashing from four or five Paisleyites with a policeman looking on: the policeman was pushing the walking-wounded marchers up the road to join the front rows and doing nothing to prevent the attack.

"What the bloody hell d'you think you're doing?" I shouted at him, here-upon he gave me a vigorous shove and said. "Get up the road to the rest of your mates, stupid bitch." (Policemen always call me a stupid bitch, and I deny that I'm stupid.) Well, that push was enough for me, unsteady as I was: I just went sprawling right into Maurice Keenan, one of the marchers, and another policeman, and Bernadette's passive mood changed to anger. Maurice got me back on my feet again, saying, "Now take it easy," and even the other policeman protested to the fellow who had pushed me. "Mind the way you throw those kids about they're getting enough." He was quite reasonable: "Go you right up and stay with the march," he said to me, "and we'll get the rest of your friends."

As I turned to walk away, an unconscious girl who was bleeding about the head somewhere was carried by two of the marchers to a police truck, and the constable in the truck pushed her away with his boot. "She must get to hospital," said the marchers pushing her in. "Take her to the hospital yourself," said the constable, pushing her out. At that, two other officers came over and threw him out of the truck. "For Christ's sake, let the child in," they said. A few policemen were at least trying to stop us from being killed, but the others were quite delighted that we were getting what, in their terms, we deserved.

I went rampaging up the road saying that if I had my way, not one solitary policeman who was at Burntollet would live to be sorry for what he had done; that there was only one way of dealing with the police force—give them three weeks for every honest man to get out of it, then systematically shoot the rest. The wee policeman who had shoved me kept pace: "You say that again and you're for it! Say stuff like that again and you'll find yourself in the tender!" And I kept on saying it, and so we kept up this barrage all the way up the road.

Back with what was left of the march, I found that Tom McGurk, well-known moderate of the PD, was arguing for the march to be stopped, and everyone else was quite willing to make a sacrifice of him to the Paisleyites; for how do you stop anything in the middle of a riot? I was frantically looking round for people I couldn't see. The last time I'd seen Gerry Lawless, he'd been scrambling over a ditch having the head thumped off him by four Paisleyites and I thought he had probably been killed. And I couldn't find Eddie Toman: these were my two "cowards," and they were both missing. I found Eamon McCann: "Look Eamon, I'll have to go back to look for people." Eamon said, "If we get out of this without having at least three people dead, we shall thank God, if he exists, for miracles; but if you go down there, there'll be four people dead; and when you don't come back, I'll go down there and I'll be dead, and it will all be lovely. All we can do is march on and hope we don't find a corpse when we get to Derry." And that was the first thing that really brought me to my senses. There were, as it happened, no deaths, but eighty-seven people were taken to hospital from Burntollet, and many more were less seriously injured. No one was brought to justice for it nor ever will be. Evidence was collected—by civilians not by the police who didn't see the necessity for doing so; but Major Chichester-Clark, when he became Prime Minister, declared an amnesty, and our attackers need never worry about the damage they did us at Burntollet Bridge.

Bernadette Devlin (now McAliskey), *The Price of My Soul*, Deutsch, London, 1969

Indeed, on January 5, 1969, Northern Ireland prime minister Captain Terence O'Neill denounced the marchers as "mere hooligans" and praised the police "who handled this most difficult situation as fairly and as firmly as they could." However, when a government-appointed commission under Lord Cameron investigated the matter and issued its report as Disturbances in Northern Ireland *(HMSO, 1969), it found "a number of policemen were guilty of misconduct which involved assault and battery, malicious damage to property in streets in predominantly Catholic Bogside (Derry)." The commission recommended the disbandment of the B Specials, the disarming of the Royal Ulster Constabulary, making it a civil police rather than a paramilitary one, and an examination of the discrimination and lack of civil rights. A few months later, on April 17, Bernadette Devlin was returned as a member of Parliament to Westminster for the Mid-Ulster constituency.*

Throughout the early months of 1969, many Civil Rights advocates were attacked by Paisley's supporters openly backed by the RUC B Specials. On Thursday, April 14, the United Kingdom deployed troops in Derry in full battle kit to protect the Catholic enclaves, following an attack by six hundred fully armed police backed by armed civilians. The Catholic Bogside became a barricaded ghetto for the protection of its citizens. The Irish Republic Taoiseach (prime minister) ordered the Irish army to the border and requested a United Nations peacekeeping force to be sent into Northern Ireland. Among the civilians killed by the RUC was Francis McCloskey, age sixty-seven, bludgeoned in Dungiven, Derry; Samuel Devenny, age forty-two, who died three months after the RUC broke into his house on William Street, Bogside, and beat him up; Patrick Corry, age sixty-one, bludgeoned in Unity Flats Belfast; Patrick Roony, age nine, shot near Divis Street Flats, Belfast; Hugh McCabe, Samuel McLarnon, Michael Lynch, Gerald McAuley, and John Gallagher, shot in Armagh.

Civil Rights Demonstration, Armagh
(August 14, 1969)

I was invited to speak in Armagh City Hall at a civil rights meeting on August 14, 1969. I was rather late in getting there and when I reached the roundabout at the Moy Road I found a large force of police and B Specials on duty.

I was told I could not go to the City Hall. I asked for a passage to be made for me but this was refused. Consequently I never reached the hall and in fact parked my car at the foot of Banbrooke Hill where I met a small number of civil rights supporters. They told me there had been police baton charges down the hill but that most of the civil rights supporters had gone into the Shambles Square.

It later transpired that the meeting in the City Hall had been abandoned because of a report that the Paisleyites were going to burn down the hall when the people were inside. The Paisleyite mob were outside the hall with police and B Specials fraternising with them.

From my position at the foot of Banbrooke Hill I could see that stones were being thrown now and again by the civil rights people in Shambles Square, and they were being returned by Paisleyites, RUC and Specials. A couple of petrol bombs were also thrown but they did no damage. I witnessed this confrontation for about three-quarters of an hour or so and at about 11 P.M. I heard several shots—it seemed to be a burst of automatic fire.

A moment later I looked around and saw to my consternation a group of eight Specials walking resolutely and steadily towards us from the Moy direction. They were armed. Myself and another man got the crowd of civil rights supporters up Banbrooke Hill away from the Specials.

I thought they were going past to join the police and Paisleyites down the road a bit, but when they came to the corner they wheeled around and went down on their knees, with their weapons pointed at us. I heard one of them shout out that they would "blow our heads off" all of us if we did not get in quickly.

One of these Specials was a man named King, a well-known Paisleyite. He is a big burly man, a resident of the Armagh area, and the people greatly fear him.

We ran up Banbrooke Hill helter-skelter into whatever house we could find cover in and the Specials followed us. The people were screaming in terror.

In the house I had entered we all lay on the floor with all lights off. I could hear the Specials out in the street shouting threats.

They eventually retreated to the bottom of the hill. People came out and huddled around the doors—and then word came that Seán Gallagher was dead.

John Gallagher, age thirty, was shot on Cathedral Road by the RUC B Specials.

Some time later I saw Mrs Gallagher and she told what happened. She heard that her husband was shot and she rushed into the street. There was a police patrol car there and she went over and asked the police about her husband's condition. They advised her to telephone the hospital, but she was unable to get through.

She went back to the patrol car and asked: "For God's sake, take me to the hospital because I am afraid to go through the Paisleyite mob down there." This the police refused to do. So, she had to make her own way through a mob to the hospital where she found that her husband was dead.

I could not face going home to Dungannon that night because it was too dangerous. [In fact, six people were shot on that one day, five by the RUC.] There were B Specials roaming around; their cars roared through the city that night. I do not regard myself as a coward; I say things publicly that indicate that I am not a coward, but I was afraid to go down the street and get my car and drive it up to the hose where I was staying because I would have had to pass a number of Specials.

I stayed in the house of some friends that night and they gave me a bed. I think it was about 3 A.M. when we got to bed, and at 3.30 A.M. I was awakened by members of the family to tell me there was a fire in the town.

The city of Armagh seemed to be ablaze and we rang the Fire Brigade. They had not been called out, although the factory, which was ablaze, was now half burned out. This seemed extraordinary since the streets in that area were being patrolled by B Specials and police earlier.

The factory—a big textile plant owned by Bairnswear Ltd—was burned down and £1 million damages done. It is significant that it gave employment to a large number of Catholics.

After that, I went back to Gallagher's house and there I met a press reporter who told me that he had been up to the RUC barracks and was told that "the police and B Specials had not fired any shots."

I then spoke to two men who had witnessed the shooting of Seán Gallagher. They stated that they had seen about four cars without lights come down Cathedral Road to the back of the civil rights demonstrators who were engaged in a confrontation with the police in throwing stone at Shambles Square. Uniformed Specials jumped out of the cars and opened fire, killing Seán Gallagher and wounding two others. This was the shooting I had heard earlier that night.

At 6.30 A.M. That morning on the BBC news bulletin I was incensed to hear a statement by the RUC to the effect that they had not fired any shots, and further that Seán Gallagher did not die by any shots fired by any police.

Aidan Corrigan, Eye-Witness in Northern Ireland, Voice of Ulster Publications,
Dungannon, 1969

On the morning of Saturday, August 16, the British army was finally deployed throughout Northern Ireland, to initially protect the Catholics from attacks from the Loyalists. There is a historical irony that the first RUC man to die in the ensuing conflict, Constable Victor Arbuckle, age twenty-nine, was shot by Loyalists on October 11, 1969, on Shankill Road, Belfast.

22

The Long War

Smarting from the 1969 graffiti in Nationalist areas, "IRA—I Ran Away," those in the Republican movement demanded action to protect the Nationalist ghettos. Toward the end of 1969, the Republican movement split. A "Provisional" Sinn Féin and IRA disowned the old leadership, now indulging in Marxist theory, which had allowed the rank-and-file IRA to become almost nonexistent. Volunteers flocked to the new organization. In the U.K. general election of June 1970, Edward Heath's Conservative and Unionist Party came to power. The Northern Ireland Unionists were an integral part of the government party. Policy changed for the army, and instead of acting as a buffer for the out-of-control forces of the Northern Ireland statelet, the British army began to turn their attention to the Nationalists, harassing and searching Nationalist areas and turning a blind eye to Loyalist extremists. The Provisional IRA began to strike back.

There were 170 bomb attacks in 1970, but it was not until February 6, 1971, that the first member of the British army was killed. By August 8, 1971, eleven soldiers, one UDR man, and three policemen had been killed. The new Unionist prime minister of Northern Ireland was Brian Faulkner (1921–1977), who created a furor among liberals when he announced on May 25 that any soldier could shoot to kill merely on suspicion and not get into trouble. He then persuaded the U.K. government to back him with the introduction of internment without trial. On the day of internment, August 9, fourteen people were killed and one hundred wounded. The shooting war had started in earnest.

Internment (August 1971)

At five o'clock on August 9, British soldiers smashed their way into the house of Patrick Joe McClean, age thirty-nine, a remedial teacher and local Civil Rights worker, in Beragh, County Tyrone. Hauled away from his wife and children, McClean was one of 342 men who were interned under the notorious Special Powers Act.

I spent the first 48 hours period with the other detainees at Magilligan Camp. At the end of these initial 48 hours, a hood was pulled over my head and I was handcuffed and subjected to verbal and personal abuse, which included the threat of being dropped from a helicopter while it was in the air. I was then dragged out to the helicopter, being kicked and struck about the body with batons on the way.

After what seemed about one hour in the helicopter I was thrown from it and kicked and batoned into what I took to be a lorry. The lorry was driven only a couple of hundred yards to a building. On arriving there I was given a thorough examination by a doctor. After this, all my clothes were taken from me and I was given a boiler suit to wear which had no buttons and which was several sizes too big for me.

During this time the hood was still over my head and the handcuffs were removed only at the time of the "medical examination."

I was then taken into what I can only guess was another room and made to stand with my feet wide apart with my hands pressed against a wall. During all this time I could hear a low droning noise, which sounded to me like an electric saw or something of that nature. This continued for what I can only describe as an indefinite period of time. I stood there, arms against the wall, feet wide apart. My arms, legs, back and head began to ache. I perspired freely, the noise and heat were terrible. My brain was ready to burst. What was going to happen to me? Was I alone? Are they coming to kill me? I wished to God they would, to end it. My circulation had stopped. I flexed my arms to start the blood flowing again. They struck me several times on the hands, ribs, kidneys and my kneecaps were kicked. My hood covered head was banged against the wall.

As I have said this particular method of torture lasted for an indefinite period, but having consulted other men who suffered the same experience I believe this period to have been about two days and nights.

During this time certain periods are blank—fatigue, mental and physical, overwhelmed me; I collapsed several times only to be beaten and pulled to my feet again and once more pushed spread-eagle against the wall. Food, water and the opportunity to relieve my bowels were denied me. I had to urinate and defecate in my [boiler] suit. I collapsed again.

I came to in what I believe to be Crumlin Road jail, having been pushed into a chair. The hood was removed and I was handed what I was told was a detention form. I was told to read it. My eyes burnt and were filled with pain; they would not focus and I couldn't read the form. . . . The hood was pulled over my bursting head. I was roughly jerked to my feet and half pulled, half kicked and beaten for about 400 yards. This was the worst and most sustained beating to date. Fists, boots and batons crashed into my numbed body, someone else's not mine. Hands behind my back, handcuffs biting into my wrists. Pain! Someone was pulling and jerking my arms. Thrown headline into a vehicle—soft seats, beating continued, boots, batons, fists. Then the noise, that dreaded helicopter again. Dragged out of the vehicle by the hair, thrown onto the floor of the helicopter. Blacked out!

Conscious again. Hands manacled in front of me. Pushed against a wall, legs wide apart. I dug my fingernails into the wall, pain all over me.

Now that I can relax and think about it I can't find words to describe the pain. Without attempting to be melodramatic, I think I can best describe it by saying I was enveloped in stretching, cramping pain.

My mind began to drift. I tried to sing to myself. I was going mad. I must already be mad to stick this.

Still standing rigid against the wall someone takes my pulse, sounds my bruised chest over my heart. Must be a doctor.

Dragged along. Pushed into a chair, hood pulled off. Screaming, blinding light, questions fast and hard, couldn't speak. "Spell your name." Tried to find the letters, swimming in my brain—couldn't spell my name. I must be insane. More questions—blows, hair pulled. Still can't see well. A table—three men at it—all writing—blinding light.

I was told I would be given half an hour to rest and think. Then I would be asked more questions and if I didn't answer them I would be taken back to the "music room"—the room with the noise—pain.

Sleep—deep, black sleep. Pulled to my feet. Back to the questions again, would not give answers. Back to "music room."

Feet wide apart, hands handcuffed—against the wall. Droning noise filled my head. By this time I could feel no pain. Just numb. Dragged away from the wall, legs buckled under me, fell to the floor. Dragged by the ankles up and down shallow steps. Didn't care—past feeling pain. Didn't have a body.

From now on it was interrogation—back to the "music room"—some sleep. The first taste of water in—how many days? Some dry bread and more water.

We were given out first "meal." This consisted of a cup of watery stew, which I had to eat using my fingers as utensil. The hood was lifted just enough to leave mouth free. We were allowed then to toilet for the first time since we arrived.

Punishment now eased off. Interrogation continued. Strict questioning —no beatings—just threats and personal insults. Food of a more substantial nature still badly cooked and served, but at least it was regular.

The hood was taken off and I was allowed to wash.

Now I was allowed to sleep, but the room was so cold that sleep was hard to come by. The fear of more beatings was still with me. I was terribly alone! They gave me one blanket—to keep me warm, they said.

I was told it was "all over," and I was to be interned in Crumlin Road jail. Didn't believe them—another trick, I thought. Still uneasy, still worried— still alone.

Hood over my head, but treated better now, no questions, no beating. Journey to Crumlin Road jail by lorry, helicopter and Land Rover. I was still alive—still sane—thank God!

Patrick Joe McClean, statement to the Association for Legal Justice,
printed in John McGuffin, *Internment*, Tralee, 1973
Also in John McGuffin, *The Guinea Pigs*, Penguin Books, London, 1974

By the end of 1971, some 2,357 people had been interned without trial or charge under the Special Powers Act. Many internees, innocent of any connection with the IRA, suffered torture by British military and RUC police interrogation. When stories about the brutality of the interrogations began to emerge in the press and media, the British government was forced to establish a commission under Sir Edward Compton. His Report of the Enquiry into Allegations against the Security Forces of Physical Brutality in Northern Ireland Arising Out of Events on 9 August, 1971 *could not deny the facts but played semantics with the words* torture *and* brutality.

Where we have concluded that physical ill-treatment took place, we are not making a finding of brutality on the part of those who handled these complainants. We consider that brutality is an inhuman or savage form of cruelty and that cruelty implies a disposition to inflict suffering, coupled with indifference to, or pleasure in, the victim's pain. We do not think that happened here.

The European Court of Human Rights at Strasbourg found, however, that the U.K. government was responsible for practices that constituted "torture, inhuman and degrading treatment of arrested persons in Northern Ireland." Patrick Joe McClean was awarded $33,600 "compensation" by the United Kingdom nine years after the event. The U.K. government paid out $4.8 million in compensation for the ill treatment that people had received at the hands of the police and army in Northern Ireland during this period.

Bloody Sunday (January 30, 1972): A Journalist's View

It was the most unbelievable. . . . I have travelled many countries, I have seen many civil wars and revolutions and wars, but I have never seen such a cold-blooded murder, organised, disciplined murder, planned murder. . . .

I was in the frontline of the march as the march approached the barricades erected by the military in William Street. There were a few exchanges, a few throws of stones, not very heavy, and afterwards, about three or four minutes, the Army moved up with this water cannon and sprayed the whole crowd with coloured water. Then the crowd dispersed.

Successively, it returned and threw some more stones, nothing as I have seen in other places in Northern Ireland, nothing really very heavy. After which gas was used massively by the Army, and the crowd dispersed towards the meeting place, which was at Free Derry Corner. As the crowd was moving away, I would say about a couple of thousand people— completely peaceful because they had been drenched with gas and they could hardly breathe, and many were sick—suddenly in the area behind Free Derry Corner—Rossville flats, I think it is called, the big square in front of those flats—the Army, the paratroopers, moved in on Saracens.

And other paratroopers followed on foot, and they jumped out. The people were thinking they would be given another dose of gas and scattered very hurriedly and they really fled towards Free Derry Corner. The Army jumped out and they started shooting in all directions. I took pictures of this, I took recordings of this, and there is no doubt whatsoever that there wasn't the slightest provocation.

There hadn't been one shot fired at them. There hadn't been one nail bomb thrown at them. They just jumped out and, with unbelievable murderous fury, shot into the fleeing crowd.

I saw a man with his son crossing the street, trying to get to safety, with their hands on their heads. They were shot dead. The man got shot dead. The son, I think, was dying.

I saw a young fellow who had been wounded, crouching against the wall. He was shouting "don't shoot, don't shoot." A paratrooper approached him and shot him from about one yard. I saw a young boy of 15 protecting his girl friend against the wall and then proceeding to try to rescue her by going out with a handkerchief and with the other hand on his hat. A paratrooper approached, shot him from about one yard into the stomach and shot the girl into the arm.

I saw a priest approaching a fallen boy in the middle of the square, try-ing to help him, give him the last rites, perhaps, and the army—I saw a paratrooper kneel down and take aim at him and shoot at him, and the priest just got away by laying flat on his belly. I saw a French colleague of mine who, shouting "press, press" and raising high his arms, went into the middle to give help to a fallen person and I saw again paratroopers kneel-ing down and aiming at him, and it's only by a fantastic acrobatic jump that he did that he got away.

I myself got shot at five times. I was at a certain stage shielding behind a window. I approached the window to take some pictures. Five bullets went immediately through the window, and I don't know how they missed.

It was panic, it was sheer despair, it was frustration, I saw people, old men crying, young boys who had lost their friends . . . crying and not understanding. There was astonishment. There was bewilderment, there was rage and frustration.

Interview with Italian photojournalist Fulivio Grimaldi
Broadcast on Radio Éireann, Monday, January 31, 1972
Reprinted in *Massacre in Derry,* Civil Rights publication, March 1972

One of our girls of the Order (of Malta—St John's Ambulance Brigade) was running to an injured man who we later found out had a heart attack and later died in the Ambulance going to the hospital.

She went over to help him and she waved her hands in the air shouting "first aid, first aid" to the soldier standing at the end of the Court behind a wooden fence, and they fired two rounds of ammunition at her. Everyone seen the dirt rising beside her feet. The girl was that much shocked that she dropped to the ground and she thought she was hit and when some passer-by came along and went over and examined her and told her she was all right—she wasn't hit—she got up and rushed forward to the soldiers, who still had their guns ready to shoot, and she said: "Don't shoot me, don't shoot me, I'm a first aid girl." And they started laughing at her.

Statement of paramedic Seán McDermott (St. John's Ambulance Brigade),
in Massacre in Derry, Civil Rights publication, March 1972

U.K. Embassy in Dublin Attacked and Burned Down (February 1972)

Seán Ó Bradaigh called me on Monday to ask if I would speak at a public meeting we were to hold outside the GPO on Tuesday night. I agreed; and on Tuesday, when the meeting was held, I had never seen O'Connell Street so jammed with people. After the meeting, which itself was cut short because it was so difficult to hold the crowd's attention, we marched on Merrion Square; the windows of British offices such as BEA were smashed, and the Dublin shopkeepers hurried out to put up their shutters. In Merrion Square, petrol bombs were being thrown at the Embassy. A tall house in an elegant Georgian terrace; I saw bottles curve through the air and smash against the wall, exploding in flames. Prominent in the crowd by virtue of their close-cropped hair was a group of Dublin skinheads, who had found a load of coal to hurl at the Embassy widows, but there were people of all ages, men and women, surging and cheering.

The real onslaught against the Embassy came on Wednesday, the day of mourning throughout the Twenty-six Counties, observed with almost complete unanimity. There was another march on the Embassy, with demonstrators carrying black flags and tricolours and three coffins draped in black, which were left on the steps leading into the Embassy. There were probably 20,000 people in the square—and the Provisionals' lorry, from which some of the Provisional leaders including Joe Cahill were vainly attempting to make speeches and direct events, was quite swallowed up.

Then the petrol bombs began again, raining against the Embassy, each one greeted by a huge cheer from the crowd, who were behaving like spectators at a football match. The Irish police made an attempt to move them, a line of about a hundred charging with their batons drawn, and the crowd partly scattered. But they soon returned when the next petrol bomb flew through the air. Some of the crowd were shouting "Up the IRA"—how many would retain their enthusiasm for us in a week's time? I wondered— and then chats began of "Burn, burn burn." Each explosion was greeted by a new cheer and a new surge forward. Then the window frames caught alight—but disappointingly, from the crowd's point of view, the flames did not spread inside the building.

Clanging bells signalled the arrival of the Dublin Fire Brigade, but their appliances couldn't get near the Embassy because the crowd refused to move. When they tried to approach down a street that led to the back of the building, they were blocked there too. The Gardaí charged again, and made some impressions on the crowd; but the next hail of petrol bombs soon brought them back again, and from that time both the Fire Brigade and the Gardaí abandoned their efforts.

. . . Suddenly I heard the news spread through the crowd: "The IRA's here." Then I saw a group of men moving quickly through the crowd, now wearing black IRA berets and carrying sledgehammers. I watched them attempt to batter down the door; to my surprise they failed. (The door, I discovered later, was reinforced with steel.) Then several men climbed up the outside of the building, one with an axe, the other with a tricolour. One tore down the Union Jack and flew the tricolour instead; there were more cheers, and a further barrage of petrol bombs.

The Embassy was still not burning, and it seemed as if our men were going to fail. Then, just as I heard someone shout the warning: "There's a bomb," there was an explosion in front of the building and the front door fell in—injuring two members of the Special Branch who happened to be standing behind it. Petrol bombs flew in through the doorway and in minutes flames were leaping from the Embassy windows. The crowd fell back because of the heat, ashes falling among them, but when the Fire Brigade moved in they found that their hoses had been cut.

All that week the burnt-out building was Dublin's principal tourist attraction. We thought it characteristic of British hypocrisy that their press and politicians expressed their horror and outrage at the burning— it contrasted too acutely with their failure to express anything of the kind over the thirteen Derry killings. The Irish Government, of course, apologised to the British—the British Government hadn't apologised to Derry—and said it would pay for the damage.

Maria McGuire, To Take Arms: A Year in the Provisional IRA, Quartet Books,
London, 1973

On March 24, 1972, the Northern Ireland Parliament was suspended and direct rule from London was imposed, with William Whitelaw (1918–) becoming the first secretary of state for Northern Ireland. Following a negotiated cease-fire instigated by the U.K. government on July 7, 1972, a Sinn Féin delegation was flown to London by the Royal Air Force for exploratory talks with Whitelaw and his junior Northern Ireland minister, Paul Channon. Two senior civil servants who had negotiated the truce, Frank Steele and Philip Woodfield, also took part. The republican delegation consisted of IRA chief of staff Seán Mac Stiofáin, Dáithí Ó Conaill, Seamus Ó Tuama, Gerry Adams, Martin McGuiness, and Ivor Bell, with a solicitor, Myles Shevlin, acting as the delegation's secretary.

We landed in England at Benson RAF station in Oxfordshire. Two very large limousines with Special Branch drivers were waiting for us. We headed for London, making one stop for a phone call in Staines to the secretary we had arranged to have with us for delegation work.

Our destination turned out to be a private house overlooking the Thames near Chelsea Bridge. It belonged to Whitelaw's junior minister, Paul Channon. We were guided upstairs to a very spacious carpeted room. A massive library of books filled an entire wall. The furniture was valuable and antique, but I would have been far more impressed had there been any signs of businesslike preparations for a conference. There were none, no proper working table, no table for notes, not even the elementary civility of a jug of water.

We were on our feet chatting when the door opened and Whitelaw came in. With him were Channon, Steele and Woodfield. [Paul Channon, Frank Steele, and Philip Woodfield]. Whitelaw came straight over and offered me his hand as we were introduced. "Oh, Mr MacStiofáin. How do you do?" He pronounced my name in Irish perfectly. Sure enough, he had also done some homework before the meeting. His manner was cordial, as if he were greeting business acquaintances. When the introductions were completed, Whitelaw said innocently to Dave, "Perhaps you'd like to sit next to me, Mr O'Connell?" [Dáithí Ó Conaill].

And, of course, Dave declined. I said that our delegation would sit together. I saw some of the British representatives look at each other sharply. I am not sure how they had expected we would conduct ourselves.

Seán MacStiofáin, *Memoirs of a Revolutionary*, Gordon Cremonesi, London, 1975

The cease-fire lasted fourteen days. The British military provoked a confrontation at Lenadoon in Belfast when they arrested two IRA men, in spite of the terms of the truce, and opened fire on the crowd. In spite of Dáithí Ó Conaill telephoning Whitelaw directly, it became clear that the U.K. forces had merely used the cease-fire to redeploy. At 9 P.M. on July 10, 1972, the Sinn Féin office in Dublin issued a statement from the IRA: "The truce between the IRA and British occupation forces was broken without warning by British forces. . . . Accordingly all IRA units have been instructed to resume offensive action." It was clear what the British army had been planning. On July 27, Operation Motorman, deploying twenty-one thousand regular soldiers with armored cars, converted tanks, bulldozers, and Land Rovers, entered the Nationalist ghettos that since 1969 had become "no go" areas controlled by the local populations. Troops smashed their way into the areas. Tactically, the IRA did not oppose the overwhelming force by an attempt to defend the areas.

As the war progressed, there was another truce called by the IRA on December 22, 1974, to allow the U.K. government to respond to a proposal from leading Protestant clergymen. It was to last until January 1, but the IRA extended it until January 22. The British government did engage in talks with Sinn Féin and the truce was renewed on February 9 but collapsed on February 17, 1975. Once more, the U.K. forces merely saw it as a means of redeployment. Although the Special Powers Act was repealed, being against all human rights conventions, it was replaced in July 1973 by an equally oppressive Northern Ireland (Emergency Provisions) Act. Unsuccessful attempts were made to set up "power-sharing" assemblies.

Mac Stiofáin (1928–2001) was arrested in the Irish Republic later in 1972 and therefore ceased to be chief of staff. He was the last IRA chief of staff to be given a media profile, and the IRA Army Council went "underground."

"Covert Action" (1974)

On October 5, 1974, Eugene McQuaid, age thirty-five, was killed in an explosion at Killeen, County Armagh.

My first knowledge of the "Case of the self-exploding motor cyclist" came when I went to Brigade HQ in Lurgan and discovered Captain D, Captain M the Brigade's explosives expert, and others of the Intelligence staff sitting round guffawing like a lot of schoolboys in the tuck-shop. The big jar of white mints they kept to celebrate successes in the field was being passed round. The killing of Eugene McQuaid—the event being celebrated—had been well planned and intelligence sources in the south were heavily involved. An arms cache had been discovered some time previously across the border. Instrumental in allowing an ordnance expert to cross into County Monaghan and take a look at it, the Garda, had also contacted an Irish Army officer with a view of getting him involved: and he claimed that he had been given leave for this approach from a higher authority in both the Eire Army [sic] and the Garda itself. But the officer reported the matter to GHQ in Dublin. A report was then compiled concerning his role as an undercover agent for the British—but to no apparent effect. Instead he was later able to arrange for a "Covert Felix" team from the north of the border to go across and, rather than simply inspect the cache, to actually interfere with its contents. (Felix the cat is the symbol of the British Army's Explosive Ordnance Disposal team and is also used by the Intelligence teams.) Such teams consisted of special Ammunition Technical officers, and usually a senior NCO who worked primarily with the SAS and members of the RUC Special Branch or with their counterparts in the Intelligence Corps, depending upon the task required.

On this occasion it was Captain M himself who went on the mission—and carefully sawed through the safety pins inside the rockets which had been found in the IRA cache. These rocks, or bombards as they are more usually known, had already been used by the IRA to attack armoured vehicles, and had a range of up to 800 feet. The discovery of these "mobile mines" was quite a coup. However, by sabotaging them in this fashion, it was quite impossible to predict when or how they would explode: any rough handling would be enough to set them off.

Of course, when Eugene McQuaid was asked to transport the bombards to the north on his motorcycle, he could not have known the risk he was taking—though he must have known what the package contained. So he set off towards Newry, as arranged—under close surveillance from the security forces. McQuaid drove quite some way before he encountered the checkpoint set up especially for him on the Dundalk-Newry road, just north of the border, with the Army team set well back from the area for their own safety's sake. McQuaid braked and turned back towards the Republic. As he did so one of the booby-trapped bombards which he had strapped by the bike's petrol tank exploded. (The detonator was struck by a pin attached to a sliding weight moving on deceleration.)

Eugene McQuaid was blown to pieces a hundred yards or so from Donnelly's Garage. A witness who heard the explosion and came out to see what had happened was greeted by the side of the motorcyclists severed head, still encased in his helmet, lying at the foot of a tree, with blood running gently from the nose. The remains of McQuaid's body and motorbike were scattered across the pavement and a field nearby and hanging from the tree itself. The witness described how the Army team arrived quickly at the spot and one soldier was seen to approach the severed head, pick up a handful of the dead man's guts, and say, "That's an end of another of you bastards."

Had McQuaid been intercepted rather than turned into a live bomb on his journey north, it is quite likely that he would have been broken under interrogation, and might have yielded useful information about the people he was working for. Far more important is the fact that the motorbike might have exploded on the streets of Dundalk in the south, or in Newry north of the border, where scores of innocent people might have been injured or killed. There was no possible guarantee, once he had set off, that this wouldn't have happened. Yet back at Brigade HQ in Lurgan the white mints were out and Captain D and his cronies were congratulating one another.

Captain Fred Holroyd, *War Without Honour*, Hull, 1989

Bobby Sands, M.P.: Republican Prisoner

In 1976, the British government had withdrawn political status from all prisoners' involvement in the Irish war in an effort to present the IRA as criminals. As a protest, republican prisoners refused to wear prison clothes, remaining naked in their cells, or wearing a prison blanket. Bobby Sands, a twenty-four-year-old former community worker and republican, had been on remand for eleven months before being sentenced in September 1977 to fourteen years in prison for the alleged possession of a revolver. He spent twenty-two days in solitary confinement, of which fifteen were in an unheated cell with his clothes removed. He began to write on toilet paper with a ballpoint refill and smuggled his work out.

Panic gripped me as the heavy steel door rattled and flew open. A wave of black uniforms swept into my cell blotting out the door space. A gruff, intimidating voice yelled, "Right you, get up!"

I was already half way to my feet before the last syllable left his rowdy mouth, wrapping my threadbare old blue towel around my shivering waist.

"Bears in the air" echoed throughout the wing as those awake and alerted by the invasion warned the rest of the lads that there were screws in the wing.

"Wing shift," someone shouted, leaving me in no doubt as to what was to come.

"Right you, out and up to the top of the wind and be quick," rowdy mouth snapped. I moved out of the cell, the corridor was black with uniforms, batons dangling by their sides.

"Not quick enough," rowdy mouth snapped again.

Two strong pairs of arms gripped me from behind. My arms were wrenched up my back and my feet left the floor. A mass of black thronged around me and moved in a sudden burst of speed dragging me along with it. I came back to earth and a well-polished pair of leather official issue boots ground into my feet. A screw on the perimeter of the now excited gang kneed me in the thigh. I felt like vomiting and creaming surrender but I remained mute. A table loomed up before me where half a dozen or so screws converged, gaping and inspecting me—their first intentional prey. I was left standing in the midst of the black horde who awaited their cue from the mouthpiece.

"Right," screamed the self-appointed tyrant. "Drop that towel, turn round. Bend down and touch your toes."

I dropped my towel, turned a full circle and stood there embarrassed and naked, all eyes scrutinising my body.

"You forgot something," the mouthpiece grunted.

"No I didn't," I stammered in a fit of bravado.

"Bend down, tramp," he hissed right into my face in a voice that hinted of a strained patience. Here it comes, I thought.

"I'm not bending," I said.

Roars of forced laughter reinforced by a barrage of jibes and abuse erupted.

"Not bending!" the confident bastard jibed.

"Not bending! Ha! Ha! He's not bending, lads," he said to the impatient audience.

Jesus, here it comes. He stepped beside me, still laughing and hit me. Within a few seconds, in the midst of the white flashes, I fell to the floor as blows rained upon me from every conceivable angle. I was dragged back up again to my feet and thrown like a side of bacon, face downwards on the table. Searching hands pulled at my arms and legs, spreading me like a pelt of leather. Someone had my head pulled back by the hair while some pervert began prodding and poking my anus.

It was great fun: everybody was killing themselves laughing, except me, while all the time a barrage of punches rained down on my naked body. I was writhing in pain. They gripped me tighter as each blow found its destination. My face was smashed against the table and blood smeared the table under my face. I was dazed and hurt. Then they dragged me off the table and let me drop on the floor. My first reaction was to wrap the towel, which lay beside me around my reddened waist. Again I was gripped by the arms from behind and dragged towards the other wing. I just caught a glimpse of one of my comrades being beaten and dragged to the table, while in the background someone else was being kicked out of his cell. A cell door opened and I was flung inside. The door slammed shut and I lay on the concrete floor, chest pounding and every nerve in my body strained. Could have been worse. I tried to tell myself in consolation. But this didn't convince me or my aching body one bit.

The cold drove me off the floor. Every part of my body protested as I made the slow ascent to my feet. A trickle of blood ran from my mouth on to my long shaggy beard and dripped on to the floor. My skin was finely emblazoned and with a host of bruises and marks. I was trembling. I hadn't really had very much time to be frightened; everything had moved too fast. Thank God I had not been asleep when they came.

"We'll get those bastards someday," I told myself. We'll see how big they are then, I thought, as I spat out a mouthful of blood into the corner.

"We'll see how great they are then."

I began pacing the floor. The cold streamed in through the open window and still clad only in a towel, I really felt it. God I was sore.

More bodies were dragged down the wind.

The bastards were shouting their sadistic heads off, revelling in the blood and pain, all of it ours, of course. God only knows how long it will be before they decide to throw us in a blanket. An empty freezing cold cell, an aching black and blue frozen body, a bunch of psychopaths beating men to pulp outside the door and it isn't even bloody well breakfast time yet!

"Suffering Jesus, can it get any worse?" I asked myself, and then answered, "you know bloody well that it will." That's what was worrying me.

Bobby Sands, *One Day in My Life*, Mercier Press, Dublin, 1983

In Long Kesh, the H-Blocks—renamed by the British HM Prison the Maze— republican prisoners finally went on a hunger strike on October 27, 1980, to restore their political status and as a protest against the ill treatment they were receiving. Brendan Hughes led the seven hunger strikers. The British authorities persuaded the hunger strikers to come off the fast by promising them a return to the political prisoner status. With the men safely off, the British authorities refused to keep their word. This made a second strike inevitable. On March 1, 1981, Bobby Sands led the new hunger strike, insisting that he begin two weeks in front of his fellow hunger strikers, so if the British proved intransigent, his death might secure for the others the five demands that would return them to the status of political prisoners.

The five demands were: (1) They wanted the right to wear their own clothes at all times. (2) Political prisoners should not be required to do menial prison work; they were prepared to do all work required for the maintenance and cleaning of the portions of the prison occupied by them. They also asked that study time should be taken into account in determining the amount of work they were required to do. (3) They requested the right to associate freely at recreation time with other political prisoners. (4) They requested the right to a weekly visit, letter, or parcel, as well as the right to organize their own educational and recreational pursuits in the prison. (5) They wanted the right to remission of sentences as is normally provided for all other prisoners.

On April 10, while in prison and on a hunger strike, Bobby Sands was elected Member of Parliament at Westminster for the constituency of Fermanagh and South Tyrone. At 1:17 A.M. on Tuesday, May 5, as he entered into his sixty-sixth day of the hunger strike, Bobby Sands, M.P., died.

The U.K. government of Margaret Thatcher was intransigent. After Bobby Sands died, Francis Hughes died on May 12, 1981; then Raymond McCreesh and Patsy O'Hara on May 21, 1981; Joe McDonnell on July 8, 1981; Martin Hurson on July 13, 1981; Kevin Lynch on August 1, 1981; Kieran Doherty, who had been elected while a prisoner as a TD, a member of the Dáil, the Republic of Ireland's Parliament, died on August 3, 1981; Thomas McElwee on August 8, 1981; and Michael Devine on August 29, 1981. Pressure was put on families by the religious authorities, so when a hunger striker slipped into unconsciousness, the next of kin was persuaded to give permission for the authorities to feed and revive this person. Under such conditions, the hunger strike was eventually called off. Irish bitterness against rule from England only increased.

The Death of John Downes (August 12, 1984)

Silvia Calamati is an Italian journalist and writer. Having earned her degree in philosophy at the University of Venice, she went to University College, Dublin, to carry out postgraduate research. She was interested in what was happening in Northern Ireland and went to see for herself. What she saw changed her life and made her become a journalist. She covered Northern Ireland for the Italian weekly Avvenimente.

On August 2, 1984, the annual Internment March took place. Thousands of people converged on Falls Road. They came from the nationalist areas of Belfast and from all over Ireland. Support groups came from Britain, America and other parts of the world. I remember it was a nice, warm, sunny day. The march went off peaceful in a kind of festive spirit. There were lots of children in the street.

When the march got to Andersonstown the people gathered in front of the Sinn Féin offices to listen to Gerry Adams speaking. A lot of them sat down on the ground. The road was closed off at each end by the armoured vehicles of the RUC and by dozens of police officers in their battle gear. On the rooftops, behind the people, British soldiers observed the proceedings. A TV camera fixed to a helicopter hovering low over our heads, filmed the scene.

The noise from the helicopter was so deafening that we could barely make out what Gerry Adams was saying. So only a few people heard that the next speaker would be Martin Galvin. He was the representative of the American association NORAID and the then Secretary of State, James Prior, had denied him entry into Northern Ireland.

In a few seconds, in an attempt to arrest him, the RUC officers climbed into their armoured cars, started their engines and began to move forward, ignoring the crowds of people sitting on the ground. Other policemen used brute force and batons to clear the way. They lashed out blindly at men, women and children who hadn't been given time to get to their feet. Photographers and reporters too were beaten and clubbed.

It was then that the police began to shoot. Again and again they fired rounds of plastic bullets into the crowd. Panic broke out. Terrified, the people didn't know which way to run. Many tried to get their children to safety by taking to the side-streets. The dozens of people sitting down could only flatten themselves against the ground to try to stay underneath the line of fire. Anyone who stood up would become a target.

John Downes, a young man of 22, was hit in the heart by one of those bullets. Though he was given help straight away, he died very soon after, there on the asphalt of Andersonstown.

Twenty people were wounded that tragic afternoon, struck by plastic bullets or injured by the armoured vehicles of the RUC.

That night on TV thousands of people witnessed video recorded images of the tragic moment when the RUC office shot John Downes from a distance of less than two metres.

In spite of this, the following morning Belfast newspapers carried the news reporting the version of the incident given by the RUC Chief Constable: John Downes had died after being hit by a plastic bullet fire at random at the crowd during riots broken out at the end of the march. Yet I knew that this was not true. There had been no riots whatsoever and the police had opened fire at an unarmed crowd.

Once I returned to Italy I checked the Italian newspapers if any had reported the news of Downes' death. Only the daily paper *La Repubblica* mentioned the incident but the version of the killing was again the one given by the RUC Chief Constable.

At this point I realised I would be an accomplice in John Downes' death if I had been silent. I realised that people in my country had a right to know the truth about the Downes' killing. When I was in Ireland I had got a photo showing the RUC officer Nigel Hegarty firing at John Downes. I therefore decided I would try to have this photo published in an Italian newspaper.

It took me more than a month. I managed to have it published in the daily paper *Il Manifesto*.

A few months later I got to know that Nigel Hegarty had been acquitted and reinstated back in the ranks of the police. And yet, during the course of the trial, evidence was presented to the court, in the form of photographs and a video, showing the sequence of the killing.

Today I can say John Downes' death marked a point of no return in my life. It was both his killing and the immunity granted to Nigel Hegarty, which was the main reason, which pushed me to become a journalist and, since then, to highlight that the truth is the first casualty in Northern Ireland.

Silvia Calamati to the author, April 9, 2003
Manuscript with author

John Downes was from Slievegallion Drive, Andersonstown. He had gone to the march with his wife, Brenda, and one-year-old baby. He became the fourteenth person to die from injuries sustained from plastic and "rubber" bullets; of the fourteen, eight were children. Three more people were later killed by the Royal Ulster Constabulary in this fashion. Many hundreds of others had been severely injured and blinded. Only the fact that this killing had been witnessed by the media, who, like Silvia, were outraged, caused the RUC to charge Constable Hegarty with manslaughter, for which he was promptly acquitted. Downes's wife was not even informed of the hearing. The U.K. government refused an inquiry. On September 14, 1984, as a direct result of Downes's killing, the United Campaign against Plastic Bullets was formed.

As a newspaper and television journalist, Silvia continued to cover the events and wrote and translated several books on Ireland. Her work includes Irlanda del Nord: Una colonia in Europa *(Rome, 1997) and* Figlie di Erin: Voce di donne dell'Irlanda del Nord *(Rome, Edizione Associate 2001), which is also published in English translation as* Women's Stories from the North of Ireland *(Belfast, Beyond the Pale, 2002).*

The Good Friday Agreement (April 10, 1998)

In 1993, Gerry Adams, M.P., leader of Sinn Féin, and John Hume, M.P., leader of the Social Democratic Labour Party (of Northern Ireland), had been secretly talking about a peaceful way forward and announced a plan to progress peace talks. They had won the support of Irish Taoiseach Albert Reynolds of Fianna Fáil. Throughout 1993, the Dublin government worked to get the U.K. government to sign up with a joint declaration based on the Hume/Adams text in which the IRA would end its campaign and Sinn Féin would be included in talks on creating a democratic society in Northern Ireland.

In December 1993, the Downing Street Declaration acknowledged the start of the peace process. On August 31, 1994, the IRA declared a "complete cessation of military activities." It was clear from the outset that London wanted to pursue its failed strategies by seeking either a military victory over the IRA or an "acceptable level of violence." After the cease-fire, conditions for republican prisoners worsened, and London newspapers conducted a vitriolic hate campaign against John Hume for talking with Gerry Adams. London civil servants recoursed to the Oxford Dictionary to allow politicians to argue what was meant by a "complete cessation." John Major's Conservatives pursued a blocking policy on any talks and sought a means of forcing a complete IRA surrender. Without any sign of progress in response to their cease-fire except renewed attacks by the police and military during eighteen months, on February 9, 1996, the IRA ended the cease-fire.

On May 1, 1997, the U.K. general election showed that the republicans were not the only people tired of the failed politics of the Tory Party, and Tony Blair and Labour swept to power. On May 16, Blair went to Northern Ireland and indicated his government was willing to respond to the Hume/Adams initiative. On July 20, the IRA renewed its cease-fire, and on August 20 Secretary of State Mo Mowlam responded by announcing that Sinn Féin were entitled to a place in the talks on the future of Northern Ireland.

We were beginning to think we had reached the end, but then as the day wore on there was a phone call from David Trimble [leader of the Ulster Unionist Party] from his rooms on the floor below. He had shown the document to his negotiating team and they had raised two key objections, on prisoners and decommissioning. Tony [Tony Blair, the U.K. prime minister] kept amazingly calm considering how long we had been going and just said it was too late now to make any changes to the agreement because it would mean that all the other parties would want to do the same and we could not carry on indefinitely. As a compromise, Tony offered to provide a side letter, which was drafted and given to the unionists. In it he offered to "support changes" to the provisions for excluding parties from executive government in N. Ireland if "during the course of the first six months of the shadow Assembly or the Assembly itself, the provisions [in the agreement] have been shown to be ineffective." It gave Trimble the cover he needed to say that if things weren't working out as he wanted and issues like decommissioning were not being properly dealt with then he had some redress through the British Prime Minister.

David Trimble called his party together and read the letter to them. In doing so, he managed to satisfy the majority of the unionist negotiating team. It was a difficult meeting but he succeeded in holding in John Taylor and Ken Maginnis, which was important. But Jeffrey Donaldson couldn't be persuaded to support the deal. He walked out of the meeting and out of the building, got into his car and drove away. Fortunately by then all the media attention was on what came to be known as the Good Friday Agreement and less on Donaldson's departure.

David Trimble then indicated, as the other party leaders had done, that he was ready to go with a final statement. [Senator] George Mitchell [of the United States] called all the parties into a plenary session for 5 P.M. Tom Kelly arranged for a pooled television camera to be there, with pictures but no sound. But the pictures were enough. George went round the table asking solemnly if they were agreed. Everyone apart from Sinn Féin said Yes. Gerry Adams said, as expected, that their negotiating team would "report back to the Ard Chomhairle [their party executive] of Sinn Féin who will assess the document," but he added that the Sinn Féin leadership would "approach this development in a positive manner." We assumed, as on previous occasions, that it was the Shinners' [English slang for a member of Sinn Féin] way of holding their followers together. But it was clear that we had made it. At the end of everyone's comments, a large cheer went up and we all started clapping.

Mo Mowlam, U.K. secretary for Northern Ireland, *Momentum: The Struggle for Peace, Politics and the People,* Hodder & Stroughton, London, 2002

The "Long War" had cost 3,523 deaths and countless injuries. Of these deaths, 1,798 were civilians. The British military had lost 714 service personnel, mainly soldiers, and 307 police, of whom 301 were members of the Royal Ulster Constabulary; 24 prison officers also lost their lives. A further 66 deaths were people who had formerly been in the British military and RUC. The IRA had lost 276 members, and 81 members of republican splinter groups. Additionally, 22 former republican activists had been killed. Loyalist paramilitaries had lost 135, with 13 former members killed. There had also been 58 political activists killed. On the border, 1 soldier of the Irish army and 9 members of the Garda Siochána (Irish police) were killed.

L'Envoi

Immediately following the signing of the 1998 Good Friday Agreement, when U.S. senator George Mitchell told the press and media that "at long last the burden of history can be lifted from our shoulders," he was being unduly optimistic. Perhaps he should have borne in mind the prophetic words of Mark Sturgis, the senior British civil servant at Dublin Castle, in 1922: "It is another milestone but if Ireland—or England—expects that the Golden Age is dawning I hope they won't be too roughly disillusioned."

Disillusion followed quickly. The continued stonewalling of the Unionists, the brutal sectarian violence of Loyalist paramilitaries and their supporters, even attacking Catholic children walking to school, and the tired but well-orchestrated chorus of blame directed almost entirely at republicans for all the delays in progressing the agreement made in 1998 have continued to the present. An illustration of this stonewalling to prevent the next step toward a just and peaceful solution is demonstrated by the fact that the Unionists have been able to pressure the U.K. government into suspending the Northern Ireland Assembly many times. The Assembly met for the first time on November 29, 1999, and was suspended on February 11, 2000. It was restored on May 29, 2000, but suspended on

August 10, 2001. It was restored on August 12, 2001, but suspended on September 21, 2001. It was restored on September 22, 2001, but suspended on October 14, 2002. In May 2003, the scheduled elections for the Northern Ireland Assembly were suspended for six months.

The reason for these continued delays and suspensions is the continuing political game of Unionist semantics. While U.K. Conservative prime minister John Major had held up the peace process for eighteen months after the IRA cease-fire of 1994—arguing the meaning of the IRA phrase "complete cessation" of its activity and whether this meant "permanent"—it was not expected that Labour prime minister Tony Blair would fall into the same semantic game. Yet six years from the last IRA cease-fire (July 20, 1997), politicians are still arguing whether the war has ceased. The Unionists seem to offer nothing except their constant demand for a total IRA surrender before they move forward. It is as if they can only suggest a return to conflict as an alternative for the future. Sooner or later, if the U.K. government really desires to shake off the colonial past, they will have to face down the Unionists who have managed to manipulate them since the day when Lord Randolph Churchill (1849–1895), as chancellor of the Exchequer, came up with the idea of "playing the Orange card" to defeat Irish self-government. In the political game of cards, he had forgotten who the dealer might be.

Yet in spite of this, there is still an underlying optimism among most Irish people that the future may bring peace and reconciliation. There is an optimism expressed by the majority of the people on the island that Ireland may one day be reunited by peaceful means as logic dictates it should. But, among a war-weary people, it is often easy to be optimistic.

Adlai Stevenson, speaking in Richmond, Virginia, on September 20, 1952, pointed out: "We can chart our future clearly and wisely *only when we know the path which has led to the present.*" So far as Ireland has been concerned, successive London governments have never acknowledged, much less accepted responsibility for, the brutally destructive force that they have exerted over the centuries in the affairs of their neighbor. James Joyce, in *Ulysses,* was expressing the feelings of most Irish people when he caused his hero, Stephen Dedalus, to observe: "History is the nightmare from which I am trying to awake." It is a nightmare from which Ireland is still struggling to awake.

Further Reading

In 1972 the Dublin publishers Gill and Macmillan launched a paperback series as *The Gill History of Ireland,* under the general editorship of James Lydon and Margaret MacCurtain. Each book was written by a reputable authority in his or her period. The series started with *Ireland before the Vikings* and covered thirteen volumes, to *Ireland in the Twentieth Century.* These are excellent introductory volumes to each period with detailed bibliographies.

However, the best single-volume general history remains:

Moody, T. W., and F. X. Martin. *The Course of Irish History.* Cork: The Mercier Press, 1967.

For a radical alternative:

Ellis, Peter Berresford. *A History of the Irish Working Class.* New York: George Braziller, 1972.

For a conservative alternative:

Foster, Roy. *The Oxford History of Ireland.* Oxford University Press, 1992.

Mythology and Pre-Christian Ireland

Ellis, Peter Berresford. *A Dictionary of Irish Mythology.* New York: Oxford University Press, 1987.
O'Rahilly, Thomas F. *Early Irish History and Mythology.* Dublin Institute for Advanced Studies, 1946.
Raftery, Barry. *Pagan Celtic Ireland.* London: Thames and Hudson Ltd., 1994.

Christian Ireland

De Paor, Liam. *Saint Patrick's World.* Dublin: Four Courts Press, 1993.
Gougaud, Dom Louis. *Christianity in Celtic Lands.* London: Sheed and Ward, 1932.
Joyce, P. W. *A Social History of Ancient Ireland,* 2 vols., London: Longmans, Green and Co., 1903.
Ó Cróinín, Dáibhí. *Early Medieval Ireland 400–1200.* New York: Longman, 1995.

Early Irish Law

Kelly, Fergus. *A Guide to Early Irish Law*. Dublin Institute for Advanced Studies, 1988.

The Irish Language

Hyde, Douglas, *A Literary History of Ireland*. London: T. Fisher Unwin, 1899.

Ó Cuív, Brían, ed. A *View of the Irish Language*. Dublin: Stationery Office, 1969.

Native Irish Rulers

Ellis, Peter Berresford. *Erin's Blood Royal: The Gaelic Noble Dynasties of Ireland*. New York: Plagrave, revised ed., 2002.

Furlong, Nicholas, *Dermot, King of Leinster and the Foreigners*. Tralee: Anvil Books, 1973.

Simms Katharine. *From Kings to Warlords: The Changing Political Structure of Gaelic Ireland in the Later Middle Ages*. Wolfeboro, New Hampshire: The Boydell Press, 1987.

The Medieval Period

Curtis, Edmund. *A History of Medieval Ireland from 1086–1513*. Dublin: Maunsel and Roberts, 1923.

O Riordan, Michelle. *The Gaelic Mind and the Collapse of the Gaelic World*. Cork University Press: 1990.

Roche, Richard. *The Norman Invasion of Ireland*. Tralee: Anvil Books, 1970.

Tudor Period

De Blácam, Aodh. *Gaelic Literature Surveyed*. Dublin: Talbot Press Ltd., 1929.

Falls, Cyril. *Elizabeth's Irish Wars*. New York: Barnes & Noble Inc., revised ed., 1970.

Cromwellian Period

Ellis, Peter Berresford. *Hell or Connaught: The Cromwellian Colonisation of Ireland 1652–1660*. New York: St. Martin's Press, 1975.

Williamite Conquest

Ellis, Peter Berresford. *The Boyne: The Battle of the Boyne 1690*. New York: St. Martin's Press.

Simms, J. G. *Jacobite Ireland, 1685–1691,* London: Routledge & Kegan Paul, 1969.

Seventeenth and Eighteenth Centuries

Corkery, Daniel. *The Hidden Ireland*. Dublin: M. H. Gill, 1924.

The United Irishmen and Republicanism

Curtis, Liz. *The Cause of Ireland: From the United Irishmen to Partition*. Belfast: Beyond the Pale Publications, 1994.

The Great Hunger, 1845–1949

Woodham-Smith, Cecil. *The Great Hunger: Ireland 1845–1849*. London: Hamish Hamilton, 1962.

The North and Irish Culture

Blaney, Roger. *Presbyterians and the Irish Language*. Belfast: Ulster Historical Foundation and Ultach Trust, 1996.

Campbell, Flann. *The Dissenting Voice: Protestant Democracy in Ulster from Plantation to Partition*. Belfast: Blackstaff Press, 1991.

Collins, Kevin. *The Culture Conquest of Ireland*. Dublin: The Mercier Press, 1990.

Ó Snodaigh, Pádraig. *Hidden Ulster: Protestants and the Irish Language*. Belfast: Lagan Press, 1995.

1916 Uprising and War of Independence

MacArdle, Dorothy. *The Irish Republic: A Documented Chronicle of the Anglo-Irish Conflict and the Partitioning of Ireland with a Detailed Account of the Period 1916–1923*. Preface by Eamon de Valéra. London: Victor Gollancz Ltd., 1937.

Ryan, Desmond. *The Rising: The Complete Story of Easter Week*. Dublin: Golden Eagle Books, 1949.

The Irish Civil War 1922–1923

Coogan, Tim Pat, and George Morrison. *The Irish Civil War*. London: Weidenfeld & Nicolson, 1998.

Ireland in the 1939–1945 War

Carroll, Joseph T. *Ireland in the War Years 1939–1945*. Newton Abbot, Deon: David & Charles, 1975.

The Struggle for Reunification

Bowyer Bell, J. *The Secret Army: A History of the IRA*. London: Anthony Blond Ltd., 1972.

Curtis, Liz. *Ireland: The Propaganda War*. London: Pluto Press, 1984.

De Baróid, Ciarán. *Ballymurphy and the Irish War*. London: Pluto Press, revised ed., 2000.

Farrell, Michael. *Northern Ireland: The Orange State*. London: Pluto Press, 1976.

Kelley, Kevin. *The Longest War: Northern Ireland and the IRA*. Ireland: Brandon Books, 1982.

Louglin, James. *Ulster Unionism and British National Identity Since 1885*. New York: Pinter, 1995.

O'Brien, Jack. *British Bruality in Ireland*. Dublin: Mercier Press, 1989.

Index